RESEARCH METHODS FOR LEISURE, RECREATION AND TOURISM

CABI TOURISM TEXTS are an essential resource for students of academic tourism, leisure studies, hospitality, entertainment and events management. The series reflects the growth of tourism-related studies at an academic level and responds to the changes and developments in these rapidly evolving industries, providing up-to-date practical guidance, discussion of the latest theories and concepts, and analysis by world experts. The series is intended to guide students through their academic programmes and remain an essential reference throughout their careers in the tourism sector.

Readers will find the books within the CABI TOURISM TEXTS series to have a uniquely wide scope, covering important elements in leisure and tourism, including management-led topics, practical subject matter and development of conceptual themes and debates. Useful textbook features such as case studies, bullet point summaries and helpful diagrams are employed throughout the series to aid study and encourage understanding of the subject.

Students at all levels of study, workers within tourism and leisure industries, researchers, academics, policy makers and others interested in the field of academic and practical tourism will find these books an invaluable and authoritative resource, useful for academic reference and real world tourism applications.

Titles available

Ecotourism: Principles and Practices
Ralf Buckley

Contemporary Tourist Behaviour: Yourself and Others as Tourists
David Bowen and Jackie Clarke

The Entertainment Industry: an Introduction
Edited by Stuart Moss

Practical Tourism Research
Stephen L.J. Smith

Leisure, Sport and Tourism, Politics, Policy and Planning, 3rd Edition
A.J. Veal

Events Management
Edited by Peter Robinson, Debra Wale and Geoff Dickson

Food and Wine Tourism: Integrating Food, Travel and Territory
Erica Croce and Giovanni Perri

Research Methods for Leisure, Recreation and Tourism
Edited by Ercan Sirakaya-Turk, Muzaffer Usyal, William E. Hammit and Jerry J. Vaske

RESEARCH METHODS FOR LEISURE, RECREATION AND TOURISM

Edited by

Ercan Sirakaya-Turk
The University of South Carolina, USA

Muzaffer Uysal
Virginia Polytechnic Institute & State University, USA

William E. Hammitt
Clemson University, USA

Jerry J. Vaske
Colorado State University, USA

www.cabi.org

CABI is a trading name of CAB International

CABI Head Office
Nosworthy Way
Wallingford
Oxfordshire OX10 8DE
UK

Tel: +44 (0)1491 832111
Fax: +44 (0)1491 833508
E-mail: cabi@cabi.org
Website: www.cabi.org

CABI North American Office
875 Massachusetts Avenue
7th Floor
Cambridge, MA 02139
USA

Tel: +1 617 395 4056
Fax: +1 617 354 6875
E-mail: cabi-nao@cabi.org

A catalogue record for this book is available from the British Library, London, UK.

Library of Congress Cataloging-in-Publication Data

Research methods for leisure, recreation, and tourism / editors Ercan Sirakaya-Turk . . . [et al.].
    p. cm.
  Includes index.
  ISBN 978-1-84593-763-8 (permanent paper)
1. Recreation--Research. 2. Leisure--Research. 3. Tourism--Research.
I. Sirakaya--Turk, Ercan. II. Title.

GV14.5.R46 2011
790'.07--dc22

2010049316

ISBN-13: 978 1 84593 763 8 (paperback)
ISBN-13: 978 1 84593 891 8 (hardback)

Commissioning editor: Sarah Hulbert
Production editor: Fiona Chippendale

Typeset by SPi, Pondicherry, India.
Printed and bound in the UK by Cambridge University Press, Cambridge.

Contents

PART IV: Analysing the Data and Testing Hypotheses

PART V: Research Write Ups: Reporting the Results

About the Editors

Ercan Sirakaya-Turk (Ercan) is a Professor of Tourism and the Associate Dean of Research and Graduate Studies in the College of Hospitality, Retail and Sport Management at the University of South Carolina (USC). Before joining USC, Dr Turk worked at Texas A&M and Pennsylvania State Universities. He received his PhD and MS from Clemson University, South Carolina, USA. He was the 2007 recipient of US State Department's prestigious Fulbright scholarship to Russia, Saint Petersburg State University of Finance and Economics. Ercan has published a significant number of articles in the area of tourism destination marketing and tourism development in prestigious tourism journals and completed numerous grants/contracts exceeding one million US dollars. He is the founding editor and current Associate Editor for an online tourism research bulletin (*e-Review of Tourism Research*). He also serves on editorial boards of numerous journals including *Journal of Travel Research, Annals of Tourism Research* (as a resource editor), and *Tourism Analysis*. He teaches tourism economics, marketing and research methods classes.

Contact: Ercan Sirakaya-Turk, Sloan Professor of Tourism and Associate Dean for Research and Graduate Programs, University of South Carolina, College of Hospitality, Retail and Sport Management, Columbia, South Carolina 29208 USA. E-mail: ercan@hrsm.sc.edu

Muzaffer (Muzzo) Uysal is a Professor of Tourism in the Department of Hospitality and Tourism Management in Pamplin College of Business at Virginia Polytechnic Institute & State University, Blacksburg, Virginia USA. He received his PhD from Texas A&M University, MBA from the University of New Haven and BS in business administration and accounting from Ankara Academy of Economics & Commercial Sciences. He has extensive experience in the travel and tourism field, authoring or co-authoring a significant number of articles in tourism; hospitality and recreation journals; proceedings; book chapters; and four monographs and two books relating to different aspects of tourism and research. He has also conducted workshops, seminars and field research in several countries. Dr Uysal is a member of the International Academy for the Study of Tourism, the Academy of Leisure Sciences, and serves as co-editor of *Tourism Analysis: An Interdisciplinary Journal*. In addition, he sits on the editorial boards of a significant number of journals, including *Journal of Travel Research*, and *Annals of Tourism Research* as resource editor. Dr Uysal received the Award for

Research Excellence, Alumni Award for Excellence in International Education, Teaching Excellence Award from the Pamplin College of Business, and Outstanding Research Award from College of Human Resources. In addition, he received the 2009 University of Delaware Michael D. Olsen Research Achievement Award in Hospitality and Tourism and a Lifetime Achievement Award in Tourism Research in 2008 from the Chinese Tourism Management Association – Taiwan. Dr Uysal is also featured in *Who's Who in America* (2001–2010). He worked as Associate Dean for Graduate Programs and Research in the College of Hospitality, Retail and Sport Management at the University of South Carolina from July 2007 to August 2008. His research interests centre on tourism demand/supply interaction, tourism marketing and quality of life research in tourism.

Contact: Muzaffer Uysal, Professor, Pamplin College of Business, Department of Hospitality and Tourism Management, Virginia Tech, 355 Wallace Hall, Blacksburg, Virginia 24061, USA. E-mail: samil@vt.edu

William E. Hammitt (Bill) is Professor Emeritus of Wildland Recreation in the Department of Parks, Recreation and Tourism Management at Clemson University. He has been at Clemson since 1990, teaching and conducting research in the area of wildland recreation. From 1975 to 1999 he was on the faculty of the Department of Forestry, Wildlife and Fisheries at the University of Tennessee. His research specialty is recreation behaviour and visitor management in natural environments. Dr Hammitt earned his first BS degree in Biology at Bluffton College, Bluffton, Ohio in 1965. He then spent three years at the University of Michigan studying Forestry, receiving a BS in Forestry in 1968 and a MF in Forest Ecology in 1969. From 1969 to 1976 Dr Hammitt was employed as Superintendent at the University of Michigan Botanical Gardens; served as a Peace Corps Park Biologist in Costa Rica; and was employed as Director of the Whitehouse Nature Center, Albion, Michigan. In 1976 he returned to the University of Michigan to complete his Doctorate in Forest Recreation, which was granted in 1978. William Hammitt is author and/or co-author of more than 150 papers and articles in professional and trade journals in his field. He is a past associate editor of the *Journal of Leisure Research* and *Leisure Sciences*. He is senior author of the text, *Wildland Recreation: Ecology and Management*, 1998 (2nd edition). He is the recipient of two Fulbright Awards, Peru and Norway, and a Fellow in the Academy of Leisure Sciences.

Contact: William E. Hammitt, Professor Emeritus, Clemson University, Department of Parks, Recreation and Tourism Management, 263 Lehotsky Hall, Box 340735, Clemson, South Carolina 29634-0735, USA. E-mail: Hammitw@clemson.edu

Jerry J. Vaske is a Professor in the Department of Human Dimensions of Natural Resources at Colorado State University and a founding editor of the journal *Human Dimensions of Wildlife*. He received his BA and MA degree from the University of Wisconsin and his PhD from the University of Maryland. For the last 30 years his research has focused on the application of social science theory and methodology to the concerns of natural resource managers and policy makers. Dr Vaske has published over 125 articles in scientific journals and authored or co-authored six books. His latest book is titled *Survey Research and Analysis: Applications in Parks, Recreation and Human Dimensions*. His primary teaching responsibilities at Colorado State University focus on research methodology and statistics. Specific topics range from survey design to applied multivariate analysis. Courses at both the undergraduate and graduate level emphasize understanding data manipulation techniques and what statistics are appropriate for addressing theoretical and applied natural resource problems.

Contact: Jerry J. Vaske, Professor, Human Dimensions of Natural Resources, Colorado State University, Fort Collins, Colorado 80523, USA. E-mail: jerryv@warnercnr.colostate.edu

Contributors

Kathleen Andereck is the Director of the School of Community Resources and Development at Arizona State University where she also holds the rank of Professor. Her research focuses on the tourism experience from the perspective of both visitors and residents particularly as it applies to sustainable tourism and marketing. Dr Andereck has done research with a diverse range of organizations and agencies at the federal and state level including the Bureau of Land Management, the USDA Forest Service, the Arizona Office of Tourism and the Arizona Department of Transportation. Dr Andereck is an associate editor for four academic journals and is the author of numerous refereed journal articles, and conference papers and professional reports.

Contact: Kathleen Andereck, Professor and Director, School of Community Resources and Development, Arizona State University, 411 North Central Avenue, Suite 550, Phoenix, Arizona, USA. E-mail: kandereck@asu.edu

Begum Aybar-Damali is an Assistant Professor at the Department of Recreation, Tourism and Therapeutic Recreation at Winona State University. She received her undergraduate degree in psychology at Middle East Technical University, in Turkey in 1999. She earned an MS degree in Industrial Management at Clemson University in 2002 and a PhD in Parks, Recreation, and Tourism Management from Clemson University in 2007. Prior to her current position at Winona State University she worked at the Institute for Engaged Aging at Clemson University as a postdoctoral fellow. She serves on the editorial board of *Therapeutic Recreation Journal* and the *Journal of Unconventional Parks, Tourism & Recreation Research*.

Contact: Begum Aybar-Damali, Assistant Professor, Recreation Tourism and Therapeutic Recreation, Winona State University, Memorial 103, PO Box 5838, Winona, Minnesota 55987, USA. E-mail: BAybarDamali@winona.edu

Seyhmus Baloglu is Professor and the Associate Dean for Research at the William F. Harrah College of Hotel Administration, University of Nevada, Las Vegas (UNLV). His teaching areas include marketing, international tourism, research methods, and multivariate statistics. Dr Baloglu has research interests in the areas of consumer behaviour and marketing in hospitality, tourism and leisure. He has extensive publications on image formation and positioning for vacation and convention destinations, destination branding, customer loyalty, segmentation, and Internet marketing in leading academic and professional journals in hospitality and tourism. His many accomplishments are chronicled in *Who's Who in America* (2001–2009).

Contact: Seyhmus Baloglu, Professor and Associate Dean, Department of Tourism and Convention Harrah College of Hotel Administration, 4505 Maryland Parkway, PO Box 456023, Las Vegas, Nevada 89154-6023, USA. E-mail: baloglu@ccmail.nevada.edu

Frederic Dimanche is Professor of Marketing and Director of the Centre for Tourism Management at SKEMA Business School, Nice Sophia Antipolis, France. After obtaining his PhD in 1990 from the University of Oregon (USA), he worked until 2001 in the College of Business Administration at the University of New Orleans. He was also Director of Research for the Olinger Group, a full service marketing research firm in New Orleans. He then moved to Europe to join SKEMA Business School where he developed academic programmes in tourism and event management. Frederic has been an active researcher, teacher and consultant, working for private companies and national or regional organizations in North and Central America, Africa, Asia and Europe. He has been a member of the Travel and Tourism Research Association (TTRA) since 1990, and is currently President of TTRA Europe. He is also a member of the International Association of Scientific Experts in Tourism.

Contact: Frederic Dimanche, Marketing Professor, Associate Dean of the Faculty, Director, Center for Tourism Management, CERAM Business School Nice - Sophia Antipolis, France. E-mail: Frederic.DIMANCHE@cote-azur.cci.fr

Harriet E.T. Dixon is an Adjunct Professor at the Department of Kinesiology & Health Promotion of Troy University, Troy, Alabama. She earned a BSc in Recreation and Leisure Studies and Master of Science in Recreation and Leisure Facilities and Services Administration from East Carolina University, and a PhD in Parks, Recreation, and Tourism Management from Clemson University. Her primary areas of research interest include: constraints to leisure, aquatic training and safety, and qualitative research methods. She has had manuscripts appear in the *Recreational Sports Journal and Parks and Recreation* and is an Associate Editor of the *Journal of Unconventional Parks, Tourism, and Recreation Research*.

Contact: Harriet E.T. Dixon, Adjunct Professor, Department of Kinesiology & Health Promotion, Troy University, Troy, Alabama, USA. E-mail: harrietdixon@gmail.com

Yuksel Ekinci is a Professor of Marketing in the Business School at Oxford Brookes University. Prior to starting his career in academia, Yuksel worked in international tourism organizations. Upon completing his PhD in Services Marketing, he was appointed as a lecturer at the University of Surrey. Yuksel teaches Global Marketing and Research Methods at Oxford Brookes University. He designed and delivered workshops in Research Methods in the UK and the EU countries. His articles appeared in the *Annals of Tourism Research, Journal of Travel Research, Tourism Analysis, Journal of Hospitality and Tourism Research, Journal of Business Research, European Journal of Marketing, Journal of Retailing and Consumer Services* and *Service Industries Journal*. Yuksel developed a customer satisfaction model for the hospitality services in 2008. His articles on service quality and destination branding received best paper awards. Yuksel is an active researcher and an editorial board member of the retail marketing and tourism journals.

Contact: Yuksel Ekinci, Professor of Marketing, Business School, Oxford Brookes University, Wheatley Campus, Oxford OX33 1HX, UK. E-mail: yekinci@brookes.ac.uk

Jacinta M. Gau is an Assistant Professor in the Department of Criminal Justice at California State University, San Bernardino. She teaches undergraduate statistics, criminal procedure, courts, and other subjects. Her research interests include policing and quantitative methods and her work has appeared in *Justice Quarterly, Criminology & Public Policy, Police Quarterly,* and *Policing: An International Journal of Police Strategies and Management.*

Contact: Jacinta M. Gau, Assistant Professor, Department of Criminal Justice, California State University, San Bernardino, 5500 University Parkway, San Bernardino, California 92407-2318, USA. E-mail: jgau@csusb.edu

Dogan Gursoy is the Taco Bell Distinguished Professor in Hospitality Business Management at Washington State University in the School of Hospitality Business Management and the editor of *Journal of Hospitality Marketing & Management.* His area of research includes hospitality and tourism marketing, tourist behaviour, travellers' information search behaviour, community support for tourism development, cross-cultural studies, consumer behaviour and involvement. His research has been published broadly in refereed Tier I journals such as *Annals of Tourism Research, Journal Travel Research, Tourism Management, International Journal of Hospitality Management, Journal of Hospitality and Tourism Research.*

Contact: Dogan Gursoy, CHE, Professor, Washington State University, School of Hospitality Business Management 479 Todd Hall, PO Box 644742, Pullman, Washington 99164-4742, USA. E-mail: dgursoy@cbe.wsu.edu

Chenchen Huang is an Assistant Professor with the Hospitality and Tourism Department at Buffalo State College. His research interests include tourism planning, tourism destination marketing and sustainable tourism. His dissertation applied theories from urban and regional planning and tourism planning to investigate US timeshare owners' willingness to participate in tourism planning. He has extensive professional and academic experience in China and has published book chapters and articles on tourism development in China. Dr. Huang teaches various undergraduate courses, including Tourism Management, Cultural Tourism and Hotel Management. His future teaching and research activities will concentrate on cultural and heritage tourism and its impacts on the local community, under the paradigm of sustainable tourism development.

Contact: Chenchen Huang, Assistant Professor, Buffalo State College, Hospitality and Tourism Department, Caudell 310, 1300 Elmwood Ave, Buffalo, New York 14222, USA. E-mail: huangc@buffalostate.edu

L. Brent Igo is an Assistant Professor in the School of Education at Clemson University. In the realm of research, Dr Igo has addressed the impact of teachers' corrective feedback on students' self-efficacy, the role of visual mnemonics in learning confusing words, and how to maximize the effectiveness of note taking in Web-based environments. His research, in addition to being presented annually at national conferences, has yielded chapters in recent books addressing Web-Based Learning and articles in professional journals, such as the *Journal of Educational Psychology, Learning Disability Quarterly* and the *Journal of Experimental Education.* Brent also serves on the editorial boards of *Educational Psychology Review* and *Journal of At-risk Issues.*

Contact: L. Brent Igo, Assistant Professor, Clemson University, Educational Foundations, School of Education, 102 Tillman Hall, Clemson, South Carolina 29634-0702, USA. E-mail: ligo@clemson.edu

Gayle Jennings is the Director of Research, Imagine Consulting Group International. Her research agenda focuses on practical and applied research for business and industry, research training and education, qualitative methodologies, and quality tourism experiences. Gayle is also an Adjunct Professor of Tourism Management, Department of Tourism, Leisure, Hotel and Sport Management, Griffith University, Gold Coast Campus. She is the sole author and editor of a number of books, written book chapters, and journal articles across a range of topics relating to theoretical paradigms that inform research processes, water-based tourism and quality tourism experiences.

Contact: Gayle Jennings, Griffith Business School, Department of Tourism, Leisure, Hotel and Sport Management, Griffith University Gold Coast Campus, PMB 50, Gold Coast, Rockhampton Campus, Queensland 4703, Australia. E-mail: g.jennings@griffith.edu.au

Sheryl Kline is an Associate Professor and the Associate Dean at the University of South Carolina, College of Hospitality, Retail and Sports Management, Columbia, USA. Sheryl Kline performs research in the area of hotel operation and management and organizational behaviour. She teaches courses in hotel management, human resources management and organizational behaviour. She has been recognized as an innovative teacher and is the recipient of several teaching awards. Before joining USC, she was a tenured faculty member at Purdue University and at Widener University. Prior to joining academia she had a successful career in the hotel and casino hotel industry where she held management positions in casino hotels in Atlantic City, New Jersey and Las Vegas, Nevada.

Contact: Sheryl Kline, Associate Professor and Associate Dean, University of South Carolina, College of Hospitality, Retailing and Sports Management, Columbia, South Carolina 29208, USA. E-mail: klines@mailbox.sc.edu

Xiangping Li obtained her PhD from Pamplin College of Business – Hospitality and Tourism Management at Virginia Tech. Her area of research includes tourism marketing, tourist behaviour and tourism development. She has published a number of academic papers in reputable tourism and hospitality journals.

Contact: Xiangping Li, Virginia Polytechnic Institute and State University, Pamplin College of Business, Department of Hospitality and Tourism Management, Blacksburg, Virginia 24061, USA. E-mail: lxpwj@vt.edu

Francis A. McGuire is an Alumni Distinguished Professor in the Department of Parks, Recreation, and Tourism Management at Clemson University, South Carolina, as well as a Fellow in the Strom Thurmond Institute. He has had manuscripts appear in a variety of publications including *The Gerontologist, The International Journal of Aging and Human Development, Journal of Leisure Research, Leisure Sciences, Activity, Adaptation and Aging,* and the *Therapeutic Recreation Journal.* He was named the South Carolina Governor's Professor of the Year in 2004.

Contact: Francis A. McGuire, Distinguished Alumni Professor, Clemson University, Department of Parks, Recreation and Tourism Management, 282B Lehotsky Hall, Box 340735, Clemson, South Carolina 29634-0735, USA. E-mail: lefty@clemson.edu

Harmen Oppewal is a Professor of Retail Marketing at Monash University in Melbourne, Australia, where he teaches research methods and consumer behaviour. His research focuses on consumer choice and decision behaviour in tourism, leisure, retail, marketing and transport. He conducted studies concerning consumer choice of vacation destination, shopping destination, travel mode and route, and urban parks. He holds degrees in psychology and geography and received his PhD from Eindhoven University of Technology in the Netherlands. He published academic papers in refereed tourism, leisure, retail, marketing, transportation and planning journals, including the *Journal of Travel Research, Tourism Management, Leisure Sciences, Journal of Retailing, Journal of Marketing Research, Transportation Research* and *Environment and Planning.*

Contact: Harmen Oppewal, Professor of Retail Marketing, Department of Marketing, Faculty of Business and Economics, Monash University, Room 09A, Building S6, PO Box 197, Caulfield East, Victoria 3145, Australia. E-mail: Harmen.Oppewal@BusEco.monash.edu.au

Lori Pennington-Gray is an Associate Professor in the Department of Tourism, Recreation & Sport Management at the University of Florida, Gainesville, Florida, USA. Her responsibilities include teaching undergraduate and graduate courses, conducting research and generating externally funded projects in Recreation, Parks and Tourism. She has been involved in numerous research projects in the state of Florida and other areas in the USA. Lori has consulted with several destination marketing organizations, designing research to identify front-end positioning and results-oriented evaluation. Lori has conducted visitor study research for many counties and regional groups. She has also been involved with international projects. As the Director of the Tourism Crisis Management Institute, her responsibilities with the Institute are mainly to facilitate interdisciplinary research projects focusing on crisis management in the tourism industry.

Contact: Lori Pennington-Gray, Department of Recreation, Parks and Tourism, Center for Tourism Research and Development, University of Florida, 325 FLG, PO Box 118209, Gainesville, Florida 32611-8209, USA. E-mail: penngray@hhp.ufl.edu

Edward Ruddell is an Associate Professor and Director of Graduate Studies in the Department of Parks, Recreation and Tourism at the University of Utah where he teaches numerous theory, research methods and statistics courses. He also teaches courses in natural resources recreation and the philosophy of leisure. His research interests are in scenic beauty and restorative environments. He also conducts research in interpretation and the social psychology of communication. Edward Ruddell received his PhD from the Department of Parks, Recreation, and Tourism Sciences at Texas A&M University and holds master's and bachelor's degrees in forestry from the University of Tennessee.

Contact: Edward Ruddell, Professor, Department of Parks, Recreation and Tourism, University of Utah, 250 South, 1850 East Office: ANNEX 1066, Salt Lake City, Utah 84112, USA. E-mail: edward.ruddell@health.utah.edu

Patrick Tierney is Professor, Chairman and Graduate Coordinator of the Recreation, Parks and Tourism Department at San Francisco State University. He is co-author of the book *Recreation, Event and Tourism Businesses: Startup and Sustainable Operations*. Pat has been actively involved in tourism research, having completed tourism and internet marketing studies for many organizations, including the California Division of Tourism, the San Francisco Convention and Visitors Bureau, Alcatraz Cruises, Resort and Commercial Recreation Association, the National Park Service, the Belize Tourist Board, U.S. Forest Service, Galapagos National Park and California Coastal Conservancy. Pat has authored numerous refereed publications and made presentations at state, national and international conferences. He is co-recipient of the 1997 Best Tourism Research Award from the California Division of Tourism, the 1991 and 2008 Excellence in Research Award from the Commercial Recreation and Resort Association, as well as recipient of the 1990 Colorado Rural Tourism Achievement Award. Pat has recently served on the Executive Committee of the California Travel Industry Association Board of Directors and the Bay Area Partners in Responsible Tourism.

Contact: Patrick Tierney, Professor, San Francisco State University, Department of Recreation and Leisure Studies, 1600 Holloway Ave, San Francisco, California 94019, USA. E-mail: ptierney@sfsu.edu

Ahmet Usakli is a Research Assistant at the Faculty of Tourism, Nevsehir University, Turkey. He received his MS in Hotel Administration from the University of Nevada, Las Vegas, and BS in Tourism Management from Gazi University, Turkey. Ahmet Usakli was the 2007–2009 recipient of US Department of State's Fulbright Scholarship to study in the USA. His research interests are in the areas of consumer behaviour, and marketing in travel and tourism, particularly in destination branding and tourist self-concept.

Contact: Ahmet Usakli, Department of Tourism and Convention, Harrah College of Hotel Administration, 4505 Maryland Parkway - PO Box 456023, Las Vegas, Nevada 89154-6023, USA. E-mail: usaklia@unlv.nevada.edu

Preface

Research is an important function in our society, global economy and in our disciplines of leisure, recreation, parks and tourism. A research methods class requires a student to be critical, detail oriented, questioning, constantly thinking, and adept at finding new ways of writing and rewriting. Research methods classes help students formulate, organize and write their thoughts in a logical manner. At the end of the research methods class, and reading associated books and research materials, students tend to become better consumers and users of research and more informed citizens of our society as they learn systems, processes and tools that are used to attack flaws in logic and arguments.

The purpose of this book, titled appropriately *Research Methods for Leisure, Recreation and Tourism,* is to have a research methods book that is friendly and welcoming while still conveying the essentials of research methods and tools. The book has 16 chapters. We began each chapter with Learning Objectives, a Chapter Summary of the main points, and end it with a Discussion/Review Questions and Key Terms of the chapters. The text also contains illustrations and figures to make the students visualize appropriate research processes and analyses. In quite a few chapters, real world examples, key points and short cases are introduced in Research Boxes. The text contains plenty of examples from leisure, recreation and tourism literature as examples or case studies where appropriate. The book's language is easy to understand. We intended the book to be a welcoming and friendly research methods book for students of leisure, recreation, parks, natural resource management and tourism. Graduate students majoring in leisure sciences, recreation, parks, natural resource management, tourism management and hospitality will find it useful and rewarding as well. Tourism professionals, practitioners and academicians who are teaching and conducting applied research will want to add this book to their library as a quick reference guide to research in leisure disciplines. In addition, tourism offices and tourism bureaus/boards at different levels (national, regional, state, city and county) will find the book valuable in their research efforts.

Why We Wrote the Book

Many of our colleagues who teach research methods classes rely on textbooks from other disciplines such as sociology, psychology or marketing. However, since these books are usually field specific, they are not always well received by our students. Many of us are compelled to change and/or modify the contents of existing books to fit and reflect our unique disciplinary knowledge. Our experiences with students over the years convinced us that teaching such classes with books borrowed from other disciplines creates discontent and confusion within the minds of our students. The lack of examples from within the leisure, recreation and tourism field is perhaps the most significant complaint we get from our students. Although there are some good research methods books currently in the market in our field they seem to follow a typical outline from methods book from other social science disciplines with examples brought in from the author's own area of expertise. We have all used these books in our classes; our students in leisure, recreation and tourism have indicated that they found these books to be content-dry and not necessarily covering all closely related disciplines of leisure studies.

A leisure methods book that covers topics for all related disciplines such as tourism, parks and recreation will add to the learning experience of a student in our disciplines. We have decided to ask our colleagues to help us write an edited book that would overcome some of the problems found in other books. Thus, we have invited internationally renowned and active researchers and authors as contributors based on their experience in teaching research methods and being known as established researchers in our field of leisure sciences. Chapter contributors bring their own unique experiences and knowledge from their field of expertise into the chapters giving the book added flavour and uniqueness.

This book is written mainly for upper level undergraduate college students as well as graduate students majoring in leisure sciences, recreation, parks, natural resource management, tourism management and hospitality departments. We have used a uniform template and guidelines to direct and guide the writing process of the chapter contributors. This process has assured uniformity of format and consistency in the flow and quality of the chapters. As editors of the book, we have streamlined the language and structured the book so that it would read in 'one voice'.

Why So Many Different Authors?

An edited text book written by renowned professors and active researchers who have experiences in teaching methods classes, and are thus familiar with pedagogic issues involved in teaching research methods classes, provided a unique opportunity for creating a textbook that transcends the international boundaries. Students and readers in mainly English-speaking countries, including the USA, Canada, UK, Australia, New Zealand, Pacific Asia countries such as Hong Kong and other countries where there is a significant number of both public and private universities in which the primary academic language is English will benefit from this unique book.

Organization and Content

This book is an introductory research methods book for mainly senior level undergraduate students and first year graduate students. The book is written with plenty of experiences from the everyday life of an upper level manager. The book introduces students to the broad area of research unique to leisure, recreation and tourism management issues. Research is a life-long learning process. This book will introduce you to the realm of research with very broad-based guidelines on not only how one can conduct proper research, but also become a better consumer and user of research, upon which our knowledge economy depends so much. One suggestion when reading the book: make sure that you read the real-world examples presented in research boxes and case studies in order to apply the concepts learned in each chapter to a real situation.

Typically, instructors teaching research methods classes require their students to learn research methods with a hands-on original research project. Thus, the book is organized in a manner that facilitates such a learning approach. From early on, starting with Chapter 1, the student is guided to think about an original research idea and the process so s/he can see the light at the end of the tunnel. While we will give the student/reader enough details about how to proceed with each step in the successive chapters, the student of methods must picture the entire process while studying Chapter 1. This approach will help the student use the time efficiently, so the research paper required by the instructor can be completed on time. Some of the concepts will be repeated over and over again to facilitate clarification and better understanding of what some might call the 'dry concepts'.

Part I provides a broad overview of the research process in leisure, recreation and tourism with a chapter specifically devoted to understanding the entire research process that will then be fully covered in successive chapters, giving the student the opportunity to think about all associated steps and processes involved in research as a whole.

Part II looks at the fundamental concepts and processes involved in conducting research. Individual chapters are devoted to the nature and importance of research, basic research concepts and designs, finding and summarizing the existing research, the measurement of variables, and writing a research proposal for scientific inquiry.

Part III looks at survey research, qualitative research methods, grounded theory methodology, evaluation research, and basic principles of the design and analysis of experimental research, and cross-cultural research issues and concerns.

Part IV deals with tools used in analysing data and testing hypotheses. Individual chapters discuss how to summarize data, use of inferential data analysis, uses of parametric (t-tests and ANOVA) and non-parametric (χ^2) tests, correlation analysis and simple linear regression.

Part V provides an extensive discussion about how to communicate and report research results via four types of research reports: class assignments, a thesis or dissertation, a research journal article and a technical report.

Features

Although the book is edited by several authors, features of the book are common elements to all of the 16 chapters. We believe the features listed below to be essential tools that facilitate a focused learning process and help students to comprehend the many aspects of the leisure research process.

Learning Objectives. Each chapter begins with a list of main learning objectives. These objective statements reflect the content of each chapter and emphasize the areas of competency, knowledge and skills that students should develop and possess before they proceed to the next chapter. These objectives are also broad enough that instructors could add specific objectives of their own.

Chapter Summary. Each chapter provides a summary of key points that are covered in the chapters. A snapshot of the chapter allows students to see the big picture and gain insights into the nature and content of the chapters before they are exposed to the detail concepts and elements of the chapters.

Key Terms. For each chapter, key terms are added to highlight and emphasize key concepts that have special meanings within the context of research process and methods. Key terms are also good learning tools for students to better relate to concepts and the underlying dimensions of such concepts. Most of these key terms included in the chapters are also repeated as needed throughout the book. Key terms are also great tools for students to navigate research and gather further information as needed beyond the coverage of the book.

Discussion/Review Questions. Every chapter ends with a list of discussion/review questions to make sure that students have comprehended the concepts and mastered the level of competency, knowledge and skill sets that are expected of them. Discussion/review questions are not always very specific and some are also intended to be directional and propositional in nature so that students are challenged to be creative in their responses and analysis of such discussion points and questions.

Research Boxes. The research boxes contain examples of research applications or scenarios that explore the nature of leisure, recreation and tourism research issues in a variety of research settings. Some research boxes present research issues and the manner in which they may be addressed. These research boxes are relevant to the subject and content matter of the chapters.

Case Studies. Cases studies are all created using a leisure, recreation or tourism setting. Most chapters begin with a case study to set the stage for the chapter content and its concepts. These cases are all real-life situations that are aimed at building knowledge and research skills. Case studies provide students with the opportunity to see the complexity of problems in leisure, recreation and tourism, and engage in research and decision-making processes in a coherent and meaningful way. Case studies allow students to investigate a research phenomenon within its real-life context. Instructors can encourage students to come up with alternative ways of approaching case situations and examples in the book. The goal is to create an environment where students can fully engage in critical thinking in a logical and informed way.

Examples. Almost all examples in this book come from the field of leisure sciences, covering leisure, recreation, tourism and hospitality examples and cases, one of the unique features of this book. Examples in the chapters reflect the authors' own teaching and research experiences in the field of leisure, recreation and tourism and hospitality. This certainly makes the book more relevant and interesting for the students of leisure, recreation and tourism.

Acknowledgements

A book like this would not have been possible without generous and full support from our outstanding contributors. We owe a great debt to our friends and colleagues from around the globe for their diligent work on the chapters and their prompt revisions. We also thank them from the bottom of our hearts for being patient with us and for not giving up on us.

We wish to acknowledge the Commissioning Editor from CABI, Sarah Hulbert, and her staff for their support and guidance in developing this book.

We are particularly in debt to the countless number of students who have passed through our research method classes and educated us in the pedagogy of teaching methods classes.

Finally, we thank our families for their support and encouragement.

Editors

Ercan Sirakaya-Turk
The University of South Carolina

Muzaffer Uysal
Virginia Polytechnic Institute & State University

William E. Hammitt
Clemson University

Jerry J. Vaske
Colorado State University

Research Methods for Leisure, Recreation and Tourism

Ercan Sirakaya-Turk and Muzaffer Uysal

Learning Objectives

After studying this chapter, you will be able to:

1. Understand the importance of studying research in leisure, recreation and tourism;
2. Understand research and research process;
3. Learn how to formulate research problems and implications of research;
4. Know research typologies.

Chapter Summary

This chapter introduces the nature and importance of research in leisure, recreation and tourism. Research in this broad field is a process by which we produce new information and knowledge to answer questions, help managers solve problems and make effective decisions. The process is planned and systematic in its approach and is free from bias. Specifically, the process may consist of the formulation of research questions and ideas, identification of research concepts, development of the theoretical model that guides and underpins the research process, data collection, testing hypotheses, analysis

and feedback to theory, and generating new questions. This chapter provides research typologies that include exploratory research, descriptive research and explanatory research. Exploratory research is intended to develop familiarity with a topic in order to generate new insights. The chapter further introduces the concept of the unit of analysis in research.

An Introduction to Research in Leisure, Recreation and Tourism

The purpose of this introductory chapter is to familiarize you with the main concepts of the entire book. We will explain why you need to learn the process of conducting research with a few examples in the realm of leisure, recreation and tourism research. We will then review the actual process involved in carrying out a research project, concepts used throughout the book, and examples from past student projects that might help you think about your own research topic for the semester. Typically, instructors teaching research methods classes require their students to learn research methods with a hands-on project in your own area of interest. Thus, we need you to start thinking about an original research idea and the process early on so you can see the end of the tunnel before you even start doing the project. While we will give you enough details about how to proceed with each step in the upcoming chapters, you must picture the entire process before you even start reading the following chapters. This approach will help you use your time efficiently, so you can complete the research paper required by your instructor on time. Some of the concepts we introduce in this chapter will be repeated over and over again, so do not worry if you don't understand it the first time. Repetition will lead to clarification and better understanding of what some might call 'the dry concepts'.

A research methods class is unlike any other course you have taken before; it requires you to be critical, detail oriented, questioning, constantly thinking, and find new ways of writing and rewriting. Don't be scared; many students like you who

have taken this class before have graduated. Some learned very well to the extent that they have decided to pursue a career in research; you may not want to go that far, but this class will help you formulate, organize and write your thoughts in a logical manner. You will become a better consumer of research and a more informed citizen as you learn to attack flaws in logic and arguments. Make sure that you read the real-world examples presented in **research boxes** and other student projects to get an idea of why research is an important function in our society, global economy and in our disciplines. The following case illustrations represent the vast realm of research and how we go about investigating these interests. The example, shown in the first research box, is about a group of students who wanted to run their own nightclub; the second box contains illustrations of a few student ideas and questions and the significance of their study answers.

Research Box 1.1. So many bars, so little time!

College students are always interested in where to go and what to do during their free weekends. One of the popular recreation activities for some is going to clubs and bars. Students who were taking a research methods class with one of the authors of this book had to conduct original research as their term project. Among the members of a student team was one student who was already managing a nightclub, thus had experience and wanted to go solo in opening up his own nightclub/bar after graduation. He convinced his fellow group members to conduct a market feasibility study to determine the business potential for such a club among the many existing clubs in a college town. He wanted to know what type of music he should play and whether or not to provide live music; why students should prefer his bar to others; and what type of students frequent which bars; how much do they spend when out and about; and more importantly how much would they be willing to spend for drinks and food during their night out.

The project began with listening to customers in the bar managed by the leader of the group. He spoke to potential customers informally while they were having their beers. After sharing what he found with his group, they went out one night to question more students and to recruit a few of them for intensive interviewing about all aspects of their research. Their focus group with bar patrons provided the necessary information for a more in-depth, longer and more standardized form of research (survey research) with appropriate scales that included like/dislike, agree/disagree statements that probed bar patrons on their motivations to frequent bars, the types of bars they frequent, the reasons and their likelihood of visitation under certain pricing of liquor and beer, and students' concept of a new bar and whether these bar patrons would like their new bar concept and, most importantly, whether they would become a customer. Their idea took a semester to form. Framing their questions in a way that was free from bias, accurate, free from value words, the design of the questionnaire, the selection of a procedure that would give them a variation of responses that might come close to being representative of all potential bar patrons (population), the implementation of data collection and so on were all part of this process.

What they found at the end of their research process was that there were plenty of bars and clubs for college-age students but none for older adults age 26 and above who liked a 'classy' atmosphere, dress-to-impress, big-city-type of club where pricing did not matter as much. They could command higher prices for the type of club they were going to offer. The student ended up opening the bar for no more than US$50K initial investment and, after having a great time and making a good living for over 3 years, sold it for US$375K and moved out of the college town to a larger city.

Research Box 1.2. Examples of student research ideas and their relevance.

Typical research questions asked by students	Real-world Connection: significance of answers
What do students do during their leisure time? How satisfied are they with leisure service offerings?	Finding the answers to these descriptive questions can help create better programming for recreation facilities and public schools, understand the role of free-time and leisure within the lives of students, and how leisure could be structured so it is beneficial for students and the society in general. For example, many university recreation centres continuously monitor the use levels of various recreation activities and facilities, and satisfaction levels with them. Accordingly, they add or discontinue some leisure activities and recreation programmes, and improve facilities' equipment and work out schedules of their clients.
How do tourists make their trip decisions and what influences them? What stages do they go through when choosing among destinations?	The answers to these types of decision-making questions help develop effective advertising and promotion strategies tailored to different stages of consumer buying process. For example, Marriott Corporation taps into this research model during their advertising. The advertising is aimed at reminding people of the solution to the potential problem of what to do with relatives when they come to town for a visit. The advertising offers Residence Inns as an alternative lodging option. It uses an upside-down house as a picture and adds 'Does this remind you of your house when relatives come to visit?' It literally suggests 'that Marriott can help avoid chaos at home. Hosting people should not be a cause for stress at home'.
Why do women not participate in traditional men's sport such as football?	Equal access to recreation and leisure facilities to female students is mandated by law. An extension of this line of management application is to understand how women could be made welcome in the existing facilities without much investment on the part of the facility management. Understanding the reasons why women do not play men's sports or participate in activities traditionally dominated by men would not only satisfy the equal access mandate of the law by modifying the existing facilities, but also make existing facilities run more efficiently and to optimum capacity.
How and why is dining important for the health of a hospitality industry?	Understanding recreational dining experiences and patterns such as frequency/time, foods consumed, entertainment, and décor can help the hospitality industry at a tourism destination determine what foods, services and environments their customers dislike or enjoy. As a result, decision makers can improve services based upon these findings and serve their target customers better.

Why Study Research Methods in Leisure, Recreation and Tourism?

You see and read research every day. Regular opinion polls about a particular societal issue, political polling, restaurant guest surveys, airport comment cards, even polling of coaches to determine the rankings of best football teams represents some types of research. Why do you have to learn such a dull topic? Are you taking it because it is a required class for most higher education programmes in our field? On top of this, you might have heard about higher expectations placed upon such a course, and that a research methods class is one of the more difficult subjects a student can take, as it requires many hours of study time and it seems impossible to satisfy the teacher's expectations. These are all legitimate concerns but most of the time they are propagated by a few former methods students who found the topic difficult because they underestimated the time requirements and felt that they were unable to complete everything they wanted to accomplish within one semester. We understand this student psychology and other time requirements placed upon students of our times. Thus, we've designed this book to give you the optimum knowledge in a precise, efficient and effective manner.

If this statement does not convince you, here is some news for you: research is everywhere, and it will not disappear anytime soon. Research does not have to be dull or boring; indeed, it could be very exciting, especially if you can find a topic that truly interests you. As a matter of fact, as competition for scarce resources, markets and people's money increases, the reliance on research, and hence quality information, will become even more evident and widespread. As a high-ranking manager, you will find yourself in situations where **accurate** (reliable) and **trustworthy** (valid) information will mean personal job security, advancement in your career, respect from your colleagues and of course success for your company. Knowledge gained through research activities, especially in our field of recreation and tourism (the 'leisure industry') will not only help you and your organization but also your customers, guests and visitors with whom you interact. They will be appreciative of the resulting decisions (when implemented correctly, of course) that will help solve their problems and satisfy their needs and wants, and thus increase their loyalty to your business or organization.

Some of you will finish university and perhaps never step foot through its doors again; others will continue with their graduate degrees to become academics, researchers or consultants who conduct research. Most likely, you will be like many of us 'consumers of research' who read the research reports, news and papers that deal with a host of issues such as market segmentation, employee satisfaction, needs assessment, or recreation programme evaluation. In other words, you will become not the 'doers of research' but the 'consumers of research'. The question then is: why do you need to learn research methods if you are not going to become a researcher or a graduate student who typically needs to conduct thesis or dissertation research for his/her degree? For those of you who may not get involved with research directly, knowledge in research methods will still be helpful, as you will become a better decision maker in this knowledge economy where access to new information means everything. You will be in a position of power when you know how information has been obtained and interpreted. Thus, you will not accept claims based on their **face value** but require higher standards when accepting claims of advertisers, educators, pollsters and people around you who assert statements to be factually correct that are, in fact, based on **pseudoscience** or **bad science**. You will have the necessary analytical tools to be able to evaluate and assess life's claims.

In fact, we all were once very good researchers as babies, but as we got older, we seem to have abandoned that frame of mind. Babies do experimental research when they learn about their new world; they create presuppositions or hypotheses (i.e. what happens if I touch this burning oven?), test them (touch the hot oven), and confirm the presupposition (hot ovens hurt) and feed it back to their own world, thus supporting an ever-growing body of knowledge (theory) that consistently tells the baby that hot objects will burn and hurt when touched. Of course, we had so much to learn in such a short timeframe, we simply had to abandon that self-testing and self-learning, and started relying on our parents, teachers, friends and other sources of information such as newspapers, television and so on for information, and thus became efficient learners. However, because of the efficiency involved in relying on others' knowledge during that process we have lost some of our innate ability to investigate and think critically.

But, here, within this book, your methods professor wants to show you how to resharpen these skills you once had when you were a baby and to add to these skill sets a little bit more by letting you question things and by teaching you how quality information is supposed to be obtained and verified. By this, we do not mean that you ought to be disputing everything you hear or read or that you should start testing everything you see and learn about, but we hope that you will be in a position to say: 'I know that a certain assertion cannot be true because this research needs various planned steps and rigor before I can accept what is said is true on its face value'. For example, you will question when someone in your management team suggests that three out of four resort guests are happy with your leisure and recreational programming, if indeed this person has literally talked to four people only and three of them said: 'yes, indeed we are happy with the programming'. You will ask tough questions such as: How did the person obtain this information? How many people were involved? Is this group representative of our larger customer base? What questions did s/he ask to get responses? Was there any bias involved when asking the questions? Were the questions leading toward a positive answer (just like the lawyers sometimes do in courts and judges warn them not to lead the witness)?

So, being equipped with such knowledge will not only help you with your professional career but also with your daily life; you will learn to be sceptical and suspicious of unsubstantiated claims. For example, some economic impact reports indicate that spending US$1 in tourism advertising results in US$28 in return-rate for a particular region or state; or the multiplier effect of tourism in a particular community is seven or twelve (i.e. a dollar spent creates additional seven or twelve additional dollars in the local economy); or during your daily life, you might hear a politician or government official asserting something using statistics that appears to be a fact; or you might see a pharmaceutical commercial on television that product X is preferred over product Y by two to three doctors. How do you sieve through so much information without doing extensive first-hand research to get the most reliable and accurate information?

Research Box 1.3. Student research settings and decisions to solve research dilemmas.

Assume, for example, that you want to conduct a survey to assess students' levels of satisfaction with a university recreation centre on your campus. You go to the recreation centre during a rush hour, perhaps between 5 and 7 pm. You start with the students who work out in the free-weight room, because that area seems so busy. You make the decision to interview the students who are waiting to obtain a spot at a crowded workout station because they are waiting and don't seem to have much to do; they seem to be excellent candidates for your interviews. When they agree to participate and start answering your questions about the level of service, especially the space, all 25 male students turn out to be unhappy about the lack of workout space in the recreation centre.

Can you trust your results; does that really mean all recreation centre clients are unhappy about the space? Do these 25 male students represent the entire recreation centre clients? What about the female students? Where were they?

A better way for you to do your survey would be to randomly select the names from a list of all enrolled full-time students, making sure that females, minorities and international students are represented as well (there will be more on random samples in Chapter 6). You could ask them maybe by using a phone interview technique, online or mailing questionnaires about what they think of the workout situation. Because your sample was randomly selected, you would expect their answers to reflect what the students as a whole felt about the workout situation. The use of random samples is just one way that researchers try to ensure that the answers they find are representative of the larger group.

Knowing the tools of research will help you identify and disclose potential trouble spots, which could prevent misinformation coming from your office, hence preventing potential embarrassment and even the dismissal of responsible people. Moreover, you will gain research skills that could come in handy in your first jobs, providing you with the opportunity to impress your superiors, hence give you an opportunity to climb the corporate ladder a little more quickly.

Your professor might choose to teach the research methods class, as is the case with many of us, by letting you carry out an original research project either on your own or as a part of a larger group so that you can learn and question every aspect involved in a quality research. You will come to appreciate that obtaining useful and quality information is not as easy or simple as it sounds when you hear someone talk about it. Learning by doing, in other words, conducting an independent research project from its start to its end-report is our recommended approach for learning research methods. Having the necessary skills and tools of research will make you marketable and extremely valuable to your organization because modern companies are looking for candidates who are knowledgeable in conducting and understanding research. Even if you do not conduct the research yourself, you would be able to assess a research report for its mistakes, deficiencies and the credibility of the information therein helping your organization to get the best from research reports.

What are Research Methods? Leisure, Recreation and Tourism Research in Action

You may be asked to solve a marketing problem of a resort destination via primary research. Let's look at one example of a typical research setting.

Problem setting

Club Ottomans-II (Club O-II) is an all-inclusive vacation club in the Caribbean targeting mainly married couples without kids and fun-seeking singles from higher income brackets. Club O-II has been known as the 'Paradise on Earth', with many indoor and outdoor recreation opportunities, exclusive cuisine and beautiful sandy beaches, including one that is set-aside for nudists and provides a variety of other activities for alternative-style vacationers. Over the years, the club has created loyal customers; up to 87% of their new customers become repeat guests who usually come from north-eastern USA for a week-long vacation. The club has also been popular with British, Australian and Turkish tourists. There are ~16,000 guests, for whom only 12,000 addresses (~7,500 in the USA; ~2,000 in England; ~1,500 in Australia, and ~1,000 in Turkey) can be located.

Club O-II has been experiencing a consistent decline in their customer base since early autumn of 2008. The Chief Operating Officer (you, in this example) suspects that the decline in service quality, concomitant increase in prices and recent resentment against tourists by local residents have something to do with the sharp decline in repeat business. A focus group of 15 new guests from various age groups revealed that the problems stem mainly from dissatisfaction with the quality of the food, attitudes of the staff towards the guests and each other during work, and hostile attitudes of locals toward tourists. Guests also seem to be extremely concerned about the drinks at the bars because they have to pay for each drink, including soft drinks. Basically, it seems that the perception of all-inclusive advertising is deceptive because not everything is included in one price. You overhear one of the guests comment on how unfair the resort's advertising is: 'If I knew that drinks were not free and this expensive, I would not have come here in the first place'. He further comments 'they are ripping us off here as they charge extremely high prices for drinks; they know we have no choice but to buy our drinks here'.

Let's look at this problem from the viewpoint of a research-minded manager like you are. First of all, would you implement changes to all of the aforementioned problem areas based on the opinions of 15 people? Of course, some managers/marketers would argue even a single complaint is too much to ignore. However, realistically you would think more in detail of all the implications that decisions related to price changes, staff allocation, and new product and service offerings would have on the resort before acting on what you heard from a small number of people that only represent 0.0001% of your customers. After all, each and every one of the management-related decisions has bottom-line implications.

So, here, well-designed research might come in handy. If you were to conduct research based on the aforementioned scenario, what and how would you do it? First of all, the most important question you should ask yourself is why you need to conduct a study at all; this establishes the need for scientific observation, the purpose of your study. Second, another important question is whether or not these 15 people are **representative** of the larger 16,000 plus guests in a year. No way, you can be sure about this. Will you change the direction of the company because you heard 15 people complain? Maybe the same 15 people always complain because they are motivated by the prospect of receiving 'freebies'. On the basis of the responses of a small group of guests, you cannot say for sure that the guests at your resort are unhappy. What do the rest of the 15,985 guests think about the resort? What if it turns out that they are all happy? Maybe a focus group of people consists of volunteers, and volunteers may not represent the general population because they could be very different from the general population. So, simply put: your focus group becomes a **biased sample**, thus should not be trusted. Anything obtained from this group of visitors cannot be generalized to the entire population of the guests. So, you should wonder if the rest of the guests have similar concerns or if these 15 people are just a **sub-sample** of biased customers who seem to complain at every occasion. In short, you need to design a **reliable** and **valid** study that would address all these issues in a way that you can **generalize** your findings to your entire customer population in a year using a **random probability sampling** method.

How do you design a quality study that addresses the aforementioned issues but is generalizable to the larger population of guests without actually getting an answer from them? Magic involved in sampling and statistical techniques will help you come very close to the true answer. In Chapter 6, we will deal more closely with sampling issues.

As you can see from above example, the method involved in acquiring information to solve the outlined problems in a resort setting, such as this, requires one to carefully plan a systematic procedure that is value-free and unbiased (free from emotions or prejudices) when implemented, and therefore produces results that are trustable and accurate. So, what then is research? Can you come up with your own definition?

For us, *research in leisure, recreation and tourism means a process by which new information and knowledge are produced to answer questions we deem valuable and beneficial for our purposes in a planned and systematic way that is free from personal bias.* It is not just a fact-finding exercise, it is not just library research of some sort by reading pieces from a book or newspaper, it is not digging up information somewhere, but it is the combination of all activities that use the information generated by others, that can be replicated when sufficient detail is provided, that provides results which can be used in other

similar settings, that generates new questions and insights at the end, and foremost that provides an understanding by allowing us to make predictions to settings similar to the one studied. Thus, it must be based on some form of theory or rationale either generated (induced) by us or deduced from already available theories. So, what does a research process look like?

What is the Research Process?

Research question

A typical research project starts with an idea or questions (see Fig. 1.1 for an outline). You might be curious about why in certain Caribbean tourist destinations locals resent tourists from Western nations. You might ask yourself a question about what happens to your clientele base when you increase the price of a monthly membership to your recreation facility by 20%? You may have heard about the effect of school recreation programmes on preventing delinquency among young adults and wonder how this process really works. Simply put, an idea generated by you or a question posed by you or your supervisor is the only thing needed to initiate a research project. Depending upon the purpose of your research, whether exploring a phenomenon or describing it or explaining it, you will have to make a formal research statement or question. Obviously, asking a question must sound like a question and end with a question mark. For example, why is repeat visitation to your resort declining? If you are to state this question in a purpose statement format, it might read something like: the purpose of this research (or study) is to determine the reasons for customer decline at our resort. Note that this statement is clear and the study area is narrow enough to guide you in the right direction.

Where do ideas come from? They can be found anywhere: listening to your customers, talking to your peers, professors, friends and relatives, reading newspaper articles or formal research reports, reviewing social networks such travel blogs or simply observing phenomena around you. The next step in research is to develop some background to the topic. What is out there? What type of information can you find that might have dealt with similar topics? What can you learn from it? Is there some sort of coherent form of study results that point

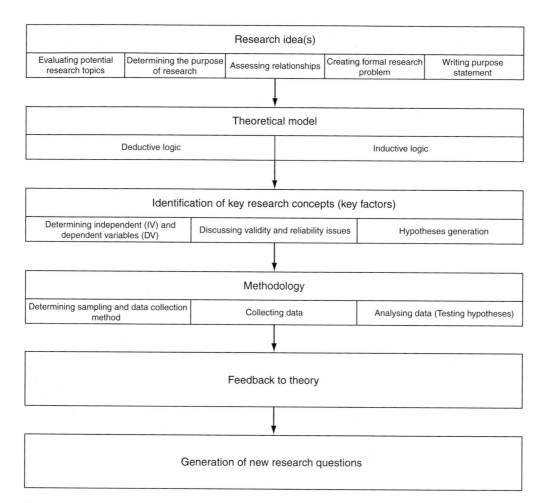

Fig. 1.1. Leisure, recreation and tourism research process.

toward a unified set of ideas (that we call **theories**) that might explain or provide you with clues as to how to tackle the problem?

Theory

Theories or rationales are important during the early phase of the research process; they will hint at possible solutions and give you a deeper understanding of the topic in which you are interested. If there is no formal theory, you may develop your own rationale as to how things might be related or working (inductive reasoning). Theories shape our world; they allow us to make sense of things, speculate and try to predict the future events. Theories allow us to make educated guesses about uncertain

future circumstances and events while taking into account all agreements and disagreements surrounding the phenomenon under study. Theories are building blocks of research but sometimes you can initiate research without a formal theory. A good theory must also be practical, so do not buy someone's assertion that 'it'll only work in theory'. Good theories should work in real life as well; there is nothing as realistic and practical as a good theory. Sometimes they may not work in the present, but a good theory may have been constructed by the theorist to work in the distant future when certain conditions are met, not necessarily in your current timeframe. Think about the famous theory of relativity by Albert Einstein. His theories were supported with evidence many years after he had first formulated them.

Theories allow a researcher to speculate on and play with unforeseen events, thus they work sometimes at the abstract level. Sometimes you may want to have a solution to some practical question without a much deeper understanding of the phenomenon, and then you may lack a firm theory. Even during those times, you may be relying on some sort of coherent ideas that may be formed while thinking and speculating about the topic. In relation to our resort scenario described above, you may use the formal **Social Exchange Theory** to describe the reactions of locals toward tourists. The theory asserts that host populations in a tourist destination will tolerate the inconveniences created by visitors if they are provided with some benefits from tourist activity.

> Theories are nets cast to catch what we call 'the world': to rationalize, to explain, and to master it. We endeavour to make the mesh ever finer and finer.
> Karl. R. Popper, *The Logic of Scientific Discovery*

Concepts and variables

The next step in research is identifying the relevant factors (concepts) and specifying the meanings of these factors (conceptualization) so the questions can be answered. In our resort example, one of the important factors is **attitudes** of locals toward resort guests and their **likelihood of return** to the resort. Concepts are building blocks of theories and make up the questions and the purpose statements. Once you know what you mean by an attitude, the next step would be to operationalize the concept of attitude, in other words, translating the concept into a measurable indicator which we call a **variable**. How will you measure the attitude variable? Using a five-point scale of agree/disagree statements or yes/no type questions?

Independent and dependent variables

Please note that we differentiate between an **independent variable** (IV) and a **dependent variable** (DV). Independent variables (IVs) refer to causes that lead to changes in the dependent variable. A DV is the effect or the outcome variable in which we are interested. One quick method of figuring out the dependent variable

is to answer the question: What is it that I am trying to explain, understand or find out the solution to? Operationalization usually leads to the formulation of hypotheses (educated guesses pointing out the likely outcome of a test between variables). We basically transform the research question into a testable statement with a clear indication of the expected relationship that might exist between variables according to our theory. For example, attitudes toward the guests might be a function of whether a person works in or has a family member working in the tourism industry. You may state: 'people who have family members working in the tourism industry are more likely to have positive opinions about tourists than the people who do not have a family member working in the tourism industry'. Your variables here are the **nature of employment** (whether or not a person works for the tourism industry) and **attitudes toward tourists**. Since the nature of employment determines (leads to) positive or negative attitudes toward tourists, it is the IV. It is independent because people work for the tourism industry regardless of their attitudes. Even if they don't have attitudes, they will still be working for the industry. Thus, we call this cause variable an independent variable. On the other hand, attitudes are affected by (depend on) the nature of employment, thus the DV. If people were *not to* work for the tourism industry, they would not have had any attitudes toward it. Because attitudes depend on where people work, we call this the dependent variable (DV).

Operationalization

The process of **operationalization** of variables and the formulation of hypotheses lead to the collection of information from relevant people or populations. There are basically two questions that need to be answered simultaneously before deciding how to proceed. You need to see the end of the tunnel before anything should happen, otherwise you might be wasting a lot of valuable time. The first question to ask is who will your study subjects be? Typically, you would go for a small group (**sample**) of people who you think is representative of the larger group (**population**). How will you collect the information? What means will you use?

Research Box 1.4. Independent variable versus dependent variable and hypothesis.

We differentiate between independent variables (IVs) and dependent variables (DVs) because we try to understand or explain things by assessing the relationship between variables. IVs refer to causes that lead to changes in the DV. This distinction is particularly relevant when you are investigating cause and effect relationships. For example, the variables such as income, cost of travel, attractiveness of the place and quality of services may all affect the demand for international tourism. Such variables would be called IVs. A DV is the effect (outcome) variable in which we are interested. In this case, the tourism demand, the number of arrivals from an originating market A to a destination place B would be the DV. The general research hypothesis should state that the demand for international tourism can be explained as a function of income, cost of travel, attractiveness of the place and quality of services.

A hypothesis can be defined as an educated guess that states a testable relationship between two or more variables. The specific null hypotheses related to the theory of demand explained above are as follows:

HO_1: The demand for international tourism is not affected by income.
HO_2: The demand for international tourism is not affected by the cost of travel to the destination.
HO_3: The demand for international tourism is not affected by the attractiveness of the destination.
HO_4: The demand for international tourism is not affected by the quality of services at the destination.

Data collection

Depending upon your purpose and budget, you might decide to collect information using a small group of people (a focus group) that might give you good insights but will not provide you with generalizable information. Perhaps you could conduct survey research via questionnaires mailed to each individual member of the representative sample of the population. In our resort example, you could choose to use the telephone interview method with your guests. Once you have the data, you will need to enter them into a computer database and test your hypotheses. Here, you will have to be familiar with the basic concepts in statistics such as measures of central tendency (Mean, Mode and Median), measures of variability (Range, Variance and Standard Deviation), test of independence or chi-square, t-test, analysis of variance (ANOVA), correlation analysis and so on; we assume that the student of this book has had an introductory course in statistics. You do not need to be expert in statistics to do well in research methods; however, being familiar with basic concepts would make understanding easier.

Data analysis and results

On the basis of what you find through using statistics, you will then either accept or reject your hypothesis relating back to the theory with which you started. Based on the results of your testing, you will either provide more support for the theory or question the predictive ability of your theory within the limits of your research setting. More questions should be generated because of this analytical decision process. If the results of your research do not make you pose new questions, you should reevaluate your research process and/or read more studies that have similar or contradictory findings in different settings. Ultimately, you will generate more research questions than you have answered. A full application of research processes can be found in Worked Example 1.1 at the end of this chapter.

Research Typologies

Generally, research can be categorized as either **experimental** or **non-experimental research**. Depending upon the nature of the investigation, they can further be divided into **exploratory**, **descriptive** and **explanatory** (causal) research. The first major category is called **experimental research**. Although you will seldom find or perform experimental research in our field, it is important to recognize the difference between experimental and other research designs in order to understand what we mean when we say a **true** cause-and-effect relationship. In other words, how can we be certain when asserting one thing leads to another?

Perhaps, the best way of understanding the impact of something on a phenomenon is experimental in nature because one is in a position to isolate the impact, and attribute the cause of the effect to that source only and nothing else. In an experimental study, you can give treatments (conditions that can be manipulated) to your group of interest to determine whether it will change their reaction/behaviour due to that treatment. In a typical experiment, you can form two groups, one that receives the treatment (our manipulation group) and the other, the control group, that receives none or different treatment by a random assignment of people to the

respective groups. By observing the reaction of the first experimental group and comparing it to that of the second group, you can determine whether your treatment had an effect on the observed outcome of the first group. There can be a number of variations in designing experimental research, each attempting to control for possible external factors and situations that are likely to impact the outcome of research. The challenge is to be able to conclude that the outcome is the result of the treatment itself only and nothing else. Box 1.5 illustrates an example of an experimental research design that could be done using the resort example in this chapter, whereas Box 1.6 shows an example study from the literature in our field. There will be more detailed discussion on experimental research design in Chapter 10.

Research Box 1.5. Experimental research scenario.

In the resort scenario presented earlier, you might be interested in isolating the impact of the quality of the food on satisfaction levels of guests. In other words, the research question you are interested in solving is: Is the quality of food responsible for dissatisfaction among your guests? From your guest list, you might randomly choose, say, 70 guest names to create two groups. You can draw 35 guest names out of the hat and assign them to the experimental group and the rest to the control group. The control group would be given regular meals that the resort has been serving, and the experimental group would be given 'higher-quality food' that was prepared elsewhere by a known chef. The difference observed between the two groups when related to their satisfaction would isolate the impact of food on satisfaction/dissatisfaction.

Research Box 1.6. Experimental research example from the literature.

The study used a novel field experiment to test the assumption that subjective feelings are important in recreation conflict. During a weekend, cross-country skiers in a popular recreation area were assigned randomly to an experimental group who were exposed to an operating snowmobile and a control group who were not exposed. In the experimental group, skiers were asked to fill out a self-administered survey shortly after encountering a snowmobile, while skiers in the control group filled out a self-administered survey without having been exposed to a snowmobile. Survey respondents were given no clue as to the relationship of the snowmobile and survey being conducted. Results showed that relative to the control group, skiers who encountered a snowmobile had the quality of their affective experiences — as measured by feelings of relaxation, peacefulness, joy, harmony and annoyance — significantly reduced. In other words, the snowmobilers reduced skiers' enjoyment on the slopes. This result points to the subjective nature of recreation conflict. Furthermore, the encounter with the snowmobile affected the participants' beliefs about the extent to which noise from snowmobiles disturbed the quality of ski touring in general.

Vitterso, J., Chipeniuk, R., Skar M. and Vistad, O. (2004) Recreational conflict is affective: The case of cross-country skiers and snowmobiles. *Leisure Sciences* 26, 227–243.

The second major category, which you might encounter more often in our field, is **non-experimental research.** In this category of research, you do not give any treatment to your group of interest or subjects but observe them in their natural settings as they process information, interview questions, or survey items and describe their reaction to your study phenomenon. In non-experimental research, you cannot truly study the cause-and-effect relationship between variables (factors); all you can point out is the **inferred relationship** (outcomes) but never the true cause. For example, if you wanted to survey visitors in your community to find out whether they came there because they saw an advertisement of your community on television, your descriptive study can only point to their presence after the fact; in no way can you truly identify whether the television advert or something else was responsible for their visit. You could find out whether they saw the advert, whether they thought it had an impact, and if so what they could recall about the advertising. However, since you cannot control the information or the setting in which they saw the advert, the study results cannot isolate the true effect of advertising on their visitation behaviour.

The non-experimental research comes in a variety of forms, some of which could help you come close to the true cause–effect relationship but you can never be certain if, in fact, your study variables really caused the outcome. As part of non-experimental research, we will briefly cover **exploratory research** (explore a new under-researched area), **descriptive research** (as the name implies it describes the characteristics of the phenomenon you are interested in), and **explanatory** or **relational research** (investigates how one or more things are related to each other). There is also another type of research category, **historical and ethnographic research** (examines the effects of past events on current events), which we will not cover in this book, as you will seldom encounter such research in our field, although it is becoming popular among a few colleagues in our field.

The first group of studies can be collectively called exploratory. Don't confuse the two terms explanatory and exploratory. Exploratory studies are done when there is not much information about a phenomenon at hand, when the subject is relatively new and thus did not attract much attention or simply to develop procedures to be used in larger follow-up studies. Frequently our students in methods classes come up with ideas that have simply not been researched well enough, or are too specific to their institution and have not attracted outside attention to produce the necessary mass of studies so they can read and compile a literature review (background information) for their research projects. We suggest that you find a well-researched area so you have enough reading material for the literature review section of your project proposal. You will find more information in Chapter 3.

The second category of studies refers to descriptive studies, which simply describe the characteristics of a population without truly understanding the underlying structure of the problem; why and how it happened in the first place. They are useful in that they describe the setting of the problem or events. Typically, we start with describing the situation and certain events before trying to explain the reasons why and how they happened in the first place. So, descriptive studies precede all other studies because they set the stage for further analysis of the situation, events or phenomena. It answers the '*what*' question. The largest and perhaps best-known descriptive study is a population census. It describes various characteristics of the population accurately and precisely. When you obtain visitor statistics such as number of visitors to your city's attractions or the percentage of guests satisfied with your resort's offerings you are basically describing the situation. You do not know why people visit your city's attractions, or why and how the guests are satisfied with recreation programmes at your resort. Surveys that seek to describe the percentage of people holding a particular opinion (e.g. the percentage of people preferring outdoor activities to indoor recreation activities) are examples of descriptive studies. Here, you are simply interested in describing the current state of preferences for recreational activities, how many tourists visit your city within a year, how many people attend your parks within summer months or how many people attend your school's basketball games. These are all questions that are descriptive in nature; in other words, when a study is designed primarily to describe what is going on or what exists we call it descriptive. Without knowing the current state of affairs, you cannot make much difference around you.

To make a difference, to change the world, to improve your business or eliminate some of the problems you encounter, you are automatically interested in explanatory studies (sometimes referred to as **relational** or **correlational** studies): studies that tell us how our causes (e.g. programmes, treatments, actions, interferences) affect the outcomes of interest. Regardless of what the situation might be, your instructor will probably ask you to do a combination of approaches because a descriptive study alone cannot explain why things really happen.

Many authors of research method books use different ways of categorizing research; instead of using the term explanatory they might call them relational, correlation, or causal-comparative studies. All these terms point toward the third general group of studies, which we call explanatory studies. The explanation of certain phenomena, whether by isolating the impact of one variable (cause, treatment, independent variable) on the outcome (effect, dependent variable) like in experimental studies or whether the purpose is to determine the existence of some sort of relationship between variables (correlations or relational research) without attributing a cause, is the reason why a researcher conducts explanatory research. What the researcher is really interested in is a true understanding, followed by explaining or predicting the phenomenon under investigation. Although the terms seem to be a matter of semantics, they do indeed help to understand a class of studies, its methods, its benefits and its limitations. Although all study types can be useful in different circumstances, the ultimate goal of doing research is to provide some sort of thorough understanding and prediction of similar cases in the future. Explanatory research helps us understand how and why things happen in relation to other events or factors. For example, if you would like to know how many customers you would lose by increasing your price by 10%, you are looking at the relationship between the price and the number of customers using your services. The underlying assumption is that as the price of a good or service increases, customer demand for it will decrease. This is the first law of demand you will recall from your introductory economics class (note: not all relational variables are causal but all causal studies are relational). The purpose of various study types along with specific examples from our field are shown in Table 1.1. When doing a study you will want to explore the topic first, then describe it and finally explain what you have observed. Let's briefly look at each category of studies.

Table 1.1. Research typologies.

Research type	Exploratory studies	Descriptive studies	Explanatory studies
General aims	Develop familiarity with the topic Yield new insights Explore an under-researched area Develop procedures for future larger studies Test the feasibility of in-depth research Break new ground via new insights Answer the 'what', 'how' questions for limited cases	Observe and describe the nature of a population or event of interest Describe what is happening Answer the 'what' questions Map out the current situation First step in research Provides broad picture	Provide true understanding and prediction of topic of interest Examine relationships Determine cause and effect relationships Answer the 'why' question
Temporal use	Beginning, when topic is new	Now	Now, past or future
Limitations	Answers not fully satisfactory	Rarely provide satisfactory answers	May not be able to determine real cause–effect relationship if the study is non-experimental

(Continued)

Table 1.1. Continued.

Research type	Exploratory studies	Descriptive studies	Explanatory studies
Common techniques used	Focus groups Case study Nominal (guided) group discussions Interviews	Surveys Observations Interviews	Correlation analysis Experimental research Causal-comparative research (surveys, historical research) Interviews
Example tourism questions	What is the opinion of a group of guests in your hotel regarding the level of services? How do travel agencies cope and deal with difficulties and competition imposed upon their business by emerging technologies such as the Internet?	What are the most frequently visited tourist attractions in your city? How can tourist be classified? What tourism market segments exist, and how large are these segments? What are the factors affecting destination choices of college students?	Is there a relationship between exchange rates at a destination and visitation rates? If yes, what is the nature of this relationship? Can we reliably predict people's choices for a vacation destination knowing what images they have of the place and their motivations for taking the trip? What are the impacts of images, and motivations in choice decisions?
Recreation example	What are the existing barriers and obstacles to participation in recreational activities?	What percentage of visitors to a recreational sports centre buys food during their visit?	How would park visitors react to a 28% price hike? What would the effect be on visitation rates?
Leisure example	How and why is dining important for the health of a leisure industry?	How satisfied are customers with various services at our resort?	What is the relationship between employee satisfaction and customers return intentions in area hotels? What roles do peoples' sensory perceptions play during a recreational dining experience? What type of effect does music have on consumption behaviour of diners?

Discussion Questions

1. Why should we do research?
2. Define research and its process.
3. Discuss typologies of research with examples.
4. Identify one research topic that may deal with some aspects of recreation, parks, tourism and hospitality and then provide justification as to why this particular topic needs to be investigated.

Chapter Assignment

You have been just hired by Washington DC Area Convention and Visitors Bureau (WDCAC&VB) to conduct a study that will, first, determine the level of satisfaction (dissatisfaction) of international travellers with respect to main amenities (attractions) in the area, and second, further understand the barriers to international travellers to visit attractions once they have arrived. Write a brief proposal for this study that would convince your boss that you are capable of conducting the study. The main effort in this proposal should centre on your methodology, operationalization and justification of the variables for inclusion in your study. Please also remember that your boss wants to make sure that you look at the problem by origin of visitors (Germany, UK and Japan) to the area. Specifically you need to provide brief written answers to the following:

1. State a general objective statement for the proposed plan of the study.
2. Provide a brief statement of justification for the importance of the study.
3. What relationships exist among study's concepts (your theory) that would help your boss understand the setting of the problem?
4. Develop at least two examples of testable hypotheses for the study.

Key Terms

Concept: A term whose meaning is agreed upon.
Dependent variable: The outcome, the effect, or the result that independent variables have in hypothesized relationships. The answer to our question 'what am I trying to explain?'

Generalizability: Ability of research findings from a small sample to be applied to the larger target population.
Hypotheses: A tentative statement or educated guess that gives direction to research by predicting relationships of our variables or outcomes of our study.
Independent variable: The treatment or cause variable – the variable that is manipulated or changed to examine its effect or influence upon the dependent variable.
Operationalization: A process of creating measurements by assigning values or definitions to variables.
Population: A collection of elements or subjects belonging to the same group.
Pseudoscience: A practice, belief or claim that is falsely being portrayed as science. Astrology, linking personalities or future events to stars, is a typical example.
Research: In leisure, recreation and tourism means a process by which new information and knowledge are produced to answer questions we deem valuable and beneficial for our purposes in a planned and systematic way that is free from personal bias.
Research methods: Techniques involved or steps taken to produce new knowledge or to study a phenomenon.
Sample: A subgroup of a population that is selected to represent the population.
Theory: Tool of mind used to help understand, explain a subject matter, and/or predict an outcome and/or events.
Variable: Concepts that can take on different values such as gender (male or female), agreement (agree or disagree) or income (dollar value of earnings).

Worked Example 1.1. Solution to Case Study Questions

1. What is the main problem? Why do you need to conduct a study?

If you think that the main problem is just the high prices for drinks or locals' attitudes toward the tourists, you would be mistaken. Remember, only a small fraction of guests expressed their dissatisfaction with various aspects of the resort. They did not list all possible problem areas that might be of concern to a larger population of guests who stayed in the resort. What would they think? So, these little useful hints are part of the problem but not the main problem. The main problem is: why is there a consistent decline in the resort's business? What is the reason for such consistent decline over a period of two or three years? A potential list of likely answers to this question would perhaps include employee dissatisfaction with pay levels, a faulty perception of advertising by the guests (fine print that has not been read by the guest), elitist attitudes toward the locals by the resort guests and hence locals' reciprocal negative attitudes toward the resort guests. So, the first step would be to identify all possible reasons that would be part of the solution (you will have to consult the relevant literature here to gain more insight and background into your research problem). By doing so, you are basically creating a list of **hypothetical answers** that, if confirmed by your collected information later, would constitute a solution verified by empirical observation. Would, for example, employee dissatisfaction with pay levels be related to poor attitudes toward the guests? When conducting your research, you will need to create **hypotheses** that will give you guidance to your research. So, you know what you expect the results will show and how you are going to test relationships once you have the information.

2. Are there any smaller problems that you think of as an important area for study while investigating the main problem and are they are in some fashion related to each other, hence to the main problem at large?

Maybe in some way, these little problems are parts of a larger problem and hence are related to the main problem? For example, what are the salary levels of workers? How many hours are they required to work? Is tipping allowed? Here again, we are talking about a **theory** of some sort that connects all concepts (variables) together to give a unified explanation of seemingly unrelated or even sometimes contradictory explanations. Is there an existing theory that describes such scenario? Or do you have to create your own theory that might explain what is going on easily? Have other people done similar studies that looked at some of these questions? What did they find? Can you list some of their findings as an input for your study? Typically, there is a real truth out there independent of what we are thinking; the relationships are there and working and there might be rules or modi operandi that control such relationships that are waiting to be discovered. We always have theories, or parts of theories that make our world around us understandable, helping us drive logical conclusions. Most examples of what we think are original, probably had been studied before, elsewhere, maybe in a different context. Nevertheless, there must be some information out there, in the library, books, research articles, newspaper clips, even unwritten, existing only in your professor's thoughts and maybe, if you are lucky, someone might have pulled all these together, and called it an 'XYZ theory'. In the context of this research example, you might use 'disconfirmation of expectations theory', which asserts that people are satisfied if the performance of whatever they are consuming or using is exceeding their prior expectations. They will be dissatisfied if the performance remains below their expectations. Or you might use Azjen's and Fishbein's theory of planned behaviour, which postulates that under certain circumstances people's attitudes will predict their behaviour. When studying the same question within this resort setting, you might try to understand why local residents are hostile towards the resort guests by using 'social exchange theory'. It argues that residents will tolerate inconveniences of tourists as long as they also benefit from their spending in their community; otherwise they will not support tourism activity in their community and, over time, they might even show antagonistic feelings towards their guests. You might deduce hypotheses from this theory and test them whether they are valid within your setting. You will learn about the importance and the role of theories and derivations that give directions to your research, the so-called hypotheses, later.

3. Who are you going to study? What is your population?

The population of resorts guests is at around 16,000 (theoretical population, theoretical because you do not have access to all of them), you know this because of the customer registrations. But, you only have 12,000 addresses (list of addresses or the so-called sampling frame), which constitutes your effective population or practical population. Then, the question becomes, shall I ask all 12,000 customers? Thanks to statistical theory, the good news is that you do not need to ask or interview all of your customers; you could select a random sample, or small group of people who are **typical customers** in your resort, and conduct your research with them. Normally, if this subset of customers is selected carefully so that they represent the larger group, you can use as few as 600–800 people. Interestingly, for a nation as large as USA, in which 190 million plus voters elect the president, political opinion polls usually do not ask more than 1200–1800 people to get an answer as close as ±4% of the true value. So, the design and selection of the sample is very important. How are you going to select the potential respondents? Are you going to use random-probability design or a convenient sample? Are there any drawbacks of each of these methods? These are typical questions that you have to answer before doing anything else. Thus, the sample will be made up of fewer people from the list of the effective population of 12,000 whom you will talk to, write to or e-mail. Typically, the sample will range from 600 to 1200, depending upon the accuracy you want. Statistical theory, here, suggests that if you would like to reach ±4 % to values that can be observed in the theoretical population (remember you never observe this because you never go to the entire population), you will have to approach at least XYZ number of people. What's really important is: can you select the sample in a way that is representative of the population without introducing unintentional and unwanted bias? There are a variety of ways to do this and you will learn about this later.

4. How are you going to go about collecting information so you can draw conclusions about the general population of guests? Are you going to design your own questions and/or scales or will you use scales and questions that have been validated before by someone else?

Typically, we avoid reinventing the wheel by using already accepted and used instruments. Only if we cannot find a measurement instrument do we create our own data collection tool/instrument. The next series of questions: are you going to talk to the guests on site, or at their home, and how, via what medium (face-to-face interviews, telephone interviews, a standard survey questionnaire sent via regular postal mailing or internet (e-mailing lists)? What type of design would be best to get the answers to your questions? Are there other methods to be used that can get you the answers to your questions easily and effectively? Do you have enough in the budget for conducting such research? How much can you spend for what method? For example, you might opt for conducting on-site surveys or interviews with guests while they are in your resort. Or you might include a list of questions and scales that are related to your questions in a survey instrument of some kind (typically self-reported questionnaires) and mail them to randomly selected guests from your list of 12,000 and hope that they fill it out and send it back to you. There are ways and guidelines for creating effective surveys so the response rate is high enough to draw reliable conclusions. Of course, survey questionnaires are one of many ways of collecting data. There are other types of data collection techniques that we typically use. Depending upon the choice of the research design, whether for example it is an experimental or non-experimental, descriptive study, exploratory or explanatory study (see the difference between them) or relational or causal-comparative, we will explain in detail how to collect information, the caveats, rules and various methods.

5. Once you have the information, what are you going to do with it? How are you going to analyse the responses? What programme will you use for data analysis? Are you familiar with a data analysis programme such as SPSS, SAS or Excel that will help you with analysis?

Typical programmes in our field ask students to complete at least one course in statistics before taking a research methods course. 'Research methods' is not a statistics course but does use statistics at one point or another. Your instructor might review statistical tools so you refresh your forgotten statistic skills. Chapters in Part IV of this book provide discussions on common statistical tools used by student projects. The next question becomes: how are you going to code and enter the responses into a computer software programme? Responses to a series of questions by one person constitute one unique entry in your database system; in other words, if you have one questionnaire filled out by one of your respondents, that questionnaire is given an ID number and entered into the database as one unique entry. So, a person becomes one observation. What happened to that person's answers in the questionnaire? They become variables or parts of variables that when put together can designate one variable. For example, in the scenario above attitudes of guests toward locals might be measured on a five-point agree/disagree scale. The sum of all responses (items) to all attitude statements can make a variable called 'attitudes toward locals'. Every response must be entered in a single column in the computer program (thus every column becomes potential variable) but it is you who will decide whether another **unique variable** that sums up all attitude items in columns shall be created and called an 'overall attitude variable'. You will learn about these types of issues, coding, programming and so on, in Part IV of this book.

6. How are you going to use this information?

The most important part of your research will be not just the design, proposal of your research, and subsequent steps to collect the information but how you can report and use the information. Potential use and implementation of research outcome is probably the most important area. There are no guidelines here except that as a researcher or consumer of research you can only read what has been found in what way, but you cannot assure the correct implementation of research results. All you can do is to suggest what the research findings are telling you. Two people doing the same research may end up implementing totally different programs to achieve their objectives. However, research is a value-free undertaking and thus cannot answer normative questions. It can only suggest or point towards the likely solutions of problems. The decision maker, you, will decide how to read the findings. Of course, knowing what others in similar situations with similar research findings have suggested would illuminate your path toward a better interpretation of your results. Thus checking back, with what other had done and written about in the past might help you during the final phase of reporting.

7. The answers to these types of questions before you even start conducting the study constitute a formal research proposal

You may not submit a formal proposal in your own resort unless you work for someone else and are required to submit a brief outline of what you will do and how much it will cost in terms of time and money. For typical methods classes in programmes in our field, you will have to write and submit a formal research proposal to your instructor for approval of your term research project. There are certain guidelines and minimum required information to be included in a research proposal. We dedicate Chapter 5 to how to write an effective research proposal.

References and Further Reading

Babbie, E.R. (1990) *Survey Research Methods,* 2nd edn. Wadsworth Publishing Company- Cengage Learning, Inc., Florence, Kentucky.

Blankenship, C.D. (2009) *Applied Research and Evaluation Methods in Recreation.* Human Kinetics Publishing, Inc., Champaign, Illinois.

Dillman, D.A. (2000) *Mail and Internet Surveys: The Tailored Design Method,* 2nd edn. John Wiley and Sons, New York.

Finn M., Elliott-White, M. and Walton, M. (2000) *Tourism and Leisure Research Methods.* Pearson, Prentice Hall, New Jersey.

Lankford, S. and Mitra, A. (1997) *Research Methods in Park, Recreation, and Leisure Services*. Sagamore Publishing, Inc., Champaign, Illinois.

Riddick, C.C. and Russell, R.V. (1999) *Evaluative Research in Recreation, Park and Sport Settings: Search for Useful Information*. Sagamore Publishing, Inc., Champaign, Illinois.

Ritchie, B.W, Burns, P.M. and Palmer, C.A. (2005) *Tourism Research Methods: Integrating Theory with Practice*. CAB International, Wallingford, UK.

Salkind, J.N. (2008) *Exploring researc*h, 7th edn. Prentice Hall, Princeton, New Jersey.

Veal, A.J. (2006) *Research Methods for Leisure and Tourism: A Practical Guide*, 3rd edn. Prentice Hall, New Jersey.

Zikmund, G.W., Babin, J.B., Carr, C.J. and Griffin, M. (2008) *Business Research Methods*. South-Western, Cengage Learning, Mason, Ohio.

Vaske, J.J. (2008) *Survey Research and Analysis: Applications in Parks, Recreation and Human Dimensions*. Venture Publishing Inc., State College, Pennsylvania, p. 635.

chapter 2

Leisure, Recreation and Tourism Research Design

William Hammitt, Begum Aybar-Damali
and Francis A. McGuire

Learning Objectives

After studying this chapter, you will have a better understanding of:

1. Purpose and types of research;
2. Steps to designing a research problem and project;
3. Types of variables and hypothesis testing;
4. Reliability and validity in research projects.

Chapter Summary

This chapter introduces some of the basic research concepts and design. The chapter starts by discussing the purpose and types of leisure, recreation and tourism research and then how to formulate and evaluate potential research topics and problems. The objective of the chapter is accomplished by a discussion of identifying/writing a research purpose, developing and writing hypotheses, concepts and constructs, variables, significance and significance testing, causality and association, and reliability and validity. The chapter concludes with examples of topics discussed in the chapter.

Purpose and Types of Recreation and Tourism Research

Research in recreation and tourism usually falls into one of the three major categories: **descriptive**, **relational** or **causal**. Descriptive research is simply a systematic recording of data on the subject matter under investigation. This type of research does not attempt to draw relationships among recreation behaviours or social phenomena and other factors. For example, a list of the messages posted on a bulletin board describes how the board is being used. Another example would be socio-demographic characteristics of members of a local YMCA such as gender, age, income level, etc. You may collect information through **observations and/or surveys**. Watching and noting the behaviours of people or listing characteristics of recreational settings are examples of how to collect information through observation. You might be interested in describing the details of an event or instance, recreation behaviour, or how people use recreational settings. You may also investigate a research interest by asking people to report their behaviour or opinions; this

©CAB International 2011. *Research Methods for Leisure, Recreation and Tourism* (ed. E. Sirakaya-Turk *et al.*)

would illustrate a survey method. In either case, the ultimate purpose is to simply describe a recreational behaviour, experience, a setting or a phenomenon.

One of the most common types of research carried out in the recreation and tourism field is **relational research**. Beyond descriptive studies, observing and describing events or behaviours, with relational research the researcher begins to explore and identify relationships among various factors, such as age, weight, height, characteristics of the environment, number of recreation areas in a city, distance travelled, how many times you hike in a week, how happy you are when you play basketball, or how often your grandfather practises playing

his old guitar. Relational studies use **correlational statements** describing how two variables, or factors, are related. Correlation indicates the possibility of a cause–effect relationship. For example, participating in yoga correlates with relaxation. However, correlation does not indicate causation. In this example, we cannot say practising yoga will cause relaxation.

Here, we briefly describe two studies that are examples of recreation and tourism research. They represent the sorts of issues that recreation researchers are interested in and how they go about investigating these interests. Both of these studies have some similarities regarding the types of questions they try to answer.

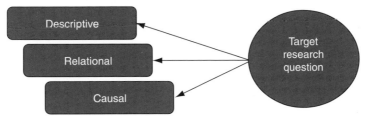

Fig. 2.1. Types of research.

Research Box 2.1. A few illustrations.

Backpacker tourist enclaves: Robert W. Howard (2007) states that today's backpackers are different than archetypal backpacker tourists. They follow well-trodden routes and many types of inexpensive accommodation are available to them, such as traveller centres, backpacker meccas, backpacker ghettos or enclaves. However, since little is known about the characteristics and types of these backpacker enclaves, along with how tourists use and view enclaves, he decided to learn more about them. He investigated five backpacker enclaves where tourist backpackers stay. Howard spent two or three days and one evening in each enclave. The researcher noted the layout and size of the enclaves, counted tourist-oriented businesses such as hotels and observed the tourist behaviours. With this approach the researcher was able to describe the characteristics of backpacker enclaves. Howard states that the tourists at the enclaves use the places to relax, plan their trips, see local attractions, use the internet, and socialize with other backpackers.

Bridge game: Do you know how to play bridge? Do your parents or grandparents know how to play bridge? Have you ever considered joining a bridge club as a hobby? David Scott's (1991) study on participation in contract-bridge activity explored the world of bridge. He was interested in understanding problems related to participation in a group leisure activity, such as bridge. Thus in his study, he discussed the diminished popularity of bridge in the USA and explored the factors that affect participation in this activity. Scott participated in several clubs to observe a range of activities; he played with players and joined informal conversations. He also conducted in-depth interviews with the members of clubs. His study describes the participants' personal history in bridge, frequency of participation, activity and setting preferences, reasons for playing, commitment to studying the game, friendship patterns within the groups, and technical terms used by the players. In addition, he also collected information about the factors related to participation frequency such as reasons for missing games or not playing with a particular group and reasons for withdrawing from a club.

The type of research least often used in recreation and tourism research is **causal research**. This type of research involves investigating the relationship between two variables with an expectation of inferring one variable to be the cause of the other. The most important difference between causal research and relational research lies in how you obtain information. In causal research the time order between the variables investigated is important; cause occurs before the effect.

How do you decide on the type of research to use? Let's assume you are interested in visitors to the Great Smoky Mountains National Park (GSMNP). Shown are example research questions you might pursue. Each question seeks a different type of answer; the target research question that is being investigated tells you if your research is going to be descriptive research, relational research or causal research.

Research Box 2.2. Research questions illustrating three different types of research.

Descriptive: What are the characteristics (i.e. socio-economic, demographics) of Great Smoky Mountain National Park (GSMNP) users and in what activities do they participate?

Relational: What is the relationship between age of visitors to GSMNP and the types of activities they participate in?

Causal: Does viewing the GSMNP visitor centre orientation film influence visitors' littering behaviour while in the park?

The Role of Theory in the Research Process

Some research is guided by a theory and uses the theory to develop research questions, hypotheses and observations. Ultimately you want to use your observations to support, or refute, the original theory. This approach, going from the general (the theory) to the specific (hypotheses), is called deduction, or a **deductive approach**. For example, you may theorize that the aging process causes a reduction in physical stamina and as a result individuals become less active as they age. Based on that you then hypothesize that people aged 65 or over will spend fewer hours engaged in physical activity than they did when they were under 30 years of age. You gather data from a sample of older individuals, determining the number of hours they currently exercise every day compared to daily exercise 40 years ago. The data indicate that older people currently spend more hours engaged in physical activity than they did when younger, causing you to rethink your theory.

Other research begins with observations, leads to hypotheses, and then evolves into the development of general statements, or theories. This approach of moving from the specific (your observations) to the general (your theory) is called induction, or an **inductive approach**. For example, you regularly go to a gym at 7pm every evening and notice that few people over the age of 65 are there. You visit several gyms and observe the same thing. Based on this observation you hypothesize the people reduce their level of physical activity as they age. You then gather data from a sample of older individuals and find that they prefer to exercise early in the day and that is why few are present during the evening hours. As a result you revise your thinking and develop an alternate explanation for link between aging and gym use.

What are Some Sources of Research Topics?

What is the ultimate goal of recreation and tourism research? The most common reasons for doing recreation and tourism research are: (i) to answer society's questions; and (ii) to contribute to explanations of a phenomenon. But, as a new researcher, you may wonder how to select a research topic. What are the sources of research topics? We consider research as a person's attempt to learn about the world, thus research topics emerge in various forms. The sources of research topics can be listed in at least four general categories:

1. Natural observation.
2. Media (Newspapers, magazines, radio/TV programmes, etc.).

3. Academic journals, text books, technical reports.
4. Experts in the field such as your advisor(s), manager, supervisor, etc.

By its nature, recreation and tourism research has implications for many aspects of social life. Although these sources may provide you a good range of research topics, it is very important that you as a recreation and tourism researcher continually communicate with others about how recreation and tourism takes place in daily life. These discussions may provide additional research topics and give you an opportunity to discuss their implications.

Developing Your Research Problem

Where do research questions come from? All research starts with a question, or at least an uncertainty, although there is no one answer to how you arrive at your research question. It may come from something that happened with your job. For example, you may wonder why people pay a membership fee at the gym but seldom come. Or it may come from something you read. For example, you read about your local recreation department's midnight basketball league and their rationale that the league will keep kids 'off the streets' and out of trouble and you wonder whether that is true. It may come from your own experiences. For example, you wonder why some parents get so vocal at high school soccer games and what impact that has on the players. Or perhaps you observe the human condition and wonder why things are as they are. For example, you may wonder what happens to poor people when parks start charging fees. Or maybe one of your professors discussed a theory and you want to know how it might apply to recreation. For example, your psychology professor talked about selective optimization with compensation and you wonder whether that may explain why some older people reduce the number of leisure activities they do as they get older. The questions are endless. However, there are some things that are important in determining your research question.

First, make sure it is a topic in which you are interested. Research is hard work and the likelihood that you will persist when things get tedious or challenging is increased if you are fully engaged with your topic. Second, read, read and then read some more. Search for what others have done in that area and find what others have written. This will help determine whether your topic is recent and appropriate. In addition, you will certainly alter your question as new information becomes available to you. Reading the work of others will let you know not only what has been done but also how it has been done. After reading you should refine your topic. That typically means you need to focus. Many research problems are too broad and not realistic. Focusing helps identify a manageable problem, one you will have the resources to address. Trochim (2005) uses the term **feasibility** to describe the need to select a problem that is doable, issues such as how long will the project take, how much will it cost, whether participants are available, are there ethical concerns, and whether agencies will cooperate with you must be addressed.

After you formulate your research problem, the next step is evaluating potential research topics. Do you know how to evaluate a potential research topic to decide how to design your research? Consider the following example.

Let's assume for a moment that you are working in a recreation centre. You are responsible for coordinating the swimming classes, and providing opportunities for both beginner and intermediate level swimmers. Your participation level is low and enrolment has been declining. As a researcher, you may begin thinking about the possible reasons for non-participation. Thus a decision tree might help you picture all possible answers to your question, visualize your thoughts and help you evaluate this potential research topic. As you see in Fig. 2.2, the lack of participation might have many reasons. The decision tree helps you see the big picture and, if necessary, narrow your focus to one or more dimensions of the topic.

Once you have identified your topic you should write a problem statement clearly stating the issue. Establishing the problem and why you need to research it are an important part of addressing that problem. There are a variety of formats for problem statements. Regardless of the format, clarity is crucial. The problem statement might lead to your research purpose, a further clarification of what you are going to do in your study. You should specify the variables you are studying, how they are linked and any contextual information, such as a specific group you are studying. Finally, you might identify your research questions or objectives and your hypotheses.

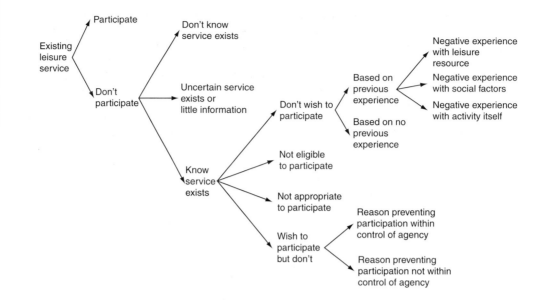

Fig. 2.2. Decision tree of non-participation in leisure services. (Adapted from Godbey, 1985.)

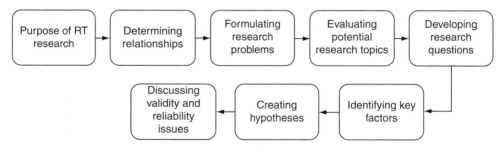

Fig. 2.3. Steps to formalizing a research project.

Next you need to develop the road map you will follow in conducting your research. This road map will include a variety of steps, many discussed in later chapters of this book. Figure 2.3 provides a brief outline of the process you will go through. Researchers follow a sequential approach based on linked activities.

Identifying the Key Components of the Research Process

A research study cannot, and should not, study every factor that is interesting to the researcher, or anyone else for that matter. Many topics are interesting to explore, but interest is not a sound

basis for a topic or factors to be included in a study. A well-focused study should only investigate those factors that are important to addressing the purpose, research questions and objectives of an investigation.

If the problem, purpose and research question or research statement of a study are well focused, clear and concise, the key factors and variables important to a study should become obvious. It is analogous to having a blueprint for the design of a house. The blueprint will dictate what materials are needed to construct the house. In a similar fashion, collecting data without specifying your research question and important variables in advance is like buying a variety of wood and hardware at a sale and then trying to construct a building. When the purpose and research question are clear and focused, you are ready to predict what you expect to find, to specify what would disprove your prediction, and decide what pieces of data and variables you must collect.

Unfortunately, many research questions are not written in a focused and clear state, where a relationship between two or more variables is stated concisely. The most important or key factors that the research design must address is data collection concerning the independent and dependent variables listed in the study objectives and associated hypotheses. The independent and dependent variables are key factors in a study because it is impossible to fulfil study objectives and/or test study hypotheses if data are not collected on these variables and their attributes.

Once the independent, dependent and other key variables necessary to address the study research question and objectives are identified then we must determine who will provide this information. This involves identifying the study population and sample. The study population, like the research question, must be focused, and the sample must be a miniature replicate of the study population. This is necessary because once the sample data are analysed and tested for inferences about the study population, we can draw conclusions about elements of the specified study population and no other populations.

Finally, researchers must predict what they think the sample data and population inference outcomes or results will be concerning variables and variable relationships. This practice is called hypothesis formulation and the resulting predictions are called study hypotheses. Hypotheses state the predicted relationships between the key variables of a study, and are tested to verify the predictions of hypothesized relationships.

Hypotheses

Empirical research consists of three main steps: prediction, discovery and verification. Prediction involves the formulation of hypotheses or the hypothesizing of data outcomes, discovery involves the collection of data, and verification is the testing of hypotheses to determine if our predicted outcomes are true or if they need to be rejected. So, the first step is to formulate and state our study predictions/hypotheses.

A hypothesis is an educated guess, a focused prediction of what we think the relationship between the variables will be in our study. They are always stated as declarative statements of what we predict the results will be of our research questions and objectives. Thus, hypotheses must include stated predictions between and among our key variables. Stated predictions are essential, for the data collected during the discovery process and the testing of data during the verification stage are dependent on the variable relationships stated in our hypotheses.

Types of hypotheses

There are two basic types of hypotheses: **null** and **research**. The null hypothesis is a prediction of equality or that there is no relationship between stated variables. Scientific research is built on the premise that the null hypothesis (i.e. no relationship) exists until there is evidence (i.e. data) to reject the null, in favour of the research or alternative hypothesis. Therefore, the research hypothesis states that there is inequality or that a relationship exists between stated variables. If we predict only that there will be a relationship, but do not state the direction of the relationship, we have a **non-directional** research hypotheses. If, on the other hand we have enough information to predict the direction of the relationship between variables, then we have formulated a **directional** research hypothesis.

Examples

Null Hypothesis ($H1_0$): There is no relationship between gender and types of recreation activity participation.

Null Hypothesis ($H2_0$): The will be no difference in the average satisfaction scores of female customers and male customers of Club Ottomans II.

Null Hypothesis ($H3_0$): The word-of-mouth will be independent of customer satisfaction and service quality among the guests of Club Ottomans II.

Non-directional Research Hypothesis (H_1): There is a relationship between gender and types of recreation activity participation.

Directional Research Hypothesis (H_1): Males will participate in a greater number of recreational activities than will females.

Examples of common mistakes made when formulating hypotheses

Research Hypothesis (H_1): Age is related to outdoor recreation participation? Not quite clear. How is it related? The only way this hypothesis can be falsified is if you fail to find statistically significant relationship of any type between the age and participation. A better way: Age is related to outdoor recreation participation, with younger adults participating more frequently (or stating exactly the opposite).

Directional Research Hypothesis (H_1): Gender is positively (or negatively) related to the support for tourism development in a community (again not adequately clear). How do you expect the gender to be related, that is, whether the men or women will be more supportive of tourism development? A better way: Gender is related to support for tourism, with women being more supportive than men (or men being less supportive). Equally legitimate would be 'women are more likely to support tourism development than men'.

Hypothesis testing

Once our predictions are made, in the form of stated hypotheses, then we collect data in order to test (verify) the hypotheses. We test the hypotheses to determine if there is evidence to keep believing in the null hypothesis, or if there is enough evidence to reject the null in favour of the research hypothesis. As previously stated, science is based on the premise that there is no evidence to stop believing in the null hypothesis until testing proves that there is evidence to reject the null. It is analogous to the law profession, where people are presumed innocent until the prosecution can produce enough evidence to reject innocence, in favour of being guilty. Along with this line of thinking is the practice of rejection, not acceptance. By this we mean that as a researcher, we never accept the null or research hypothesis but rather, we fail to reject or we reject the null in favour of the research hypothesis.

Another reason we test hypotheses is so we can make inferences about population parameters with a certain level of confidence from our sample data. In applied research, we can seldom collect data on all elements of the population, simply because the population is too large. So, we collect data on only a representative portion of the population, called the sample. However, the sample data only represents or describes elements of the sample. Since our ultimate aim is to examine relationships between variables in the population, we have to test our hypothesized relationships using sample data, make a decision to reject or not reject hypotheses, and infer the predicted relationship either holds true or not for the study population. Inferential statistics, which will be discussed in Chapter 13, are used to test the sample hypotheses and to infer back to the population with an acceptable level of confidence.

Hypothesis testing procedures

Steps to test your hypothesis:

1. Identify the population and population parameter of interest (i.e. rate of participation of recreation majors by gender (male and female).
2. Define the null hypothesis and research hypothesis.
3. Collect a random sample of variable(s) of interest (participation rate of male and female).
4. Compute a sample statistic to estimate population parameter (average participation rate by gender).
5. Use a statistical test to decide whether null hypothesis is true (not rejected) or to reject in favour of the alternative or research hypothesis.

Example:

Research question: Do females have higher recreation participation rates than males?

Objective: To determine if the recreation activity participation rate of females is significantly greater than males.

Hypothesis: There is no significant difference in the recreation participation rate of females and males at Great Smoky Mountains National Park.

Hypothesis testing: Is it reasonable to believe that the value of the population activity participation rate of females is greater than the male participation rate of the population?

Hypothesis testing is the use of **decision rules** to determine (decide) if our hypothesis about the value of a population parameter is reasonable.

Elements of hypotheses

There are certain basic characteristics that all good hypotheses should have:

Be a declarative statement, not a question.
Posit an expected relationship between two or more variables.

Be based on or reflect theory or literature, in order to represent an expectation or prediction.
Be brief, focused and to the point.
Be testable.

- Although any hypothesis is a direct extension of the original research question(s) posited, the formulated hypothesis is always stated as a declarative statement.
- The declarative statement should posit a predicted relationship between two or more variables, but more importantly, a focused relationship between the variables.

- A good hypothesis reflects the theory or literature upon which it is based; it has a substantive link to the past accomplishments of science.
- Your hypothesis should be brief and to the point so that there is no doubt as to the variables being tested and the decision rule to be made.
- If a hypothesis is not stated in a testable form, it is not a hypothesis. For example, it is better to hypothesize that 'backpackers cause more trail erosion than day hikers' than to say 'backpackers are worse hikers than day hikers'.

Research Box 2.3. Developing a research question.

Rationale for Study:

It appears that young people, when they leave home for college or for any other reason, stop attending religious services or at least reduce attendance at these events. Many believe this affects family values.

Problem Statement:

Does attendance at religious services decrease when young people leave home (versus those who stay at home), and if so, what are the major reasons?

Objectives:

To determine if young people (18–25) attend religious services less than other age groups.
To determine if young people (18–25) living away from home attend religious services less than those living at home.
To determine the major causes for this decrease in attendance at religious events.

Hypotheses:

H1: All young people (18–25) will have lower rates of attendance at religious services than other age groups.
H2: Young people (18–25) living away from home will have lower rates of attendance at religious services than young people living at home.
H3: The major cause for less attendance at religious services is the lack of parental pressure to attend.

Variables:

H1: dependent variable = attendance (religious services)
  independent variable = age (groups) young versus others
H2: dependent variable = attendance (religious services)
  independent variable = home and residence
H3: dependent variable = attendance (religious services)
  independent variable = parental pressure

Conceptualization and Concepts

Hypotheses, in essence, involve ideas and relationships we have formulated. But, how does the hypothesis formulation begin and result in a focused, testable statement? It begins with the process of conceptualization. Conceptualization is the mental process by which we give meaning to ideas, images and thoughts. For example, our idea of recreation may involve the following associated images: fun, free time, non-work, leisure, relaxation, recovery, restoration, activities and skills. These are terms we use to define the meaning of our mental image of **recreation**. That is, we have a mental conception of recreation, and these terms help to communicate an agreed upon meaning for the concept of recreation. The process of coming to an agreement about what terms mean is **conceptualization** and the result is called a **concept**. Thus, recreation is a concept derived from a 'family of associated terms or images'. We cannot define the variables to be researched and how we will operationalize those variables unless we go through the mental process of research conceptualization.

Concepts and constructs

In behavioural sciences and recreation research, we often speak of studying behavioural **constructs**. A construct is a particular type of conceptualization of a concept, which tends to be more abstract and theoretical, than real and observable. Perhaps an example will help to clarify the distinctions between a concept and a construct.

Abraham Kaplan (1964) distinguishes three classes of things that researchers measure. In the context of recreation, the first class involves direct observables: those things we can observe rather simply and directly, such as the number of people in a recreation group (i.e. party size). The second class refers to indirect observables, which require 'relatively more subtle, complex, or indirect observations' (1964, p. 55). We often ask recreation visitors to indicate their job occupation, so that we can indirectly determine the relationship of work occupation to rate of recreation participation. The final class of observables consists of constructs. Constructs are theoretical creations that are based on observations but that cannot be observed directly or indirectly. A good example is recreation motivations. We cannot observe a person's motivations for participating in a specific recreation activity, either directly or indirectly. Instead, we often have participants rate the importance of numerous reasons for participating and then use statistical tools to identify underlying motivational themes. Thus, motivations are a behavioural construct that have their grounding in motivation theory.

Variables

Variables are the most important element of hypotheses. They are the things or ideas we measure in a study. The various characteristics of the things we measure are called **attributes**. For example, recreational activity is a variable and hiking, camping, fishing, and so on could be attributes or the values recorded for the variable.

There are many classes of variables (see Table 2.1), each defined by the role they serve in the hypothesized relationship. The **dependent variable** is the outcome, the effect or the result that independent variables can have in the hypothesized relationship. We often say the dependent variable is the one measured to see if a treatment, stimulus or manipulation has the predicted outcome. The **independent variable** is commonly referred to as the treatment or cause variable – for it is the variable that is manipulated or changed to examine its effect or influence upon the dependent variable. We often say that the outcome or effect observed in a study is caused by the independent variable(s). It is common to have more than one independent variable in a study, for the outcome in research is seldom due to only one variable.

Other types of variables that may or may not be part of a hypothesized relationship are **control**, **extraneous** and **moderator**. Control variables are variables that have a potential influence on the dependent variable outcomes, and we often want to focus our hypotheses so as to remove or control this influence. For example, if we want to examine the rate of recreation participation among men and women, we might want to control for the place, because place can influence participation rate. We may want to hold place of activity constant in order to examine the real relationship between recreation participation rate and male/females. An extraneous variable can be related to the dependent or independent variable, but not in a predictable manner. For example, income may influence the recreation participation rate or even the type of visitor participating and therefore function as an extraneous variable that might affect participation rate between males and females. A moderator variable is a variable that interacts with the independent or dependent variable, masking the true relationship between the independent and dependent variable. For example, if you are studying the relationship between swimming and soft drink consumption, you need to examine temperature because it moderates that relationship.

Table 2.1. Types of variables in recreation research. (Adapted from *Exploring Research*, N.J. Salkind, 2006.)

Type of variable	Definition	Other terms you might see
Dependent	A variable that is measured to see whether the treatment or manipulation of the independent variable had an effect	Outcome variable Results variable Criterion variable
Independent	A variable that is manipulated to examine its impact on a dependent variable	Treatment variable Factor Predictor variable
Control	A variable that is related to the dependent variable, the influence of which needs to be removed	Restricting variable
Extraneous	A variable that is related to the dependent variable or independent variable that is not part of the experiment	Threatening variable
Moderator	A variable that is related to the dependent variable or independent variable and has an impact on the dependent variable	Interacting variable

Units of analysis

The most common units that we analyse in recreation research are the individual and/or the group. We may need to know the camping preferences of individual backpackers or the effect of camping on family group cohesion, respectively. It is important to select the appropriate unit to analyse, because we can only infer or generalize our sample data back to the unit of analysis. For example, we cannot study individual behaviour and infer it will be the same when that individual functions within a group. Units of analysis, then, are those things we examine in order to create summary descriptions of all such units and to explain relationships among them. Other common units of analysis in recreation other than the individual or group, are managing agency or organizations, recreation associations, and large social aggregates. Also the unit of analysis in recreation may be artefacts, impacts and objects associated with recreation behaviour. As examples, varieties of litter, trail/erosion impacts and classes of recreation vehicles may be the unit of analysis in certain studies.

Concept of Statistical Significance

There is no such thing as a perfect sample. Because sampling can never select a portion of elements that exactly matches the profile of those in the study population, there will be a sampling error (the difference between sample data and data of the population). And, because there is an error in the sample data, the testing of our hypothesis, which is always based on sample data, cannot be inferred back to the population without the risk of error. For example, we may arrive at the decision to reject a stated null hypothesis when in reality there truly is no difference (i.e. the null hypothesis) in the population data. Therefore, we must always accept a degree of risk (i.e. making the wrong hypothesis decision rule) when inferring a conclusion about the population from our imperfect sample data.

The actual amount of risk you are willing to accept or error you are willing to make in your inferences about the study population is called **level of significance**. You might remember from your statistics classes a term called **confidence level**. It tells us how confident we want to be before believing our research findings. Usually, in our field we use 95% confidence level; in other words, we would like to tell others of our findings when we are 95% sure that what we have found is good enough to be believed. For some strange reason, no statistical packages report that; they report exactly the opposite. They will instead show you 0.05, meaning that our research finding from the sample has a 5% (0.05) chance of not being true; as smart as you are, you will figure that this is exactly the converse of a 95% chance of being true. This is probably the most confusing yet the most important issue in hypotheses testing; thus, you may want to reread this section until you understand it well.

Statistical significance is the degree of risk that you are willing to take that you will reject a null hypothesis when it is actually true. Statistical significance does not have anything to do with the everyday use of the word importance. In statistical terms, significance means probably true (not due to chance), in other words, it says we might have found something in our sample that is worth telling to others. Hence, when we say a result is significant we actually mean the results are probably true and we do not (necessarily) mean they are important; although the research or the findings could be important too. Accordingly, a research finding may be true without being important.

The significance levels show you how likely a result is due to chance. In recreation research, we commonly set the significance level at 0.05. When reporting level of significance and/or whether we have a statistically significant difference, it is usually stated as $p < 0.05$, and is often expressed in a scientific report simply as 'significant at the 0.05 level'. This means that on any one test of the null hypothesis, there is a 5% chance we will reject the null when it is really true, or similarly there is no relationship between variables.

Again, statistical significance is the degree of risk you are willing to take that you will reject a null hypothesis when it is actually true. For our example (H2$_0$), displayed in the Hypotheses section of this chapter, the null stated that there is no difference between the two groups (remember, the null is always statement of equality). In our sample data, however, we find a difference. That is, given the evidence so far, gender seems to have an effect on customer satisfaction scores. Maybe in reality (in the population), however, the scores of male and female customers do not differ from each other, and if we reject the null we stated, we make an error. The risk we take in making this kind of error (or the level of significance) is also known as a **type 1 error**. The good news is that we can control the chances of making this type of error. This topic will be covered in great length in Chapter 13.

When you ask around, you will see that the 0.05% seems to be a sacred number. What if a test shows you a 0.06 probability level of making an error, which, in other words, means that your results still have a 94% chance of being true? Would you dismiss your findings? It's a judgement call which needs to be determined before you start running your analysis.

Research Box 2.4. Transforming research topics into research questions: refining the research question/problem statement.

Your friend told you that she has a genuine interest in backpacking, because it allows her to be with herself and experience solitude. While reviewing the literature related to backpacking, you discovered something interesting and shared it with your friend after hearing her interest in backpacking. According to literature when the number of people in the wilderness increases, people are usually less satisfied with their experience. This information made you think even more about your friend's interest in backpacking. You told your friend that 'perhaps, solitude may reach an unacceptable level based on the number of visitors at a wilderness site'.

Your friend responded that this could be a nice research topic and convinced you to explore it more. You remember the basic qualities of a good research question. Good research questions:

1. Investigate the relationship between two or more variables;
2. State the question clearly, concisely and in a focused manner;
3. Allow for empirical testing.

Thus, based on these criteria you wrote a research question: How many visitors can a typical wilderness user experience before solitude is lost?

(Continued)

Research Box 2.4. Continued.

Comparing the research question to the criteria, you see that it is still less than ideal. Now you and your friend brainstorm and discuss the following questions:

1. What type of wilderness users should be considered?
2. Should you identify a specific wilderness area?
3. Should you expand visitors to visitor encounters?
4. Should you identify locations of visitor encounters?

Based on your brainstorming process, your research question became more specific. Your revised research question is now similar to this:

'How many parties of other backpackers can a typical Ellicot Rock Wilderness backpacker see at the trailhead, on the trail and at the campsite before solitude reaches an unacceptable level?'

According to this research question, you expect that solitude, and subsequent satisfaction with the wilderness experience, is dependent upon the number of encounters with other backpackers (and perhaps other variables as well). So solitude becomes your dependent variable (effect) and number of encounters your independent variable. Location is a control variable.

Now you and your friend are examining the components of solitude, and the link between solitude and wilderness experience. Can you write a null hypothesis and a research hypothesis? Before you write your hypotheses, it is important to have clear objectives that would drive each hypothesis. Below are example objectives and hypotheses:

Objectives

To answer the research question, you may develop the following objectives:

Objective 1: Determine the relationship between number of party visual contacts and level of perceived solitude.
Objective 2: Determine the influence of location on the contacts to solitude relationship.
Objective 3: Determine if level of solitude received varies by type of use contact (backpacker contacts versus horseback user contacts).

Hypotheses

To test your research question and objectives, you develop the following hypotheses:

H_1: As the number of visual contacts with other parties of backpackers increase, the level of perceived solitude will decrease.
H_2: Solitude will decrease different amounts depending on the location where visual contacts occur.
H_3: Perceived solitude will be less for visual contacts with horseback users than for contacts with other backpackers, given the same number of party contacts for each.

Concepts of Causality and Association

Recently there was a discussion on the radio about whether eating together is beneficial to families and the children in those families. The question was simple: are children in families that eat dinner together better off than children in families that do not eat together? Much of the evidence discussed indicated they are better off because they are healthier leading to the conclusion that eating as a family results in healthy children. But at that point the commentator said an interesting thing: maybe it is not eating together that matters, but maybe having parents who are organized enough to pull off the coordinated effort to bring the various members of family together at the same time to share a meal that also required coordination and planning was what mattered, not the act of eating.

Perhaps any activity done as a family on a regular basis would have the same effect. So maybe playing together on a scheduled basis would have the same impact as eating together. Maybe the family that plays together has healthier children. Or perhaps there is another explanation for this eating together–healthier children link. Perhaps families that eat together have more nutritious meals than families eating on the run to soccer practices, Girl Scout meetings and other activities. Perhaps the nutrition is what matters rather than the communal meal. Obviously determining what caused the health impact is more complicated than it first seemed.

That brings us to the concept of causality, or cause and effect and its concomitant, internal validity. The issue is simple: **did A cause B**? Did eating together cause children to be healthier? However, the actual establishment of the linking a cause to an effect is more difficult than it might appear.

Perhaps the story should have focused more on the issue of association than cause. There clearly seems to be a link between eating as a family and healthy children. These two things, eating together and healthy behaviour in children, occur together, one is accompanied by the other. In families where eating together was the norm, children were more healthy than in families that did not eat together. That may be true but there are many explanations for why that may occur. Only one explanation is truly causal. Association does not indicate cause and effect.

So how does one establish cause and effect? Trochim (2005) identified three criteria for causal relationships:

1. There must be temporal precedence. This seems the most obvious of the criteria. Simply put, the cause must occur before the effect. If the family that stays together, plays together and if the playing causes the staying then playing must occur first. That seems obvious but the actual temporal relationship may not be clear. Maybe families only play together after they have bonded as a cohesive unit. The playing comes after the staying! Or maybe there is a cyclical relationship (Trochim, 2005) where a little playing causes a little staying and then a little staying causes more play, and the more playing causes more staying and . . . well, you get it. As Trochim describes this type of ebb and flow, establishing causality is difficult because 'it's likely that the *variables* influence each other causally' (p. 137). Nevertheless, the cause must always precede the effect to establish causality.

2. The second criterion is the cause and effect must co-vary, that is they must be related to one another. Trochim expresses this in a syllogism framework (if x then y; if not x, then not y). In the playing together and staying together link we might write: if families play together they stay together, if families don't play together they don't stay together. Notice what we are saying here, playing and staying are linked; they are associated. However, we are not saying that one causes the other. In fact, neither is necessarily a cause or an effect. Perhaps something else, like a highly organized parent, is causing both the playing and the staying. Nevertheless, this linked nature of the variables must be present for causality.

3. The final criterion for causality discussed by Trochim is that no other explanation for the relationship exists. The possibility of a third variable (remember the highly organized parent) is an alternative explanation. The possibility is that any of many threats to internal validity are the explanations for the relationship. Internal validity refers to the confidence that the cause–effect relationship is real. Threats to internal validity are alternative explanations for the link between the presumed cause and the effect other than causality. The term internal validity is typically used in experimental research (see Chapter 10) and establishing internal validity requires the elimination of alternative explanations.

Concepts of Validity and Reliability

You get up every morning and you go to your bathroom, hop on the scale and weigh yourself. Your nickname for your scale is old reliable since it delivers consistent results. Then one morning you wake up and feel ill so you visit the student health centre. The first thing they do there is ask you to step on the scale so they can chart your weight. You are shocked to find that the weight on the clinic's scale is 14 pounds higher than the weight on your scale at home. Something is clearly wrong with the clinic' scale since your scale has been the same for months. You explain this to the doctor but she assures you their scale has been recently calibrated and is tested monthly by the Bureau of Weights and Measures. Upon returning home you get on your scale and your weight is exactly what it has been every other morning. Something is wrong here since you know you didn't lose 14 pounds in your walk from the health centre to your room. It is obvious that your scale has been consistent, consistently wrong! In research terms the measurement you are getting from your scale is reliable but not valid.

Reliability refers to several aspect of measurement, all focused on consistency. There are several types of reliability (Babbie, 2001; Trochim, 2005) including:

- *Inter-rater reliability*. This is fairly self-explanatory; it is the extent of agreement between two or more observers of a targeted behaviour. Suppose you are studying the play of children on a playground and you are measuring how frequently they interact with one another. Two of your friends agree to observe the playing children and record the frequency of interaction. You assign them to observe the same child and tell them to look at that child every 30 seconds, and record whether they observe him interacting with any other child. They work independently and after 30 minutes they have finished their observation and report the result to you. Each has reported 60 observations (remember, they observed every 30 seconds). You then calculate the percentage of time they agreed that they observed interaction. Your friend Joshua recorded 40 incidents of interaction for the 60 observations made. Your other friend Elaine recorded 10 incidents of interaction. You note that they agreed (interaction or not) for 20 of the 60 observation points, a 33% agreement rate. Upon discussing this with Joshua and Elaine you discover that Joshua defined interaction as verbal or non-verbal (such as eye-contact or touching) behaviour, whereas Elaine limited it to verbal contact. You realize you should have trained your observers and clearly defined what you meant by 'contact'. You do so and then they return to the playground to observe another child. This time Joshua records 45 incidences of contact and Elaine records 50 such incidents. Furthermore they agree on 50 of the 60 observation points, an 83% rate of agreement.
- *Internal consistency*. This type of reliability refers to the relationship among items in a test or instrument. It is based on the assump-

tion that if several items are measuring the same dimension, for example, your knowledge of research or your satisfaction with recreation activities, then they should be related to one another. For example, suppose you are interested in measuring student satisfaction with your university's intramural program and you develop a scale with 32 items designed to measure satisfaction. If they are reliable then they should be related to each other. A common statistic to measure internal consistency is Cronbach's Alpha. This test essentially divides your scale into all possible combinations of two scales, each with half the items in our original scale, and then computes the correlation between all those halves (this is referred to as a split-half method, dividing the test in half and computing the relationship between halves). The higher the Cronbach's Alpha then the higher the reliability.

- *Test–re-test reliability*. This type of reliability refers to the consistency of a test across time, typically measured by the repetition of testing at different times. For example, if an IQ test is given to a group of students on a Monday and then the same test is given to them on Tuesday, and assuming IQ is a stable trait, then we would expect their scores on the two tests would be highly correlated, or have high test–re-test reliability.
- *Parallel-forms reliability*. This type of reliability refers to the extent to which two versions of a test yield similar scores. For example, the teacher of your course is concerned that students may cheat on the final exam. So she develops two versions of the exam and asks students count off by twos. The ones receive version A and the twos receive version B. One of the students complains that version A was easier than version B. So after grading the exams, because she is concerned that perhaps the two exam versions were not equivalent, she correlates the scores of the two exams and finds a high correlation. As a result she is confident the two versions are parallel and equivalent.

Validity might be considered the gold standard when evaluating research. Simply put, validity is the extent to which your results are congruent with reality. If reliability is synonymous with consistency, then validity is synonymous with accuracy.

There are different types of validity, some related to measurement, some related to study design, and some related to conceptualization. Nevertheless, all validity meets under one umbrella: 'the quality of various conclusions you might reach based on a research project' (Trochim 2005, p. 16). That quality encompasses all the components of your research. There are several components of validity (Trochim, 2005), including:

- *Conclusion validity*, also called statistical conclusion validity, is the extent to which there is a statistical relationship among variables and the 'degree to which conclusions you reach about relationships in your data are reasonable' (Trochim, p. 206). This reasonableness includes concepts such as Type I (concluding there is a relationship when there is not one) and Type II (concluding there is not a relationship when there is one) errors and statistical power.
- *Construct validity*, referring to the measurement of your constructs, relates to whether your instruments are capturing the variables they are measuring, or as Babbie (2001) succinctly stated: 'tests of construct validity, then, can offer a weight of evidence that your measure either does or does not tap the quality you want to measure' (p. 144). Trochim includes several types of validity under the construct validity category: face validity, content validity, predictive validity, concurrent validity, convergent validity and discriminate validity.
- *Internal validity*, commonly seen in experimental designs, refers to the accuracy of ascribing causality to a relationship. Chapters 4 and 6 discuss internal validity in more detail.
- *External validity* refers to the generalizability of a finding. This type of validity reflects whether findings hold up in settings or situations other than those involved in the actual research.

Discussion Questions

1. Compare and contrast types of research.
2. List four sources you would use to find research topics.
3. List and explain formalizing and focusing the research topic.
4. What is the difference between a concept and a construct? Compare concepts and constructs, give an example for each.

5. Write hypotheses with IV and DV.
6. Why can gender not be a dependent variable?
7. Identify the IVs and DVs in statements 8 and 9.
8. People who hike in large groups do not perceive as much solitude as people who hike alone.
9. Experienced wilderness users are more likely to seek solitude than inexperienced users.
10. Can something be reliable but not valid? Why?
11. How can something be valid but not reliable? Why?
12. Read the following statement and indicate whether it reflects a causal relationship: In summer, ice-cream sales go up, and the number of people who drown goes up.

Key Terms

Descriptive research: A type of research that attempts to describe attributes of behaviours or social phenomenon and other factors.

Exploratory research: A type of research attempting to explore relationships among various factors.

Relational research: A type of research drawing relationships among recreational behaviours or social phenomenon and other factors.

Causal research: A type of research investigating the cause/effect relationship between two variables.

Applied research: A type of research that addresses a specific question or concern, done for practical purposes related to solving problems.

Basic research: A type of research that is primarily conducted to expand knowledge; in a more general sense it is focused on transcending a specific problem and may not necessarily produce immediate value.

Hypothesis: Educated guess, a focused prediction of what we think the relationship between the variables will be in our study.

Deductive approach: Reasoning that moves from the general phenomenon to a specific question.

Inductive approach: Reasoning that moves from a specific question to a general phenomenon.

Confidence level: The level of chance of results being true.

Construct: Theoretical creations that are based on observations.

Conceptualization: Process of coming to an agreement about what terms mean.

Concept: A term whose meaning is agreed upon.

Dependent variable: The outcome, the effect, the result that independent variables have in hypothesized relationships.

Independent variable: The treatment or cause variable – the variable that is manipulated or changed to examine its effect or influence upon the dependent variable.

Control variable: A variable that is related to the dependent variable, the influence of which needs to be removed.

Extraneous variable: A variable that is related to the dependent variable or independent variable that is not part of the experiment.

Moderator variable: A variable that is related to the dependent variable or independent variable and has an impact on the dependent variable.

Unit of analysis: Something researchers examine in order to create summary descriptions of them and to explain relationships among them.

Statistical significance: Degree of risk that you are willing to take that you will reject a null hypothesis when it is actually true. The level of chance of tests results not being true.

Null hypothesis: A prediction of equality or that there is no relationship between stated variables.

Research hypothesis: A prediction of that there is inequality or that a relationship exists between stated variables.

Level of significance: Actual amount of risk you are willing to accept, or error you are willing to make in your inferences about the study population.

Inter-rater reliability: The extent of agreement between observers of a targeted behaviour.

Test–re-test reliability: The consistency of a test across time, typically measured by repetition.

Parallel-forms reliability: The extent to which two versions of a test yield similar scores.

Internal consistency: The relationship that is expected to occur among items in a test or instrument

Validity: Extent to which a measurement tool captures reality or extent to which it measures what it meant to measure.

Construct validity: Whether a measurement instrument can capture the variables it intends to measure.

Conclusion validity: The extent to which there is a statistical relationship among variables and the extent to which the conclusions reached about relationships in the data are reasonable.

Internal validity: The accuracy of ascribing causality to a relationship.

External validity: The generalizability of a finding.

References

Babbie, E. (2001) *The Practice of Social Research*, 9th edn. Wadsworth, Belmont, California.

Godbey, G. (1985) Nonuse of public leisure services: A model. *Journal of Park and Recreation Administration* 3, 1–12.

Howard, R.W. (2007) Five backpacker tourist enclaves. *International Journal of Tourism Research* 9, 73–86.

Kaplan, A. (1964) *The Conduct of Inquiry*. Chandler Publishing Company, Scranton, Pennsylvania.

Salkind, N.J. (2006) *Exploring Research,* 6th edn. Pearson Education, Inc., New Jersey.

Scott, D. (1991) The problematic nature of participation in contract bridge: A qualitative study of group-related constraints. *Leisure Sciences* 13, 321–336.

Trochim. W.M.K. (2005) *Research Methods: The Concise Knowledge Base*. Atomic Dog Publishing, Cincinnati, Ohio.

chapter 3

Finding and Summarizing Research Literature

Jerry J. Vaske

Learning Objectives

After reading this chapter you will have a better understanding of:

1. The functions of a literature review;
2. Where and how to find the relevant literature for addressing a research problem;
3. How to summarize the literature in tables and figures.

Chapter Summary

This chapter is concerned with finding and summarizing the existing research. Finding the research involves conducting a literature review of the professional journals and academic books. Literature reviews serve a variety of functions (e.g. becoming familiar with the concepts used to understand a problem, developing a theoretical framework, providing a rationale for research questions/hypotheses), and can be done manually or electronically. The chapter outlines a series of six steps that should be followed when conducting a literature review. Taking notes on each article is a good starting point, but sometimes it is helpful to construct tables or figures that highlight the 'big picture'. After identifying and reading the pertinent literature, the chapter provides strategies for summarizing what is learned and discusses how to think critically about existing research.

Introduction

In the early 1980s, the author was working on a project designed to integrate and synthesize the literature on ecological and social aspects of recreation carrying capacity (Kuss *et al.*, 1990). One of the products from that effort was a menu-driven bibliographic database (VIMDEX) containing 2714 references related to visitor impact management (Vaske *et al.*, 1989). In the early stages of the project, a graduate student was assigned the task of continuing the literature search on the general topic of carrying capacity. After a few days, she informed us that her search had produced no (zero) books, articles or research reports on the topic. Although one would not have expected the student to have found all of the pertinent documents, producing zero was a mystery, especially since our reference database at the time had approximately 1000 entries. Upon further inquiry, we learned that the student had simply entered the words 'carrying capacity' into a search engine on the university's mainframe. When the computer returned the message 'No Matches Found', she mistakenly assumed that nothing existed.

Although the search engines on today's computers are vastly better than what was available in the early 1980s, the general problem of finding and understanding relevant literature continues to be a 'magical mystery tour' for many students. This chapter is concerned with the topics of finding and summarizing the pertinent literature. The chapter begins with a general discussion of the functions of the literature review process.

Functions of a Literature Review

Virtually all research projects begin with a literature review. This process generally involves searching professional journals and academic books to find writings similar to the current project. Students sometimes do not appreciate the importance of building upon the work that already exists. Science and theory development are a never-ending story. All theories are tentative explanations of the way the world works, dependent on empirical verification. Each specific study can be thought of as a piece of a picture puzzle. Studies that build upon each other contribute to the picture (or theory); the more studies that fill in the blanks in the puzzle, the clearer the picture.

Conducting a thorough literature search highlights what is currently known and, more importantly, what remains unknown. Identifying and understanding the prior literature helps to focus a project, provides guidance for measuring the concepts of interest, and may suggest strategies for avoiding mistakes. There are at least five functions of the literature review process (Riddick and Russell, 1999). These functions are briefly reviewed below as separate topics, but should not be thought of as mutually exclusive categories.

Become familiar with historical background and concepts

From a historical perspective, the initial carrying capacity model predicted that visitor enjoyment with a recreation experience should be negatively correlated with the number of people in the area. Although this hypothesis was logical given the wilderness context of most early studies, none of the 14 studies reviewed by Kuss *et al.* (1990) supported

the predicted negative relationship between actual density and satisfaction. Subsequent researchers theorized that other variables (e.g. reported encounters, perceived crowding) may lower the correlation between actual density and visitor satisfaction (see Box 3.1 for definitions of these concepts). The frequently used capacity model (actual density → reported encounters → perceived crowding → visitor satisfaction) was a logical extension of the original hypothesis, but still failed to account for much of the variation in what constitutes a quality recreation experience. As predicted, for example, perceived crowding was negatively related to overall satisfaction in 8 of the 12 studies examined by Kuss *et al.* (1990). The strength of this relationship, however, was minimal. In retrospect, the perceived crowding measure (a specific attitude) should not have been a good predictor of visitors' overall satisfaction (a general attitude) because of the mismatch in levels of measurement specificity (i.e. specific → general). As predicted by social psychological theory (Whittaker *et al.*, 2006), when there is a direct correspondence between the two measures of interest (specific → specific or general → general), stronger correlations are more likely (Vaske, 2008). Understanding both the social psychological and recreation literature helped clarify these relationships and explain the relatively low correlations in the traditional capacity model.

Develop an appropriate theoretical framework

Different theorists define and use concepts differently. Some social psychologists, for example, emphasize the structural characteristics of norms (e.g. norm intensity, consensus, range of tolerable conditions), while others focus on the variables that serve to activate a norm (see Vaske and Whittaker, 2004, for a review). If the research problem involves developing standards for an acceptable number of people in a recreation area, the structural approach has proven useful. On the other hand, if the research question is concerned with getting people to behave appropriately (e.g. not littering, recycling), the norm activation model can serve as a helpful theoretical orientation. Knowing how different researchers use the same basic concept (e.g. norms, attitudes) clarifies what theoretical framework is most appropriate for examining a given situation or problem.

Research Box 3.1. Definitions of recreation/tourism concepts.

Concept	Definition
Actual density	Objective count of the number of visitors in an area. Typically measured using infrared monitors, time-lapse cameras or traffic counters.
Reported encounters	Visitors' reports of encounters with other recreationists (i.e. a belief).
Crowding	Visitors' negative evaluation of a certain density or number of encounters (i.e. a specific attitude).
Visitor satisfaction	Visitors' overall evaluation of an experience (i.e. a general attitude).
Conflict	*Interpersonal conflict:* Occurs when the presence or behaviour of an individual or group interferes with the goals of another individual or group. *Social values conflict:* Occurs when groups do not share the same norms and/or values; independent of the physical presence or actual contact between groups.
Visitor displacement	A shift in visitors' behaviour in response to changing conditions such as higher entrance fees or increased crowding.
Motivation	Goals or reasons for engaging in an activity.
Attitude	Alternative definitions: *Descriptive attitude research:* An individual's evaluation of an entity. In applied descriptive recreation/tourism research, concepts such as perceptions, beliefs, opinions, crowding and satisfaction are considered relevant in the context of this definition. *Conceptual attitude research:* This type of research consists of 'concept-driven studies that, in addition to the functions described with descriptive research, also (a) attempt to predict behaviour, attain a deeper understanding of why attitudes are held, or suggest ways of affecting attitudes, (b) clearly identify a theoretical orientation, and (c) test a theoretical or methodological model' (Manfredo *et al.,* 2004, p. 273). Studies utilizing Fishbein and Ajzen's (1975) theory of reasoned action (TRA) illustrate conceptual attitudinal research.
Norm	Alternative definitions: *Descriptive norm:* What most people are doing in a given situation. *Injunctive norm:* What people should or ought to do in a given situation. *Evaluative standards:* Perceived acceptability of individual behaviour or conditions created by behaviour in a given context. Descriptive attitude research might consider evaluative standards an attitude. *Personal norm:* An internal norm, enforced by an internal sense of obligation to other people or the environment, regarding what is appropriate in a given situation. *Subjective norm:* Beliefs about what others think you should do in a given situation (e.g. my friends think that I should vote for the open-space amendment).
Norm prevalence	The proportion of individuals in a population who can articulate a norm in a given evaluation context.

**Provide a rationale for research questions/
hypotheses and study importance**

Studies are sometimes guided by a desire to solve a practical problem (question). Other times the motivation for the research is driven by an interest in testing a theoretical hypothesis. The importance of a study should never be viewed as either an applied or a theoretical problem. Good theoretical research has applied consequences and good applied research has theoretical implications. Theory and application go hand-in-hand and both are important. The Colorado Division of Wildlife, for example, sponsored a study of recreation conflict between non-hunters and hunters on Mount Evans (Vaske *et al.*, 1995). The impetus for the study arose because of complaints received from wildlife viewers who had observed a hunter shoot a bighorn sheep. The Division was interested in knowing the extent to which similar situations occurred on the mountain (i.e. an applied problem). To address this question, the researchers reviewed both the applied and theoretical conflict literature. The review and subsequent survey analysis suggested that interpersonal conflict (i.e. negative interactions between non-hunters and hunters) rarely happened. Rather, the conflict between non-hunters and hunters mainly related to differences in social values (i.e. simply knowing that hunting occurred in the area was enough to initiate perceptions of conflict for non-hunters irrespective of actual contact with hunters). Had the investigators only reviewed the applied recreation literature (i.e. interpersonal conflict), the distinction between interpersonal versus social values conflict may not have been as apparent. The literature review helped to establish the theoretical importance of the study and facilitated an understanding of the applied problem.

**Provide context for filling gaps
in earlier research**

Research does not always produce consistent findings. When differences occur, the search for clues that will explain the discrepancy begins. Such gaps in knowledge can occur because of differences in theoretical orientation (e.g. interpersonal versus social values conflict), seemingly small differences in the concepts (e.g. general versus specific measures

of a concept), or differences in the way researchers ask the questions.

Norm prevalence, for example, refers to the proportion of individuals in a population who can articulate a norm in a given evaluation context (see Box 3.1 for definitions). Past research (Donnelly *et al.*, 2000; Hall and Roggenbuck, 2002) suggests that norm prevalence is influenced by the way the question is asked. To address this question format issue, an experiment by Vaske, Donnelly and Lehto (2002) randomly assigned Rocky Mountain National Park visitors to one of two treatment conditions. In the surveys with a 'semi-open' response format (treatment 1), respondents were asked to 'write in a number' for the acceptable number of other visitors. Norm questions using the 'closed' format (treatment 2) asked individuals to 'circle a number' of acceptable encounters along a range of possible responses provided in the survey. In both treatment conditions, norm questions allowed respondents to indicate that the number of encounters 'makes no difference', or check a category 'makes a difference, but can't give a number'. Results indicated a statistically higher percentage of the visitors reported a norm (i.e. norm prevalence) for the closed version of the survey than the semi-open treatment condition. Among those who reported a norm, however, the average norm tolerance levels for the closed and semi-open question formats were statistically equivalent. Thus, question format influenced norm prevalence, but not the reported tolerance level.

The literature review on norm prevalence provided a context for the Vaske *et al.* (2002) experiment and the study filled a gap in existing knowledge. When reviewing the literature, the researcher needs to develop an ability to critically evaluate why the findings from studies on the same topic do not always yield consistent conclusions. Are the differences due to the activities/resources studied or the methodology used (e.g. question format)?

**Facilitate interpretation of results
relative to other research**

To better understand concepts of interest to practitioners and researchers, investigators have expanded their focus from single resource descriptive studies to comparative analyses of data aggregated across a variety of contexts (Vaske and Manning, 2008).

By contrasting identical measures of the same concept across a number of activities, resources, and visitor characteristics, aggregated data sets can reveal patterns in the findings and identify causal factors that typically cannot be manipulated in a single study. An analysis of 181 crowding studies (615 evaluation contexts – see Box 3.2), for example, indicated that crowding varied across recreational settings, time or season, resource availability, and accessibility (Vaske and Shelby, 2008). This and other comparative studies highlight the importance of placing empirical findings within the context of multiple studies to facilitate interpretation of a given result.

Research Box 3.2. Definitions of methodological concepts.

Concept	Definition
Evaluation context	A specific situation where an evaluation is given. For example, one evaluation context on a river might involve kayakers' evaluation of motorboaters on the river (or access/egress locations). A second evaluation context might concern motorboaters' reactions to kayakers at different locations along the river.
Primary references	Publications (typically journal articles) that contain results from actual studies.
Secondary references	Publications that summarize or compare the works of others. Common secondary references include text books or research review articles.
General references	Indices, abstracts or bibliographies on a given topic.
Indices	List basic information such as author, title and place of publication.
Abstracts	Succinct summaries of research published in journals, dissertations or presentations at professional conferences.
Bibliography	List of books and articles relevant to a specific topic and may or may not be annotated.
Comparative analysis	A synthesis and analysis of multiple studies that utilize a common metric and set of variables.
Meta-analysis	There is no single well-accepted definition of meta-analysis. Glass (1976), for example, referred to meta-analysis as 'the statistical analysis of a large collection of analysis results from individual studies for the purpose of integrating the findings' (p. 3). With this definition, a meta-analysis and a comparative analysis are identical. Stricter definitions of meta-analysis are more common. Gliner *et al.* (2003) define 'meta-analysis as a research synthesis that uses a quantitative measure, effect size, to indicate the strength of the relationship between the independent and dependent variables of studies making up the synthesis' (p. 1376).

In summary, the literature review process facilitates an understanding of the prior research. Knowing this historical background and the theoretical approaches that have been used provides the foundation for building on a body of knowledge, clarifies what concepts are important to study in a given context, and demonstrates how those concepts have been measured. It is important that the literature search covers a broad spectrum of past research. If a researcher approaches the literature review with tunnel vision, (s)he may miss a creative angle for the study. When a considerable body of literature has focused on the same measure (e.g. crowding, norms), summarizing the findings in a single table helps to visualize where similarities and differences have been observed. This tabular approach to reviewing the literature is detailed at the end of this chapter.

Finding the Literature: Knowing Where and How to Look

Literature reviews can be done manually or electronically using a computer. As noted in the introduction to this chapter, the well-meaning but misguided graduate student assigned to the carrying capacity project fell into one of the traps of computerized searches. She assumed that the results of the computer search – no matches found – reflected the current state of knowledge. Although both manual and electronic literature reviews have advantages and disadvantages, Fraenel and Wallen (1993) identify six basic steps involved in any literature search. The following is an adapted version of their logic.

1. Identify the general problem or research question

The question of where to start is often a major stumbling block for students new to a discipline. Sometimes the student's advisor outlines the initial problem or question. Such advice may have its origin in a problem area of interest to the mentor or it may be dictated by a funding agency. In recent years, for example, the US Congress mandated that the four federal land management agencies (i.e. US Forest Service, National Park Service, US Fish and Wildlife Service, Bureau of Land Management) implement a recreation fee programme and evaluate its impact on the visiting public (see *Journal of Leisure Research*, 13, 1999; *Journal of Park and Recreation Administration*, 17, 1999). Similarly, the National Fire Plan (USDA Forest Service, 2000) called for intensified research to support efforts to reduce human and ecological losses from wildfires. Not surprisingly, many researchers developed an interest in studying the impact of wildfires on humans.

Recreation fees and wildfires, however, represent broad topics that can be approached from a variety of theoretical and methodological perspectives. Economists, for example, might be interested in respondents' willingness to pay fees as a function of the distance they travelled. Psychologists, on the other hand, might focus a fee study on the concept of 'visitor displacement'. Visitor displacement refers to a shift in visitors' behaviour in response to changing conditions (e.g. higher entrance fees or increased crowding). Such behavioural shifts may take a variety of forms (Shelby, Bregenzer and Johnson, 1988). For example, increases in entrance fees may lead individuals to visit a natural resource less often or stop visiting altogether. If the fees are specific to particular types of recreation, the person may still visit the resource but choose a different activity that does not have a fee.

Visitor displacement studies necessitate different methodologies depending on the research question of interest. If the question is whether or not current visitors are likely to be displaced because of the fees, an on-site survey may be sufficient for providing the information. If the question involves the extent to which fees have already displaced visitors from coming to an area, on-site surveys will fall short of meeting the research objective. A researcher cannot interview people who are not present at the site. Answering actual displacement questions requires obtaining a sample of individuals who used to visit the resource, but have stopped because of the fees. In this instance, a mail or phone survey may be more appropriate.

In summary, while the literature search begins with a broad problem, researchers working in different disciplines narrow this focus to more specific questions. Narrowing the focus influences: (a) what theories will do better in explaining variable relationships; and (b) what methodologies are most appropriate for answering the questions. Both of these considerations impact the literature review process.

2. Narrow the problem by examining secondary references and review articles

Secondary references are publications that summarize or compare prior research findings (Riddick and Russell, 1999). Common secondary references include **text books** or **research review articles**. Specific to recreation/tourism concepts, several review articles have appeared in the literature

Table 3.1. Sample review articles on selected aspects of the recreation/tourism literature.

Concept	Citation
Motivation	Manfredo *et al.* (1996) Kuentzel (1990) Légaré and Haider (2008)
Satisfaction	Vaske *et al.* (1982)
Crowding	Vaske and Shelby (2008) Shelby and Vaske (2007)
Conflict	Graefe and Thapa (2004)
Norms	Vaske *et al.* (1986) Shelby *et al.* (1996) Donnelly *et al.* (2000) Vaske and Donnelly (2002) Kuentzel *et al.* (2008)
Specialization	Scott and Shafer (2001) Kuentzel and Heberlein (2008)

(Table 3.1). Manfredo *et al.* (1996) and Kuentzel (1990), for example, conducted meta-analyses of the recreation experience preference (motivation) scales. A **meta-analysis** is a method of reviewing the empirical literature that focuses on the statistical integration and analysis of empirical findings (see Box 3.2 for alternative definitions and Shelby and Vaske, 2008 for an example). Rather than collecting original data on a sample of individuals, meta-analysts obtain a sample (or the population) of studies that have been conducted by others or themselves on a given topic. In a single research project, the 'unit of analysis' is typically the individual respondent. In a meta-analysis, the unit of analysis is the study. Data from these studies are pooled (aggregated) and analysed statistically. Such analyses usually involve: (a) describing the characteristics of the original studies; and (b) transforming the results of the original studies into a common metric called an effect size (Gliner *et al.*, 2003).

Many of the review articles in Table 3.1 can more accurately be characterized as comparative studies rather than true meta-analyses. Vaske *et al.* (1982), for example, compared the overall satisfaction ratings of consumptive (e.g. hunting) and non-consumptive (e.g. wildlife viewers) recreationists as reported in 12 separate studies. The inductive theorizing that followed this comparative analysis stimulated

several deductive hypotheses and subsequent studies (see Vaske, 2008 for details). The comparative analyses of the crowding, conflict, norms and specialization concepts have also helped clarify why different findings sometimes occur in the literature.

From a literature review perspective, meta-analyses and comparative analyses offer at least three advantages. First, because these analyses succinctly synthesize findings from many studies, they facilitate an understanding of the current state of knowledge on a topic (e.g. motivations, crowding, norms, satisfaction). Second, the analyses can identify the most important variables and their associated relationships. This information allows researchers to concentrate on these concepts when new projects are designed and implemented. Third, the approach can highlight both consistencies and inconsistencies in the empirical findings. Understanding where the knowledge gaps exist helps to set priorities for future research.

3. Identify relevant primary references

Primary references are publications (typically journal articles) that contain results from actual studies (Riddick and Russell, 1999). A variety of applied (Table 3.2) and discipline specific journals are relevant to recreation/tourism researchers. For example, the broad issue of wildfire impacts on humans can be approached from different disciplinary perspectives. Economists might measure the impact relative to the US dollar loss in residential homes. Sociologists may concentrate on how different segments of society react to changes in Forest Service policies regarding wildfires. Economics and sociology, however, are themselves broad disciplines. Researchers working in these fields have a diversity of theoretical and conceptual interests. Within the general discipline of psychology, for example, researchers may use different specific concepts to explain the relationship between wildfires and humans.

Some social science wildfire research (e.g. Daniel *et al.*, 2007) has emphasized attitude theory or more specifically, **the theory of reasoned action** (Fishbein and Ajzen, 1975). Results from these investigations suggest that situational responses to wildfires are influenced by respondents' perceived knowledge of fire management policies and prior experiences with forest fires. Perceived knowledge is a belief that individuals have about the outcomes of fire management practices and an evaluation of

Table 3.2. Sample list of recreation/tourism journals.

Broad-topic-area journals

Journal of Leisure Research	Leisure Sciences
Leisure Studies	Journal of Park and Recreation Administration
World Leisure	Journal of Environmental Management
Environmental Management	Environment and Behavior
Society and Natural Resources	Society and Leisure
Human Ecology Review	Leisure/Loisir: Journal of the Canadian Association for Leisure Studies

Interest-area journals

Journal of Interpretation Research	Journal of Environmental Education
Therapeutic Recreation Journal	International Journal of Sport Psychology
Human Dimensions of Wildlife	Journal of Wildlife Management
Biological Conservation	Environmental Conservation
Rivers	Coastal Zone Management
Journal of Travel Research	Annals of Tourism Research
Tourism Analysis	Journal of Travel and Tourism Marketing
International Journal of Tourism and Hospitality Research	Tourism Management

those outcomes. Perceived knowledge and prior experience are important precursors to one's attitudes toward specific fire management practice. Prior experience with forest fires, for example, shapes an individual's attitude toward forest management practices. Attitudes formed as a result of previous experience (i.e. with forest fires) will be more consistent with subsequent behaviour (i.e. support for forest management practices) than attitudes formed as a result of indirect experience (e.g. reading about forest-fire management in a newspaper). This conclusion is derived from **the process model of attitudes** (Fazio, 1986).

From a literature review perspective, what began as a general problem of understanding the relationship between wildfires and humans was narrowed to more specific questions derived by the researchers' discipline (e.g. economics, sociology, psychology). Within the sub-discipline of social psychology, the search was further narrowed

to two theories (i.e. theory of reasoned action and the process model of attitudes) and several specific concepts (i.e. perceived knowledge, prior experience, attitudes). Different social psychologists may have narrowed their approach to the same problem using different theories and concepts. A wildfire study, for example, assessed the structural characteristics of recreationists' norms regarding specific fire management policies, and examined the influence of value orientations on norms about acceptable management actions (Kneeshaw *et al.*, 2004).

4. Critically review all primary journals

Do not assume that previous researchers uncovered all relevant articles in the primary journals. A critical review of all primary journals pertinent to your topic helps to ensure a thorough literature review. A few decades ago, there were only a handful of recreation/tourism-related professional journals. Becoming familiar with or staying current with the literature was a relatively simple matter of reviewing these journals, most of which were quarterly publications. Student questions about how far back in time one should search was not really an issue, since most journals did not have a long history. Today, the number of journals and the frequency of publication have expanded greatly. Some journals that previously published four issues a year now produce 10 or 12 issues a year.

Table 3.2 shows a sampling of recreation/tourism related journals. These journals do not constitute an exhaustive listing, but rather a starting point for understanding the literature. The expansion of broad topic area journals (e.g. *Leisure Sciences, Society and Natural Resources*) to special interest journals (e.g. *Human Dimensions of Wildlife, Coastal Zone Management*) reflects the growing interest in recreation/tourism research among academics. Critically reviewing *all* previous issues of these primary sources can identify references that may not have been discovered by other researchers.

5. Consult appropriate general reference works

General references refer to indices, abstracts or bibliographies on a given topic. **Indices** list basic information such as author, title and place of publication. **Abstracts** are succinct summaries of research published in journals, dissertations, or presentations at professional conferences. A **bibliography** contains a list of books and articles relevant to specific topics and may or may not be annotated. In addition to their traditional print format, many general references can be accessed via the Internet. Electronic versions of these databases may contain indices, abstracts, bibliographies, and/or full-text versions of the references.

Many of the theories and methods discussed in the recreation/tourism literature have their origins in specific disciplines such as anthropology, economics, psychology and sociology. A thorough literature review should include not only the recreation/tourism journals, but also the ideas and concepts as discussed in the core disciplines. Good starting points are the Annual Reviews found in anthropology, psychology, and sociology. These articles tend to focus on a given concept and provide excellent summaries of the current state of knowledge.

6. Summarize and organize sources

When done properly, a thorough literature review tends to produce piles of journal reprints, book chapters and books. Sorting through and making sense of this information poses a significant challenge. There are, however, several strategies that can help in this matter.

First, unless the person has a photographic memory, keeping track of which studies examined specific concepts and particular variable relationships, what activities were involved in the study, what resources were examined, what the findings suggested, and what conclusions were drawn is virtually impossible without some assistance. One useful strategy is to summarize the key points in each article that is read. Such notes might be simply written down on note cards or they can be entered into software programs such as Endnote or Procite. These referencing packages allow the researcher to enter brief (or extensive) notes on the article, as well as the bibliographic data for an article (e.g. author, date, title, publication source). Summarizing the article's key points allows the researcher to become more organized. Entering the bibliographic information into Endnote or Procite is useful when it comes time to produce the 'references' section of a journal article.

Second, summarizing the key points in articles reduces the page count of material to be reviewed from thousands (i.e. the original articles, books) to hundreds (i.e. the summarized key points). Such a reduction clearly helps in terms of understanding the literature. Sometimes, it is possible to summarize the findings more succinctly by collapsing the information into one or two tables.

Summarizing the Literature in Tables and Figures

Carefully reading the literature and taking notes on what you read are good starting points for understanding the literature. Sometimes it is also useful to summarize the articles in tables and/or figures to provide a 'big picture' overview of a topic. The following tables illustrate some suggestions for summarizing the literature.

Table 3.3 shows one approach to summarizing the recreation conflict literature. Cell entries categorize recreationists as either sensitive to, or tolerant of, the presence of others. Column 3 of

Table 3.3. Synopsis of sensitive versus tolerant user groups.[a]

Sensitive	Tolerant	Citation
Paddling canoeists	Motorboaters	Adelman, Heberlein and Bonnicksen (1982) Ivy, Stewart and Lue (1992) Lime (1975, 1977) Lucas (1964) Nielsen and Shelby (1977) Schreyer and Nielsen (1978) Shelby (1980) Stankey (1973) Todd and Graefe (1989)
Anglers	Other water sports	Confer, Thapa and Mendelsohn (2005) Driver and Bassett (1975) Gramann and Burdge (1981) Heberlein and Vaske (1977) Knopf et al. (1973) Lynch et al. (2004) West (1982)
Hikers	Trailbikers	Andereck, Vogt, Larkin and Freye (2001) Hendricks, Ramthun and Chavez (2001) Jacobi and Manning (1999) McCay and Moeller (1976) Wang and Manning (1999)
Hikers	Mountain bikers	Carothers, Vaske and Donnelly (2001) Cessford (2002) Heer, Rusterholz and Baur (2003) Ramthun (1995) Watson, Williams and Daigle (1991)
Hikers	Stock users	Blahna, Smith and Anderson (1995) McCay and Moeller (1976) Moore and McClaran (1991) Stankey (1973, 1980) Watson and Niccolucci (1992) Watson, Niccolucci and Williams (1994)
Skiers	Snowmobilers	Davenport and Borrie (2005) Dustin and Schneider (2005) Jackson and Wong (1982) Jackson, Haider and Elliot (2002) Knopp and Tyger (1973) Lindberg et al. (2001) Vaske, Needham and Cline (2007) Vittersø, Chipeniuk, Skår and Vistad (2004)
Skiers	Snowboarders	Edensor and Richards (2007) Thapa and Graefe (1999, 2003, 2004)

(*Continued*)

Table 3.3. Continued.

Sensitive	Tolerant	Citation
		Vaske, Carothers, Donnelly and Baird (2000)
		Vaske, Dyar and Timmons (2004)
		Williams, Dossa and Fulton (1994)
Backcountry skiers	Helicopter skiers	Gibbons and Ruddell (1995)
Non-ORV users	ORV users	Dellora, Martin and Saunders (2004)
		Noe, Wellman and Buhyoff (1982)
		Noe, Wellman and Hull (1982)
		Behan, Richards and Lee (2001)
Non-hunters	Hunters	McShea, Wemmer and Stuwe (1993)
		Schuster, Hammitt, Moore and Schneider (2006)
		Vaske, Donnelly, Wittmann and Laidlaw (1995)

[a] This table is a sample of articles examining conflict between different types of recreationists. Full citations are not provided because the articles may not reflect the most recent research on conflict; the focus here is on 'how to' summarize, not 'what is' summarized.
ORV, off-road vehicle.

this table gives the citations supporting this categorization. Such a table points to which activity pairings have been studied the most; activity comparisons that have received minimal attention in the literature; and comparisons between activities that have not been previously examined (i.e. no listing in the table). Examining the literature at this level offers several advantages. First, for those activity comparisons that have been studied frequently, one can ask whether the findings have been consistent or inconsistent. Second, knowing that there are no listings in the table for a given pair of activities might suggest an interesting future investigation. Third, such a table proves useful when writing the introduction to an article or dissertation. The table provides an outline for summarizing what has occurred in the published literature.

This approach to reviewing the literature and making inferences about its current status works when the researcher has confidence that his/her literature search was as thorough as possible. Table 3.3 does not reflect the most recent research on conflict; the focus here is on 'how to' summarize, not 'what is' summarized.

Table 3.3 used 'words' to characterize the findings from multiple studies. When numerous studies have examined the same variable using similar methodologies, the findings can be compared 'numerically'. Table 3.4 illustrates this

approach for the concept of norm prevalence. As noted previously, norm prevalence refers to the proportion of a population who can articulate a norm in a given situation. Prevalence can range from 0% to 100%. If prevalence is high, the norm is probably relevant for respondents. If norm prevalence is low, the issue may not be as important to respondents.

Several trends emerge when findings from different studies are summarized in a table. Across the 68 evaluation contexts (Table 3.4), for example, the percentage of respondents who reported an encounter norm (i.e. norm prevalence) ranged from a high of 97% for the Colorado bow elk hunters' evaluations of other hunters to a low of 16% for visitors at the Alpine Visitor Center in Rocky Mountain National Park. The average (mean) norm prevalence was 66%, the median was 67%, and the standard deviation was 20%. These descriptive statistics suggest that across all evaluation contexts, two thirds of respondents, on average, reported a numerical encounter norm when asked.

Studies conducted in back-country settings tend to be grouped in the upper half of the table where norm prevalence is highest. Sixteen of the 36 evaluation contexts with norm prevalence greater than the median (67%) are from studies conducted in Alaska. Data for other evaluation contexts in this group come from locations with known low densities. For example, use on the Rogue River (Oregon)

Table 3.4. Ranking of norm prevalence for different resources and evaluation contexts.[a]

Study site	Evaluation context		% Reporting an encounter norm[b]	% 'It matters but cannot give a number'	% 'It does not matter to me'
	Evaluations by:	**Evaluations for:**			
Colorado	Bow elk hunters	Other hunters	97		3
Colorado	Bow elk hunters	Other archers	96		4
Talkeetna River Canyon	Rafters	Other rafters	96		4
Upper Kanektok River	Floaters	Powerboats	94		6
Colorado	Bow elk hunters	Recreationists	92		8
Lower Kanektok River	Floaters	Powerboats	92		10
Rogue River (1984)	Rafters	Other rafters	90		10
Goodnews River	Floaters	Powerboats	90		10
Upper Kanektok	Floaters	Other float groups	90		10
Illinois River	Rafters	Other rafters	90		10
Talachulitna River	Rafters	Other groups	89		11
Upper Lake Creek	Rafters	Other rafters	88		12
Goodnews River	Floaters	Other float groups	87		13
Gwaii Haanas	Kayakers	Motorboaters	86	11	3
Upper Kenai River	Bank anglers	Other anglers at high use times	86		14
Grand Canyon	Rafters	Other rafters	84		16
Lower Lake Creek	Boaters/rafters/anglers	Other groups	84		16
Rogue River (1977)	Rafters	Other rafters	82		18
Lower Kanektok	Floaters	Other float groups	82		18
Talkeetna River at Clear Creek	Boaters/anglers	Other groups	81		19
Togiak River	Fly-in anglers	Other angling groups	80		20
Upper Deshka River	Rafters/boaters	Other groups	80		20

(Continued)

Table 3.4. Continued.

Study site	Evaluation context		% Reporting an encounter norm[b]	% 'It matters but cannot give a number'	% 'It does not matter to me'
	Evaluations by:	Evaluations for:			
Middle Kenai River	Bank angler	Other anglers at low use times	78		22
Rogue River (1991)	Rafters	Other rafters	78		22
Klamath River	Summer rafters	Other rafters	78		22
Poudre River	Kayakers	Rafters	77		23
Deschutes River	Rafters	Other rafters – Segment 1	73		27
Bear Lake Shuttle Lot (closed question)	Visitors	Other visitors	72	8	20
Lower Deshka River	Rafters/boaters	Other groups	72		28
Gwaii Haanas	Motorboaters	Motorboaters	71	29	0
Columbia Icefield	Snowcoach visitors	Other visitors	71		29
Klamath River	Anglers	Float groups	70		30
Columbia Icefield	Toe of glacier visitors	Other visitors	69		31
Little Susitna River	Rafters/boaters	Other groups	68		32
Bear Lake trail (closed question)	Visitors	Other visitors	67	15	18
Middle Kenai River	Bank anglers	Other anglers at high use times	67		33
Mt. Evans	Wildlife viewers	Hunters	62	28	10
Deschutes River	Rafters	Other rafters – Segment 2	62		38
Deschutes River	Rafters	Other rafters – Segment 3	62		38
Mt. Shasta	Hikers	Other hikers while camping	61		39

(Continued)

Table 3.4. Continued.

Study site	Evaluation context		% Reporting an encounter norm[b]	% 'It matters but cannot give a number'	% 'It does not matter to me'
	Evaluations by:	Evaluations for:			
Mt. Evans	Hunters	Other hunters	60	34	6
Poudre River	Kayakers	Other kayakers	60		40
Longs Peak summit (closed question)	Hikers	Other hikers	59	18	23
Longs Peak trailhead (closed question)	Hikers	Other hikers	57	18	25
Longs Peak trail (closed question)	Hikers	Other hikers	57	19	24
Mt. Evans	Hunters	Wildlife viewers	57	33	10
Poudre River	Rafters	Other rafters	56		44
Clackamas	Rafters	Other rafters	56		44
Klamath River	Anglers	Other anglers	56		44
Mt. Shasta	Hikers	Other hikers while climbing	54		46
White Salmon	Rafters	Other rafters	52		48
Alpine Visitor Center (closed question)	Visitors	Other visitors	51	18	31
Mt. Shasta	Hikers	Other hikers at summit	51		49
New River	Rafters	Other rafters – as wilderness	50	34	16
Gwaii Haanas	Kayakers	Other kayakers	48	44	8
Mt. Evans	On-site visitors	Other visitors	48		52
New River	Rafters	Other rafters – as scenic experience	45	25	30
Mt. Evans	Wildlife viewers	Other viewers	43	47	10
Longs Peak summit (semi-open question)	Hikers	Other hikers	42	16	42

(Continued)

Table 3.4. Continued.

| Study site | Evaluation context | | % Reporting an encounter norm[b] | % 'It matters but cannot give a number' | % 'It does not matter to me' |
	Evaluations by:	Evaluations for:			
Clackamas	Rafters	Other rafters	39	38	23
Poudre River	Rafters	Kayakers	39		61
Longs Peak trail (semi-open question)	Hikers	Other hikers	38	25	37
Gwaii Haanas	Motorboaters	Kayakers	34	41	25
Longs Peak trailhead (semi-open question)	Hikers	Other hikers	30	20	15
Bear Lake trail (semi-open question)	Visitors	Other visitors	30	25	45
New River	Rafters	Other rafters – as social experience	29	18	53
Bear Lake Shuttle Lot (semi-open question)	Visitors	Other visitors	21	13	66
Alpine Visitor Center (semi-open question)	Visitors	Other visitors	16	32	52

[a]An earlier version of this table appeared in Donnelly *et al.* (2000) – see Table 3.1 for reference.
[b]The percentage reporting an encounter norm represents norm prevalence.

is limited to 120 people per day, and norm prevalence ranged from 78% (1991 data) to 90% (1984 data). Use on the Colorado River in the Grand Canyon was limited to 150 people per day during the time of the study, and averaged about 75 per day during the season (norm prevalence = 84%).

By comparison, evaluation contexts with norm prevalence scores lower than the median are more often higher density, front-country settings. The New River (Virginia), for example, is a day-use area with use levels averaging more than 1000 people per day on summer weekends. Norm prevalence for the New River ranged from 29% when the setting was evaluated as a social experience to 50% when it was evaluated as wilderness. The debate in the literature regarding norm existence can be traced to this investigation (Roggenbuck *et al.*, 1991). This study ranked third from the bottom in

terms of norm prevalence among the 68 evaluation contexts examined in Table 3.4. By summarizing the studies that have examined the prevalence of encounter norms, and evaluating variables influencing norm prevalence (e.g. back-country versus front-country, response format), the debate can be placed on a more empirical basis.

Vaske (2008) summarized the bivariate relationships between four variables (actual density, reported encounters, perceived crowding and visitor satisfaction) in the traditional capacity model. The matrix in Table 3.5 illustrates another approach to summarizing those same relationships. The row and column headings are the variables in the model. The cell entries show the studies that examined specific pairs of variables along with the findings reported in those investigations. Table 3.5 uses symbols to indicate the results. A plus (+) sign indicates that a positive and statistically significant relationship was observed. A minus (–) sign is used when the relationship was negative and statistically significant. Zeros (0) are given when no statistical relationship for a given pair of variables was reported in the study.

In the cell comparing 'actual density' against 'reported encounters', seven studies are shown. Each of these investigations found a positive and statistically significant relationship between the two variables. This suggests that as actual density increases, the number of reported encounters with other individuals increases. The use of symbols (+) makes this pattern intuitively obvious. The consistency of these findings across all studies examining this bivariate relationship suggests that the pattern generalizes regardless of where the study was conducted.

In the opposite corner of the matrix, the relationship between 'perceived crowding' and 'visitor satisfaction' is displayed. Eleven studies are shown in this cell. Seven of the studies found the predicted negative relationship between the two variables, whereas four studies reported no statistical relationship. Again, the pattern is obvious when symbols are used to display the results. The advantage of this approach to summarizing the literature is the ease of understanding. The disadvantage is that the reader does not know the specifics (e.g. the effect size of the reported relationship or what activities and resources were studied). In reality, both numeric and symbolic approaches might be used to better understand the capacity model. Table 3.5 provides a 'big picture' overview.

From a more general perspective, the matrix approach to summarizing the literature offers several advantages. First, when there are numerous citations in a given cell and they all report the same finding (+, – or 0), the researcher has more confidence in the findings. The results in this case generalize for the two variables of interest. Second, when the studies reported in a specific cell show different symbols (i.e. +, –, 0), discrepancies in the literature are intuitively apparent. Such differences lead to new research questions regarding why the differences occurred. Was it because of differences in the activity studied, the resource included in the investigation, or the methodology used to collect the data? Third, a literature search that produces no entries in a given cell may signal the need to fill this knowledge gap.

In summary, three different methods for summarizing the literature were presented here. Table 3.3 used words to give an overview evaluation of the recreation conflict literature. Table 3.4 summarized the findings from a single concept (norm prevalence) using numbers. Table 3.5 illustrated the bivariate relationships between variables. Any or all of these strategies may be used to better understand a given phenomenon. Other strategies might also be applied. What is important is that the researchers use some strategy to distill the status of existing research.

Discussion Questions

1. Why is it important for a research project to build on the work that already exists?

2. Identify three functions of the literature review process.

3. Explain why the following statement is important: 'Good theoretical research has applied consequences and good applied research has theoretical implications'.

4. List six basic steps involved in conducting a literature review.

5. What is a 'secondary' publication reference?

6. Define 'meta-analysis' and discuss the distinction between a meta-analysis and a 'single survey research project'.

7. Discuss three advantages of meta- and comparative analyses.

8. Identify five major recreation/tourism journals.

9. Define 'general references'.

10. Discuss two alternative ways of summarizing scientific articles. Why is it important to adopt a strategy for summarizing the literature?

Key Terms

Literature review functions: Steps and processes involved in searching professional journals and academic books to find writings similar to the current project and to develop overall understanding of what has been done in the past.

Primary references: Publications (typically journal articles) that contain results from actual studies.

Secondary references: Publications that summarize or compare prior research findings.

Meta-analysis: A method of reviewing the empirical literature that focuses on the statistical integration and analysis of empirical findings.

Table 3.5. Example matrix format for summarizing a body of literature.

Variables	Actual density	Reported encounters	Perceived crowding	Visitor satisfaction
Actual density		Shelby (1976) + Heberlein and Vaske (1977) + Heberlein et al. (1982) + Randall (1977) + Blackwood (1977) + Shelby and Colvin (1979) + Donnelly (1980) +	Lee (1975) + Shelby (1976) 0 Heberlein and Vaske (1977) + Randall (1977) + Heberlein and Laybourne (1978) 0 Heberlein and Baumgartner (1978) +/0 Absher (1980) + Shelby and Colvin (1979) + Gramann and Burdge (1981) 0 Absher and Lee (1981) + Ditton et al. (1982) + Hammitt et al. (1982) + Heberlein et al. (1982) +	Shelby (1976) 0 Heberlein and Vaske (1977) 0 McConnell (1977) 0 Randall (1977) 0 Heberlein and Laybourne (1978) + Heberlein and Baumgartner (1978) 0 Shelby and Colvin (1979) 0 Becker (1981) 0 Ditton et al. (1982) 0 Heberlein et al. (1982) +
Reported encounters	(see upper diagonal of matrix)		Blackwood (1977) + Heberlein and Vaske (1977) + Heberlein and Laybourne (1977) + Heberlein and Baumgartner (1978) +/0 Schreyer and Nielson (1978) + McDonald and Hammitt (1979) + Shelby and Colvin (1979) + Donnelly (1980) + Bultena et al. (1981) + Vaske et al. (1982) + Hammitt et al. (1982) + Schreyer (1976) + Vaske and Graefe (1983) + Vaske et al. (1983) +/0	Blackwood (1977) 0 Heberlein and Vaske (1977) –/0 Becker (1981) 0 Heberlein and Laybourne (1977) 0 Heberlein and Baumgartner (1978) 0 McDonald and Hammitt (1979) +/0 Shelby and Colvin (1979) 0 Donnelly (1980) 0 Manning and Ciali (1980) 0 Bultena et al. (1981) 0 Vaske et al. (1982) 0 Vaske and Graefe (1983) 0 Vaske et al. (1983) +/0

Perceived crowding	(see upper diagonal of matrix)	(see upper diagonal of matrix)	
			Shelby (1976) —
			Blackwood (1977) 0
			Heberlein and Vaske (1977) —
			Randall (1977) —
			Shelby and Colvin (1979) 0
			Donnelly (1980) 0
			Bultena et al. (1982) —
			Ditton et al. (1982) —
			Vaske et al. (1982) —
			Vaske and Graefe (1983) 0
			Vaske et al. (1983) —

Zero (0) = non-significant relationship reported; Plus (+) = Positive and significant relationship reported; Minus (−) = Negative and significant relationship reported

Complete citations for the referenced articles can be found at: http://welcome.warnercnr.colostate.edu/~jerryv/

References

Daniel, T.C., Carroll, M.S., Moseley, C. and Raish, C. (2007) *People, Fire, and Forests: A Synthesis of Wildfire Social Science*. Oregon State University Press, Corvallis, Oregon.

Donnelly, M.P., Vaske, J.J., Whittaker, D. and Shelby, B. (2000) Toward an understanding of norm prevalence: A comparative–analysis. *Environmental Management* 25, 403–414.

Fazio, R.H. (1986) How do attitudes guide behavior? In: Sorrentino, R.M. and Higgins, E.T. (eds) *Handbook of Motivation and Cognition: Foundations of Social Behavior*. Guilford Press, New York, pp. 204–243.

Fishbein, M. and Ajzen, I. (1975) *Belief, Attitude, Intention, and Behavior: An Introduction to Theory and Research*. Addison–Wesley, Reading, Massachusetts.

Fraenel, J. and Wallen, N. (1993) *How to Design and Evaluate Research in Education*, 2nd edn. McGraw–Hill, New York.

Glass, C.V. (1976) Primary, secondary, and meta-analysis research. *Educational Researcher* 5, 3–8.

Gliner, J.A., Morgan, G.A. and Harmon, R.J. (2003) Meta analysis: Foundation and interpretation. *Journal of the American Academy of Child and Adolescent Psychiatry* 42, 1376–1379.

Graefe, A.R. and Thapa, B. (2004). Conflict in natural resource recreation. In: M.J. Manfredo, M.J., Vaske, J.J., Bruyere, B.L., Field, D.R. and Brown P. (eds) *Society and Natural Resources: A Summary of Knowledge*. Modern Litho, Jefferson, Missouri, pp. 209–224.

Hall, T.E. and Roggenbuck, J.W. (2002) Response format effects in questions about norms: Implications for the reliability and validity of the normative approach. *Leisure Sciences 24*, 325–337.

Kneeshaw, K., Vaske, J.J., Bright, A.D. and Absher, J.D. (2004) Acceptability norms toward fire management in three national forests. *Environment & Behavior* 36, 592–612.

Kuentzel, W. (1990) Motive uniformity across recreation settings: A meta-analysis of REP scales. Paper presented at the Annual National Recreation and Parks Association.

Kuentzel, W.F. and Heberlein, T.A. (2008) Life course changes and competing leisure interests as obstacles to boating specialization. *Leisure Sciences* 30, 143–157.

Kuentzel, W.F., Laven, D., Manning, R.E. and Valliere, W.A. (2008) Understanding the role of norm strength at multiple national park settings. *Leisure Sciences* 30, 127–142.

Kuss, F.R., Graefe, A.R. and Vaske, J.J. (1990) *Visitor Impact Management: A Review of Research*. National Parks and Conservation Association, Washington, D.C.

Légaré, A. and Haider, W. (2008) Trend analysis of motivation–based clusters at the Chilhoot Trail National Historical Site of Canada. *Leisure Sciences* 30, 158–176.

Manfredo, M.J., Driver, B.L. and Tarrant, M.A. (1996) Measuring leisure motivation: A meta-analysis of the recreation experience preference scales. *Journal of Leisure Research* 28, 188–213.

Manfredo, M.J., Teel, T.L. and Bright, A.D. (2004) Application of the concepts of values and attitudes in human dimensions of natural resources research. In Manfredo, M.J., Vaske, J.J., Bruyere, B.L., Field, D.R. and Brown P. (eds) *Society and Natural Resources: A Summary of Knowledge*. Modern Litho, Jefferson, Missouri, pp. 271–282.

Riddick, C.C. and Russell, R.V. (1999). *Evaluative Research in Recreation, Park and Sport Settings: Search for Useful Information*. Sagamore Publishing, Inc., Champaign, Illinois.

Roggenbuck, J.W., Williams, D.R., Bange, S.P. and Dean, D.J. (1991) River float trip encounter norms: Questioning the use of the social norms concept. *Journal of Leisure Research* 23, 133–153.

Scott, D. and Shafer, C.S. (2001) Recreation specialization: A critical look at the construct. *Journal of Leisure Research* 33, 319–343.

Shelby, B., Bregenzer, H. and Johnson, R. (1988) Displacement and product shift: Empirical evidence from two Oregon rivers. *Journal of Leisure Research* 20, 274–288.

Shelby, L.B. and Vaske, J.J. (2007) Perceived crowding among hunters and anglers: A meta–analysis. *Human Dimensions of Wildlife* 12, 241–261.

Shelby, L.B. and Vaske, J.J. (2008) Understanding meta–analyses: A review of the methodological literature. *Leisure Sciences* 30, 96–110.

Shelby, B., Vaske, J.J. and Donnelly, M.P. (1996) Norms, standards and natural resources. *Leisure Sciences* 18, 103–123.

USDA Forest Service. (2000) Protecting people and sustaining resources in fire-adapted ecosystems. http://www.fs.fed.us/publications

Vaske, J.J. (2008) *Survey Research and Analysis: Applications in Parks, Recreation and Human Dimensions*. Venture Publishing Inc., State College, Pennsylvania.

Vaske, J.J. and Donnelly, M.P. (2002) Generalizing the encounter–norm–crowding relationship. *Leisure Sciences,* 24, 255–269.

Vaske, J.J., Donnelly, M.P., Heberlein, T.A. and Shelby, B. (1982) Differences in reported satisfaction ratings by consumptive and nonconsumptive recreationists. *Journal of Leisure Research* 14, 195–206.

Vaske, J.J., Donnelly, M.P. and Lehto, X. (2002) *Visitor Crowding and Normative Tolerances at Congested Areas of Rocky Mountain National Park*. (Project Rep. No. 50). Project Report for the National Parks Service. Colorado State University, Human Dimensions in Natural Resources Unit, Fort Collins, Colorado.

Vaske, J.J., Donnelly, M.P., Wittmann, K. and Laidlaw, S. (1995) Interpersonal versus social–values conflict. *Leisure Sciences* 17, 205–222.

Vaske, J.J., Graefe, A.R., and Drogin, E.B. (1989) VIMDEX: An index of visitor impact management references. *In Proceedings: 1989 Northeastern Recreation Research Symposium*. USDA Forest Service General Technical Report NE–132. Saratoga Springs, New York, pp. 77–84.

Vaske, J.J. and Manning, R.E. (2008) Analysis of multiple data sets in outdoor recreation research: Introduction to special issue. *Leisure Sciences* 30, 93–95.

Vaske, J.J. and Shelby, L.B. (2008) Crowding as a descriptive indicator and an evaluative standard: Results from 30 years of research. *Leisure Sciences* 30, 111–126.

Vaske, J.J., Shelby, B., Graefe, A.R. and Heberlein, T.A. (1986) Backcountry encounter norms: Theory, method and empirical evidence. *Journal of Leisure Research* 18, 137–153.

Vaske, J.J. and Whittaker, D. (2004) Normative approaches to natural resources. In Manfredo, M.J., Vaske, J.J., Bruyere, B.L., Field, D.R. and Brown P. (eds) *Society and Natural Resources: A Summary of Knowledge*. Modern Litho, Jefferson, Missouri, pp. 283–294.

Whittaker, D., Vaske, J.J. and Manfredo, M.J. (2006) Specificity and the cognitive hierarchy: Values orientations and the acceptability of urban wildlife management actions. *Society and Natural Resources* 19, 515–530.

chapter 4

Measurement of Variables

Yuksel Ekinci

Learning Objectives

After reading this chapter you should be able to:

1. Understand the characteristics of the four types of measurement scales – nominal, ordinal, interval, ratio – and describe why and when we use each of them in leisure, recreation, and tourism research;
2. Appreciate the principles of construct measurement;
3. Discuss goodness of measures and how they are established;
4. Develop an understanding of various forms of reliability and validity when developing and using measurement scales.

Chapter Summary

This chapter introduces how tangible and intangible variables are measured. Generally, variables can be measured by the four types of scales: nominal, ordinal, interval and ratio. A valid and reliable scale should be used to measure intangible variables to engage in scientific research. Goodness of measure can be established through various reliability and validity tests such as Cronbach's Alpha, content validity, construct validity and criterion validity. If a good (reliable and valid) scale is not

available, a new scale can be developed by following the scale-development process. As developing a multi-item scale would be laborious task, leisure, recreation and tourism researchers can borrow the instruments that are already reputed to be 'good'.

Introduction

Measurement is an essential part of the research process and research design. Unless the variables are measured in some ways, we will not be able to test our hypothesis and find answers to research questions. Certain variables lend themselves to easy measurement through the use of established instruments, such as blood pressure, pulse rates, body temperature, height and weight. But when we get into the realm of people's subjective feelings, attitudes and perception, measurement becomes complicated. This is one of the unique characteristics of leisure, recreation and tourism research.

For example, consider the issue of whether quality of service influences a tourist's intention to revisit a destination. This is a question of significant interest to researchers, policymakers, managers and destination marketers. And it is common to see newspaper headlines or holiday programmes that discuss how service quality affects tourist satisfaction and loyalty. But such stories and headlines raise questions about, for example, what we mean by quality of service in a resort hotel. The concept of service quality is very complex, including a number of different dimensions. Despite the lack of physical devices to measure service quality, there are ways of tapping it. For example, we may measure the quality of service based on a hotel's physical elements, driven by cleanliness of the rooms or visual attractiveness of the décor. Alternatively, we may focus on the perceived attitudes and behaviours of the hotel employees (e.g. friendliness and competence) when serving the guests. These may be typical indicators of service quality, but using different measures raises another very important question. Do these items provide reliable and valid measures for assessing the perceived service quality? What is the amount of error in measurement, if there is any? In this chapter, we will discuss how tangible and intangible variables (e.g. the quality of service, tourist loyalty) are measured. We will also discuss methods used for assessing 'goodness' of measurements.

About Measurement

All social science research including leisure, recreation and tourism requires some form of measurement. Measurement is an essential part of a research design, since most research begins with broad constructs (e.g. quality of service) and then these constructs are translated into specific variables for questionnaire development, data collection and data analysis. Measurement refers to grouping objects (e.g. firms, machines and people) according to their score on a measurement scale. For example, hotels can be grouped according to their size and location. After carrying out such a measurement, hotels can be classified into various categories such as big, small or medium. Similarly, tourists can be grouped into three broad categories according to their level of satisfaction experience with a particular tourism destination: satisfied, dissatisfied, neither satisfied nor dissatisfied.

There are at least two types of variables: tangibles and intangibles. A **tangible variable** lends itself to objective and precise measurement. An **intangible variable** is abstract and does not easily lend itself to accurate and easy measurement because of its subjective nature. The intangible variables can be related to tourists' feelings or perceptions and are known as constructs such as the quality of service, destination image or attitudes towards a tourism destination. Measuring an intangible variable is usually done indirectly and usually involves measurement error. For example, thirst is abstract and measured indirectly. The degree of thirst can be measured through a number of ways that include typical indicators of this concept. Let's suppose that after a safari tour we want to find out how thirsty the outdoor recreationists are. We ask them to drink water from a measurable glass. We then count the amount of water consumed by each traveller and draw conclusion about their degree of thirst. Accordingly, we may be able to group them into three broad categories: not thirsty at all, thirsty, and very thirsty. If we are not satisfied with the quality of this measurement, other forms of measurement can be applied such as observing their skin condition or examining a blood sample.

Unlike intangible variables, tangible variables are measured by standardized physical instruments and pose little or no measurement error. For example, the height of a rope course or the length of a hotel lobby can be measured using a tape measure and grouped into various categories with little measurement error. Similarly, people too can be measured and grouped based on some tangible characteristics using the following questions:

- What is your gender?
- What is your age?
- What is your occupation?
- What is your marital status?
- How long have you stayed in this leisure complex?
- How many times have you visited this recreation complex?

Why Measure?

Measurement is an essential component of the quantitative methodology. There are three fundamental reasons for measurement (Bryman and Bell, 2007, p. 72):

- Measurement allows us to delineate the fine differences between objects in terms of the characteristics in question. This is very useful because we can often distinguish between objects in terms of extreme categories but finer distinctions are much more difficult to recognize. For example, we can detect clear variations among visitors' satisfaction with their destination experience – visitors who like the destination and visitors who dislike the destination – but smaller differences are much more difficult to detect.

- Measurement gives us a consistent device or a yardstick for making such distinctions and estimating differences among the objects. This relates to two things: our ability to be consistent over time and our ability to be consistent with findings of other studies. Hence, when a measurement is repeated under the same conditions, the measurement score should not be influenced by the timing of its administration or by the person who administers it. This is not meant to say that measurement scores do not change over time. They do, because they are bound to be influenced by social change. For example, the anxiety of a child who plans to visit Disneyland would normally be high. If a measurement is applied to capture her anxiety just before and after the visit, her anxiety score will probably change because of the timing effect. But the overall score should very similar if it was administered after 30 or after 40 days of the visit.

- Measurement provides the basis for more precise estimation of the relationships among variables and theories through statistical analyses such as correlation, regression and structural equation modelling. Thus, if we measure a tourist's satisfaction with a tourism destination along with other variables that might be related to this concept, such as the destination loyalty or value for money, we would be able to produce a more precise estimation about these relationships than if we had not accounted for such variables.

Measurement of Variables

What is a variable?

A variable can be anything that takes on differing or varying values. The value can differ at various times for the same variable (e.g. job satisfaction measured before and after a pay rise) or

at the same time for the same variable (e.g. job satisfaction for different employees before a pay rise). Examples of variables we use in our field are: job satisfaction, tourist loyalty, absenteeism, number of golf courses, number of urban recreational parks, number of after school recreation programmes, amount of leisure time within a week, and motivations to participate in women's football.

A variable can be discrete (e.g. gender: male/female, nationality: American, British, German, Turkish) or continuous (e.g. age of a tourist, income of recreationists, or number of fitness clubs). A variable can also be tangible (e.g. age, number of visits) or intangible (e.g. attitudes toward work, motivation). The concept of motivation has to be reduced from its level of abstraction or operationalized in a way that it becomes measurable. For example, an individual's motivation to visit a leisure complex can be measured on a 10-point scale. The level of motivation may take varying values from (1) being 'very low' to (10) being 'very high'. However, how the level of motivation should be measured from a visitor's point of view is an entirely different matter. In this chapter, we will primarily concern ourselves with tangible and intangible (abstract) variables and their level of measurement using different scales.

Scales of measurement

Now that we have learned the types of variables, we need to measure them in some meaningful way. To this end, we will examine the types of scales that can be applied to the measurement of tangible variables in general and intangible variables (or construct measurement) in particular.

A scale is a tool or mechanism by which individuals are distinguished on how they differ from one another on the variables of interest of our research. The scale can be a gross one in the way that it would only broadly categorize individuals on certain variables; or it could be a fine-tuned tool that would differentiate individuals on the variables with varying degrees of qualities including **difference**, **magnitude**, **equal intervals** and **absolute zero** (Sekaran, 2003). Difference means the ability of distinguishing individuals based on their scores on the scale. Magnitude refers to the ability to know if one score is equal, greater or less than another score. Equal intervals mean that the scores have equal distance from each other. And finally, absolute zero refers to where none of the scales exists or where a score or zero can be assigned.

On the basis of these qualities, the four types of scales are formed: **nominal, ordinal, interval** and **ratio**. Table 4.1 shows scales of measurement and their properties.

As can be seen from Table 4.1, the degree of scale qualities and the power of statistics increase progressively as we move from the nominal scale to the ratio scale. That is, information on the variables can be obtained with a greater degree of detail when we use an interval or a ratio scale. As the calibration of or fine-tuning of the scale increases in quality, so does the power of the scale. With more powerful scales, increasingly sophisticated data analysis can be performed. In turn, we can find more meaningful answers to our research questions.

Nominal scale

A nominal scale means objects are assigned into mutually exclusive and collectively exhaustive groups. For example, with respect to the variable of religion, tourists could be grouped into three categories – Christian, Muslim and Hindu. These three groups can be represented by three code numbers 1, 2 and 3. These numbers serve as simple and convenient category labels with no intrinsic value, other than assign tourists to one of the non-overlapping categories. Note that the categories should also be collectively exhaustive. In other words, there will be no fourth category into which respondents would normally fall. The information that can be generated from nominal scales is used to calculate the percentage (or frequency) of religion in our sample. For example, if we had surveyed 200 travellers, and assigned code number 1 to Christians, number 2 to Muslims and number 3 to Hindus, our arithmetic analysis of the data would show that 100 Muslims, 80 Christians, and 20 Hindus participated to this survey and the frequency distribution would show that 50% of the respondents are Muslim, 40% of them are Christians and 10% of them are Hindu. Other than this marginal information, no other arithmetic calculation can be performed on the data. For example, because 1 plus 2 is equal to 3 we cannot say that when we arithmetically add all the 1s and 2s in the data we would be able to find the total number of Hindus which is coded as 3. This would represent a fatal flaw in logic.

Table 4.1. Scales of measurement and their properties.

Scale of measurement	Scale qualities	Example(s)	Measures of central tendency	Some tests of significance between the variables
Nominal	Difference	Gender, religion, nationality, occupation	Mode	Chi (χ^2) square
Ordinal	Difference Magnitude	Anything rank ordered	Median	Rank-order correlations
Interval	Difference Magnitude Equal intervals	Temperature	Arithmetic mean	Linear correlations, t, F
Ratio	Difference Magnitude Equal intervals Absolute zero	Age, height, weight, income, number of visits	Arithmetic or geometric mean	Linear correlations, t, F

The interval scale has 1 as an arbitrary starting point. The ratio scale has the natural origin 0, which is meaningful as it indicates no quantities in terms of measurement.

Example 4.1

Let us take a look at another variable that lends itself to nominal scaling – the mode of transportation used by leisure travellers:

Airplane	(1)
Bus	(2)
Car	(3)
Foot	(4)
Motorbike	(5)
Ship	(6)

We could use a nominal scale to group the mode of transportation into mutually exclusive and collectively exhaustive categories. In summary, a nominal scale only shows that categories of the variables are different and displays some gross information.

Ordinal scale

An ordinal scale not only classifies the variable in such a way as to indicate differences among the various categories, it also locates its relative position (or rank orders) in relation to others in some meaningful way. In other words, an ordinal scale has the power of showing differences and magnitude among the objects (from greatest to lowest) but it has no absolute zero point and no equal intervals. The ordinal scale can be used with any variable that may be ordered according to ranking criteria such as taste, distance, competition, size, importance, etc. For example, four attributes of a leisure complex (e.g. convenience of location, value for money, friendliness of staff and quality of physical environment) could be ranked in order according to their level of importance to the visitor's choice.

Example 4.2

Let us take a look another variable that lends itself to ordinal scaling: preference of job in the tourism industry.

Rank the following four tourism job characteristics from 1 to 4 in terms of how important they are for you. You should rank the most important item as 1, the next in importance as 2 and so on, until you have ranked each of them, with 4 indicating the least important item to you.

Tourism job characteristics	Ranking of importance
Interacting with others	_____
Working independently	_____
Serving others	_____
Using a number of different skills	_____

We can now argue that the ordinal scale has more information than the nominal scale because the ordinal scale goes beyond differentiating the categories to providing information on how respondents are discriminating among them according to rank ordering. Note, however, that the ordinal scale does not give any indication of the magnitude of the rank ordering. For instance, in the job characteristics example, the first job characteristic may be only marginally preferred over the second characteristic, whereas the job characteristic that is ranked third might be preferred considerably more than the job characteristic ranked fourth. Thus, in ordinal scaling, although we would know that there are differences in the ranking of objects, we would not know the magnitude of these differences. This deficiency is overcome by interval scaling which is discussed next.

Interval scale

An interval scale possesses both magnitude and equal intervals but not the quality of absolute zero. Clinical temperature is a classic example of an interval scale because we know that each degree is the same distance apart and we can easily tell if one temperature is greater than, equal to or less than another. The temperature, however, has no absolute zero because there is (theoretically) no point where temperature or heat does not exist on level zero. Hence the starting point of the clinical thermometer is arbitrary. However, the interval scale allows us to perform certain arithmetical operations on the data. For example we can say that the magnitude of the difference between 40° and 50° is the same as the magnitude of the difference between 70° and 80°. Note, however, that we cannot say that 80° is twice hot as 40° because the starting point of the temperature scale is arbitrary.

The nominal scale allows us only to qualitatively differentiate groups by categorizing them into mutually exclusive and collectively exhaustive sets and the ordinal scale is to rank-order the preferences. In addition, the interval scale allows us to display the distance between any two measurement points on the scale. We can compute means and standard deviations of the measures collected by interval scales. In other words, the interval scale not only group respondents according to categories and includes the order of these groups, it also measures the magnitude of the differences in the preferences among the individuals. Such a scale could be exhibited for the job design example as shown below.

Example 4.3

Please indicate the extent to which you agree or disagree with the following statements that are related to your job in the leisure centre by *circling* the appropriate number against each on the five-point scale.

The following opportunities offered by the job are important to me:

Interacting with others	1	2	3	4	5
Working independently	1	2	3	4	5
Serving others	1	2	3	4	5
Using a number of different skills	1	2	3	4	5

Strongly disagree, 1; disagree, 2; neither agree nor disagree, 3; agree, 4; strongly agree, 5.

Let us demonstrate the equality of the magnitude on the above example. Let us suppose that employees circle the numbers 1, 2, 3 and 4 for the four statements. That is, the magnitude of difference represented by the space between 2 and 3 on the scale would be the same as the magnitude of difference represented by the space between 3 and 4.

Ratio scale

The fourth and most powerful scale of measurement is the ratio scale which overcomes the deficiency of the arbitrary origin point of the interval scale. The ratio scale has an *absolute* (as opposed to an *arbitrary*) zero point which is meaningful. Thus, the ratio scale contains all four qualities and is often the scale that researchers prefer because the data

can be analysed with all sorts of statistical methods. Examples of variables measured by ratio scale would be age, height, weight and knowledge (as measured by test scores from being 0 to 100). With a ratio scale, we have a zero point where no quantities exist. For example when a person is born his or her age is zero. If you are 30 years old, you not only know that you are older than someone who is 15 years old (magnitude) but also know that you are 15 years older (equal intervals). Thus we would be able to say that a traveller who is 30 years old is *twice* as old as 15 years old.

You may also infer by now that some variables such as gender can be measured only on the nominal scale, while others such as income can be measured on the nominal (low, high), ordinal (low/medium/high) or the interval scale that increase by equal intervals (US$10,000 to $19,999 and US$20,000 to $29,999). Whenever it is possible to use a more powerful scale than a lesser one, it is wise to do so. When data manipulation is needed, it would be also be easy to merge a powerful scale into a less powerful one. If we recorded the age of travellers with a ratio scale, we would be able to categorize the respondents into three groups: young (e.g. 16–30), middle age (e.g. 31–45) and senior (45 and over). However, we would not be able to identify the real age of the respondents if we had already collected data using the three age groups.

Rating scales

Now that we know the four different types of scales that can be used to measure variables, it is necessary to examine the methods of scaling to elicit the responses of subjects at some point along a numerically valued continuum using rating scales. The rating scale allows us to express our evaluations of the object's characteristics. Some of the most frequently used rating scales are the **Likert scale**, the **numerical scale**, the **semantic differential scale**, **the itemized rating scale, the graphic rating scale**, the **fixed or constant sum scale** and the **consensus scale**. Example 4.4 shows a sample Likert scale.

Example 4.4

A sample Likert scale:

Strongly disagree	Disagree	Neither disagree nor agree	Agree	Strongly agree
1	2	3	4	5

Construct measurement

Constructs are abstract. Examples of constructs are poverty, safety, love, friendship, terrorism or trust. Although we do not physically see constructs, we feel that they exist. In everyday life, we deal with many constructs and form positive or negative opinions about them. Their image is formed by our perception and therefore they are subjectively evaluated. Some of the constructs are very important because they not only represent our emotions, beliefs and social identities (e.g. love, friendship, safety, security) but also influence our behaviour (e.g. tourists' religious beliefs motivate them to visit a specific tourism destination).

Another unique characteristic of the constructs is that it can be unidimensional (one-dimensional) or multidimensional. The dimensions of a construct are usually determined by its complexity and levels of abstraction. We can say that the dimension of a construct represents how its image is formed in our mind. When we describe the human body we may talk about its components such as heads, arms and legs. Similarly, when we describe a construct we talk about its dimensions. If a construct is simple, it will be unidimensional. On the contrary, a complex construct is multidimensional and usually consists of two or more dimensions.

There are many constructs that we must understand and deal with in leisure, recreation and tourism research. Some of them are quality of service, tourist satisfaction, an attitude towards a tourism destination, tourist loyalty, destination branding, tourist motivation, destination image and destination brand image. Furthermore, we study constructs to explain tourist behaviour to develop theories in recreation, leisure and tourism research.

As constructs are abstract, they can be described by its **dimensions** and/or **elements** which are less abstract. Quality of service is an important construct in tourism because it would have a positive influence on tourist satisfaction and tourist loyalty. Perceived quality is often measured to understand tourist satisfaction with services. Then benchmarks are developed in order to control the level of service quality. Let us demonstrate characteristics of the constructs using the concept of perceived service quality in resort hotels (Fig. 4.1).

As can be seen from Fig. 4.1, perceived service quality consists of two **dimensions**: physical quality and staff behaviour. It is likely that tourists will be satisfied with the quality of the hotel service when they find various aspects of the hotel's physical environment and hotel employee behaviour pleasant.

Dimensions such as physical quality and staff behaviour are still abstract even though less abstract compared to the main construct: service quality. It is possible to define these two service quality dimensions using even less abstract concepts or

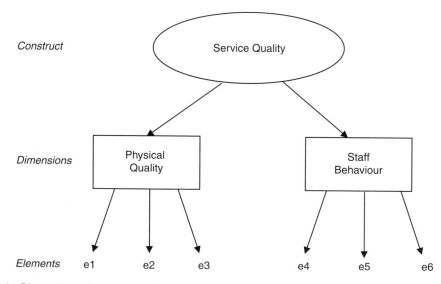

Fig. 4.1. Dimensions of service quality.

elements. Elements of the physical quality can be related to beauty of the hotel décor, cleanliness of the hotel environment and attractiveness of the hotel room, whereas elements of the staff behaviour can be related to competence, friendliness or politeness of the hotel employees. A hotel manager can find out whether customers are satisfied or dissatisfied with the level of hotel service quality by asking questions using elements of the construct. These questions can be rated on a 10-point scale where (1) indicates very poor quality and (10) indicates extremely good quality. If a customer rated below the mid point of the rating scale, such as (3), managers would know that customers are not satisfied with the quality of the hotel service or vice versa. As we move from the main construct to its elements, we progressively increase the level of tangibility or reduce the level of abstraction and better define the construct.

Conceptualization and Operationalization

Tangible variables such as age or income are easily measured through simple straightforward questions and do not have to be operationally defined. Conceptualization is the process of specifying what is meant by the construct. An operational definition is a necessary process before measuring the construct. Operationally defining a construct requires identification of the behavioural dimensions, facets, properties or elements to render it measurable. In other words, it involves taking portions of an abstract theory and translating them into testable hypotheses using its elements. In the previous example, quality of service is operationalized by six elements or questions.

As important as it is to understand what an operational definition is, it is equally important to remember what it is not. An operational definition does not indicate the other theoretically related variables of the construct. For example, intention to recommend cannot be a dimension of service quality, even though service quality is likely to influence the tourist's intention to recommend. Thus, the operational definition of a construct does not include delineating the reasons, antecedents, consequences or other theoretically related variables of the constructs. Rather it identifies its observable elements in order to

measure the construct. This is important because if we operationalize the construct incorrectly or unable to differentiate it from other constructs, we will introduce bias (error) in measurement (Sekeran, 2003).

Having seen what an operational definition is, and how different scaling techniques are applied to measure constructs, it is important to assure that the instrument we used to measure a construct (e.g. service quality) is indeed reliable and accurate (or valid). This would mean that we have not overlooked some important dimensions and elements of the construct. Therefore a measurement scale should produce reliable and valid data. Reliability and validity are the two benchmarks for 'goodness of measurement'. If our instrument is not reliable then the data are at best worthless, and at worst, misleading. It is important to note that reliability is necessary but not sufficient for goodness of measure. The instrument must also be valid. We would know if an instrument is reliable if it produces stable and consistent responses when administered at one point in time or multiple time intervals. The instrument will be valid if it produces accurate responses. In other words, reliability is concerned with stability and consistency of the measurements whereas validity is concerned with accuracy of the measurements. The two criteria will now be discussed in developing a multi-item scale for measuring constructs in leisure, recreation and tourism research.

General guidelines for developing a multiple-item scale

Developing a multiple-item scale is a complex procedure that requires quite a lot of technical expertise (Churchill, 1979). Suppose you need to develop a measurement scale for measuring a construct in tourism research such as destination image or tourist satisfaction. How would you proceed? Let us now examine how we can develop a multiple-item scale that is reasonably good, as illustrated in Fig. 4.2.

As can be seen from Fig. 4.2, if a reliable and valid instrument does not exist, we may need to develop a new measurement scale (assuming that the time and money would be available) and determine the goodness of the measure by applying a number of reliability and validity tests. Note that if such an instrument is already available, we do not

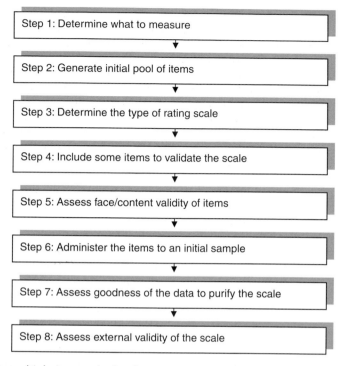

Fig. 4.2. Steps in multiple-item scale development.

need to develop a new scale but assess the goodness of this scale by applying the same reliability and validity tests explained in the following sections. The stages of scale development are discussed below.

Step 1: Determine what to measure: This requires the development of a conceptual definition for the construct. Note that if you cannot define a construct, you cannot measure it. For example, if we aim to measure quality of service in the travel industry, we need to define what is meant by service quality from a traveller's point of view. Thus, the construct definition involves answering questions such as: 'Exactly what do we mean by this construct service quality or destination loyalty in the travel industry? How does it differ from similar constructs such as customer satisfaction and customer loyalty? Should service quality be defined from the manager's or consumers' perspective?' Reviewing past studies, interviewing experts on the subject (managers, academics, researchers and other experienced customers) would assist in the development of a sound construct definition.

Step 2: Generate initial pool of items: This step involves generating a list of scale items (survey questions, statements or phrases). This is called operationalizing the construct. If quality of service is multi-dimensional, specific items (or elements) must be identified for each dimension. Systematic literature review, discussion and/or focus groups with key stakeholders (customers, travellers, frontline employee, supervisors, managers, distributors, trade officials and researchers), content analysis of brochures and brainstorming are all useful for generating the scale items.

If new items are to be developed for the construct, they must be written with creativity. The conceptual definition of the construct may be used to stimulate the researcher's creativity. The content of each item should reflect positive and negative aspects of the construct to avoid any potential 'yeah' or 'nay' in response to the survey. After generating a sufficient pool of items they must be edited for clarity. So, the revised items should be short and simple.

Step 3: Determine the type of rating scale to be used: The third step in the scale development process is to determine the type of rating scale. This could be a Likert-type scale, a semantic differential scale or a numeric scale. In fact, the type of a rating scale has to be determined quite early for two reasons. First, the wording of the items should match with the scale format and second, the choice of the scale should be consistent with the conceptual definition of the construct. For example, the attitude surveys usually employ a Likert-type scale ranging from 'strongly agree' to 'strongly disagree', to capture the individual's favourable or unfavourable feelings towards an object (Oppenheim, 1992). This also reflects the conceptual definition of an attitude towards an object. Performance measurement surveys tend to employ numeric rating scales ranging from 'extremely poor' to 'extremely good'. The labels and response categories of the rating scales vary. Managers should determine whether all the response categories should be labelled rather than the two opposite ends. A suitable rating scale can be determined after reviewing past studies on the topic.

Step 4: Include some items to validate the scale: New questions are usually added the survey to assess the validity of the scale. These questions should be theoretically related to the construct (its antecedents and consequences). For example, if we wanted to measure service quality in hotels, we would expect the measurement scale to be correlated with customers' intention to recommend, so a new question should be designed to measure intention to recommend. If we wanted to measure job satisfaction, we would expect it to be correlated with employee motivation. So a question about employee motivation should be included in the survey. After completing the survey, the data should be checked to see whether the scale items would be correlated with these theoretically related questions.

Step 5: Assess content and face validity of items: **Content validity** concerns the extent to which a measure adequately includes all items of the construct (Carmines and Zeller, 1991, p. 20). Consider a set of questions that serve as items (or indicators) of service quality in hotels (e.g. attractiveness of the hotel décor, quality of the food, cleanliness of the room). If some critical elements (e.g. competence, politeness, empathy of hotel employees) were omitted from the initial pool of items, the content validity of the scale would be undermined.

Face validity concerns whether the scale appears to measure what is supposed to measure (Fink, 1995). In other words, do the scale items seem to relate to the construct that we intent to measure? Unlike content validity, face validity is very practical. Subject experts such as managers, academics or potential candidates who are likely to participate in the survey could confirm or reject the face validity of the scale. They can also judge the relevance and clarity of scale items. Following their feedback, the scale items may be modified. Some may be dropped from the initial pool of items and some new items can be added. The final measurement instrument should include at least three items for each dimension. This is essential to assess reliability of the scale. As some of the scale items may be deleted in steps 6 and 7, which concern scale validation, it would be better to start measurement of the construct/dimension with four or five scale items.

Step 6: Administer the items to an initial sample: After determining the initial pool of scale items and the additional survey questions, the next step in scale development is to administer the measurement instrument to a sample of respondents. This is essential to check its reliability and validity. It is also essential to determine a suitable and large enough sample to represent the study population. The sampling design and sample size should be determined according to the population or the type of data analysis methods (e.g. correlation, regression, exploratory factor analysis) that will be used to assess validity and reliability of the scale. Churchill (1979) recommends that a sample size of 200 would be sufficient for assessing reliability. However, the sampling decision should be determined based on the study topic and the number of scale items.

Step 7: Assess goodness of the data to purify the scale: Step 7 concerns determining goodness of the scale by administering the reliability and validity tests. The scale items should be correlated with other theoretically related questions (e.g. service quality and customer loyalty). Some of the scale items may be eliminated so as to purify the scale. To do this, correlation tests, Cronbach's Alpha and exploratory or confirmatory factor analysis are common used (Fink, 1995; Hair *et al.*, 2006). The various forms of reliability and validity are shown in Fig. 4.3.

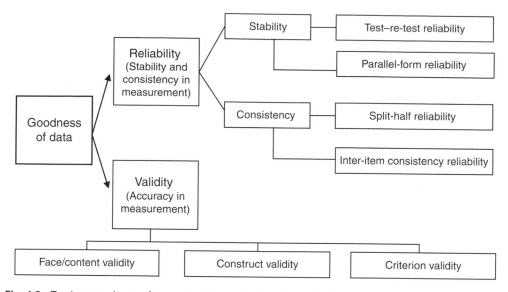

Fig. 4.3. Testing goodness of measures: forms of reliability and validity. (Reproduced from Serakan, 2003, p. 204.)

Reliability

Reliability is the extent to which the scale yields the same result on repeated trials or consistency across the scale items. In other words, the reliability of a scale is an indication of the *stability* and *consistency* of measurement.

There are several ways in which we can assess reliability. If we wanted to assess the stability reliability through repeated measures, a correlation test might be appropriate. When the two measures are correlated, a very strong correlation (e.g. 0.90) would be an indication of high reliability. Another test for assessing stability reliability is the split-half reliability which can be done using the Kuder-Richardson method (Kuder-Richardson, 1937).

There are several ways of examining reliability when looking at reliability in terms of internal consistency. For example, item analysis is often used via the Cronbach's Alpha test. The alpha coefficient is computed by correlating all the scores on individual items, with the overall score on the scale. Tests with high reliability, i.e. those with high internal consistency, will achieve an alpha coefficient of 0.70 or more and a high coefficient indicates high reliability. Generally speaking, an alpha coefficient of 0.70 indicates a good reliability in leisure, recreation and tourism research. The

remaining part of the reliability score (30%) represent the amount of error in measurement.

Stability reliability. Stability reliability indicates the scale's ability to produce the same score over time. Two tests of stability are called **test–re-test reliability** and **parallel-form reliability**. To determine test–re-test reliability, a scale is administered to the same subjects on multiple occasions (at least twice). For example a service-quality scale is administered to the same group of tourists now and several days/weeks later. Results are compared and correlated with the initial test to assess the stability of the measures. The higher the correlation between the two scores the higher the test–re-test reliability. However, this form of reliability is not practical because it is difficult to convince the same individual to respond to the survey twice.

Parallel-form reliability. Parallel-form reliability is obtained when responses on two comparable sets of scales tapping the same construct are highly correlated. Both scales should have similar items and the same response format. The only difference may be the wording and the order of the items. For example, service quality can be measured by two multi-item scales. The first and second scale may have the same number of items and the same respondents may complete the two scales at the same time. Then the two scales are compared using the data. If the two comparable forms are highly correlated (say 0.90 and above), we may be fairly certain that the scales are reasonably reliable, with minimal error variance caused by wording or other factors. A major deficiency of this method is that there may not be another form to test the scale reliability. Moreover, if an alternative scale is available, the application of the two scales may cause fatigue on the respondents due to large number of scale items.

Internal consistency reliability. The internal consistency reliability indicates the degree to which the scale items are homogenous. In other words, the scale items should 'hang together as a set' and be capable of independently measuring the same dimension or construct so that the respondents attach the same overall meaning to each of the items. This can be observed by examining whether the scale items or the subsets of items are correlated highly so that one item produces consistent scores with another. Two tests of internal consistency are **split-half reliability** and **inter-item consistency reliability**.

Split-half reliability. It assumes strong relationship between two halves of the scale. For example, if a scale consists of six items, the first three items should be correlated with the last three items. However, this is one of the deficiencies of the split-half reliability because reliability estimates would vary depending on how the scale items are split in two halves.

Inter-item consistency reliability. It assumes that the respondent's answers to the multiple scale items would be consistent when the items measure the same construct. From the theoretical point of view, all the items are independent but as they measure the same construct they should

be correlated with one another. The most popular inter-item consistency reliability test for assessing a multi-item scale is Cronbach's Alpha test (Cronbach, 1951). The alpha coefficient of the physical quality scale is shown in Example 4.5 to illustrate how it works within the SPSS software.

Example 4.5

Reliability statistics:

Cronbach's Alpha	Number of items
0.792	3

The results in the first SPSS output table indicate that the alpha score of the three-item physical quality scale is 0.79. The corrected item-total correlation in the second column of the SPSS output table (Table 4.2) indicate how much each scale item correlates with the total score. Low correlation scores (e.g. less than 0.30) indicate that the item is not producing consistent results with other scale items. If the Alpha statistic is too low (e.g. less than 0.70) we may need to consider removing the items with low item-total correlations in order to improve scale reliability. The column headed 'Alpha if item deleted' shows the impact of this action. As shown in the above example, the Alpha score of the physical quality scale is higher than 0.70, there is no need to remove any item from this scale.

Validity

Validity refers to the degree to which a scale accurately assesses the construct that are being measured. While reliability is concerned with stability and consistency of the measurement, validity is concerned with the success at measuring what we

Table 4.2. The SPSS output of reliability.

	Scale mean if item deleted	Scale variance if item deleted	Corrected item-total correlation	Cronbach's Alpha if item deleted
Décor of the hotel	7.011	2.902	0.635	0.724
Cleanliness of the hotel	7.897	2.386	0.604	0.761
Attractiveness of the hotel room	7.016	2.527	0.679	0.667

set out to measure. Although there are several terms to denote the term validity (e.g. internal validity, external validity and statistical validity), Sekeran (2003) introduces three commonly used validity measures: **content/criterion validity**, **criterion validity** and **construct validity**. As we already discussed content/criterion validity, we will explain criterion and construct validity in the next section.

Construct validity. Construct validity seeks agreement between a theoretical formulation of the concept and its operationalization via the measurement scale. Construct validity can be established in three steps. First, a theoretical relationship between the construct and the measurement scale must be justified. Second, theoretical relationships between the concepts and other variables must be established. Third, the relationships between the construct and other theoretically related variables must be examined (Carmines and Zeller, 1991, p. 23). For example, researchers examining the construct validity of a service-quality scale should spend a great deal of time defining what is meant by quality of service and whether service quality is unidimensional or multidimensional (e.g. physical quality, staff behaviour). Then they seek evidence to establish the relationship between dimensions of service quality and other constructs such as tourist loyalty. Finally the relationship between the dimensions of service quality and tourist loyalty is examined by an empirical study.

Construct validity can be assessed through **convergent** validity and **discriminant** validity. Convergent validity assumes that the relationship among the scale items measuring the same concept would be strong. Discriminant validity assumes the lack of a relationship among the scale items that are theoretically unrelated. For example, if we aimed to assess convergent validity of the service-quality scale, we would obtain strong correlations among the items that measure physical quality. At the same time, we would obtain very weak correlations between the physical quality and staff behaviour scale items. In addition to linear correlation, convergent and discriminant validity can be established through exploratory factor analysis, confirmatory factor analysis and multi-trait, multi-method matrix where appropriate (Churchill, 1979).

Criterion validity. Criterion validity is known as instrumental validity. Criterion validity shows how accurate the scale is by comparing its score against other theoretically related measures. For example, a theory test is used to assess a person's knowledge about driving and his driving ability. The test can be validated by using other scores such as the person's score on the practical test. That is to say, if the test is good, the theory test score should correlate with people's driving ability score. Criterion validity can be established by two types of validity tests: **concurrent** and **predictive** validity.

Concurrent validity is established when the scale is correlated with pre-existing items; something that is already designed to measure the same construct. For example, if a six-item scale is developed to measure perceived service quality in hotels, the scale should also correlate with another measure designed to capture individual's overall perception of service quality using a single item scale such as this one; 'Please indicate your satisfaction with the quality of services received on this occasion on a 7-point scale where (1) indicates very poor and (7) indicates very good'.

Predictive validity indicates the ability of the scale to predict a theoretically related variable as to a future criterion. For example, if a multi-attribute scale is administered to measure the customers' perception of service quality, it is expected that the score obtained from this scale would predict the customer's intention to recommend behaviour. Concurrent and predictive validity can be assessed through **correlation analysis**, **regression analysis** or **structural equation modelling**.

Note that construct and criterion validity may overlap when the scale is unidimensional. This would not pose an issue. It is important to remember that the measurement scores should work in the expected direction in relation to the other theoretically related variables. As indicated in Fig. 4.2, if the reliability and validity results are unsatisfactory in stage 7, the conceptual definition of the construct and wording of the existing items should be revised. Moreover new items should be generated to improve validity of the scale.

Step 8: Assess external validity of the scale: External validity refers to the extent to which the results of the scale can be generalizable or transferable. Most discussions of external validity focus solely on generalizability and causal relationships (e.g. Campbell and Stanley, 1966). We include a reference here to transferability because many scales are not designed to be generalized. Accordingly, when a satisfactory measurement is obtained, the scale should be administered to a new sample in order to assess its transferability. It is particularly important if the scale produces similar results when it is it used in multiple samples or on different occasions.

Generally speaking the larger the scale, the greater the reliability, but shorter scales are easy to respond to and administer. Researchers may assess goodness of the existing scales through the reliability and validity tests explained above. This process determines the meaning of the scores and the length of the scale. A sample of the measurement scales that is validated through this process is provided in Worked Example 4.1 at the end of this chapter.

Key Terms

Measurement: Measurement is grouping objects (e.g. firms, machines and people) based on their rating on the same scale.

Scale of measurement: A scale of measurement is a tool or mechanism by which individuals are distinguished on how they differ from one another on the variables of interest to the research topic.

Nominal scale: A nominal scale assigns subjects to mutually exclusive and collectively exhaustive categories or groups.

Ordinal scale: An ordinal scale indicates differences among the variables and locates its relative position (or rank-orders) in relation to others in some meaningful way.

Interval scale: An interval scale measures variables on equal intervals without an absolute zero point.

Ratio scale: The ratio scale measures variables on equal intervals with an absolute zero point.

Reliability: Reliability is a form of test that indicates stability and consistency of the measurements.

Validity: Validity is a form of test that indicates accuracy of the measurements.

Discussion Questions

1. What is meant by measurement?

2. What is a construct?

3. How can we evaluate quality of the measurement data?

4. Whenever possible, it is recommended that you should use the measurement scales that have already been developed and repeatedly used in published studies, rather than develop our own instrument for our research. Do you agree? Discuss the reasons for your answer.

Worked Example 4.1. Examples of the Multiple-item Scales, their Reliability and Validity

Service quality in the hospitality industry

A five-point Likert-type scale with (1) indicating strongly disagree and (5) indicating strongly agree.

Physical Quality (Internal Consistency Reliability = 0.70; Average Variance Extracted = 0.61)
The décor was beautifully co-ordinated with great attention to detail (0.70)[a]
The hotel (restaurant) was tidy (0.81)
The hotel (restaurant) provided a comfortable room (0.83)
Staff Behaviour (Internal Consistency Reliability = 0.85; Average Variance Extracted = 0.68)

Staff were helpful and friendly (0.80)
Staff seemed to anticipate what I wanted (0.80)
Staff listened to me (0.85)
Staff were talented and displayed a natural expertise (0.84)

[a]Numerals in parentheses denote measurement model loadings. Taken from Ekinci, Dawes and Massey, 2008.

Tourism destination personality

A 5-point Likert-type scale in which: 1, not at all accurate description of Destination X; 2, somewhat inaccurate description of Destination X; 3, neither accurate nor inaccurate; 4, somewhat accurate description of Destination X; 5, extremely accurate description of Destination X (Table 4.3).

Table 4.3. Tourism destination personality.

Destination personality	Factor loadings	t values	Sig.	AVE[b]	Mean	Standard deviation
Conviviality				68	4.20	0.67
Friendly	0.86	19.51	0.00[a]		4.08	0.80
Hospitable	0.86	19.53	0.00[a]		4.18	0.80
Family oriented	0.75	15.97	0.00[a]		4.34	0.76
Sincerity				52	3.29	0.55
Intelligent	0.99	10.11	0.00[a]		3.33	0.72
Reliable	0.87	14.05	0.00[a]		3.27	0.83
Successful	0.79	13.94	0.00[a]		3.36	0.74
Wholesome	0.67	10.90	0.00[a]		3.35	0.79
Spirited	0.51	5.79	0.00[a]		3.21	0.74
Sincere	0.26	6.44	0.00[a]		3.20	0.77
Exciting				50	3.30	0.53
Exciting	0.86	11.96	0.00[a]		3.22	0.79
Charming	0.76	15.21	0.00[a]		3.40	0.75
Daring	0.68	9.27	0.00[a]		3.01	0.83
Cheerful	0.45	7.00	0.00[a]		3.65	0.80

[a]Significant at the 0.001 level. [b]AVE = Average variance extracted. (Taken from Ekinci, Baloglu and Sirakaya, 2007.)

References

Bryman, A. and Bell, E. (2007) *Business Research Methods*. Oxford University Press, Oxford.

Churchill, G.A. (1979) A paradigm for developing better measures of marketing constructs. *Journal of Marketing Research* 16, 64–73.

Campbell, D.T. and Stanley, J.C. (1963) *Experimental and quasi-experimental designs for research*. Houghton Mifflin, Boston.

Carmines, E.G. and Zeller, R.A. (1991) *Reliability and validity assessment*. Sage Publications, Newbury Park, California.

Ekinci, Y., Dawes, P. and Massey, G. (2008) A model of consumer satisfaction for hospitality services. *European Journal of Marketing* 42, 35–68.

Ekinci, Y., Baloglu, S. and Sirakaya, E. (2007) Host image and destination personality. *Tourism Analysis* 12, 433–446.

Fink, A. (1995) *The Survey Handbook, v.1*. Sage, Thousand Oaks, California.

Fink, A. (1995) *How to Measure Survey Reliability and Validity, v.7*. Sage, Thousand Oaks, California.

Hair, J.F., Black, B., Babin, B., Anderson, R.E. and Tatham, R.L. (2006) *Multivariate Data Analysis*. Prentice-Hall, New Jersey.

Haynes, N.M. (1995) How skewed is 'the bell curve'? *Book Product Reviews* 1–24.

Kirk, J. and Miller, M. (1986) *Reliability and Validity in Qualitative Research*. Sage Publications, London.

Kuder, G.F. and Richardson, M.W. (1937) The theory of the estimation of test reliability. *Psychometrica* 2, 151–160.

Oppenheim, A.N. (1992) *Questionnaire Design, Interviewing and Attitude Measurement*. Pinter Publishers, London.

Sekaran, U. (2003) *Research Methods for Business: A Skill Building Approach*. Wiley, London.

chapter 5

Proposal Writing

Sheryl Fried Kline

Learning Objectives

After reading and studying this chapter the student will be able to:

1. Begin the process of writing a research proposal;

2. Explain the purpose of the research proposal;

3. Outline the format and define the elements of a research proposal;

4. Create a timeline for writing a proposal.

Chapter Summary

This chapter introduces the importance of writing a research proposal and discusses the elements of a good proposal for scientific inquiry. It stresses that research proposals must contain extensive literature reviews and offer convincing support of a need for the research study being proposed. It covers several steps of writing a proposal. The areas such as identification of a research topic, conducting a relevant literature review on the topic, developing propositions and hypotheses, data analysis and designing data collection instruments, reporting and citation styles and related issues are also introduced as elements of writing a research proposal. A short proposal example is also provided.

The Purpose of the Proposal

A research proposal has been compared to a plan designed to execute a large complex project. Whether you are designing a building, planning a large event, or preparing to climb Mount Everest, the success and execution of the final product is dependent upon a well-conceived and executed plan. The purpose of the research proposal is to communicate your research plan, in detail. A well-written proposal is clear, precise and well organized. A proposal is a well-defined plan and, as with any plan, the more thought given and detail provided the better! Students need to dedicate a good deal of effort to ensure that their proposal describes each and every aspect of their research thesis or dissertation. This is a research and writing exercise that is not to be taken lightly and should be given serious thought and consideration. It is for this reason that the proposal is considered to be the foundation of the thesis and dissertation process. A strong foundation is essential for a strong final research thesis that is completed on time and as planned. A weak, ill-conceived proposal is likely to result in delays, false starts and unexpected problems that can plague a student throughout the research process.

The proposal is designed to answer questions. The classic questions include who will conduct your research, what is the research focus, where will you find and collect the data, and when and how will you conduct your research? Nothing is left to question or chance. The well-written proposal will specifically answer these questions and others.

As with any written document it is important to consider your audience. Research proposals are written for two specific audiences. One is the thesis or dissertation committee and the other is the grant review board. Although these two groups evaluate proposals in similar ways there are subtle differences in the purpose of these proposals. This chapter will focus on the former audience, the committee, which is led by your major advisor who is also your committee chair. This committee's goal is to evaluate your proposal and to determine if it is a well-conceived plan that at its core will answer research questions that are relevant and have not been answered. A good proposal will build on the existing literature and add to the body of knowledge in the field.

Most thesis committees have three to four members and dissertation committees may have four to five. You will work with all your committee members while developing the proposal and you work most closely with your committee chair. The proposal must inform your committee as to the nature of your proposed research. It must also convince them that this is a worthy research project to undertake.

Through your proposal you convey the idea that your research will be able to answer your research questions and two larger questions. At the end of your research project you need to answer the questions 'So what?' and 'Why is this research project important to the field?' You will be spending many days, months and perhaps years doing research and answering those well-crafted research questions. Make sure that you can justify the reason that that your research will be relevant to the field and will make a difference to academics and industry practitioners. At the end of your proposal you should be able to clearly say that your research will have meaning and will answer those unanswered questions that are central to your research proposal.

Contents of the Proposal

The content of the proposal is directly related to how it is organized. Essentially, research proposals have five main sections and an appendix. The first is the **Introduction** that defines the research question and its significance. Proposal introductions should capture the reader's attention and compel him/her to want to read more. It is a first impression that clearly states the problem and the need to solve the problem. The second part is the **Literature Review** that intertwines your research question to the relevant literature to date. The third section is the **Methodology** that explains how the research question(s) will be answered. The fourth section usually includes **Expected Findings** but it can be more varied in form and in content from the others and may include the biography of the researcher, the budget and relevant appendices. The last part of the proposal is a complete **Reference List**.

Proposals may be organized differently based upon the institution's requirements, your professor's personal preference and the nature of your particular study. As an example, quantitative and qualitative studies have very different content elements due to the different methods used to collect the data. Box 5.1 shows sample outlines that list the content headings for research proposals. It is recommended that you have your committee chairperson approve your proposal outline before you write the first word of your proposal. At the beginning of the process of writing your proposal it is helpful to check with your institution to determine if there is a standard proposal format for a thesis or dissertation. You may also want to talk with your committee chair to find out his or her preference. It is also a beneficial to talk with other students who have gone through this process, ask to see copies of their proposals and ask your professor if you can read examples of excellent proposals from his or her other students. Appendix 5.1 gives an example of a research proposal.

Research Box 5.1. Samples outlines for proposal content.

Quantitative Proposal

1. Introduction
   (a) The Problem
      (i) The statement of the problem
      (ii) Sub-problem statements

(Continued)

Research Box 5.1. Continued.

    (b) The Hypothesis

        (i) Sub-hypotheses

    (c) Definition of terminology

    (d) The importance of the study

    (e) Summary of the problem

2. Literature Review

    (a) Review of related literature

    (b) Current state of the literature

    (c) Relationship of the statement of the problem to the literature

        (i) Explanation of how the hypothesis will expand the literature and body of knowledge

3. Methodology

    (a) Describe the data

        (i) Source of the data and how it will be collected

            Describe the instrument used to collect the data

    (b) Describe how the data will be analysed

        (i) Define all the variables

        (ii) Methods used to measure validity and reliability

        (iii) Pilot test results

    (c) Proposed outcome and results

4. Implications and limitations

5. Reference list

6. Appendices

    (a) Include copies of survey instruments

    (b) Copy of IRB approval form

    (c) Biography of researcher

    (d) Budget for the project

        (i) Costs and sources of funding

    (e) Timeline for the project

Qualitative Proposal Outline

1. Introduction

    (a) Background for the study

    (b) Purpose of the study

    (c) Guiding questions to be studied

    (d) Intended audience for this study

    (e) Delimitations for the study

    (f) The importance of the study

    (g) Summarize the purpose of the study

2. Literature Review

    (a) Review of the relevant literature

    (b) Theoretical framework for this study

3. Methodology

    (a) Design for the study

        (i) Underlying assumptions

    (b) The role of the researcher

        (i) Researchers' expertise and qualifications

(Continued)

Research Box 5.1. **Continued.**

    (c) Description of the site and participants

        (i) Selection process used to determine the site

        (ii) Selection process used to determine the participants

        (iii) What relationship will the researcher have with the participants?

    (d) Data collection strategies employed

        (i) Detailed description of the entire data collection process

    (e) Data analysis strategies employed

    (f) Validity and reliability strategies employed

4. Proposed Findings

    (a) Relate the research to the literature

        (i) Describe how the literature influenced this research study

    (b) Provide the relationship of this study to the theory

    (c) Provide the relationship of this study to practice

    (d) Limitations

5. Reference list

6. Appendices

    (a) Include interview questions

    (b) Copy of IRB approval form

    (c) Budget for the project

        (i) Costs and sources of funding

    (d) Timeline for the project

Format of the Proposal

The format refers to the layout, design and style used to write the proposal. In our field the American Psychological Association (APA) style guide is perhaps the most popular format guideline used when writing and publishing research proposals, theses, dissertations and articles. There are other style and format guides including the Modern Language Association (MLA), Chicago Manual Style and Turabian Style. You need to check with your institution and major professor to determine if there are particular fonts, page headings and other style issues that are preferred or required for your proposal. Purchasing and using the official and current style guide is best when writing a proposal. However, most universities have websites that provide helpful and friendly guides for formatting and writing research papers. Purdue University's English Department and Ohio State's University Libraries have extensive websites with a comprehensive APA formatting

style guide. They can found at the following URLs: http://owl.english.purdue.edu/owl/resource/560/01/ and http://library.osu.edu/sites/guides/apagd.php. APA and the University of Southern Mississippi also have helpful tutorials regarding APA formatting and style at these URLs: http://flash1r.apa.org/apastyle/basics/index.htm and http://www.lib.usm.edu/legacy/tutorials/apatutorial/tutorialindex.html.

The front matter for the proposal includes a title page, table of contents and some institutions require a page where your committee approves the proposal with their signatures. The first part of the proposal is an abstract, which is a summary of your proposal. This may be 100 to 250 words in length. It is a single paragraph that includes your research topic and problem statement, a brief description of your methodology and questions and proposed findings or reason for the study.

What is most important is that the proposals format follows a style and it is consistent throughout. The mechanics of the paper should follow a consistent formatting scheme that takes in consideration the font style and size, margins, line spacing and headings. Even tables and appendices have a style and format that is prescribed by style manuals including APA. Box 5.2 includes a sample for formatting the proposal. It is recommended that you create a similar formatting guide before writing the first draft of your proposal. As you write your proposal this guide will be very useful reference that will save you time and editing.

Research Box 5.2. Example of a formatting guideline for a proposal.

- Paper size 8.5 by 11 inches
- Margins are one inch on all sides
- The font size is 12 point (10 point may also be a common font size)
- The font is Times New Roman (font styles should be easy to read, the Arial font is another commonly used font style.)
- Include a header at the top of every page so that it is flush to the left margin and printed in all capitals "THE TITLE OF YOUR PAPER"
- The pages are numbered with a page number located flush to top right margin on every page but the title page
- A model of a five heading system is used to define the content of the paper.
  - Level 1 is centred, boldface and lower case heading
  - Level 2 is left aligned, boldface, uppercase and lower case heading
  - Level 3 is indented boldface, lowercase heading with a period
  - Level 4 is indented, boldfaced, italicized, lowercase heading with a period
  - Level 5 is indented, italicized, lowercase heading with a period
- Citations both in text and in the reference section follow an exacting format based on the style manual
- Tables and Appendices follow a prescribed format

Research Box 5.3. Data coding sheet.

Variables	Range of the data	Example
Subject ID	001 to 500	421
Gender	1 or 2	1 is Male
Highest level of education	0 to 6	0 attended high school but did not graduate, 1 is graduated from high school, 2 attended college but did not graduate, 3 has an associate degree, 4 graduated from college, 5 attended graduate school but did not graduate, 6 has a graduate degree
Length of trip	01 to 12	6 days

The Literature Review and Note Taking

The literature review is a key component of your proposal and of your thesis or dissertation. Finding relevant material, understanding it, and being able to organize and retrieve it is essential to writing a good research proposal. Doing a thorough review, locating germane articles, takes many months, including hours in the library and on the Internet surfing search engines. Good note taking and note-taking habits will make it easier to retrieve, organize and synthesize vast amounts of information.

Note taking can be done at four levels:

1. The reference. This includes the author's name, title of the work and other information that is cited in a bibliography. This should be recorded in the same format as the reference list found at the end of your proposal.
2. Summarize the main points in the material.
3. Paraphrase in your words the key ideas or concepts. This should include the page number where the original information is found within the work cited.
4. An exact quotation or passage that is transcribed word for word.

Note taking is a practice that has been done for decades using note cards or notebooks. Today, students use computers and software programs that assist with the process of organizing articles and literature. Computers make it easy to transfer electronic resources from the library, search for key words within documents and back up information in more than one location. There are numerous software packages that help with the note-taking task. One is part of the Microsoft family of software products. It is called *OneNote*. This is similar to a filing system with files folders and subcategories in an easy to organize electronic media. Another software program used for note-taking and reference creation is called *Endnote* which is a program that creates references and can put references in different formats with a click of a mouse.

Review of Relevant Literature

Literature reviews need to be thorough and relevant. Most people consider literature reviews to be a summary of the literature on a topic. A true literature review is more than a summary and synthesis of the relevant literature. It is a critique of the knowledge base for a carefully defined topic area. In addition, it should highlight the relationship between your study and the previous literature. The review can also identify areas where there are gaps in the literature. This is also done to underscore the need to answer your research questions. Most importantly, the literature review must support and build up to your problem statement.

It is very helpful to read other literature reviews to gain a sense of the flow and organization of this part of the proposal. The review should be organized around a topic or themes. In most cases the literature is in chronological order from the oldest to the most recent literature. Chapter 3 goes into much more detail about how to write a literature review. The literature review in our proposal would be similar to the one described in that chapter.

The literature review in your proposal needs to be thorough but may not be as long or as thorough as the literature review in your final research paper. At some institutions the literature review in the proposal is the same as the review in the final research paper. At other institutions it is a narrower review of the literature as it relates to the problem statement. Although the literature review in the proposal may not be complete, it always includes the most relevant material. When the proposal has a shorter review of the literature, the student should be selective and only include the literature and studies that directly relate to the research questions. In both situations, the literature review in the proposal will certainly be the basis of the literature review in your final thesis or dissertation.

The Problem Statement

The problem statement is at the beginning of the proposal. This section of your proposal needs to get the reader's attention; it puts the problem within the context of the literature and convinces the reader that this question is worth answering. The problem statement is where you clearly define what you plan to study. This statement must be written as clearly and concisely as possible. It is a research question formulated in the form of a sentence. Simply, succinctly worded, straightforward sentences are best to use when writing a problem statement. This statement usually expresses a relationship between variables unless it is a descriptive study. It also expresses a measurable relationship and it identifies the population that will be studied. The following are examples of problem statements:

- What is the relationship between the number of flights a person takes on XYZ Airlines and their level of satisfaction with air travel on that airline?
- A destination's ability to prepare for a crisis is not a factor when meeting planners select a location for a citywide convention.

The problem statement is both delimiting and testable. The problem statement area of the proposal should also state what would not be studied. The statement by its nature should limit the focus of the study. It identifies a population and topic that will be studied and, in doing so, eliminates other potential topics and populations. The statement must also be able to be tested or the research study ends here. This means that the problem statement can be answered. Finally, the problem statement leads to the formation of research hypotheses.

Significance or Rationale of the Study

The proposal must address the reason for taking on this study and the rationale for doing this research. This is perhaps one of the most important persuasive points that you will make in your proposal. This is where you convince your audience that this study is worth doing. The rationale for the significance of a study can be achieved in three ways and the more ways your research is significant the better chance you have of convincing your committee to support your project. The first rationale for doing a study is that it will fill a gap in the body of knowledge and literature. The second is that it will answer an unanswered question or solve a problem that has not been solved. The third is that the outcome of the study will result in a finding that is important to the field. Finally you need to communicate directly the significance of the study to your audience. Be explicit and tell your audience most directly why this research is significant and a value to the field.

Theory

Good research is steeped in theory. A theory explains phenomena and is based on hypotheses and backed by empirical evidence. As researchers, part of our job is to generate and verify theories. Your literature review will probably reference theories that have been posited, proved, disproved, modified or are in need of testing. Your research proposal will probably include a theoretical model where you seek to explain a relationship between variables. As you write your proposal you will need to define the theory that you plan to explore, give it context within literature and explain how your study will impact, explain or possibly change that theory. Theories can be deconstructed into variables and the relationships between the variables are the basis for a hypothesis.

Dependent variables

Dependent variables are the variables that are the outcome of the research. When you are doing experimental research, the dependent variables are the ones that the researcher does something to or changes. These variables are on the receiving end of the treatment. For example, if you are measuring the difference between men and women's purchase behaviour based on a destination's marketing campaign, the purchase behaviour is the dependent variable.

Quite often dependent variables may be a test or measures on a survey instrument or on a scale. It is very important to select a dependent variable with care. It is best to utilize a test or scale that has been used before in other studies. These measures are more likely to have a higher level of validity and reliability. In our example in the previous paragraph, purchase behaviour is the dependent variable. You would need to determine how you will measure purchase behaviour. As part of your literature review you would want to search for other studies that have measured purchase behaviour in travel destination studies that are similar to yours. Finding a credible measure that has been used on the same population and sample is best. It is also important to use the newest version of the measure.

Hypotheses

A research hypothesis is a statement of the expected relationship between two or more variables. The statement is a description of the predicted results. It is also a well-informed educated statement that can be tested. This description may sound very similar to a problem statement. However, a research hypothesis is a declarative statement and is much more specific than a statement of the problem. One statement of the problem may have several hypotheses that support and further explain the statement of the problem.

There are some things that characterize well-written research hypotheses. A research hypothesis states an expected relationship or difference between variables. Sometimes it is stated in an if/then statement. A research hypothesis must be testable. This means that you can test it empirically and verify it either by supporting it or not supporting it. A well-grounded hypothesis is born out of a theory or set of theories based on previous studies and serves to extend the existing body of knowledge. The hypothesis should be clearly and concisely written.

For example, the following hypothesis follows the if/then format. The population of this study includes college alumni who graduated in the year 2005 or earlier:

If an individual participated in a study-abroad programme while in college then he or she will take more international vacations than those college graduates who did not participate in a college-abroad programme.

Sampling

Quite often the research hypothesis refers to a group or identifies a particular population that will be studied. It is usually a group of people. For example a population could be students attending a university; women who have purchased a cruise-ship ticket; Turkish travellers who visit Germany; or members of the United States Golf Association. In most cases it is not possible to study every member of that group or population. Therefore as a researcher you need to determine what proportion or sub-group of the population you are able to study. A sample is the group of subjects that you will study.

The selection of a population and then the process used to select a sample of the population is something that must be well described in the proposal. Samples need to be selected in such a way that they are most similar to the population. Chapter 6 goes into detail about how to select a sample that best represents the population. Your proposal should clearly describe how you selected your sample and how you ensured that it is truly representative of the population that you plan to study. Both the population and the sample must be defined based on demographic characteristics including distinctions such as age, gender, level of education, location and other relevant attributes and behaviours. Samples that truly represent the population allow you to make assumptions and theorize about the entire population. If your sample does not represent the population you cannot generalize your results. If you are unable to generalize your results to the population then the value of your research is diminished.

Data collection method

Although the actual collection of the data may be in the near future, the proposal is the place and time to explain in detail the steps you will use to collect your data. This is one part of your proposal that you will need a great deal of input from your major professor and committee. You need their agreement as to the best way to gather your data.

The proposal must include a description of how, who and when the data will be collected. How refers to the method used to collect the data. This could be through the use of many different methods including phone interviews, survey instrument mailed to subjects and students in a tourism class collecting information from a website. The process should be described thoroughly.

The data, once it is collected, needs to be organized and stored in a neat, obsessively organized way. Your proposal should describe how to collect and store the data. The data needs to be labelled including the subject information and date that the data was collected and by whom. Sometimes data on paper will need to be transferred to a file on the computer. This process needs to be described. It is also good to explain how the data are stored so as to prevent the loss of data. Most security experts recommend that you store your data in two or more places. You may plan to keep your database at school, on a USB stick around your neck and another copy in your e-mail account hosted by your institution. Keeping it in three different locations is best to ensure that you can recover it in case of an emergency or computer crash.

Who will be collecting the data? In many cases you will be collecting your own data. In other cases you might have undergraduate students or other individuals collecting the information. Collecting data in a prescribed way involves training. If you plan to have others help you collect data you will need to provide a set of clear step-by-step instructions so that all the data are collected in the same way. Lastly, you want to ensure that you collect the data in an unbiased manner. Training, and keeping with the plan, will unsure that you have a solid unbiased plan to collect your data.

Data instruments

Many research projects include the use of a survey or data collection instrument. A copy of the instrument should be included in the appendices section at the end of the proposal. A description of how the data instrument was developed and its relationship to the literature should be provided in the body of the proposal. If the instrument involves entering the data into a database or spreadsheet then the coding sheet should also be included in the appendix. A coding sheet explains the number coding system, or initials and terms used to describe the data. It is very helpful to use when transferring data from the instrument to a database. This coding sheet is invaluable when the researcher revisits the data at a later date. An example of a coding sheet is given in Box 5.3.

Data analysis

This section of the proposal explains in detail how the data will be analysed. You should include the name of the software package or program you plan to use to analyse the data. Many proposals follow the flow of stating the hypothesis followed by the statistics or analyses used to support or not support the hypothesis. This section can be repetitive and will certainly explain in detail how each hypothesis will be tested. It is appropriate to reference the literature in citing cases that have used similar data analysis to your study. This section should also describe any tests for validity and reliability being performed on the data. Chapters 11 to 14 go into more detail about how to analyse data.

Budget

A well-conceived proposal leaves little room for surprises and this includes the budget projections. The budget should include the cost of doing the research project and the source of the funding. Typical budgets have major categories for research projects. They will vary, however, based on the type and scope of research to be performed.

Funding sources typically come from grants. These can be internal grants that are supplied by the institution where the student is studying. Many graduate schools have funds that students may compete for in order to fund their thesis or dissertations. Sometimes your major professor has funds available that can be used for student research projects.

Outside agencies can also be a source for funding. Governments, industry associations and corporations offer grants for projects that are of interest to them. Sometime the student must fund his or her own study. In either case it is important to get accurate information that informs the budget. Many institutions have a business office that a student can work with in order to determine the appropriate costs for each line in the budget. Budgets include labour costs and other costs associated with the collection of data. Many universities require an additional expense to be added to the budget and it is usually called an **indirect** (overheads) expense. This is a percentage of the total project that is added to the budget to cover facility and administrative costs. Many institutions have a set percentage for indirect costs. Some funding agencies limit the percentage of indirect costs. Box 5.4 is an example of a budget.

Time chart

A time chart is a description of each step of the research process; it is a budget of your time. Experience has shown that the research process usually takes longer than planned, so you will need to revise your plan as you go through each step of the process. Start your time chart by listing every element of the process. Begin by listing the time it takes to think about the research idea and end with the date you plan to submit your thesis or dissertation. Present your timeline to your major professor for feedback and input. Remember you are not doing this research alone and many key milestones depend upon gaining feedback from your committee and on the key deadline dates established by your institution.

One effective way to create a time chart is to utilize the same tools that meeting planners and business project planners use to plan large-scale projects and events. A Gantt chart visually depicts a schedule of tasks and activities. It can be easily created in a chart or by using an Excel spreadsheet. The tasks are listed on the vertical axis and the time is listed horizontally across the top from the closed date to the end point. A sample Gantt chart is depicted in Fig. 5.1.

Research Box 5.4. Example of a research budget framework.

Title of the Project

Identify the sponsoring agency or source of funds if any

Timeframe of the budget: Start Date_____ End Date _____

Labour Expenses	Number of hours, weeks, or months	Amount (US$)
Senior personnel (PI)	2 months	15,000
Other personnel		
Students for data collection	2 students at 100 hours each	2,000
Graduate students for data analysis	1 student at 100 hours	1,500
Fringe benefits		5,920
Total labour		24,420
Equipment		5,000
Telephone		2,000
Travel		3,000
Materials and supplies		2,000
Sub-contractors		1,000
Printing		2,500
Total direct costs		39,920
Indirect costs	@44%	17,565
Total cost of the project		57,485

Ethics in Research and the Institutional Review Board (IRB)

When doing research all practitioners should follow the mantra that they should do no harm. Many institutions have review boards that are established to monitor and protect both human and animal subjects. The purpose of the IRB is to review and approve protocols for research that involves human subjects. This board is interested in what you will be asking your subjects and who your subjects are. They evaluate research to ensure that subjects will not be harmed either emotionally or physically. In particular they work to protect subjects that are part of vulnerable populations such as children, prisoners or the mentally ill. The IRB may ask you to take a training programme before undertaking your research. The IRB will require information before granting approval for you to do your research. No data collection can occur until the IRB has approved the research study. There are many guidelines and policies regarding ethics in research. The US Department of Health and Human Services has several good websites where you can learn more about the regulations and compliance regarding ethical issues and research using human subjects. The URLs are http://www.hhs.gov/ohrp/ and http://www.hhs.gov/ohrp/.

The following are a list of items that the IRB typically requests.

- Project abstract/summary
- Consent form
- Full description of the study (research proposal/dissertation/thesis)
- Survey instrument(s)/questionnaire(s)
- Cover letter (if appropriate)
- Subject recruitment materials (e.g. flyers, advertisements)
- The research methods and procedures
- Letter of support from Faculty Advisor (required for students)
- Letter verifying permission to recruit at the site, school, destination or location where data will be collected.

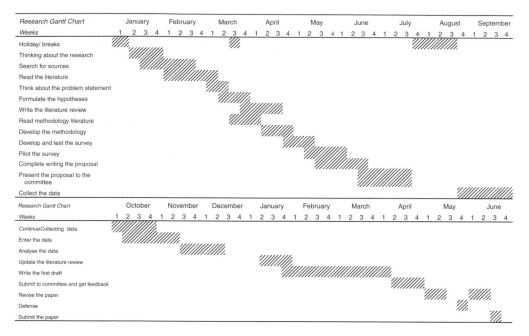

Fig. 5.1. Gantt chart example with timeline for a research project.

Case Study 5.1. Graduate student research proposal.

This case study is a likely scenario of how a graduate student develops and presents her research proposal.

Sarah Smith is a doctoral student who is finishing her coursework and is preparing to give her research dissertation proposal to her committee. Her major advisor, Dr Sirakaya-Turk, is an expert in sustainable tourism and she has worked closely with him and her committee to ensure that the proposal is in the correct format and her research questions are clear and precise. Her literature is thorough and complete and she is about to prepare her presentation that summarizes her proposal. She knows that as part of her presentation she will describe how her research will build on the current body of knowledge. She plans to make the connection to the existing literature and to impress on her committee that her proposed hypothesis has not been tested. In fact her research problem was suggested in a recent journal article's suggested future research recommendation.

Her literature includes some of the first studies on sustainable tourism through to the most recent published works. Although her committee chair praised her diligence with finding and reporting on the literature she knows that she will need to revise it before her final defence. She has selected a survey instrument based on Dr David Weaver's seminal work in that field. Her research design is based on several notable tourism studies and she plans to test one part of Dr David Weaver's theory on sustainable tourism.

She is about to create her PowerPoint presentation slides for her proposal presentation. Her presentation will take a total of 45 minutes. It will be an outline of her proposal for which she has 30 minutes to present with 15 minutes set aside for questions.

What should she include in the presentation? What are the headings on the slides and what should she present to the committee? In anticipation of questions she may be asked, she plans to write up several questions and prepare to answer them. What questions would the committee ask?

Key Terms

Dissertation: A research paper written by doctoral students. It is written at the end of the PhD degree programme.

Indirect costs: Costs of doing business that are included in grants to recover the cost of facilities and administration. They are usually a set percentage of the grant and the institution sets the percentage.

Population: The entire group.

Proposal: A research proposal is a plan that describes the problem and exactly how the research will be conducted.

Reliability: Consistency of your measure.

Sample: A representative sub-group of the population

Thesis: A research paper written by masters' students. It is written at the end of the masters degree programme.

Validity: The degree that the technique accurately measures what you are trying to measure. It is the best approximation of the truth.

Discussion Questions and Exercises

1. Select a research article from a recent research journal article. Create an outline for a proposal based on that article.

2. Form a small group of students and generate ideas for a research study. Based on the ideas generated take one and try to create a Problem Statement, and then create a hypothesis.

3. Create a formatting guide for your proposal based on a style guide and your institution's formatting requirements.

References

American Psychological Association (2009) *Publication Manual of the American Psychological Association*, 6th edn. American Psychological Association, Washington, D.C.

Booth, W., Colomb, G.G. and Williams J.M. (2007) *Kate L. Turabian, A Manual for Writers of Research Papers, Theses, and Dissertations*, 7th edn. The University of Chicago Press, London.

Booth, W., Colomb, G.G. and Williams J.M (2008) *The Craft of Research,* 3rd edn. The University of Chicago Press, London.

Chastain, E. (2008) *How to Write a Research Paper: The Ultimate Guide to Putting it all Together in your Head and on the Page.* Sparknotes, New York.

Leedy, P.D. and Ormrod, J.E. (2005) *Practical Research Planning and Design*, 8th edn. Pearson Prentice Hall, Upper Saddle River, New Jersey.

McMillan, J.H. and Schumacher, S. (2001) *Research in Education, A Conceptual Introduction*, 5th edn. Longman, New York.

Modern Language Association (2009) *MLA Handbook for Writers of Research Papers*, 7th edn. MLA, New York.

Salkind, N.J. (2006) *Exploring Research*, 6th edn. Pearson Prentice Hall, Upper Saddle River, New Jersey.

Schloss, P.J. and Smith, M.A. (1999) *Conducting Research*. Pearson Prentice Hall, Upper Saddle River, New Jersey.

Appendix 5: An Examination of Effects of Self-Concept, Destination Personality and SC-DP Congruence on Tourist Behaviour

Xiangping Li and Muzaffer Uysal

Abstract

Tourism literature has explored some critical concepts such as motivation, image, expectations and the like and their influence in tourist behaviour. However, such constructs as self-concept, destination personality and self-congruence, have received little attention. This study makes an effort to address these concepts by proposing and empirically testing a theoretical model that attempts to investigate the structural relationships between destination personality (DP), self-concept (SC), congruence between self-concept and destination personality (SC-DP congruence) and tourist behaviour. This study will use an Internet survey to collect data with the help from Zoomerang, a commercial online market research company. Pearson correlation and structural equation modeling will be used to empirically test the model. It is expected to find that destination personality, self-concept and SC-DP congruence will have significant influence on tourist behaviour. It is believed that an understanding of what influences tourist behaviour can aid in designing and implementing appropriate marketing programmes.

Keywords: destination personality, self-concept, self-congruence, tourist behaviour.

Table of Contents

1. Introduction

The purpose of this dissertation is to propose a theoretical model that attempts to investigate the influence of self-congruence on tourist behaviour. Specifically, this study attempts to examine the structural relationships among the following constructs: self-concept, destination personality, self-congruency (congruency between self-concept and destination personality, hence SC-DP congruence hereafter) and tourist behaviour. In addition, self-concept consists of four aspects, including actual self-concept, ideal self-concept, social self-concept and ideal social self-concept; hence SC-DP congruence also includes fours facets: actual SC-DP congruence (congruency between actual self-concept and destination personality), ideal SC-DP congruence (congruency between ideal self-concept and destination personality), social SC-DP congruence (congruency between social self-concept and destination personality) and ideal social SC-DP congruence (congruency between ideal social self-concept and destination personality).

(a) Statement of the problem

Factors influencing tourist behaviour have been a focal point in tourism research for decades. Efforts to unveil the determinants that shape travel behaviour stem not only from pure academic interest, but from practical business considerations (Pizam and Mansfeld, 1999). Sirgy and Su (2000) pointed out that past research efforts have focused on the issues of what, when, where and how to purchase, but not much on why to purchase. Therefore, further analysis of why tourists make their choices is much needed (Beerli *et al.*, 2007), such as the constructs of destination personality, self-concept, and self-congruence. These concepts have been largely ignored in tourism research (Ksatenholz, 2004; Beerli *et al.*, 2007).

In order to better understand the relationships among self-concept, destination personality,

SC-DP congruence and tourist behaviour, this study aims to conceptualize, develop and test a model which describes the above mentioned relationships. In particular, research questions related to the purpose of the study include:

Research question 1: What is the relationship between self-concept and destination personality?

Research question 2: How is tourist behaviour influenced by self-concept, destination personality and SC-DP congruence individually?

(b) Research hypotheses

Based on the research questions, research hypotheses are proposed to determine how tourist behaviour is influenced by the following factors: self-concept, destination personality, and SC-DP congruence.

H1: **There is a relationship between self-concept and destination personality.**

H1.1: There is a relationship between actual self-concept and dest ination personality.

H1.2: There is a relationship between ideal self-concept and destination personality.

H1.3: There is a relationship between social self-concept and destination personality.

H1.4: There is a relationship between ideal social self-concept and destination personality.

H2: **Self-concept has a direct positive influence on tourist behaviour.**

H2.1: Actual self-concept has a direct positive influence on tourist behaviour.

H2.2: Ideal self-concept has a direct positive influence on tourist behaviour.

H2.3: Social self-concept has a direct positive influence on tourist behaviour.

H2.4: Ideal social self-concept has a direct positive influence on tourist behaviour.

H3: **Destination personality has a direct positive influence on tourist behaviour.**

H4: **SC-DP congruence has a direct positive influence on tourist behaviour.**

H4.1: Actual SC-DP congruence has a direct positive influence on tourist behaviour.

H4.2: Ideal SC-DP congruence has a direct positive influence on tourist behaviour.

H4.3: Social SC-DP congruence has a direct positive influence on tourist behaviour.

H4.4: Ideal social SC-DP congruence has a direct positive influence on tourist behaviour.

(c) Definitions of terminology

Destination personality: It can be defined as the set of human characteristics associated with a destination as perceived from a tourist (Ekinci and Hosany, 2006). Destination personality is made up of three dimensions: sincerity, excitement and conviviality.

Self-concept: In the literature, self-concept and self-image are interchangeable. Self-concept denotes the 'totality of the individual's thoughts and feelings having reference to himself as an object' (Rosenberg, 1979, p. 7). Sirgy (1982) pointed out that, generally, consumer researchers have used four aspects of self-concept in explaining and predicting consumer behaviours. He described four aspects of self based on the individual's perspective: namely, actual self-concept, social self-concept, ideal self-concept and ideal social self-concept.

- **Actual self-concept:** It can be defined as how a person sees himself or herself. For instance, a person may think of himself or herself as modern.
- **Social self-concept:** It can be defined as how others see him or her. For instance, others may think of him or her as somewhat modern.
- **Ideal self-concept:** It can be defined by how a person would like to see himself or herself. For instance, a person would like himself or herself to be very modern.
- **Ideal social self-concept:** It can be described as how a person would like others to see him or her. For instance, a person would like others to think of him or her as very modern.

Self-congruence: In the consumer research, self-congruence can be defined as a process of cognitively matching a consumer's self-concept with the product-user image (Sirgy, 1982, 1985). In this study, self-congruence is defined as the cognitive matching process between a tourist's self-concept and the destination personality, SC-DP congruence. Similarly, as four aspects of self-concept are explored in this study, there are four aspects of SC-DP congruence.

- **Actual SC-DP congruence:** It is defined as the cognitive matching process between a tourist's actual self-concept and the destination personality.
- **Social SC-DP congruence:** It is defined as the cognitive matching process between a tourist's social self-concept and the destination personality.

- **Ideal SC-DP congruence:** It is defined as the cognitive matching process between a tourist's ideal self-concept and the destination personality.
- **Ideal social SC-DP congruence:** It is defined as the cognitive matching process between a tourist's ideal social self-concept and the destination personality.

(d) The Importance of the study

The potential contribution of this study can be discussed from both theoretical and practical perspectives. This study contributes to the theoretical advancement in the field of tourism research by introducing congruence between self-concept and destination personality, and investigating the impact of such congruence on tourist behaviour. This study provides empirical tests of the relationships among self-concept, destination personality, congruence between self-concept and destination personality, and tourist behaviour.

From the practical perspective, the findings of this study explain how tourist behaviour is influenced by self-concept, destination personality, and congruence between self-concept and destination personality. The results will help destination managers and marketers with the planning of strategic marketing programmes, such as how to build a strong and distinct destination personality that is congruent with their targeted tourist markets through advertising messages and promotion programmes.

2. Literature Review

(a) Destination personality

The idea that brands can be described in terms of a set of personality traits can be traced back to Gardner and Levy (1955) and Martineau (1958). The concept of brand personality has also been accepted by most marketing academics and practitioners (Aaker and Fournier, 1995; Gardner and Levy, 1955). A destination can also have a personality, thus being described with personality traits. Research has demonstrated that a distinctive destination personality can help differentiate among destinations (Murphy, Moscardo and Benckendorff, 2007), influence destination preference and choice behaviour (Crockett and Wood, 1999, 2002; Murphy, Benckendorff and Moscardo, 2007), positively improve destination image (Hosany et al., 2006, 2007), and enhance tourist loyalty (Ekinci and Hosany, 2006). Although

destination personality is an important topic of study, its research is only on its infancy. In addition, despite the growing body of literature on destination branding, there is little empirical evidence that visitors can and do associate brand personality characteristics with destinations (Ekinci and Hosany, 2006). Neither have the links between brand personality and self-concept been explored (Murphy et al., 2007). As a result, more academic effort is needed in this area (Ekinci, 2003; Ekinci and Hosany, 2006; Hosany et al., 2006, 2007; Murphy et al., 2007).

(b) Self-concept and self-congruence

Self-concept and self-congruence are two important concepts in consumer behaviour research. Research focusing on the impact of consumer self-concept, and self-congruence on their choice process has been proliferating in the marketing literature, especially during the 1960s, 1970s and 1980s. It is argued that the perceived congruency between a product's user image and the consumer's self-concept can positively influence the consumer's purchase intention (Grubb and Grathwohl, 1967; Birdwell, 1968; Grubb and Hupp, 1968; Dolich, 1969; Hamm and Cundiff, 1969; Grubb and Stern, 1971; Hughes and Guerrero, 1971; Kassarjian, 1971; Ross, 1971; Landon, 1974; Stern, Bush and Hair, 1977; Sirgy, 1982, 1985; Sirgy and Samli, 1985; Onkvisit and Shaw, 1987; Malhotra, 1988). Chon (1990) first introduced the constructs of self-concept and self-congruence into tourism research. He found that the higher the congruence between self-concept and destination image, the greater the satisfaction of the tourists. Sirgy and Su (2000) also proposed that the greater the match between the tourist's self-concept and destination visitor image, the more likely the tourist has a positive attitude toward that destination, thus the more likely the tourist would prefer and visit that destination. Although several articles have attempted to verify the roles of self-concept and self-congruity in the setting of the tourism and hospitality industry (Chon and Olsen, 1991; Chon, 1992; Goh and Litvin, 2000; Sirgy and Su, 2000; Goh and Goldsmith, 2001; Todd, 2001; Litvin and Goh, 2002; Ekinci and Riley, 2003; Litvin, Litvin and Kar, 2003; Back, 2005; Beerli et al., 2007), self-image-destination-image congruity is still a topic that has been under-studied in the discipline of tourism and hospitality marketing. Therefore, more empirical evidence is needed to clarify the role of self-congruity in tourist's destination choice process (Sirgy and

Su, 2000; Beerli *et al.*, 2007). Furthermore, the mixed results of self-congruity research also suggest further validation of the application of self-congruity, the relationship between self-image, destination image, and destination selection (Litvin and Goh, 2002).

In addition, the application of self-concept in tourism research focuses mostly on actual self-concept. However, self-concept is a multidimensional construct. According to Sirgy (1982), consumer researchers have generally used four aspects of self-image in explaining and predicting consumer behaviour. These four aspects of self-image are actual self-concept, social self-concept, ideal self-concept and ideal social self-concept. Therefore, more empirical study is needed to examine the application of all the four dimensions of self-concept in the context of tourism (Sirgy and Su, 2000; Todd, 2001).

Most of the studies focusing on self-congruity in tourism literature conceptualize self-congruity as a matching process between a tourist's self-concept and destination visitor image (Chon, 1990; Chon and Olsen, 1991; Goh and Litvin, 2000; Sirgy and Su, 2000; Litvin *et al.*, 2001; Litvin and Goh, 2002; Litvin and Kar, 2003; Beerli *et al.*, 2007). However, the congruence between tourist's self-concept and destination personality (SC-DP congruence) has rarely been tested. Ekinci and Hosany (2006) suggested future studies could assess the direct impact of SC-DP congruence on destination choice. Murphy *et al.* (2007) also requested further research to investigate the link between self-concept, brand personality and visitation.

(c) Relationship of the statement problem to the literature

This study will expand the current literatures by examining the dimensions of destination personality with an American sample. In addition, this study will expand the current literature by introducing congruence between self-concept and destination personality, and establishing the relationship between the SC-DP congruence and tourist behaviour.

3. Methodology

(a) Sample

This study targets leisure tourists. A leisure tourist is one who is at least 18 years old or above and took at least one leisure trip for at least two nights away from home during the past 18 months. The target sample size is 600. As the major statistical technique used in this study is structural equation modelling (SEM); SEM in general requires a larger sample.

One rule of thumb is that the minimum sample size is to have at least five times as many cases as the number of variables to be analysed. The more acceptable sample size would have a 10:1 ratio (Stern *et al.*, 1977). Stevens' (2002) rule of thumb is to have at least 15 cases per measured variable or indicator. In the literature, sample sizes commonly run 200–400 for models with 10–15 indicators. Hoyle (1995) recommends a sample size of at least 100–200. Schumacker and Lomax (2004) surveyed the literature and found sample sizes of 250–500 to be used in many articles. Hair *et al.*'s (1977) recommended sample size is 200, as they think 200 would provide a sound basis for estimation. In addition, they suggest that as the sample size becomes larger than 400, the test becomes more sensitive and almost any difference is detectable. As a result, sample sizes in the range of 150 to 400 are suggested. Based on the literature, the target sample size is 600. Three hundred will be used for the model testing and the other half for model validation.

(b) Data collection

An Internet survey will be utilized to collect the data, since it allows researchers to reach a large audience, and secure confidential answers quickly and cost-effectively (Zikmund, 2003). This study will use a commercial online market research company (Zoomerang) to post and distribute the questionnaires to their ZoomPanel, an online panel of some 2.5 million customers.

(c) Instrument

The questionnaire consists of four parts. The first part gathers information concerning the leisure travellers' most recent trip of a two-night minimum stay. Part two asks about their demographic characteristics. Parts three, four and five ask respondents to rate destination personality, and their self-concept with five-point Likert type scales.

Destination personality

One of the ways to conceptualize and measure brand personality is the trait approach. Based on the Five Factor Model of human personality, Jennifer L.

Aaker (1997) developed a theoretical framework of brand personality dimensions, and created a reliable, valid and generalizable scale to measure these dimensions across 37. She proposed a 42-item Brand Personality Scale (BPS hereafter) that measures five salient dimensions: sincerity, excitement, competence, sophistication and ruggedness. Since BPS's inception, it has received tremendous attention and extensive application in different cultures. Ekinci and Hosany (2006) also adapted Aaker's BPS scale to tourism destination and created an 11-item destination personality scale consisting of three dimensions: sincerity, excitement and conviviality.

During the purification process, Ekinci and Hosany (2006) pretested the content validity of Aaker's scale. This test reduced the original 42 items to 27 items. These 27 items split across five dimensions: *sincerity* (down-to-earth, family-oriented, sincere, wholesome, original, cheerful, friendly), *excitement* (daring, exciting, spirited, imaginative, up-to-date, independent), *competence* (reliable, secure, intelligent, successful, confident, secure), *sophistication* (upper class, glamorous, good-looking) and *ruggedness* (outdoorsy, masculine, Western, tough, rugged). In this study, these 27 items were used to capture destination personality (Table A5.1). Respondents were asked to rate the adjectives using a five-point Likert scale where 1 = strongly disagree, 2 = disagree, 3 = neutral, 4 = agree and 5 = strongly agree. The response cue is as follows:

'The following statements are about the destination of your most recent leisure trip (the leisure trip specified in Part I). We would like you to think of the destination as if it were a person. Please circle the appropriate number that indicates your agreement or disagreement to the following adjectives that can describe the destination of this trip.'

Self-concept

In self-concept and user image literature, it is traditional that self-concept and user image are utilizing the same measurement scales. In this study, thus, the measurement of self-concept is consistent with that of destination personality. Therefore, the same adjectives will be used to measure the four aspects of self-concept with a five-point Likert scale where 1 = strongly disagree, 2 = disagree, 3 = neutral, 4 = agree, and 5 = strongly agree (Tables A5.2 and A5.3). Different response cues will be used to guide the respondents to rate

their actual, ideal, social, ideal social self-concept (Sirgy and Samli, 1985; Sirgy *et al.*, 1991).

- **Actual self-concept:** the sort of person you think you are, or the way in which you actually see yourself; e.g. I am the type of person who is stylish.
- **Ideal self-concept:** the sort of person you would most like to be (or being), or the way in which you ideally see yourself; e.g. I like to be the type of person who is stylish.
- **Social self-concept:** the sort of person you are seen by others, or the way you believe other people see you; e.g. those people who are close to me see me as being stylish.
- **Ideal social self-concept:** the sort of person you like to be seen by others, or the way you want others to see you; e.g. I like those people who are close to me to see me as being stylish.

(d) Data analysis

Three major statistical techniques will be used to test the hypotheses. Pearson correlation analyses will be used to test the first hypothesis. Structural equation modelling (SEM) will be performed to test hypotheses two to four. In addition, before SEM is conducted to test hypotheses two to four, confirmatory factor analysis will be utilized to test the measurement model and examine the reliability and validity of the constructs.

(e) Proposed outcome and results

Based on the prior studies, it is expected that there is a positive relationship between destination personality and self-concept. In addition, it is proposed that dimensions of destination personality and self-concept will have significant influence on tourist behaviour. Similarly, the congruence between self-concept and destination personality will impact tourist behaviour significantly.

4. Implications and Limitations

(a) Implications

This study has proposed and will test a theoretical model that attempts to investigate the influence of destination personality, self-concept and SC-DP congruence on tourist behaviour. The findings will

Table A5.1. Measurement scale of destination personality.

Down-to-earth	1	2	3	4	5
Family-oriented	1	2	3	4	5
Sincere	1	2	3	4	5
Wholesome	1	2	3	4	5
Original	1	2	3	4	5
Cheerful	1	2	3	4	5
Friendly	1	2	3	4	5
Daring	1	2	3	4	5
Exciting	1	2	3	4	5
Spirited	1	2	3	4	5
Imaginative	1	2	3	4	5
Up-to-date	1	2	3	4	5
Independent	1	2	3	4	5
Reliable	1	2	3	4	5
Charming	1	2	3	4	5
Intelligent	1	2	3	4	5
Secure	1	2	3	4	5
Successful	1	2	3	4	5
Confident	1	2	3	4	5
Upper class	1	2	3	4	5
Glamorous	1	2	3	4	5
Good looking	1	2	3	4	5
Outdoorsy	1	2	3	4	5
Masculine	1	2	3	4	5
Western	1	2	3	4	5
Tough	1	2	3	4	5
Rugged	1	2	3	4	5

Table A5.2. Measurement scale of actual and ideal self-concept.

Actual self						Ideal self				
1	2	3	4	5	Down-to-earth	1	2	3	4	5
1	2	3	4	5	Family-oriented	1	2	3	4	5
1	2	3	4	5	Sincere	1	2	3	4	5
1	2	3	4	5	Wholesome	1	2	3	4	5

(Continued)

Table A5.2. Continued.

Actual self						Ideal self				
1	2	3	4	5	Original	1	2	3	4	5
1	2	3	4	5	Cheerful	1	2	3	4	5
1	2	3	4	5	Friendly	1	2	3	4	5
1	2	3	4	5	Daring	1	2	3	4	5
1	2	3	4	5	Exciting	1	2	3	4	5
1	2	3	4	5	Spirited	1	2	3	4	5
1	2	3	4	5	Imaginative	1	2	3	4	5
1	2	3	4	5	Up-to-date	1	2	3	4	5
1	2	3	4	5	Independent	1	2	3	4	5
1	2	3	4	5	Reliable	1	2	3	4	5
1	2	3	4	5	Charming	1	2	3	4	5
1	2	3	4	5	Intelligent	1	2	3	4	5
1	2	3	4	5	Secure	1	2	3	4	5
1	2	3	4	5	Successful	1	2	3	4	5
1	2	3	4	5	Confident	1	2	3	4	5
1	2	3	4	5	Upper class	1	2	3	4	5
1	2	3	4	5	Glamorous	1	2	3	4	5
1	2	3	4	5	Good looking	1	2	3	4	5
1	2	3	4	5	Outdoorsy	1	2	3	4	5
1	2	3	4	5	Masculine	1	2	3	4	5
1	2	3	4	5	Western	1	2	3	4	5
1	2	3	4	5	Tough	1	2	3	4	5
1	2	3	4	5	Rugged	1	2	3	4	5

Table A5.3. Measurement scale of social and ideal social self-concept.

Social self						Ideal social self				
1	2	3	4	5	Down-to-earth	1	2	3	4	5
1	2	3	4	5	Family-oriented	1	2	3	4	5
1	2	3	4	5	Sincere	1	2	3	4	5
1	2	3	4	5	Wholesome	1	2	3	4	5
1	2	3	4	5	Original	1	2	3	4	5
1	2	3	4	5	Cheerful	1	2	3	4	5
1	2	3	4	5	Friendly	1	2	3	4	5

(Continued)

Table A5.3. Continued.

Social self						Ideal social self				
1	2	3	4	5	Daring	1	2	3	4	5
1	2	3	4	5	Exciting	1	2	3	4	5
1	2	3	4	5	Spirited	1	2	3	4	5
1	2	3	4	5	Imaginative	1	2	3	4	5
1	2	3	4	5	Up-to-date	1	2	3	4	5
1	2	3	4	5	Independent	1	2	3	4	5
1	2	3	4	5	Reliable	1	2	3	4	5
1	2	3	4	5	Charming	1	2	3	4	5
1	2	3	4	5	Intelligent	1	2	3	4	5
1	2	3	4	5	Secure	1	2	3	4	5
1	2	3	4	5	Successful	1	2	3	4	5
1	2	3	4	5	Confident	1	2	3	4	5
1	2	3	4	5	Upper class	1	2	3	4	5
1	2	3	4	5	Glamorous	1	2	3	4	5
1	2	3	4	5	Good looking	1	2	3	4	5
1	2	3	4	5	Outdoorsy	1	2	3	4	5
1	2	3	4	5	Masculine	1	2	3	4	5
1	2	3	4	5	Western	1	2	3	4	5
1	2	3	4	5	Tough	1	2	3	4	5
1	2	3	4	5	Rugged	1	2	3	4	5

provide important implications for destination marketing strategies. An understanding of what influenced tourist behaviour tested in this model can aid in designing and implementing marketing programmes for creating and enhancing tourist destination personality; tailoring unique destination personality to attract particular markets; differentiating and positioning tourist destinations; and designing and promoting tourism advertising and programmes.

(b) Limitations

As expected in all research, this one is not without its limitations. First, this study will only focus on residents in the USA. Therefore, the findings will be culturally bound and not generalizable. More research is needed for other cultural groups. Second, this study will survey tourists who have been to the destination, and social desirability could be an intervening effect. Future study could examine the role of social desirability in self-congruence study. Third, different studies utilize different items to measure self-concept. In this study, the self-concept will be measured with the same items that measure destination personality, but with different instructions. Therefore, the measurement problem of self-concept should be further explored. It would be of great significance if a generalizable measurement scale for self-concept could be developed in tourist research. Lastly, this study will only explore the relationship between destination personality, self-concept and SC-DP congruence on tourist behaviour. There are other relevant factors that could influence tourist behaviour, such as destination image and tourist motivation. Future research could try to integrate these elements.

References

Aaker, J.L. (1997) Dimensions of Brand Personality. *Journal of Marketing Research* 34(3), 347–356.

Aaker, J.L. and Fournier, S. (1995) A Brand as a Character, a Partner and a Person: Three Perspectives on the Question of Brand Personality. *Advances in Consumer Research* 22, 391–395.

Back, K.-J. (2005) The Effects of Image Congruence on Customers' Brand Loyalty in the Upper Middle-Class Hotel Industry. *Journal of Hospitality and Tourism Research* 29(4), 448–467.

Beerli, A., Meneses, G.D. and Gil, S.M. (2007) Self-Congruity and Destination Choice. *Annals of Tourism Research,* 34(3), 571–587.

Birdwell, A.E. (1968) A Study of the Influence of Image Congruence on Consumer Choice. *The Journal of Business* 41(1), 76–88.

Chon, K.-S. (1990) *Consumer Satisfaction and Dissatisfaction in Tourism as Related to Destination Image Perception.* Unpublished Ph.D dissertation, Virginia Polytechnic Institute and State University, Blacksburg, Virginia.

Chon, K.-S. (1992) Self Image/Destination Image Congruity. *Annals of Tourism Research,* Vol. 19, pp. 360.

Chon, K.-S. and Olsen, M.D. (1991) Functional and Symbolic Congruity Approaches to Consumer Satisfaction/Dissatisfaction in Consumerism. *Journal of the International Academy of Hospitality Research,* Vol. 3, pp. 1.

Crockett, S.R. and Wood, L.J. (1999) Brand Western Australia: A Totally Integrated Approach to Destination Branding. *Journal of Vacation Marketing* 5(3), 276–289.

Crockett, S.R. and Wood, L.J. (2002) Brand Western Australia: Holidays of an Entirely Different Nature. In N. Morgan, A. Pritchard and R. Pride (eds) *Destination Branding: Creating the Unique Destination Proposition.* Butterworth-Heinemann, Oxford, pp. 124–147.

Dolich, I.J. (1969) Congruence Relationships between Self Images and Product Brands. *Journal of Marketing Research* 6(1), 80–84.

Ekinci, Y. (2003) From Destination Image to Destination Branding: An Emerging Area of Research. *e-Review of Tourism Research (eRTR)* 1(2), 21–24.

Ekinci, Y. and Hosany, S. (2006) Destination Personality: An Application of Brand Personality to Tourism Destinations. *Journal of Travel Research* 45(2), 127–139.

Ekinci, Y. and Riley, M. (2003) An Investigation of Self-Concept: Actual and Ideal Self-Congruence Compared in the Context of Service Evaluation. *Journal of Retailing and Consumer Services* 10(4), 201–214.

Gardner, B.B. and Levy, S.J. (1955) The Product and the Brand. *Harvard Business Review,* 33(2), 33–39.

Goh, H.K. and Litvin, S.W. (2000) *Destination Preference and Self-Congruity.* Paper presented at the Travel and Tourism Research Association Annual Conference, 11–14 June 2000, San Fernando Valley, California.

Grubb, E.L. and Grathwohl, H.L. (1967) Consumer Self-Concept, Symbolism and Market Behavior: A Theoretical Approach. *Journal of Marketing* 31(4), 22–27.

Grubb, E.L. and Hupp, G. (1968) Perception of Self, Generalized Stereotypes, and Brand Selection. *Journal of Marketing Research* 5(1), 58–63.

Grubb, E.L. and Stern, B.L. (1971) Self-Concept and Significant Others. *Journal of Marketing Research* 8(3), 382–385.

Hamm, B.C. and Cundiff, E.W. (1969) Self-Actualization and Product Perception. *Journal of Marketing Research* 6(4), 470–472.

Hosany, S., Ekinci, Y. and Uysal, M. (2006) Destination Image and Destination Personality: An Application of Branding Theories to Tourism Places. *Journal of Business Research* 59(5), 638–642.

Hosany, S., Ekinci, Y. and Uysal, M. (2007) Destination image and destination personality. *International Journal of Culture, Tourism and Hospitality Research* 1(1), 62–81.

Hoyle, R.H. (1995) The Structural Equation Modeling Approach: Basic Concepts, and Fundamental Issues. In: R.H. Hoyle (ed.) *Structural Equation Modeling: Concepts, Issues, and Applications.* Sage Publications, Thousand Oaks, California, pp. 1–15.

Hughes, G.D. and Guerrero, J.L. (1971) Automobile Self-Congruity Models Re-examined. *Journal of Marketing Research* 8(1), 125–127.

Kassarjian, H.H. (1971) Personality and Consumer Behavior: A Review. *Journal of Marketing Research* 8(4), 409–418.

Ksatenholz, E. (2004) Assessment and Role of Destination-Self-Congruity. *Annals of Tourism Research* 31(3), 719–723.

Landon, E.L., Jr. (1974) Self Concept, Ideal Self Concept, and Consumer Purchase Intentions. *The Journal of Consumer Research* 1(2), 44–51.

Litvin, S.W. and Goh, H.K. (2002) Research Note: Self-Image Congruity: A Valid Tourism Theory? *Tourism Management*, Vol. 23, pp. 81.

Litvin, S.W., Goh, H.K. and Goldsmith, R. E. (2001) Travel Innovativeness And Self-Image Congruity. *Journal of Travel and Tourism Marketing* 10(4), 33–45.

Litvin, S.W. and Kar, G.H. (2003) Individualism/collectivism as a moderating factor to the self-image congruity concept. *Journal of Vacation Marketing* 10(1), 23–32.

Malhotra, N.K. (1988) Self Concept and Product Choice: An Integrated Perspective. *Journal of Economic Psychology* 9(1), 1–28.

Martineau, P. (1958) The Personality of the Retail Store. *Harvard Business Review* 36(1), 47–55.

Murphy, L., Benckendorff, P. and Moscardo, G. (2007) Destination Brand Personality: Visitor Perceptions of a Regional Tourism Destination. *Tourism Analysis* 12(5/6), 419–432.

Murphy, L., Moscardo, G. and Benckendorff, P. (2007) Using Brand Personality to Differentiate Regional Tourism Destinations. *Journal of Travel Research* 46(1), 5–14.

Onkvisit, S. and Shaw, J. (1987) Self-Concept and Image Congruence: Some Research and Managerial Implications. *The Journal of Consumer Marketing* 4(1), 13–23.

Pizam, A. and Mansfeld, Y. (1999) *Consumer behavior in travel and tourism*. Haworth Hospitality Press, New York.

Rosenberg, M. (1979) *Conceiving the Self*. Basic Books, New York.

Ross, I. (1971) Self-Concept and Brand Preference. *The Journal of Business* 44(1), 38–50.

Schumacker, R.E. and Lomax, R.G. (2004) *A Beginner's Guide to Structural Equation Modeling*, 2nd edn. Lawrence Erlbaum Associates, Mahwah, New Jersey, p. 84.

Sirgy, M.J. (1982) Self-Concept in Consumer Behavior: A Critical Review. *The Journal of Consumer Research* 9(3), 287–300.

Sirgy, M.J. (1985) Self-Image/Product-Image Congruity and Consumer Decision-Making. *International Journal of Management* 2(4), 49–63.

Sirgy, M.J., Johar, J.S., Samli, A.C. and Claiborne, C.B. (1991) Self-Congruity Versus Functional Congruity: Predictors of Consumer Behavior. *Journal of the Academy of Marketing Science* 19(4), 363–375.

Sirgy, M.J. and Samli, A.C. (1985) A Path Analytic Model of Store Loyalty Involving Self-Concept, Store Image, Geographic Loyalty, and Socioeconomic Status. *Journal of the Academy of Marketing Science* 13(3), 265–291.

Sirgy, M.J. and Su, C. (2000) Destination Image, Self-Congruity, and Travel Behavior: Toward an Integrative Model. *Journal of Travel Research* 38(4), 340–352.

Stern, B.L., Bush, R.F. and Hair, J.F., Jr. (1977) The Self-Image/Store Image Matching Process: An Empirical Test. *The Journal of Business* 50(1), 63–69.

Stevens, J. (2002) *Applied Multivariate Statistics for the Social Sciences*, 4th edn. Lawrence Erlbaum Associates, Mahwah, New Jersey.

Todd, S. (2001) Self-Concept: A Tourism Application. *Journal of Consumer Behaviour* 1(2), 184–196.

Zikmund, W.G. (2003) *Business Research Methods*, 7th edn. Thomson, London.

chapter 6

Survey Research: Sampling and Questionnaire Design

Ercan Sirakaya-Turk and Muzaffer Uysal

Learning Objectives

After studying this chapter, you will be able to:

1. Understand the underlying logic and principles of survey research;
2. Know sampling terms and processes for choosing a sampling frame;
3. Know how to select a sampling procedure;
4. Develop data collection survey instruments;
5. Understand design and applications of mail surveys;
6. Understand the advantages and disadvantages of online Internet surveys and panel data.

Chapter Summary

This chapter covers three major areas of data collection and generation: (i) underlying logic and principals of survey research; (ii) issues in designing survey instruments; and (iii) means of data collection. It introduces sampling and design of survey research as one of the most important areas of data collection methods in applied research leisure, recreation and tourism. The chapter begins

with issues surrounding the logic of sampling and representativeness, sampling process and methods, choosing representative units of analysis, the concept and terminology of sampling, sampling size, sample error (variability) and confidence intervals. The chapter then addresses a number of issues including: questionnaire development, developing questions, constructing a survey instrument, evaluating questionnaires, conducting surveys and secondary analysis of survey data. Furthermore, the chapter briefly covers some of the special issues involved in Internet and panels surveys with some of the advantages and disadvantages of different data collection methods.

Introduction

Recall the problem setting introduced in Chapter 1 where Club Ottomans-II, an all-inclusive vacation club in the Caribbean, was experiencing a decline in their customer base. You, the COO (Chief Operating Officer), are thinking that a number of issues were suspect in explaining the sharp decline in repeat business. You could not trust the answers provided by a small group of guests because they do not represent the entire customer base. To whom will you ask the questions? Will you go to all 16,000 customers who stay in the Resort Club in a year? It would be too expensive, and impossible to reach all since you don't have the contact information of all the customers. What do you do? You need to design a study that will address all these issues in a way that you can generalize your findings to your entire customer base using one of many sampling methods. How do you design such a study and instruments that can be used to obtain the information you need to solve your problem?

Underlying Logic and Principles of Survey Research

One of the most important reasons to conduct survey research is the cost savings. Indeed, going to an entire population for information is costly. You probably have heard about the cost of conducting a population census. Mandated by the law in the USA, it is done every ten years, costs billions of dollars and surprisingly misses millions of people. The census bureau must then correct the population figures using scientifically obtained samples. A tourism company or a recreation organization is not different. It can have thousands of customers in a given year. Going to the entire customer base (population) is simply unreasonable and costly, especially when you are familiar with sampling. Thus, we use the methods of sampling and statistics to make inferences about population parameters.

A parameter usually refers to a piece of information (such as income or satisfaction ratings). Statistics is used to estimate the population parameter from a smaller group (sample), or a **mini population** you might call it, if you will. Since we do not know the population parameter, because we never go to the population in the first place, we use the next best method by using information obtained from a sample to make inferences about it. Of course, we might make errors doing this, but mathematically we can control this error. The key is to obtain a sample that closely matches the characteristics of the population so the statistics would be very close to the true population parameter; we call this generalizability. Leisure, recreation and tourism researchers as well as managers are interested in finding something that would apply to the larger population of interest or to a different setting; we don't want to waste

precious resources in obtaining something that we cannot use for the larger group or in a different setting. In other words, we are interested in discovering generalities using the laws of mathematical probability; we don't want to believe in something that does not apply to other situations and/or are restricted to the sample at hand only. Thus, representativeness of a sample and generalizability of the results are the two key issues that need to be addressed in any given research.

In order to understand the function and role of these concepts, we must turn our attention to two sampling methods: **probability** and **non-probability sampling**. The probability sampling method refers to the chance of any member of a population being included in the sample, and that figure is known. For example, if there are 28,000 students in a university and there are 5,000 members who use the university's recreation centre, the odds of selecting any one recreation member as part of our sample is 5,000:28,000 or 0.178. When the odds of including any one person from a population is not known, we cannot calculate this probability; we call this case a non-probability sampling method. In the aforementioned example, if you were to start haphazardly interviewing students until you hit some sort of quota, you would not be giving the same chance to everyone to be included in your sample; thus, you would bias the design of the sample (notice that statistical randomness does not mean haphazardness like in the vernacular use of the term in our daily language). The results then would not be generalizable. However, in the practice of research, depending upon the need of the researcher, both methods are used. For your own classroom research project, it is most likely you will not use the probability sampling but will rather opt for a convenience or non-probability sampling method. If you are writing a thesis or dissertation your professor or advisor might want you to use a probability sampling method.

Sampling Terms and Process

Defining the population is the first step in a sampling process. To whom will the results apply? The population refers to the entire universe of elements being studied. An element is usually an individual or a household. We use elements to generalize study findings to our entire population of interest. Obviously, the population must be determined before anything else. Do not confuse a typical understanding of a population or census of a given country or city with a study population. The term 'population' in research has a much broader meaning. The population of a study might be different for different studies. If you are interested in generalizing your results to the students in your institution, your population is the university students. However, what defines a student? Will the part-time students be part of your population? What about international students? Thus, when defining the population as university students, we need to qualify what a student means in your study.

When studying travellers, most studies delimit the boundaries of a population to the travellers who have taken a trip within the last two years or are planning to travel within the next year and are 18 years or older. Your population in this case is the travelling adults who are considered active travellers. If you were to sample from a population that has no intention to travel or have not had any travel experience before, your population would be defined incorrectly. The unit of analysis here is an individual. You may be interested in a traveller's attitudes toward a destination or motivations of recreational boaters. Attitudes and motivations are constructs that can only be studied meaningfully at the individual level. However, sometimes we are interested in families as the unit of analysis. If, for example, you would like to find out what percentage of family income is used in typical recreation activities monthly, your unit of analysis would be a household. If you are interested in studying how travel decisions are made within a family, again, your unit of analysis is the family; thus, your population of interest would be the family. However, you will still have to qualify what you mean by a family. Do the couples have to be married or would same-sex couples be considered a family? Thus, it is important to recall the purpose of your study to correctly identify the population of interest.

Choosing a sampling frame

Choosing a sampling frame is an important next step in a sampling procedure. A list or a frame that identifies every member of the population needs to be created. Lists typically are not freely available, although they can be obtained from a number of sources. In leisure, recreation and tourism research, resident attitude surveys are conducted with lists obtained from a utility or a phone company. However, phone-company lists can be inaccurate as they can miss unlisted phone numbers, rich or poor households who do not have home phones or people who moved recently from their home. Of course, you can use other types of lists such as voter registrations or property tax records with each having problems with completeness because some groups and/or individuals will always be excluded. In these instances, you run the danger of creating a sample that under-represents certain groups. The good news is that a technique called Random Digit Dialling (RDD) can help in reaching unlisted numbers. RDD is an effective, but an inefficient way of creating a sample since a computer randomly generates a large list of phone numbers that can include businesses and non-working phone numbers in addition to working numbers, making it a very costly procedure. There are many companies such as Survey Sampling, Inc., Info Survey or Claritas, Inc. that specialize in creating representative samples.

If you are interested in conducting your term project using your institution's student population, you may be allowed to obtain a list from the registrar's office. Recreation centres do have their own list of their members as well. If you are interested in conducting business surveys, then your unit of analysis is the business entity. The chamber of commerce of a city or yellow pages of a telephone book can be consulted. In short, often the sampling frame we create will not match our study population exactly. We will have to make some compromises and work with what we have, acknowledging the potential pitfalls. There is no perfect list; however, if carefully planned and potential weaknesses of each list or technique used in selecting a frame are known, we will still have a good study we can live with. We need to remember two guiding rules in this discussion: we must be very careful in defining our study population and give an equal chance to each element to be included in the final sample. Regardless of how careful we are in constructing a sample, no sample(s) will generate exact answers (statistics) that perfectly match that of the population. This error, however, can be controlled; we can, for example, state that we would be happy if our statistics were to come close, perhaps plus or minus 4% of the true population parameter, or 2% or 5%, whatever that desired outcome might be. This error can be specified before we select the sample size.

Research Box 6.1. Sampling frame for the Club Ottomans-II.

Now that you have decided on the composition of the sample, you will have to decide on the method of inclusion. Assuming that you have a list of names and addresses of customers in front of you, the best method is to give each customer an equal chance of being included in the final sample. You could make four boxes with names of each country written on them and include all customer names based on their nation of origin into the boxes. These boxes would represent your quota sample; since this is a scientific sample let's call this a proportional stratified random sample, nation of origin being your stratification factor. Now, you need to draw the names from each of the four boxes according to the numbers you've calculated above: 500 Americans, 134 British etc. When you hit the total numbers allocated to each nation, you will stop. Now, what you have in your hand is a scientifically drawn sample. Well, not quite! What if you have not been able to mix the names thoroughly enough and names that were at the bottom of the box were not given an equal chance of being included in the final sample! What if you were for some reason consistently drew names from one corner of the box because of convenience and that corner happened to contain last names starting with same letters! All these will affect the randomness clause of a sampling procedure. You need to find a better way of drawing names from a hat (box).

Fortunately, we have computers that can help. We can make the computer generate a random list of numbers and assign them to each name and address. That way, we would make sure every single name has an equal chance of being included in the sample. This sample would then represent the entire population. Anything we find out would be also found in the general population of customers, of course with some margin of error. How can this small sample be representative of the larger group (population)? Well, it's the magic of a particular theorem in statistics called **central limit theory**.

The following sections will provide you with details about how this theorem is being put into use in our disciplines. Suffice to say for now, it works; the magic involved in sampling and statistical techniques will help you come very close to the true answer. Recall the past presidential or party elections; based on a small, sometimes even less than 1000 likely voters, the majority of public opinion polls do predict the election outcomes quite accurately within a small percentage of error (somewhere ±3%). How is this hocus-pocus pulled off? You may want to consult your introductory statistics text book to understand how the central limit theorem is able to create this magic.

Deciding the sample size

After determining the population of interest and the associated sampling frame, the next question that needs to be answered is the size of the sample. How big should the sample size be? Obviously, the sample size must be a mini representation of the population. How many population elements will it take to make the sample representative of the larger population and how many sample units will it take to minimize the potential errors involved in estimating population parameters? The answer is: it depends. It depends on whether the population is homogenous or heterogeneous, which will affect the variability of key variables of the study and the precision involved in our estimation of these variables, which we call **confidence intervals** (a degree of precision in our estimates of the population

parameters). The formulas developed by statisticians to estimate a sample size based on various variances and desired precision levels of estimates are beyond the scope of this book, thus this topic will not be discussed within this text; however, a few tips can be suggested (Rosnow and Rosenthal, 1998).

The more the merrier might be the motto when it comes to determination of a sample size. Most researchers in our field look at previous similar studies done in the area to figure out the needed sample size or a rule-of-thumb guesswork to set the sample size. For populations smaller than 100, we can go ahead and survey the entire population. Our experiences dictate that any sample size from 600 and 800 should suffice for most analysis purposes. Some studies you will come across have even less than these numbers. Again, the key here is that the sample is a mini representation of the population; thus, the size is not as much important as the **representation**. If we could create a mini population (sample) by only obtaining one sample (when, for example, doctors draw blood from somebody's bloodstream to determine the blood type), we would do just that. One does not obtain several blood samples to determine the blood type; one sample is enough because blood is ubiquitous (homogenous throughout one's body), the same no matter which body part you take the sample from. Since we are trying to understand human behaviour most of the time, we do need more than one element in our sample. We know that people differ from each other in a number of ways; they can be young, old, liberal, conservative, low income, high income, liking or hating things that we ask and so on. Thus, creating a mini population requires a larger sample than one.

The numbers most researchers use are dictated by experience and previous studies. When conducting surveys, for example, you need to adjust the sample size based on expected return rate (response rate). Experience dictates that you will receive much less than initially required numbers. Typical response rate will not exceed 30%, in other words, if you send out 100 surveys you will perhaps receive 30 back. Thus, you will have to adjust your printing according to these expected returns. An analysis based on 30% is obviously not desirable and would be misleading. How would the rest of 70% of sample of non-respondents feel about your survey? Even when you have a representative sample, the response rate will play a major role in your conclusions. Since you do not know how the non-respondents would have answered your questions, at best your study will remain a good intellectual exercise, but nothing more. Optimally, you would like to have a 75% response rate to have a statistically meaningful analysis, but we never reach that unless we conduct face-to-face interviews. If we cannot reach this level, then we will have to find out the sources for non-response and ultimately conduct a separate study of the non-respondents that will help us make leapfrog arguments about the non-respondents. If somehow we were able to determine that the non-respondents actually do not differ much in terms of how they respond to our questions, we would have a basis for making logical argument about the representativeness of the returned surveys. One way to do this is contacting small group (usually 30–40) of non-respondents via telephone or other means. We ask a few key questions from the original survey instrument and compare their responses to those of the respondents. If we were to find no differences, we would conclude that non-respondents do not show systematic bias in their responses; in other words, they are not much different from a typical respondent. The logic goes like this: 'If the non-respondents were to answer the original questions, they would have responded the same way the respondents did'. Now, you have established a rationale that allows you to trust your results. We call this **non-response bias check**. We check whether there is bias involved in survey returns. Survey experts have developed other methods as well.

The second method for testing the presence of non-response bias is based on the determining the timing of survey returns. We record and tabulate return dates and then compare the answers of early respondents with those of late-respondents, people who return their surveys after repeated contacts. If we were to find any differences in their responses, we report a non-response bias. Then our job is to find ways to deal with this bias. What can we do? You either confine the study results to the sample you studied or dump the results in the trash. However, you will read and come across many studies with a low response rate that do not report any non-response bias check but claim important marketing and management implications. Indeed, the results and conclusions based on a biased sample and/or low response would do more harm than good. In the questionnaire design section of this chapter, you will learn about techniques involved in increasing response rates. A well-designed, interesting study by a university faculty or a student, for example, has a higher chance of achieving better response rates than a study done by a private market research firm. Why? Because the public still trusts universities more than they do private research and/or consulting firms. As good a student as you are, we believe you will be very creative when designing your study so you can achieve higher response rates. Do not forget, people do respond to incentives. For example, when we conducted a funded study with tour guides, we not only promised sharing the study results with the participants but also have distributed five small gold pieces (US$150 worth) through a lottery system. We have achieved 78% response rate, a much higher rate than a typical survey method. In another study, we have given away pens and calendars to all participants achieving over 70% response. When conducting a convenient study as part of the requirement for many research methods classes, our students have given cold coke during a hot summer day or pizza coupons to increase participation. We need to remember that people are not dying to respond to our surveys; they are busy and they have things on their mind other than helping us with our class projects or theses. It is incumbent upon us to make participation an interesting, fun and rewarding experience for our target sample.

Research Box 6.2. Club Ottomans-II case continued.

Recall that a sample is a small group of people that represents the entire population, in this case customers who use the Club in a year. How can you make sure that the sample is representative of the larger customer population that it represents? If you had information about the composition of the population, you could design a process by which to draw customers that resemble the composition of the target population. Again, referring back to the case scenario in Chapter 1, we do know their country of origin and the associated proportions for each citizen group. But there is no other information available other than their addresses. For example, we do not know the gender distribution of the customers, nor do we know other characteristics such as their age, income and education levels. We work with what we have; if you think that the country of origin might make a difference in how they feel about the issues presented in the case, same proportions need to be presented in the sample you will draw. Let's assume the country of origin is important. Accordingly, you might use a quota sampling or a stratified random sampling proportionate to size to obtain information. Again recall that there are approximately 16,000 guests, for whom only 12,000 addresses can be located (~7,500 in the USA; ~2,000 in England; ~1,500 in Australia, and ~1,000 in Turkey). Twelve thousand customers make of the sampling frame (not the total 16,000 because it is a theoretical sample and not the available sample). So, we'll work with 12,000 customer base. Let's assume you would like to draw a sample of 800 customers. If you were to apply the proportions presented in the available sample, you will discover that you need to include 62.5% or 500 US Americans into your sample, 16.6% or 134 British guests, 12.5% or 100 Australians and 12% or 96 Turkish guests.

Selecting a sampling procedure

As you recall we can select one of two main sampling procedures; namely, non-probability or probability sampling procedures (Czaja and Blair, 1996). Typically, when you conduct research for your class project, you will use a non-probability sampling procedure. Recall our previous discussion about giving an equal chance to elements to be included in our sample. Non-probability means that we do not know the odds of including any one element into our sample, in other words, not every person has an equal chance of being selected. Consequently, the resulting sample will be a biased sample. **Snowball sample**, finding out the information about the elements from known subjects, is one such method. Another would be when you enlist your subjects haphazardly; anyone who is close or convenient to you is included in the sample. This will result in a biased sample as well; of course, nothing is wrong with this approach, if you do not want to generalize your results to the rest of the population. For example, if you go to an urban or a national park to conduct a study of day visitors by approaching anyone who walks through the door (note that random does not mean haphazard in statistical terms), you are not giving an equal chance to every single visitor since you are not working with a known sampling frame. Thus, collected data will be biased favouring those who have agreed to participate, not every possible visitor who might be walking through the doors in a given year. Of course, you could use different days of the week and times of the day throughout a year to obtain a more representative sample but in the end you would still fail to give an equal chance to everyone. **Purposive sampling**, for example, involves approaching subjects with certain characteristics. If you were interested in finding out students' motivations for participating in underground raves or motivations for engaging in risky sexual activities while travelling, you might use your fellow classmates to start with. If you wanted to match this with some sort of predetermined number that limited the number of participants at some level, such as 15% adult bicyclists, 10% unemployed females, you would call this a **quota-sampling method**.

The second major method is when you create a probability sampling, a more scientific process; in other words, when you give an equal chance to everyone (element) to be included in your sample (Rosnow and Rosenthal, 1998). The method might be different depending upon the nature of your study. In some cases, it might be possible to select elements based on a simple method. **Simple random sampling** is used when you have access to a sampling frame and it is possible for you to select 'n' units from your sampling frame. Assigning numbers to each sampling element and drawing them from a well-mixed hat or a box or a turning ball just like during a lottery ticket draw, would constitute a good example of a simple random sampling method. Of course, we use computers these days to do this, and not hats. If, however, you were to bring in some sort of system such as drawing every 'n'th number (e.g. every 4th person is included in your sample), it would be a good example of a **systematic random sampling**. Again, you will have to have access to the entire sampling frame to be able to do this correctly. However, even with these procedures, we cannot guarantee representativeness. In many cases, people live in different towns, in different concentrations, neighbourhoods and so on. To improve the accuracy of sampling, we can use **stratification**. Dividing the sampling frame into several strata with similar characteristics, such as gender, race, public versus private recreation clubs, would enable us to compose a better, representative sample. If we were to use the simple random sampling method, by pure coincidence, we might include more males than females. However, stratification according to gender will guarantee us a more representative sample.

One step further, **probability proportionate to size** (PPS), would make the sample even more representative. If we could devise a plan to create a sample according to their proportions in their respective populations, we would be even more precise in the representation of the sampling elements. If you knew there were 30% foreign visitors to a national park, or to be exact, if you knew that there were 12% Australian visitors to your park among those foreign visitors, 10% Americans and 8% British, you could allocate the total sample size according to these proportions to arrive at a more representative sample. Typically, a researcher combines various probability sampling procedures according to the nature of their study. For example, conducting national studies would require one to use **clustering techniques**. Clustering cities (small, medium and large), followed by city blocks or streets and then systematically surveying residents within these blocks according to simple random technique would be called **multistage sampling**. More detailed information about sampling could be found in Babbie (1990) and Salkind (2008). Suffice to say, one can be creative in obtaining representation; the only principle we need to obey is to always question whether we have given an equal chance to every possible element (person) in our target population. In reality, this is harder to achieve when you do not have the necessary resources (funding and labour). If your project was funded and you had enough money to purchase a sampling frame and be able to contact those in the sampling frame, you would have a better chance of conducting a study that is truly generalizable. Thus, we encourage students who write a thesis or dissertation to obtain funding to conduct their studies. For other students, we suggest that you adopt a convenient sample of size 100 or 150 to complete a semester project.

The role of central limit theorem in sampling and inferential statistics

Generalizability of results or findings that apply to different situations is the major aim of a social scientific research. We use the principles of **central limit theorem** when predicting the values of variables (parameters) in our target population. Central limit theorem refers to normal sampling distribution, or what you might call a **bell curve**. In any given analysis, our aim is to predict (estimate) parameters in the population based on values we obtain in our sample. But how do we do this? Finding out what population parameters are without probing the population, by using only a small fraction of the population, what do we call a sample? The answer lies in probability theory of mathematics, more precisely the central limit theorem. The central limit theorem tells us that if we were to take infinite number of samples from our population and calculate the means of a particular variable for each one of these infinite

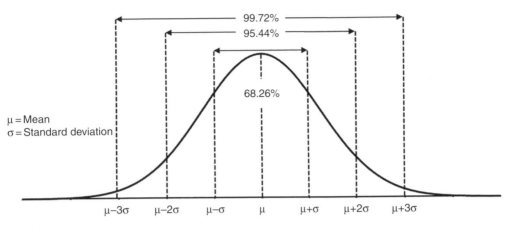

Fig. 6.1. A typical bell curve.

samples (e.g. customer satisfaction scores or incomes of respondents), the distribution of these means would look like a normal curve or a bell curve (because it is shaped like a bell). Basically, the bell curve represents the distribution of the means around a mean with a standard deviation. The curve describes all data points; in other words, the area under the entire curve contains 100% of means. We also know that about 68% of the cases can be found within one standard deviation of the mean; 95% are within two standard deviations of the mean; and 99% are within three standard deviations of the mean. Because the inherent properties of a bell curve are known to us, if we knew the mean and the standard deviation of a variable, we could pretty much know the likelihood of observing it in the population if we were to survey the population (but we never go to the population, remember). In other words, the known properties of a bell curve help us predict probabilities of observing parameters in the population. Later, in Chapter 13, we will discuss how this is put to use in inferential statistics. Figure 6.1 shows the bell curve and the probability of observing values with a given standard deviation from the mean. For example, according to Fig. 6.1, the probability of encountering values within one standard deviation from its mean is 68.26%.

Data Collection

So far, you have learned the process of selecting a suitable sample and issues surrounding the sampling process. Once you decide on whom to use as your information source, how will you collect the needed information? What are you going to use? Are you going to mail a survey form to your respondents, or telephone them, ask them to visit a website where you have your survey, or what? If your target population is tourists living in many different countries, you will need to decide on a feasible method of contacting them. If your visitors to a national park come from within your own country then you might use a different method too. A sampling frame (list) of the members of organizations such as the NRPA (National Park Recreation Association) might be easier to obtain and their level of education might be high enough to respond to a mail survey as opposed to a non-resident household whose native language might be different from the prevailing majority language in your country, in our case, English. Who the target population is will dictate the type of data collection method you will use. When the sampling frame comes from a geographically dispersed area such as the whole nation or a state, then face-to-face interviews might be a very difficult and costly choice. In this case, a mail survey of questionnaires might be your best option. Or if you could generate a list from an online panel of recreationists, you might conduct an online survey, which might be easier and faster than a mail survey that might take several months to complete. In this section, we will not dwell on face-to-face or telephone interviews much but our main goal is to discuss the design of a form or a survey instrument which can be used in self-reported mail surveys, with some modification in telephone surveys as well as interviews and online sources. The section will not discuss the strengths and weaknesses of each data collection method. Generic introductory research methods books that can be found in your schools library contain much of this debate. Here, we would like to address one crucial topic: data collection using a survey instrument (a questionnaire, a form). Survey instruments (questionnaires) are standard forms that can be useful and be adapted easily to a variety of data collection circumstances. The basic principles surrounding questionnaire design are valid whether you conduct a telephone, mail or online survey.

Data collection, according to Salkind (2008) and Rosnow and Rosenthal (1998), consists of four steps: (i) developing an instrument or form that will be used to record information from your sample; (ii) coding the information to be obtained in a most efficient way; (iii) collecting the actual information (data); and (iv) entering the information onto the instrument.

Survey instrument design

How do we know what questions to ask? How many questions shall we ask? How do we ask the right questions? Is there any limit to the number of questions? All these questions will drive the development of the survey instrument before any other design issues are addressed. Recall the discussion in Chapter 1 about the dependent and independent variables and the issues outlined in the Club Ottomans-II case scenario. Your survey instrument needs to contain questions related to your dependent (DV) and independent variables (IVs) that are part of your research questions and hypotheses. Of course, depending upon how these variables are measured, the length of your instrument will change. Again recall the measurement issues discussed in Chapter 4. If, for example, you have one DV measured as a single item, and one IV measured with two items, your questionnaire should contain a minimum of three questions. Typically, we also get information related to subjects' socio-demographic background such as their race, gender, income and education levels. Each of these may be represented by a single question and associated response set. However, we need to make sure that we include all our study variables because they will be used to test the hypotheses we developed. Sometimes we are tempted to ask 'what if we were to find out this or that?', auxiliary questions that are not pertinent to

the main research problem at hand. Experts agree that lengthening the survey instrument unnecessarily would decrease the response rate, plus your professor or advisor or the sponsoring agency may not be interested in the extra information anyway. Just stay focused and obtain as much information as is necessary to test your hypotheses and/or satisfy the purpose of your research objectives. All questions need to match with your hypotheses, dependent and independent variables or your research problem outlined in your proposal.

As we are aware, today's issues are complex and our proposal will perhaps contain variables that are measured at multiple levels and from many different aspects. For example, if you were to measure attitudes toward something, say, local host population of a tourism destination, you will have to develop multiple constructs, each of which may be measured by a battery of items that might take a few pages. Adding one dependent variable, 'satisfaction with the resort', and perhaps another two proxy dependent variable(s) to validate the measurements, such as 'the likelihood of return' and 'word-of mouth', to the instrument along with some socio-demographic background would give you an instrument with a minimum of a few pages. See the Table in Worked Example 6.1 for a questionnaire developed to obtain data in the Club Ottomans-II example. You will also notice that we have included explanatory comments in footnotes that identify problems, give hints and explain common mistakes when designing survey instruments.

When designing a data collection form, instrument or questionnaire, there are several principles that need to be kept in mind. Ideally, we would like the highest possible number of complete returns with the least possible omissions to questions. Although there is no one prescribed way of constructing a data collection instrument, an ideal survey should contain, at the minimum: a cover letter explaining the study and asking for cooperation; a confidentiality statement disclosing expected problems and procedures handling individual's privacy and data protection; enough white-space around the questions; well-thought-out opening questions to spark interest; clear, unbiased, non-leading questions designed at the level of education of the intended target population; sufficient instructions to guide the respondents toward the completion of the survey; and contact information in case of questions and/or complaints. Never assume that the respondents will know how to fill out a survey or how to respond to a scaled battery of items. Do not cram in questions so the questionnaire looks short but crowded; maintain at least 12 point font-type avoiding fancy script designs. Do say 'thank you'. Do pamper the respondents' intelligence where needed. Do not use potentially insulting language. Know the culture of the sample and be sensitive to different religions. Avoid conflicting and double-barrelled questions. Avoid using double negatives when constructing questions and scale items. Make sure that the design looks professional and neat with no grammar and spelling mistakes. Make sure that all possible answer choices are exhausted. When using categories, make sure that all categories are mutually exclusive, that is, one respondent should not be tempted to check two answers.

After designing a draft instrument, do test it using a small group of people, ideally your target sample but practically anyone you can get cooperation from, your fellow classmates, friends, relatives, co-workers, parents and so on. They will need to be instructed to give you feedback in terms of the language, flow, grammar and the clarity of questions (Czaja and Blair, 1996). Our experience dictates (learned the most expensive way!) that we should never print our first draft as our final instrument. Work and rework until you get it right. This is the most important step in your study as you may have only one shot to collect the data; if for some reason you fail to see an obvious problem, or miss something that you should have not missed, pilot testing will allow you to catch mistakes before your data collection. Thus, the data-collection instrument (questionnaire) must be flawless; otherwise, it will be too late for you to do anything if data are collected wrongly. Always check to see whether you included all possible variables of your study; we have seen students who have omitted their dependent variable (the outcome variable, the main purpose of the study). Failure to re-examine your instrument before final printing may give you data that are useless and cannot be remedied in any way.

We usually use surveys in a booklet format with an attractive purposive picture and the university's logo on the title page. We always include some sort of incentive to boost the return rate. When using a battery of items in a scale format, we use shading available in MS Word to make the items to stand out. To break a hallow effect (responding to scale items in similar ways) or the reading habit, we use alternatively worded statements and disperse positively and negatively worded scale items. In summary, the above-mentioned suggestions come from our experiences but there is no one best way of constructing surveys. Sometimes, you need to be very creative in soliciting answers from your respondents. No textbook can give you enough information about designing questionnaires; however, if you were to follow our suggestions you would come very close to creating an instrument that would do the job, namely collecting unbiased, accurate and valid data. Working with your professor and/or his/her assistants and tutors will make you an expert in survey design. Ultimately, your instructor will guide you toward the best possible design for your study. Also, professional companies, such as Qualtrics (http://www.qualtrics.com/) could design questionnaires once the content of the study questionnaire is determined. Now it's time for you to get involved. Start by restating the purpose of your study. What is your dependent and independent variable? Have you operationalized them yet? If yes, transfer them onto your survey instrument. Check for omissions, language and design following our suggestions above. You can now move to the next step: creating a coding for the instrument in preparation for data entry.

Coding

What is coding? How do we code our instrument? Coding refers to the process of data transfer from original survey instrument into a computer program in a format that is easier for computer manipulation and analysis (Czaja and Blair, 1996; Salkind, 1997). In essence, what we are trying to do is assign numbers to data entries so we speed up the data entry and analysis by saving space. For example, recording a five-point agree/disagree type of Likert scale, assigning 1 to strongly disagree and 5 strongly agree, will save you valuable space, and speed up the data entry and analysis. Categorical variables, such as the gender of a person, male or female is typically recorded as 1 representing male and 2 representing female. If you are running a regression analysis, recording zero for one category, such as zero for female and 1 for the male, is a better way for coding dichotomous variables that can take on two values. Recording like this would enable you to run two regression analyses separately for males and females if needed. Coding of other socio-demographical variables such as employment, education, age and income using numbers is the norm; however, you must be careful not to be fooled by or tempted to calculate a mean of an inherently categorical variable. How would you respond to a question: what is the average gender of the sample? If you ask the computer to calculate a mean (average) for gender, the computer will do that. But how meaningful is this generated number? What does, for example, a mean gender value of 1.33 mean? Nothing! We cannot do this, as the variable gender is categorical in nature and hence no statistics other than frequency distribution or percentage can be calculated for this variable. When coding, typically computer programs we use, Excel, SPPS, or SAS, will allow you to qualify those numbers. You can, for example, label the variables and add any description you want.

Practical Applications in Mail Surveys

Mails surveys are becoming a thing of the past, a rare method used by the larger research community. However, the cost and availability of high-quality sampling frames still make them attractive to researchers who would like to generalize their findings to a larger population but do not want to use other costly methods such as face-to-face interviews or telephone surveys. A well carried out mail survey can generate an acceptable response rate. However, reaching an acceptable response rate is not easy; it requires several rounds of mailing and re-mailing. According to the renowned Dilman's (1978) Total Design Method, mailings of surveys start with an initial contact (postcard notice) that describes and seeks cooperation for an incoming survey study. This initial contact is followed by immediate first-class mailings of the survey instruments along with a cover letter. After 2 weeks, a postcard reminder is sent followed by a second round of mailing containing a new cover letter and the survey. A final mailing can include overnight mail or registered mail for which a potential respondent makes a trip to a post office to pick up the survey.

This method combined with an attractive, clear survey design enhanced with incentives might produce enough response for you to decide to cut off the study after the first or second round of mailings. This process can be long, and might

make you nervous. You will have to develop a procedure for tracking mailing dates, coding return dates and addresses so you do not mail the same survey to people who've already responded. For a typical classroom project, we do not recommend mail surveys, although we did have students who wanted to produce generalizable results and ended up completing their projects on time. Typically, a mail survey would last as long as 3–5 months. Even then, there is no guarantee that you will have enough returns. To obtain responses to key questions, hence identifying the presence of non-response bias, you might need to resort to contacting non-respondents directly using phones. Nevertheless, in the field of leisure, recreation and tourism, you will see many researchers still resorting to mail surveys because of availability of representative sampling frames and cost issues.

Akin to mail surveys, online surveys have become very popular since the advent and upsurge of Internet use in the past two decades.

Online Internet surveys and use of panels

In the past two decades, we have seen a tremendous increase in Internet use and computer-mediated communication. Advances in computer technology and applications have created new opportunities for researchers to communicate with research subjects. Computer-assisted interviews, voice-activated telephone interviews, text-message surveys, e-mail surveys, fax surveys, and online self-administered questioners are very common data collection devices in today's research environment. Each with its advantages and disadvantages has to be considered as an alternate data generation instrument. The technology for online survey research is still evolving. Until recently, creating and conducting an online survey was a time-consuming task, requiring familiarity with web-authoring programs, HTML code and scripting programs (Wright, 2005). Today, survey authoring software packages and online survey services make online survey research much easier and faster. Most of you may have even used some of these means of generating data in your other classes. You are probably familiar with SurveyMonkey (http://www.surveymonkey.com/) and SuperSurvey (http://www.supersurvey.com/). In this section of the chapter, our goal is to focus on Internet surveys and briefly discuss advantages and disadvantages of using them. We can define an Internet survey as a self-administered questionnaire posted on a website and completed interactively.

As you recall, self-administered manual surveys take a considerable amount of time to create, distribute and collect, not to mention the amount of time and effort required to get the desired result from it. One of the major advantages of online Internet surveys is their speed and cost-effectiveness. Internet surveys allow us to research a large audience and thus help us to solve the distribution and data collection problems in a great manner. Collecting data starts even within minutes after the survey is activated. Online surveys are much faster than the traditional printed surveys. Most of the studies show that the respondents reply to online surveys within 48 h. Another benefit of the online surveys is that e-mail surveys cost 30–50% less than traditional surveys in which the surveys are printed and mailed to the individuals. There are a number of online survey companies available on the Internet and they are able to provide much cheaper options. Naturally, you get the results faster and this in turn reduces research time and effort. Online self-administered questionnaires can be visually very attractive. You can adjust backgrounds, add colour and animation to make the questionnaire interesting and appealing. Visual appeal and interactivity may also increase respondents' cooperation and willingness to do the questionnaire. This may also help increase responses. Companies such Qualtrics (http://www.qualtrics.com/) can provide help in designing online questionnaires. Several other companies such as Zoomerang (http://www.zoomerang.com/) can create surveys for different markets, analyse results, and provide panels and lists of email addresses for sampling. Other companies such as Newfangled (http://www.newfangled.com/) has a website survey application with the ability to create unlimited custom online surveys using the simple NewfangledCMS interface. The use of online surveys will continue to grow.

Disadvantages of online survey research include uncertainty over the validity of the data and sampling issues, issues of time and space, and concerns surrounding the design, implementation and evaluation of an online survey. If you as a researcher want to keep a survey on the provider's server for an extended period of time (such as more than a year), this costs extra. In addition, some online survey providers often charge more for longer surveys and when the number of respondents exceeds a certain amount.

Purchased software, in contrast, generally does not have space or response number restrictions.

One of the key challenges of Internet surveys lies in the area of sample representation. Naturally, the nature of the population to be studied, the purpose of the research and the sampling methods are necessary considerations in determining the quality of Internet samples (Zikmund *et al.*, 2008). A questionnaire that is made available to anyone who voluntarily fills out a questionnaire is not likely to be representative of the study population. The online survey also has to target the study population within the boundaries of the scope of the study. Researchers who use a company's e-mail lists to generate a sample are limited by the quality of this type of sampling frame. In cases where a company uses the same lists again and again for different clients, the individuals who receive the advertisements about a survey on these lists may become weary of being targeted by multiple surveys, and this could negatively impact response rates (Wright, 2005).

It is a common belief that Internet users tend to be younger, better educated and more affluent than the general population. Thus, you as a researcher should be aware of potential sampling problems that may stem from the nature people who use the computer frequently. Let's remember that there is no best form of survey, each has advantages and disadvantages. We have to determine the best form of survey on the basis of our particular study purpose, needs and resources.

Researchers also use panel samples to conduct surveys. Either using a mail survey or electronic questionnaire, researchers can generate data. It is known that sampling from a panel yields a high response rate. Often panel members are compensated for their time and effort through cash- or product-based incentives. Panels are usually representative of a select group, e.g. US consumers, businesses and the like. Panels can be very large in their coverage of individuals and businesses. Thus, these databases as panels would allow the researcher to draw a simple random sample, stratified samples and quota samples from panel members (Zikmund *et al.*, 2008). Drawing a probability sample from an established consumer panel is a popular and effective method for creating a sample of Internet users as well. It is not unusual in academia that some researchers may also outsource part of their data collection to a research company that may simply collect the data from its panel based on the screening questions that the research may provide.

Key Terms

Census: A survey of an entire population.

Coding: The process of data transfer from the original survey instrument into a computer program in a format that is easier for computer manipulation and analysis (Salkind, 1997).

Generalizability: The extent to which research findings can be applied to the population in general.

Internet survey: A self-administered questionnaire posted on a website and completed interactively.

Panel: Usually representative of a select group, e.g. US consumers, businesses and the like.

Non-respondents: Individuals who choose not to participate in a survey.

Parameter: Some characteristic of a population (Jaeger, 1983). It is the summary description of a given variable in a population (Babbie, 1986).

Population: Any collect of objects or entities that have at least one characteristic in common (Jaeger, 1983). In leisure recreation and tourism research, our population may consist of individuals, households or entities.

Probability sample: All members of the population have an equal chance of being selected in the sample (Babbie, 1986).

Representative sample: The aggregate characteristics of the sample closely approximate the same aggregate characteristics of the population (Babbie, 1986).

Sample: A part of a population . . . consisting of those objects or people we have observed or measured (Jaeger, 1983).

Sampling frame: The actual set of population units (individuals, households, entities) from which we draw our sample.

Discussion Questions

1. What are the principles of survey research?

2. What is the importance of sampling in research?

3. Compare and contrast probability and non-probability sampling?

4. How do you determine a sampling frame for a given study that is done by a mail survey? What are the advantages/disadvantages of a mail survey?

5. What are the advantages/disadvantages of an Internet survey?

Useful Websites

Site Name: SurveyMonkey
URL: http://www.surveymonkey.com/
Site Name: SuperSurvey
URL: http://www.supersurvey.com/
Site Name: Qualtrics
URL: http://www.qualtrics.com/
Site Name: Zoomerang
URL: http://www.zoomerang.com/
Site Name: Newfangled
URL: http://www.newfangled.com/
Site Name: Wilkins Research Center
URL: http://www.wilkinsresearch.net/

Worked Example 6.1. An Analysis of a Questionnaire

Vacation Expectations and Experiences of Guests to Club Ottomans-II

This survey is being conducted to obtain visitors' opinions about various aspects of their shopping and travel experiences in City X, Country Y. Your assistance in completing this survey is crucial. The survey will not take more than 15 minutes of your time.

YOUR CHANCE OF WINNING A MINI VACATION!
AND CASH[1]

☺

(SEE DETAILS INSIDE)

In cooperation with and sponsored by
The University XYZ

Address and the University Logo[2]

GOT A MINUTE?
TELL US HOW WE'RE DOING?

Dear Guest

Thank you for selecting our resort as your destination. We know that continued customer satisfaction is the key to success. With that in mind, we invite your comments and suggestions regarding our SERVICE, ACTIVITIES and FOOD. We want to make your vacation experience as enjoyable as possible. Your responses will be kept strictly confidential.[3]

Why participate?

You are one of 800 possible respondents representing the entire 120,000 visitors vacationing in our Club Ottomans-II. Our goal is to use this information to improve vacation and travel experiences of guests like you and provide guidance for future Club management policy and practices. This is an excellent opportunity to voice your opinions.

Your personal opinion is important

In order to answer these questions, you don't have to be an 'expert'. We are confident that everyone will be able to take part, not just those with strong views or particular viewpoints. Please remember that there is no right or wrong responses to the questions and that your thoughtful answers are appreciated. Your participation is entirely voluntary. The information you provide will be *kept confidential,* final results of the research will not reveal the respondent's identity because the responses from all study participants will be added together in the final analysis. The data collected will be destroyed soon after a report is written.

By completing this survey, you will be automatically entered into a draw for a mini vacation[4] (airfare and all-inclusive vacation) in one of our Clubs throughout the world for a week. Also, every respondent will receive $100 coupon toward their next vacation in our resorts. Please write your name and address along with your e-mail on the back of this survey.

Please contact us if you have any questions regarding this study. When you have finished the questionnaire, please return[5] your completed questionnaire to Club Ottomans-II management[6] using prestamped envelope. Your name will be entered in a lottery for a free 5-day vacation at any of the Club Ottomans' resorts.[7]

Insert researcher's (your name) name or the contact person's name and address
And a thank you note

1. We appreciate your opinion on the following (please check boxes below).[8] (Alternatively, we could have the following: 'Please indicate the degree to which you agree or disagree with the following statements')

(Overall service quality)	Very dissatisfied	Dissatisfied	Neither satisfied nor dissatisfied	Satisfied	Very satisfied[9]
ACTIVITIES					
Nightlife opportunities	1	2	3	4	5
Types of recreational activities	1	2	3	4	5
Activities for singles	1	2	3	4	5
Activities for couples	1	2	3	4	5
Activities for kids					
QUALITY OF FOOD					
Taste	1	2	3	4	5
Eye-appeal presentation	1	2	3	4	5
Freshness of food served	1	2	3	4	5
Nutritional content[10]	1	2	3	4	5
STAFF ATTITUDES					
Friendliness of our employees	1	2	3	4	5
Courtesy of our employees	1	2	3	4	5
Promptness of our employees to your needs	1	2	3	4	5
Speed of service	1	2	3	4	5

2. Compared to service received and price paid, how would you rate your vacation at Club Ottomans? (Please check one)
Low in value ☐   *Somewhat low in value* ☐   *Somewhat high in value* ☐   *High in value* ☐[11]

3. Overall, how satisfied were you with your vacation experience at Club Ottomans. (Check one)
Very dissatisfied ☐   *Somewhat dissatisfied* ☐   *Somewhat satisfied* ☐   *Very satisfied* ☐

4. Would you recommend our resort to your friends and relatives?
    (Check one)
Definitely not ☐   *Probably not* ☐   *Probably yes* ☐   *Definitely yes* ☐   *I just don't know* ☐

5. How likely is it you would come back to vacation in one of our Clubs?

	Highly unlikely	Somewhat unlikely	Neutral	Somewhat likely	Highly likely
Based on your vacation experiences in our Club Ottomans-II, how likely[12] is it that you would come back to vacation at one of our Clubs?	1	2	3	4	5

6. Please indicate the level of your agreement with the following statements on a Likert scale where 4 means strongly agree and 1 strongly disagree.

(Attitudes of locals)	Strongly disagree	Disagree	Agree[13]	Strongly agree
I think locals are very friendly toward tourists	1	2	3	4[14]
I think locals resent tourists	1	2	3	4
I feel welcomed in this community	1	2	3	4

Background Information

In this section, we would like to know you, our customer. Please check the appropriate box.

7. Are you male or female? Male ☐ Female ☐

8. What year were you born? _____ [15]

9. Please indicate your nationality. (_____)

Note: Alternatively we can also simply provide a list of possible response categories that would capture the majority of the visitor market to Club Ottomans-II. In this case, the list could be quite long. Along with a list of possible response categories, you will also include 'Other'. Use your judgment.

10. Please indicate your approximate household income before taxes (from all sources)?[16] _____

11. What category best describes your current employment status? (*Check one*)

☐ Employed full-time ☐ Employed part-time
☐ Full-time homemaker ☐ Student
☐ Retired ☐ Not currently employed

Other (be specific) _____

12. What is the highest level of formal education you have completed? (*Check one*)

☐ 10 years or less ☐ Graduated from 4-year college or university
☐ 11–13 years ☐ Some graduate school
☐ Some college ☐ A graduate degree
☐ A degree from a 2-year college or school ☐ Other: _____

Please return your completed survey to ……..[17]

If we have not covered things that you consider important, use the space below for additional comments[18]

THANK YOU

[1] Some would question the ethics of offering such a reward and potentiality of biasing response rate in favour of people who value these things.

[2] An official logo from an institute like a university will increase the credibility, thus the response rate.

[3] Depending upon the institution you are in, you will have standard language that could be inserted here that makes references to confidentiality or anonymity of responses. A typical classroom project is exempt from Institutional Review Board's (IRB) full examination. IRB is the official body that tries to protect individuals in human subject research. If you are to survey minors or confined populations such as prisoners the rules are more stringent. Your proposal will go to the review by the full IRB board.

[4] You need to disclose the odds of winning the vacation.

[5] They will not return it unless you pay for the postage. So, include a self-return prepaid envelope to make it easier for people to return. If this is an online survey, then it is not a problem. In either case, you will need to send a reminder (a post-card for the mail survey and an e-mail reminder for the Internet survey).

[6] This will not be viewed as an independent assessor. A better choice would be a third, independent, party such as a university.

[7] Let the respondents know what to do with the survey after completing.

[8] Always guide your respondent. Never assume that they know how to fill in this questionnaire.

[9] Likert scale items measure intensity and give the researcher variance needed in quantitative data analysis and use of sophisticated statistical tools. % point is the norm but you will see 7-point or 10-point scales.

[10] Do you and I understand nutritional content the same way as your potential respondents will? This is the question of validity. You need to make sure that each item measures what it intends to measure and nothing else. If not, you will need to create new items or explain it the way you want your respondents to understand. Remember validity is the most important issue when creating measurements.

[11] The design of the scale is almost up to the researcher's taste. We do use shades when using battery items in order to create visual effect that would help differentiate one box from the next. Also, we use 5-point scales with 3 signifying neutral or neither/nor. It is also a good idea to offer a 'no answer' choice.

[12] You will notice that we have included extra questions to establish validity of the dependent variable. We would expect that highly satisfied customers would want to return to the resort and/or recommend it to their friends and relatives.

[13] It's better to have a 5-point scale with a neutral point (3), thus you need to insert another box with neither/nor (3).

[14] This is an example of an attitude measure. By no means do we claim these to be valid and reliable measures. It is presented here for instructional purposes. Attitude measurement is one of the most researched areas in social science research. Typically you might see 30 to 60 items that measure several aspects of an attitude. Also, notice that the second item needs to be reverse-coded to align it with the two items that are positively worded. In addition, rather than having a 4-point scale, you may consider having a 5-point scale.

[15] Unless you are interested in exact age of your respondents, it's better to provide age categories rather that asking for the birth year. This way you will exactly know how old people are, but people don't like to reveal their ages, do you?

[16] People do not like to be questioned about their income. They might think that you will report them the tax agency of your country. Assuring confidentiality might help. Since the market of Club Ottomans-II is rather international in its make-up, it is not logical to have a list of possible categories of household income levels expressed in one particular currency unit such as $ or Euro. If the household income is expressed in one particular currency unit, say, US$, other nationalities whose currencies are not in US$, may feel uncomfortable to respond to the chosen currency unit. If the questionnaire is intended for one country or nationality, then expressing household income levels in that country's currency unit would make sense. Remember to exhaust all response options

and make sure that all response categories are mutually exclusive. We place questions related to place socio-demographic information to the last page.

[17] Remind them what to do with the completed questionnaire. Show your human side. They sacrificed their time for you. So a 'thank you' note is in order.

[18] People like to be asked their opinion. Sometimes, you will uncover issues that you could not with close ended questions. Sometimes, you may not even analyse these. Typically you should reserve at least a half page for comments so you give a chance to your subjects to utter their opinions and reactions. As you have noticed the instrument looks very crowded right now, you should avoid this as much as you can. The more white space the better it looks. A larger font needs to be used too. You will also come across nasty or insulting comments. Don't get discouraged if the respondents don't like what you are doing or take it a step further to even complain to your superior. It's the nature of survey research. Do you think we have left enough space for this to happen?

References and Further Reading

Babbie, E. (1986) *The Practice of Social Research,* 4th edn. Wadsworth Publishing, Belmont, California.

Babbie, E.R. (1990) *Survey Research Methods,* 2nd edn. Wadsworth Publishing Company- Cengage Learning, Inc., Florence, Kentucky.

Czaja, R. and Blair, J. (1996) *Designing Surveys*. Pine Forge Press, Thousand Oaks, California.

Dillman, D.A. (1978) *Mail and Telephone Surveys: The Total Design Method*. Wiley & Sons, New York.

Jaeger, R. (1983) *Statistics: A Spectator Sport*. Sage Publications, Beverley Hills, California.

Katzer, J., Cook, K.H. and Crouch, W.W. (1982) *Evaluating Information: A Guide for Users of Social Science Information,* 2nd edn. Random House, New York.

Leedy, P.D. and Ormrod, J.E. (2001) *Practical Research*, 7th edn. Merrill Prentice Hall, Upper Saddle River, New Jersey.

Rosnow, R. and Rosenthal, R. (1998) *Beginning Behavioral Research*, 3rd edn. Prentice Hall, Upper Saddle River, New Jersey.

Salkind, J.N. (2008) *Exploring Research*, 7th edition. Prentice Hall, Princeton, New Jersey.

Wright, K.B. (2005) Researching Internet-based populations: Advantages and disadvantages of online survey research, online questionnaire authoring software packages, and web survey services. *Journal of Computer-Mediated Communication* 10, article 11. http://jcmc.indiana.edu/vol10/issue3/wright.html

Zikmund, G.W., Babin, J.B., Carr, C.J. and Griffin, M. (2008) *Business Research Methods*. South-Western, Cengage Learning, Mason, Ohio.

chapter 7

Qualitative Research in Leisure, Recreation and Tourism

Edward Ruddell

Learning Objectives

After reading and studying this chapter you should be able to:

1. Describe the key differences between qualitative and quantitative research;
2. Describe the key advantages of qualitative research;
3. Distinguish between emic and etic perspectives;
4. Describe under what conditions qualitative or quantitative research would be most appropriate;
5. List and describe four qualitative research techniques.

Chapter Summary

This chapter describes the broad family of techniques called qualitative research methods. Although the specific techniques vary, there are some over-arching themes that unite qualitative methods into one larger family. Qualitative research focuses on descriptions based in kind rather than in quantity. It emphasizes the meanings people construct surrounding events in their lives. It also emphasizes the importance of understanding those meanings as they are embedded in context. The perspective is **emic** rather than **etic**. As such, text rather than numbers is its primary data source. Finally, its approach is inductive and interpretive rather than deductive. Qualitative methods take extensive training to master and are time consuming to conduct. However, the effort to conduct such research can be engaging and exciting as one frequently feels on the edge of discovery. Indeed, qualitative research is a powerful and engaging tool for understanding the local, lived experience of a person's meaning making.

A Little Word Play

One of the most common ways of describing the difference between qualitative and quantitative research is that qualitative research is based on words while quantitative research is based on numbers. Although largely true in practice, this distinction is a bit superficial. Nevertheless, in the tradition of western thought, two of the oldest and longest-standing categories of knowledge are quantity and quality. The origins for this development can be found in the teachings of Socrates and writings of Plato. These categories get further development in Aristotle's epistemological (study of knowledge) and logical writings. Thus, the distinction between quality and quantity is as ancient as it is fundamental.

It is sometimes informative to trace a word's origins to get a sense of its long-standing and deepest meanings. If we did so for the idea's quality and quantity, we would find that the origins of each term are derived directly from Latin, but are influenced by Greek notions of these categories. Our word 'qualitative' derives from the Latin *qualis*, a term meaning 'of what kind'. Conversely, our word 'quantitative' comes from the Latin *quantus*, meaning 'how great'. From these word origins we get a sense of the difference between qualitative and quantitative research. Qualitative research focuses on differences in kind; quantitative research focuses on differences (often expressed as variance) represented by quantity. From this brief historical tour we should also get a sense that the qualitative/quantitative distinction in inquiry is much older than we often realize.

The ancient civilizations considered quality to be something separate from the thing itself being studied. That is, qualities describe properties of a thing that differ in kind. Qualitative research does not seek to describe the essence of a thing, but seeks to describe properties associated with a phenomenon in question with an emphasis on kind rather than number. Perhaps these ideas explain why words are such an enchanting source of data in qualitative research.

Like quality and quantity, our modern word 'analysis' has Greek origins. 'Analysis' derives from a Greek compound *ana* which means 'up' and *luein* which means 'to loosen'. Thus, *analuein* means to get on top of a problem and 'undo' it. In qualitative research this is often done by collecting huge amounts of verbal data. Even in the simplest qualitative study, transcripts and field notes can run into hundreds of pages full of richness and complexity. By 'undoing' the confusing complexity of such data we identify themes and simplify them into categories. Incidentally, the word 'category' also has Greek origins. 'Category' is from the Greek compound *kata* which means 'against' and *agora* which means 'assembly'. Assembly means to gather, collect, or put together. Thus, category literally means against assembling into a larger whole. To create a category is to divide a whole into smaller parts for the purpose of analysis or loosening things up

so as to understand them better. This brief excursion into the word origins associated with the term 'qualitative research' should suggest that qualitative research is far more than 'word play'.

Introduction

This chapter will first describe qualitative research as a family of techniques that seek to describe phenomena associated with differences in kind (not quantity) based on verbal data. Following that, a few of the most important advantages and disadvantages of qualitative research will be listed and described. Following that, the four most commonly used qualitative methods in leisure, recreation and tourism will be described.

A word of caution is in order here. There is no single qualitative research method. There are several. Much complexity can be added to qualitative research through the use of multiple methods in combination. Further, qualitative methods can be used alongside quantitative methods. To get a sense of how large and extensive the body of literature on qualitative research is, it might be noted that several excellent book-length treatments of qualitative methods exist. Among the more popular of such books are Patton's (2002) 600-page textbook which gives an extensive treatment of qualitative methods with an emphasis on evaluation research, Denzin and Lincoln's (1998, 2003) three-volume series on qualitative research, Strauss and Corbin's (1998) treatment of qualitative methods with an emphasis on grounded theory, Lindof and Taylor's (2002) treatment of qualitative methods in communication research, and Henderson's (2006) treatment of qualitative methods in leisure, recreation and tourism. In addition, book-length texts exist for single approaches to qualitative research. Among the best known are Spradley's (1980) treatment of participant observation, Krueger's (1988) treatment of focus groups, Yin's (2003) book on case study research, and Miles and Huberman's (1994) book on analysing qualitative research data. Since there are book-length treatments of qualitative methods generally, as well as for specialist topics, this should suggest that no single chapter can possibly do justice to the enormity and complexity of topic. At best, a chapter such as this can provide only an overview and brief introduction to this family of research methods.

Qualitative Research Described

Qualitative research methods can be likened to a large, extended, and frequently squabbling family. There is no single monolithic qualitative method. In fact, the family is so large that its members are claimed by researchers of widely varying epistemological stances. Among those claiming qualitative methods are positivists, post-positivists, interpretivists, social constructionists, and post-modernists. As each of these paradigm stances claims qualitative methods as its own, they in turn shape the nature of the methods. Thus, how a positivist using participant observation would collect and interpret qualitative data would be different from how a social constructionist would use the same approach. Also, like defining a large and extended family, few writers attempt to define directly what qualitative research is. Some textbook writers start with vivid examples of qualitative research, and then work toward a descriptive characterization of this family of techniques. Others work *via negativa*, that is, they start with what qualitative methods are not. Essentially, these writers claim that qualitative research is that which collects and analyses data that is non-quantitative. Such data might include interview transcripts, behavioural observations, observations of site characteristics such as vandalism or gang graffiti, film, videotape or websites. A final definitional strategy is to enumerate the purposes of qualitative research and show how such research is different from traditional quantitative research. Very important in these definitional strategies is the importance of preserving context, of emphasizing the role of focusing on meaning from the participant's point of view, and emphasizing how qualitative methods allow for detailed and rich descriptions of phenomena that summary statistics (such as mean scores) cannot capture. In sum, qualitative research is a mode of inquiry that seeks to emphasize differences in kind over differences in quantity. Data are in the form of words and among its purposes is emphasis on describing and understanding meaning, preserving context, and providing rich description.

Advantages of qualitative research

Because the qualitative approach to research is fundamentally different from that of quantitative research, it offers several advantages. Many of these advantages are overlapping and interrelated. The most important of these advantages are listed below:

- Qualitative methods are particularly good at deriving meaning. Although the world is full of behaviours, objects, constraints, choices, relations among variables and facts, these things that are the objects of quantitative research, are never stand-alone phenomena that exist strictly 'outside of us'. Humans are interpretive animals and are always imposing meaning even on the most 'objective' of facts. It is this meaning that qualitative research is particularly good at capturing, cataloguing, describing and preserving.

- Qualitative methods are particularly good at eliciting the **emic**. Emic refers to the 'insider' perspective. Not only are qualitative methods good at preserving meaning, they are also good at capturing, describing, displaying and preserving such meaning from the perspective of those whose lives are being studied. This is opposed to an **etic** or 'outsider' perspective that is characteristic of quantitative research. When the purpose of the research is to be able to view peoples' meaning making from their own points of view, the emic stance of much qualitative research is a powerful advantage.

- Because of their ability to capture emic meaning making, qualitative methods are frequently celebrated as **verstehen**. Verstehen refers to 'empathetic understanding'. It recognizes that humans are not sterile objects of study but are a swirl of emotions, passions, desires, thoughts, beliefs, anticipations, deliberations, all of which come in layers of cultural context that, in turn, influence meaning making and behaviour. Qualitative researchers adopt a stance of verstehen, and in doing so collect data that speak to the complexity of lived experience.

- Because of the verstehen attitude, qualitative research is good at collecting, describing, interpreting and preserving the context from which meaning making is derived and behaviour is influenced.

- Context is rarely, if ever, universal. Rather it is local. Qualitative methods are good at helping researchers describe and understand how local contexts influence meaning making and shape behaviour. The emphasis on local context is frequently described as **idiographic** rather than **nomothetic**. The term idiographic is a compound of the Greek prefix '*idios*' meaning 'own', 'personal', or 'private', hence unique, and '*graphikos*' signifying 'writing' or, later, 'picture'. The idiographic means to make a picture – in words – of the unique or local. This is opposed to the nomothetic, derived from the Greek word '*nomos*' which meant 'law', thus the attempt to draw universal law-like statements. This latter idea is the ideal goal of quantitative research. Qualitative research is good at eliciting, describing and understanding how meaning making is embedded in local context rather than stripped of local context to aid in the process of testing universal law-like propositions.

- Because qualitative research is emic and contextual, it is particularly good at eliciting serendipitous findings. Traditional quantitative research, because it emphasizes etically derived (researcher-driven) hypothesis testing, often fails to generate data that allows for serendipitous findings.

- Because serendipitous findings frequently accompany qualitative research it offers another advantage and that is it can generate new theoretical insights.

Disadvantages of qualitative research

Aside from the several advantages that qualitative research offers, it does have weaknesses. A few of the important ones are highlighted below:

- Qualitative methods are labour intensive. Data collection often lasts from months to years. Further, mounds of field notes or interview transcripts can easily lead to data overload and, in turn, take many more months to process and analyse.

- Qualitative research continues to suffer from nagging questions about sampling. In quantitative research, probability sampling is the norm. Probability sampling is a powerful way to ensure that a sample is truly representative of a population of interest. As such, generalizations can be legitimately made from a sample to a population. **Purposive sampling** is generally the method of choice in qualitative research. As the name implies, cases are

selected for a specific purpose related to the research. Sample sizes are usually very small and cases are chosen, not because they are representative, but because they are information rich and thus, add to the larger story. As such, confidence in generalizability can be weak.

- Data in qualitative research are usually in the form of words. Although words preserve richness, they are, in themselves, ambiguous. Such ambiguity of words in natural language is an avenue (some might say highway) for researcher bias to enter into the research. The term 'researcher-as-instrument' reflects this idea that the researcher's understanding of terms, coloured by his or her own personal contexts, very much can influence a study's results. After all, the researcher must interpret meaning from both text and context. Unlike quantitative research, qualitative research is still struggling with developing well-agreed-upon standards of analysis to protect against researcher bias.

- In reported research, analysis methods are rarely reported in sufficient detail. Readers frequently cannot figure out how the researcher got from reams of transcripts or field notes to the final conclusions. As such, results are frequently not replicable and the reader is asked to accept the conclusions almost as an act of faith.

The above summary of advantages and disadvantages should help provide a sense of when qualitative methods are best used or not used. The next section will provide an overview of how the research is done.

Doing Qualitative Research – the Overall Process

Although the several methods of qualitative research vary in their detail, many qualitative researchers describe an overall process that involves four stages. These stages are entry, data collection, analysis, and reporting. Each of these will be described in turn.

Entry

When doing qualitative research on organizations, programmes, organized communities or events, it is often important to 'gain entry' into the situation before actual data collection can begin. Gaining entry can be as simple as sitting in the stands of a spectator event where no permission is required to having to gain permission from key gatekeepers. Patton (2002) describes gaining entry as a two-phased process. Phase one comprises negotiation with gatekeepers. Phase two is actual physical entry into the scene itself. Assuming one has been granted permission to gain entry, negotiation with gatekeepers centres on rules and conditions for data collection. Key items for discussion might include how to gain entry into the scene, how to develop trust and rapport with those being studied and how to do so without compromising the integrity of the study. This can be particularly challenging with evaluation research because people often feel uneasy about being evaluated. One technique for mitigating issues of trust and for gaining rapport is to describe the study's purpose to those being studied in non-threatening language. Another technique is to use the 'known sponsor approach'. In the known sponsor approach a gatekeeper with legitimate authority publicly grants permission and seeks to establish trust. As one example of this approach, I, as a researcher, was asked to interview concession employees about their experiences and sense of community at Yosemite National Park for the purposes of writing a social impact assessment. The president of Yosemite Park and Curry Company (the Yosemite concession at the time) wrote a letter to concession employees explaining that a researcher would request interviews of them, explained the purpose of the interviews, and asked that they participate and give full and honest answers. Thus, my entry into the Yosemite concession community was facilitated by the legitimacy and authority of the company president.

The second phase of gaining entry involves two things – managing your own uncertainty and managing the uncertainty of those being studied. Entering into new surroundings as a stranger can be a stressful and emotionally draining experience. As a researcher you may find yourself wondering if you are behaving properly. You might spend a lot of mental and emotional energy searching for cues for how to behave. You may also spend a lot of mental and emotional energy wondering how those being studied are judging you. You may wonder whether you will be able to gain enough trust and rapport to gather the data you need to successfully carry out the study. It is helpful to recognize that all field workers go through these anxieties and to recognize that by acting with good character and integrity, with patience and time, trust and rapport will be established and such anxieties will subside. With regard to managing the uncertainties of those being studied, it is often a good idea not to stand out too much or too early. It may also be useful to time more sensitive or stressful data collection episodes to later parts of the study. The researcher may need to appear to not be collecting data at all for a while. The researcher may simply need to be seen by those being studied. For example, one researcher conducting ethnographic research on cultural impacts of tourism in a small indigenous community in China obtained permission to live with one family in the community. For several weeks she lived with the family and participated in the life of the community before being more obvious about her research efforts. In-depth interviews were delayed until the trust and rapport of community members had been established.

Data collection

Data collection refers to those activities designed to determine what constitutes data for a particular study, who or what to gather those data from, and the techniques for gathering such data. Because data overload is an easy trap to fall into, some sideboards should be established before data collection begins. Perhaps the most important activity for bounding data collection is to formulate specific research questions. Research questions should be consistent with the study's purpose, yet provide enough focus to help the researcher determine what constitutes relevant data. There is no magic formula for writing good research questions in qualitative research. However, a good place to start in formulating research questions is to consider the role of breadth in the context of your study purpose. Ask yourself, 'is the research question so broad that it fails to focus my data collection efforts?' 'Is the research question so narrow that it sets boundaries too narrow to accomplish my study's purpose?' Parameters for helping ask research questions include **settings**, that is, physical or social surroundings associated with a phenomenon of interest; **actors**, that is, the major personalities and figures surrounding the phenomenon; **events**, that is, the actions that take place surrounding a phenomenon; **processes**, that is, steps through which a phenomenon unfolds. More than one of these parameters may be used in formulating questions for any one project. Let's take one example from a study of cultural impacts of tourism. A researcher is interested in the identity politics of touristic festival performances in a minority ethnic enclave in China. Identity politics refers to the ways that people negotiate identities (accept and reject) because identities are, in part, foisted on us by others. The purpose of the study was to understand how cultural performances serve in the identity politics of a minority ethnic enclave. A research question that would help determine what constitutes data in this study might be 'how are public performances and private performances of a ritual dance similar and different?' 'Are those differences meaningful in preserving cultural identities and if so, how?' These questions would suggest that what constitute data are variations in festival performances; such differences might include elements of dance that are omitted, subtle differences in costume, gesture and tempo. Data might also include interview transcripts from community elders expounding on how elements of performance speak to cultural identity.

A second key element in data collection is sampling. In qualitative research, sampling is nearly always purposive. Cases are chosen because they are information rich; not because they are representative of a larger population. As with parameters for developing research questions, the same parameters of settings, actors, events and processes can be used for sampling. That is, one or more of the parameters can be sampled. What constitutes richness varies from study to study. In one study the researcher may want to focus on key informants. These are individuals with either inside knowledge or special expertise. In another study the researcher may be interested in a wide breadth of participants. In yet another study the researcher may find a pattern emerging from the data and single out **negative cases**, that is, those persons or events that contradict the emerging pattern. Such cases help tell a larger and more complete story. In qualitative research, sampling often ends when one of two things happens: either resources or time are exhausted (this often happens with funded contract research such as evaluation studies), or **data saturation** is reached. Data saturation means that no new information is forthcoming when one continues to collect more data.

Techniques of data collection vary depending on the kind of method being used. However, key skills in the repertoire of the qualitative researcher include interviewing techniques and the ability to collect adequate field notes.

Analysis

Common to nearly all research in the behavioural sciences, both quantitative and qualitative, are the following four steps of analysis: categorizing, ordering, manipulating and summarizing. The purpose of such analysis is not to recapitulate the world, but to reduce it in order to draw meaning. In qualitative research, categorizing often refers to identifying and pulling out the main themes or categories from a body of verbal data. Ordering means to place those categories in relation to each other; in doing so, one can look for relations among themes such as same or different, and subordinate to superordinate. Manipulating refers to making data displays and matrices in order to see more complex relations among categories. Summarizing refers to making meaning from the above steps.

A key difference between qualitative and quantitative research is that in qualitative research data collection and analysis occur simultaneously. The reason for this is that as patterns and themes emerge from the initial data, such patterns and themes suggest topics to follow up on and who to sample. For example, one may not be able to identity a key informant until a pattern of data emerges that suggests a topic for which someone might be a key informant. One cannot ferret out negative cases until one knows what an emerging pattern is.

Essentially, qualitative data analysis involves reading and re-reading either transcripts, field notes or other data sources and looking for themes in the data. Such themes are often called categories. For some research projects, category identification and description is sufficient. For more sophisticated projects, categories are placed in relation to each other and interpretation of larger meaning is made. For yet more sophisticated projects, these interpretations are made from the lens of theory. That is, existing theory helps frame the interpretation and at the same time the data inform modifications to the theory. In some approaches, such as in grounded theory (Glaser and Strauss, 1999), data, perhaps across several studies, help to generate theory. Beyond these broad ideas the two most concrete activities involved in data analysis are: (i) coding and 'memoing'; and (ii) developing data displays.

Coding and writing memos is a crucial part of data analysis. **Memos** are essentially notes to oneself. They are the researcher's personal reflections on the data. They may include thoughts about the data as they are emerging, tentative interpretations, questions the researcher might want answered as the analysis and further data collection proceed, and thoughts on directions for further data collection and analysis. In essence, memos are a written personal record of the researcher's thoughts and reflections as data collection and analysis proceed. Such memos provide a road map to further refinement to data collection, interpretation and theory development.

Coding begins with **microanalysis** (Strauss and Corbin, 1998). Strauss and Corbin describe microanalysis as a 'line-by-line analysis at the beginning of a study to generate initial categories…' (p. 57). **Categories** are concepts that stand for phenomena. Categories, in turn, have **properties.** Properties are characteristics of a category that help to define it and give it meaning. In the example of the cultural identity politics study given above, a category might be 'acts of resistance to an imposed identity'. A property might be 'ritual performance not open to outsiders'. Microanalysis proceeds to **open coding**. Strauss and Corbin define open coding as 'the analytic process through which concepts are identified and their properties and dimensions are discovered in data' (p. 101). Practically, this often means placing in square brackets [**parking**] and bold type identifying a category after a line of text. For example, one respondent in the Yosemite study mentioned above said in an interview: 'Parking, my God parking it's impossible. I mean, you want to go to the store and get groceries and you can't because the tourists are taking up all the parking.' [**Parking**]. Placing the bold type 'parking' in square brackets after the line of transcribed text would be an example of open coding. It seeks to give an initial category to an idea expressed in the text.

Axial coding follows open coding. Axial coding involves relating a category to its subcategories. Axial coding helps to anchor and at the same time give richness to a category. For example the category 'parking' might be related to dimensions and subcategories such as location within Yosemite Valley (proximity to essential services), and

weekday versus weekend use by park visitors. At a more abstract level, parking could be a subcategory of a larger category 'hardships'. In this case axial coding might relate parking, primitive living conditions, crowded living conditions, lack of security, and low pay to the larger category, hardships.

Following coding, data displays further refine data analysis in order to discover relationships among categories. **Data displays** are representations of the major concepts and categories emerging from data that summarize and present such data in relation to each other. Among the more popular forms of data displays are matrices, graphs, network diagrams and charts.

Coding and data displays are designed to give the researcher 'eyes to see'. The next step in data analysis, **interpretation**, calls for making meaning from data summaries. An important distinction between qualitative and more traditional quantitative methods is that qualitative interpretations of data are **inductive**. Traditional quantitative methods, on the other hand are deductive. That is, they force the researcher, before data are collected, to specify hypotheses (usually derived from existing theory) and to collect and analyse data in such a way that the hypotheses are either supported or not supported. Traditional quantitative studies work from the general (theory and hypotheses) to the specific (data). Conversely, qualitative strategies work the other way; they work from the specific (the data) to the general, that is, working hypotheses or theory. Data interpretation in qualitative studies is such an inductive act.

Reporting

Reporting is a highly artistic act, especially so with qualitative research. Reporting means communicating the results and impressions of your research to a wider audience. Reporting can run the gamut from oral reports to interested parties or conference presentations to formal written documents such as contract reports, dissertations and journal articles. In reporting your research it is important to determine who your audience is and write for that specific audience. A piece of evaluation research directed toward agency management should emphasize the practical results of the study. It might include clear statements about programme or agency strengths and weaknesses. It might also include suggestions for change and improvement. All such claims should be anchored in the data from which those claims emerge. Reports to agencies may include more detail about method and analysis than could be included in a journal article for an academic audience. Conversely, report writing aimed toward an academic audience should be directed toward theory. Results should be interpreted in terms of new emerging theoretical insights that emerge from the study's data. Data may also be interpreted from the lens of existing theory. That lens and how it influences your interpretations should be made clear to the reader. Journals have greater space limitations than do contract reports. Theoretical insights are emphasized over the details of method. The *Journal of Leisure Research* and *Leisure Sciences* publish research articles using various qualitative methods. These articles can serve as models for how to write qualitative research for academic journals. The *Journal of Park and Recreation Administration* also publishes articles based on qualitative research. This journal differs from the other two in that it has a more pragmatic and managerial emphasis. Qualitative articles published in the *Journal of Park and Recreation Administration* can serve as good models for how to write condensed research reports intended for more pragmatic audiences. In some cases you may be writing a book-length manuscript or dissertation. In such cases, theoretical framing, theoretical insights gained, and a wealth of detail about entry, data collection and analysis should be presented. In all the above cases, direct quotes from the data can liven up the document, provide deeper insight to the meanings behind your categories, and give power to your supporting arguments.

Four Qualitative Methods

Four qualitative methods are popular in leisure, recreation, and tourism. These are the in-depth interview, participant observation, focus groups and case studies. Each will be described below. The descriptions will begin with an exemplar illustrating a research study. Following the exemplar a more general description of the method will be provided.

In-depth interviews

Example 1. The Bonneville Shoreline Trail is (BST) located along a wildland–urban interface.

As the name implies, much of its corridor follows the shoreline of the ancient Lake Bonneville in Utah. Where the trail passes along the University of Utah campus, a plot of undeveloped land is slated for development for a new museum of natural history. To the east of the trail corridor is undeveloped Forest Service land. To the south, north and west of the trail corridor is considerable development. Because the trail lies at the urban–wildland interface and because many groups in the Salt Lake area are becoming increasingly upset at development along the interface, the museum proposal has become controversial. Further, because federal funds were involved in the museum project an Environmental Impact Statement (EIS) was required. Part of that EIS involved collecting information from trail users about how their experiences might be affected by developing a museum along the BST corridor.

One approach to collecting such information involved in-depth interviews with trail users. Entry for these interviews was accomplished in conjunction with a more traditional quantitative survey. To gather a representative sample of trail users for the quantitative part of the study researchers were assigned to contact trail users, on-site, at randomly assigned time blocks. In conjunction with these interviews, trail users were asked if they would like to participate in a more in-depth interview lasting from 1 to 2h. Rather than using random sampling, interviewees were selected from this list based on their presumed ability to capture the range of experiences and motives for trail use along the BST. An interview guide was established with basic questions designed for users to talk about their motives for using the trail, their experiences associated with using the trail, their thoughts about how their experiences might be affected if a museum were to be developed along the trail site, and mitigation measures they thought the museum might take to minimize experience-related impacts. An open-ended and broad interview guide of six questions was developed (see Table 7.1). Follow-up questions and probes were used to encourage trail users to give in-depth narratives of their experiences and hopes. Interviews were tape recorded and transcribed. Transcripts were read and re-read for theme identification and coding (microanalysis). Open coding was performed on the transcripts and final themes were identified as categories of impact that may affect trail user experiences should the museum site be developed.

Our quantitative data showed that the BST gets most of its use from long-term and repeat users. Such extensive contact with the trail resource should provide fertile ground for forging vivid memories and since we specifically asked about it, not surprisingly, 'memories' emerged as a strong theme. Also important to the BST is that it is one of the few remaining dog-walking venues where dogs run free in a semi-wildland setting in the Salt Lake City area. So, dog walking, and preservation of this unique recreational opportunity, also emerged as a central theme in this research. Table 7.2 illustrates these themes and shows how the open coding appeared in fragments excised from the transcripts.

Once a broad theme such as 'memories' emerges, these fragments of texts can be placed together and a further level of coding (axial coding) can take place to develop the richness of the theme.

Reporting of this research was published in the Utah Museum of Natural History Final Environmental Impact Statement (National Park Service, 2007).

Description of the technique

The in-depth interview is among the most popular of qualitative methods used in leisure, recreation and tourism research. As the name implies, the in-depth

---

Table 7.1. Interview guide for the Utah Museum of Natural History (UMNH) EIS.

In-depth interviews template for UMNH EIS

1. Can you tell me about your/your agency's history with this section of the BST?
2. What is the most memorable experience you've had on this section of the BST?
3. Can you describe your attachment to the BST?
4. Can you describe your thoughts about the proposed relocation of the Utah Museum of Natural History to the site near Research Park?
5. What are some concerns of (_____ e.g. bicyclists) that we should be aware of?
6. Are there amenities that would enhance your experience of the BST?

Table 7.2. Example themes and open coding from the Utah Museum of Natural History EIS Research.

Respondent: I uh actually was hiking the day I gave birth to my son [**Memories**]. On that trail.
Interviewer: (laugh) Oh my god!
Respondent: So I have a lot of personal memory [**Memories**]. And hiking up there right after 9/11, when the troops were training and you know everything was so heightened, and I guess reserves were up there training and they had their guns and I just thought, you know, you see, and they do training up there, and it's so interesting to see them up there, but after 9/11 it was kinda spooky [**Memories**].
Respondent: Um, and I actually was up there the day after that whole side that I call fire (inaudible) caught fire. . .[**Memories**]
Interviewer: Ohhh. . .
Respondent: beyond where the research park, they closed it off on the road. And I remember seeing one of the researchers on TV the next day, so emotional about all of that. But then like closed for 10 years or something to see what it would do without man, without man's interference, and then it all burns [**Memories**].
Interviewer: Yeah, it sounds like it. (background noise) Can you, can you describe. . .you've kind of already done that, but can you describe your attachment to the trail?
Respondent: Umm, like I said it's close. I live in the 9th and 9th area so it takes 10 minutes for me to get up there [**Convenience**]. . . .theoretically it's off leash for the dog, although I know that there's signs posted now that you're not supposed to have dogs off leash, but I think most people up there have them off leash a lot. Um and so it's easy to get the dogs out and exercise em [**Dog use**].

interview is a conversation between the researcher and respondent designed to explore a topic in greater depth than can be had in the traditional quantitative survey. Such interviews are a powerful tool for discovering meanings that people ascribe to issues, events or other people. Once a respondent has agreed to participate in an interview (entry) a free-flowing exploration of a topic occurs between the interviewer and interviewee. Such conversations are usually shaped by an interview guide.

The interview guide is a list of broad, open-ended questions used to facilitate and shape the conversation. Patton (2002) provides several good suggestions for guide development such as considering opinion and value questions, feeling questions, knowledge questions, sensory questions and background and demographic questions. As the word 'guide' implies, the researcher should not mechanically and in too strict a manner limit the interview to the questions in the guide. Probes, follow-ups and interesting leads should be explored. The tone of the interviews should be informal and conversational. The setting should be comfortable, informal and relaxed. Empathetic listening is a tool all qualitative interviewers should develop highly. Interviews are typically tape-recorded (one should always gain permission from the respondent to tape record the interview). In order to have good quality tapes, analyse the setting in which the interview will take place for background noise and distraction.

A few of our Bonneville Shoreline Trail interviews were conducted in coffee shops. While such coffee shops offered the advantages of being in a comfortable and neutral site, background noise sometimes made parts of the tapes inaudible. Also, never forget to take backup batteries. In addition, resist the temptation to fiddle with the equipment while the interview is taking place. It calls attention to the fact that one is being interviewed and makes an easy conversational flow more difficult. Make sure the tape recorder is working before the interview begins. Once the interview begins, pay attention to the respondent and the conversation, not the equipment. Tapes should be transcribed as soon as possible after the interview has taken place. Analysis is conducted from the transcriptions. Although the interview, per se, is a data-collection technique, data analysis should begin with the first interview. As themes and new directions emerge, interview guides should be modified to take advantage of the newly emerging knowledge.

Participant observation/ethnography

Example 2. Dehang Village is a Miao ethnic enclave located in western China. The Miao (more commonly known in the west as the Hmong), are an ethnic minority living within Han-dominated China. The Miao often live both physically and culturally on the margins of Chinese society. Living within tightly bound, linage communities, often in remote villages, the Miao have preserved a unique social identity and cultural heritage. Such heritage is ripe for incursions of cultural tourism. One such place where tourism is now well established is Dehang Village. While such tourism has brought a number of economic advantages to Dehang Village, some villagers worry about the loss of cultural identity and heritage. Of particular importance to the touristic experience of Dehang Village are ritual performances. These performances are rich in music, dance, and colourful authentic costume. Yet, to the Miao of Dehang Village these performances are more than a means of generating income from tourists; they are a re-enactment of cultural identity. This study sought to understand the identity politics surrounding touristic festival performances. The primary author of this research (Liu, 2008) is Han Chinese, but with Miao heritage. She had made previous trips to Dehang Village before beginning the research. Thus, she was able through her heritage and previous contact with the community to gain entry into the scene. Still, she initially lived with a single family in the village and participated in village life before commencing more intrusive 'western' forms of data collection such as in-depth interviews. Although in-depth interviews were conducted, the primary form of data collection took the form of field notes. As one might do with interview transcripts, field notes were examined for themes and connections among themes. Analysis took place alongside data collection to allow for participating in experiences that might yield fruitful information about the identity politics of festival performances. This study's theoretical frame, methods, and results and interpretation were reported as a doctoral dissertation (Liu, 2008).

Description of the technique

Participant observation is a face-to-face encounter with research participants in their natural scene. Field notes are the primary form of data collection. Field notes are rich and vivid descriptions of the lived scene and events and reactions to those events made by the researcher as an observer of those events. Levels of participant observation can range from an outsider looking in without participating in the events or life of a community to full participant. For example, I had been a member of a single karate school (dojo) for 18 years. I went to classes several nights per week, trained for and took belt tests, and participated in tournaments. Should I have wanted to conduct an ethnography of this karate school, I would have done so from the perspective of a full participant. I would have participated in the life of the school, and after events occurred made my field notes. On the other hand, a university student with no background or interest in participating in such a school may observe classes from a foyer. She may watch tournaments and interview instructors and students about their experiences. Field notes may be taken in real time. Should this researcher conduct the same ethnography, but from a non-participatory point of view, she would do so from the perspective of full observer. These two positions, full observer and full participant, are two ends of a continuum. Differing levels of participation and observation can occur. Liu (2008), in the Dehang Village study cited earlier, was able to participate in the life of the community to a large extent. Yet, it is unlikely she would ever be embraced as a full-fledged community member. The advantages of participant observation should be obvious. Participant observation allows the researcher to connect the reported experiences and meanings of those being studied to the environment (physical, cultural and social) in which those meanings are being made.

Focus groups

Example 3. Fear of crime in parks is a significant concern for those women who wish to safely use park resources for the recreational benefits associated with their use. Responses to such fear can range from choosing not to use a resource at all to engaging in coping strategies that, while allowing for participation, may not yield the full benefits that safe environments have to offer. In one such park near Chico, California, the researcher wished to explore women's fear associated with a particular park and how those women coped with the fears they might experience in that setting. In order to bring out the synergy of what might be a shared experience, focus group interviewing was the method of choice. Three separate focus groups were conducted with approximately

seven women in each group. Participants were selected by first making on-site contact with users of the park and soliciting their participation. Questions exploring women's perceptions of fear, what physical and social situations aroused those fears, and how women coped with those fears were developed and presented to the groups to respond. Data were analysed for themes. Important among the coping themes that emerged from the data were: (i) altering time of day for park use in order to feel safe; (ii) recreating with others, rather than alone; and (iii) carrying self-defence aids when recreating. The conceptual framework that guided the study, a description of the study's methods, a reporting of the results, and finally interpretation and implications for management were reported as a master's degree thesis (Jorgensen, 1998).

Description of the technique

Focus groups are a form of interview. They differ from the in-depth interview in that they are *group* interviews and typically have more structure. Focus groups typically involve from seven to ten participants each with some common interest in the topic being researched. As with the in-depth interview, questions are designed beforehand and are open-ended in nature. The interviewer acts as a moderator and facilitator of the discussion. Generally a welcome, overview and establishment of ground rules begin the focus group session. Participants are reminded that all points of view are to be respected and that no one should dominate the session. The interview commences with a group discussion based on the interview questions. A powerful advantage of the focus group is the synergy of description that emerges from collective discussion. Interviews are typically videotaped. Transcriptions are made and analysed for themes and 'big ideas' (Henderson, 2006).

Case studies

Example 4. A little more than a decade ago the Montana Department of Natural Resources (DNR) was tagged as being responsible for the shooting deaths of potentially brucellosis-infected bison as they wandered outside the boundaries of Yellowstone National Park. The shooting deaths were claimed to be a means of controlling the spread of the disease and an effort at protecting the cattle industry in the area. The shooting of the Yellowstone bison became a media event and for the agencies involved, a public relations nightmare. Media events such as this one are ripe materials for case study research. In this case we (Fleener and Ruddell, 1998) treated the media event as a case and analysed the media presentation of the event as a case study. The primary data source for this study was newspaper reports of the controversy. We also interviewed the Chief Information Officer for Yellowstone National Park to see if we could determine how information disseminated from the Park Service might influence the framing of the story. We began with two ideas. The first was based on a phenomenon called 'pack journalism'. This is a metaphor for the phenomenon that for large news stories an 'alpha journalist' will get to set the frame for subsequent reporting on the event. Frames are metaphors that give a story its focus, interest, and make it understandable to the general public. The second idea was to frame our research within a theoretical stance of social constructionism. Social constructionism is a theoretical framework that argues that our realities are not purely objective reflections of the world beyond us, but rather, are constructed by us as we engage in social interaction, especially through language. In a sense, language creates reality. Thus, we studied the media reporting of the event to determine how the reality of the event was being socially constructed by media framing and how that frame got influenced. A content analysis of the media stories suggested a simple but graphic Biblical frame of the 'slaughter of the innocents'. Conversations with Park personnel suggested that the National Park Service had been pro-active in helping establish the media frame. By the time Montana DNR got involved in the media event, it was too late. The frame had already been set in the public's mind and Montana DNR was caught on the defensive (eliciting the memorable comment 'we're not a bunch of Neanderthal up here . . .').

Description of the technique

Case studies take single events, issues, organizations or even people and study them in great depth. One might want to study a single national park, a single wilderness challenge programme, or single policy decision in great depth. Although the sample is usually small (one unit, although studying that unit might involve interviewing several people) the data sources are many. Interviews, observations, documents, memos, e-mails, flyers, posters, physical artifacts, and videotapes may all be used in a single study. In addition, several variables are examined simultaneously to help tell the complete story. As with other

forms of qualitative research, these data are examined for themes and relations among themes until a coherent interpretation can be made.

Key Terms

Axial coding: An analysis strategy that involves relating a category to its subcategories and dimensions. Axial coding helps to anchor, and at the same time give richness, to a category.

Categories: Concepts that stand for phenomena.

Data displays: Representations of the major concepts and categories emerging from data that summarize and present such data in relation to each other. Popular forms of data displays are matrices, charts and network diagrams.

Data saturation: Data saturation occurs when no new information is forthcoming by sampling more participants.

Emic: Insider perspective. The perspective of seeking to understand a phenomenon from the research participant's point of view.

Etic: Outsider perspective. The perspective of seeking to understand a phenomenon objectively. The researcher stands as an outsider dispassionately looking in at the phenomenon.

Idiographic: A research perspective that seeks to provide full and rich descriptions of the local and contextual.

Inductive: In its most general sense, inductive is a form of reasoning that works from specific pieces of evidences to more general conclusions. In qualitative research it frequently means drawing out larger ideas from data.

Memos: Notes to oneself. They are the researcher's personal reflections on the data.

Microanalysis: An analysis technique wherein one engages in a line-by-line analysis in order to generate initial categories. It is one of the initial stages of data analysis.

Negative cases: Those persons or events that contradict the emerging pattern. Such cases help tell a larger and more complete story.

Nomothetic: A research perspective that seeks to derive and test universal law-like statements.

Open coding: A part of data analysis wherein the researcher identifies concepts along with their properties and dimensions. These concepts must be grounded in the data.

Properties: Characteristics of a category that help to define it and give it meaning.

Purposive sampling: A family of sampling strategies wherein cases are selected not because they are representative of a larger population, but because they are information rich and satisfy information needs of a given study.

Verstehen: 'Empathetic understanding'. Verstehen is a perspective that recognizes that humans are not sterile objects, but that emotions, passions, desires, thoughts, beliefs, anticipations, deliberations and cultural context influence meaning making and behaviour.

Discussion Questions

1. Describe the key differences between qualitative and quantitative research and discuss the advantages and disadvantages of each.

2. What are the key factors that would come into play if you had to choose between adopting a qualitative or quantitative approach to studying a research problem in leisure, recreation and tourism?

3. What are examples of *emic* and *etic* stances applied to a research problem in leisure, recreation and tourism?

4. What is purposive sampling and how does it differ from probability sampling? Explain why purposive sampling is appropriate for qualitative methods.

5. Create a fictional transcript of an in-depth interview. How would you code it? Give examples.

6. Among the four qualitative techniques described in this chapter, which is your favourite? Why?

References

Denzin, N. and Lincoln, Y. (1998) *The Landscape of Qualitative Research: Theories and Issues*. Sage, Thousand Oaks, California.

Denzin, N. and Lincoln, Y. (2003) *Strategies of Qualitative Inquiry*, 2nd edn. Sage, Thousand Oaks, California.

Denzin, N. and Lincoln, Y. (2003) *Collecting and Interpreting Qualitative Materials*, 2nd edn. Sage, Thousand Oaks, California.

Fleener, N. and Ruddell, E.J. (1998) Socially constructed realities and the news: An analysis of media framing of the Yellowstone bison controversy. In: *Proceedings of the Seventh International Symposium on Society and Resource Management*, Columbia, Missouri, p. 29.

Henderson, K. (2006) *Dimensions of Choice: Qualitative Approaches to Parks, Recreation, Tourism, Sport, and Leisure Research*, 2nd edn. Venture, State College, Pennsylvania.

Glaser, B. and Strauss, A. (1999) *The Discovery of Grounded Theory: Strategies for Qualitative Research*. Aldine DeGruyter, New York.

Jorgensen, L. (1998) Coping with fear of violence: Women's negotiation through leisure constraints during outdoor recreational activities. Unpublished master's thesis, California State University at Chico, Chico, California.

Krueger, R. (1988) *Focus Groups: A Practical Guide for Applied Research*. Sage, Newbury Park, California.

Lindlof, T. and Taylor, B. (2002) *Qualitative Communication Research Methods*, 2nd edn. Sage, Thousand Oaks, California.

Liu, L. (2008) Performing place and ethnic identity among the Miao of Dehang Village, Western Hunan, China. Unpublished doctoral dissertation, University of Utah, Salt Lake City, Utah.

Miles, M. and Huberman, M. (1994) *Qualitative Data Analysis: An Expanded Sourcebook*. Sage, Thousand Oaks, California.

National Park Service (2007) *Final Environmental Impact Statement, Utah Museum of Natural History, New Museum Facility*. Utah Museum of Natural History and National Park Service.

Patton, M. (2002) *Qualitative Research and Evaluation Methods*, 3rd edn. Sage, Thousand Oaks, California.

Spradley, J. (1980) *Participant Observation*. Thompson Learning, New York.

Strauss, A. and Corbin, J. (1998) *Basics of Qualitative Research: Techniques and Procedures for Developing Grounded Theory*, 2nd edn.

Yin, R. (2003) *Case Study Research: Design and Methods*, 3rd edn. Sage, Thousand Oaks, California.

chapter 8

Grounded Theory Methodology in Research

Harriet E.T. Dixon, L. Brent Igo and Fran A. McGuire

Learning Objectives

After reading and studying this chapter you will be able to:

1. Explain the purpose of grounded theory research;
2. Explain what type of research question guides grounded theory studies;
3. Describe sampling techniques used in grounded theory research;
4. Identify the primary source of data in grounded theory research;
5. Describe data analysis procedures in grounded theory research;
6. Explain what a member check is and how to conduct a member check;
7. Describe how grounded theory research is evaluated.

Chapter Summary

This chapter introduces the grounded theory methodology of Strauss and Corbin (1990, 1994, 1998). Grounded research is used to develop theories that may be useful to practitioners in understanding a phenomenon or behaviour. This type of research relies on theoretical sampling, interview data and analytic coding. Member checks are conducted to determine if you understand what study participants are communicating. Research results (the theory) are presented in a flowchart or diagram, narrative or propositional statements. Theoretical results may be used by researchers and practitioners to develop interventions and facilitate a change in behaviour.

Grounded Theory Applied to Swimming

The example study presented in this chapter used the specific recreation activity of swimming as the activity in question. However, methods described in this chapter may be applied to any leisure, recreation or tourism setting.

The primary purpose of the example study was to develop a theory of constraints to leisure and the process of successfully coping with constraints to leisure. Constraints to leisure refers to 'factors that limit people's participation in leisure activities, people's use of leisure services (e.g. parks and programmes), or people's enjoyment of current activities' (Scott, 2005, p. 280). The example study used adults that had previously experienced constraints to swimming participation or learning to swim and had been successful at coping with the constraints, therefore taking swimming lessons. More simply stated, the purpose of the study was to find out why the adults had not learned to swim earlier in their lives and how or what made them finally take swimming lessons and learn to swim. Study participants were adults taking group or private swimming lessons at a community recreation centre, private wellness centre, or university recreation centre in the upstate region of South Carolina. Twenty-eight adults participated in the study, with ages ranging from 22 to 70 years old.

The example study followed the grounded theory methodology of Strauss and Corbin (1990, 1994, 1998). Theoretical sampling techniques were used. Data were collected through in-depth interviews conducted either face-to-face or over the telephone by the primary researcher. Interviews were audio recorded and then transcribed for analysis. Interviews were analysed using analytic coding and memos. Open, axial and selective analytic coding procedures facilitated in the development of a theory answering the study research question.

Unlike quantitative research studies with numerous research questions, grounded theory research studies have only one guiding research question. The research question of this study was: *How do constraints to leisure develop and what coping strategies are used to overcome constraints to leisure?* From this research, a theory describing constraints to leisure and the successful process of coping with constraints was developed. The specific activity of interest was swimming; therefore, the example study answered: *How do constraints to swimming participation and learning to swim develop* and *how do people successfully overcome these constraints and learn to swim or participate in swimming?*

Theoretical results from the example study can assist recreation practitioners in understanding why people do not learn to swim or participate in swimming. Recreation practitioners may then develop strategies that will facilitate the process of coping with constraints to swimming participation, increasing attendance in swimming and swimming lessons at his or her facility. The resulting theory

may also be made more abstract or generalizable and applied to other leisure, recreation and tourism activities or settings. In addition, results may be used to develop a survey if further quantitative research is desired.

The example study used swimming as the specific recreation activity of interest. However, the methods described in this chapter may be applied in any leisure, recreation or tourism setting to better understand a phenomenon and develop appropriate interventions if necessary. The ability to facilitate a deep understanding of a specific phenomenon or situation and develop interventions specific to the situation or make the theory more abstract and generalizable make grounded theory research a unique and practical research option.

What is Grounded Theory?

In order to understand behavior, action, and reaction to situations or events, researchers often develop theories that both describe and predict behaviour. Theories may then be used by practitioners in the field to direct action or interventions. However, for a theoretical framework to successfully be applied in the field, it must be an accurate representation of the situation or event (Strauss and Corbin, 1994). The purpose of this chapter is to provide step-by-step instruction on how to use grounded theory methods to develop theory specific to leisure, recreation and tourism.

The phrase 'grounded theory' represents both a research method and a research outcome (Schram, 2006). As a research method, grounded theory uses structured, systematic procedures of data collection and analysis to develop theory. As a research outcome, grounded theory is an inductive, independent theory, derived by systematically gathering and analysing research data.

For this reason, you do not begin a grounded theory study with a preconceived theory in mind, nor are you testing an already existing theory. Instead, you begin with a theoretical research question, and collect data in order to answer the question. Do not get overwhelmed with the idea of developing a theoretical question. In order for a question to be theoretical, all you need to ask is how an event, behaviour or phenomenon happens. For example, the study presented in this chapter asked: How do people develop and cope with constraints to leisure? Therefore, the answer to this question will be a theoretical description of how these events happen. When asking a theoretical question, some type of action must be present. How the action occurs is the answer to the research question and is what is described by the theory.

The study presented in this chapter followed the grounded theory design of Strauss and Corbin (1990, 1994, 1998). Strauss and Corbin (1990, 1994, 1998) require systematic and structured methods in their grounded theory design. Other less systematic options for conducting a grounded theory study are outlined by Glaser (1992) and Charmaz (1990, 2000, 2002).

The purpose of this study was to develop a theory that describes, explains and predicts constraints to leisure experienced by adults who had been previously constrained from swimming but were successful in coping with constraints. Methods include: (i) sampling; (ii) data collection; (iii) data analysis; (iv) member checks; (v) theory presentation; and (vi) research evaluation.

Data for grounded theory studies comes primarily from personal interviews. Individuals that have knowledge or experiences that may answer the research question are interviewed. Then, through systematic data analysis, a theory is developed from interview data. A theory resulting from a grounded theory study is specific to the people and place being studied. However, the theory may be made more abstract, and in turn, more general. Elements of theory include: (i) categories; (ii) characteristics of those categories; and (iii) relationships among categories and properties (Strauss and Corbin, 1998). Relationships among categories are 'the action' part of the theory.

Sampling

Unlike quantitative research, in grounded theory research, a random sample that is representative of a population is not the goal. Rather, you purposefully sample participants who will contribute to theoretical development, which is called theoretical sampling.

In the example study, theoretical and convenience sampling methods were used to identify potential study participants. Following theoretical sampling, research participants were selected based on how their experiences or knowledge may contribute to developing a theory that would

answer our research question: *How do constraints to leisure develop and what coping strategies are used to overcome constraints to leisure?* We decided to focus on swimming as the recreation activity that had been constrained. Therefore, the following participant criteria were established: (i) potential study participants needed to have been constrained from participation in the recreation activity (swimming) earlier in their life; (ii) study participants must have been successful at coping with constraints to the recreation activity (swimming), meaning they were able to participate in swimming or take swimming lessons; and (iii) he or she must be willing to participate in the research study.

Using theoretical sampling, and in order to best answer the research question, adults stating they had previously been constrained from learning to swim, and were currently participating in swimming lessons were chosen as participants for the study, as these individuals would have experiences relevant to the purpose of the research. Therefore, at the time interviews were conducted, all study participants stated they had the desire to swim or learn to swim at various points in their life, yet did not, and were presently taking either group or private swimming lessons for leisure, thereby participating in swimming. Convenience sampling was also used because study participants were easily accessible at local recreation centres.

Data Collection

Data were collected through in-depth, open-ended, interviews. In the example research, each interview lasted from 45 min to 1.5 h. Interviews were conducted individually, except for one sister pair and one husband and wife pair, per their request. Interviews took place either face-to face in a public area, such as a public library or a coffee shop, or over the telephone. Interviews were audio recorded and later transcribed. Interview data were stored and managed using a qualitative data analysis software program.

A qualitative data analysis software program is not necessary in order to analyse qualitative data. As the researcher, you sort, code and categorize interview data. However, qualitative data analysis software programs make the task of storing, organizing and managing qualitative data easier. Some researchers create tables in word processing programs to assist in data analysis, while others simply use pen, paper and/or notecards. The method you use to store, organize and manage qualitative data is a matter of personal preference.

Saturation

In grounded theory research, interviews are conducted until categories and the theoretical framework are sufficiently saturated based on the subjective decision of the researcher. Saturation is considered to be reached when no new concepts or categories emerge during interviews. Once saturation is reached, data collected during interviews does not contribute any further to theoretical development. Continuing to interview after saturation has been reached yields no new information and is therefore unproductive.

In the example study, saturation began to be reached at approximately the 17th interview. However, the researcher continued conducting interviews to order to be certain saturation had been reached. Creswell (1998, 2007) suggests saturation of a grounded theory is typically reached upon interviewing between 20 and 30 participants. The example study was consistent with Creswell's (1998, 2007) recommendation, as saturation was fully reached upon interviewing 28 participants. At this point, the researcher made the decision to stop interviewing.

Interview questions

Before interviewing participants, you should develop interview questions that will yield the information you are trying to uncover. However, you may add, change or delete interview questions as interviews and the study progress. Keep in mind that interview questions should try to answer the guiding research question. In addition, you should try to ask interview questions that do not have a simple yes or no answer. Instead, interview questions should attempt to uncover detailed descriptions of when, where, why and how behaviours, events, actions or phenomena occur.

In order to answer the research question of the example study – *What is a theoretical description of how people develop and cope with constraints*

to leisure? – the following interview questions were developed before interviews began:

1. How did you come to be ___ years old and not learn how to swim?
2. What people, events, issues or happenings kept you from learning to swim?
3. How did you feel not knowing how to swim?
4. How did you deal with not knowing how to swim?
5. When did you first realize you wanted to learn to swim?
6. What made you realize you wanted to learn to swim?
7. Why is now the right time for you to learn to swim?
8. What steps did you have to take to learn to swim now?
9. How is learning to swim going to change things for you?

As interviews progress, you may probe and ask other non-scripted, spontaneous questions as needed. Interview questions may also be rewritten if you do not feel like you are getting to the information you are trying to uncover.

Ideally, each interview should be analysed before the next interview is conducted. This is an important component of grounded theory procedures that allows you to make decisions about theoretical sampling in order to reach saturation. For example, if a woman describes an event you think only a woman may experience, you may intentionally interview other women to get more descriptions of the experience, or you may intentionally interview men in order to determine if men have similar experiences as women or not. But remember, getting a sample that is representative of a population is not the goal. Your goal is to sample people that will provide information for you to accurately develop the theory.

Data Analysis

Data analysis is based upon multiple readings and interpretations of data. During data analysis, interview data are repeatedly compared, coded, and sorted. Data analysis follows standard grounded theory procedures of: (i) constant comparison; (ii) analytic coding; and (iii) memoing, as outlined by Strauss and Corbin (1990, 1994, 1998).

Constant comparison

Constant comparison refers to the continual (or constant) comparison of data. As interviews are conducted, data are analysed. New data are compared to previous data. You search for discrepancies as well as similarities in research data. Constantly comparing existing data with new data and looking for gaps in data helps you modify interview questions if necessary, saturate concepts and categories, and make theoretical sampling decisions.

Analytic coding

Analytic coding refers to analysing, grouping and labelling data. In grounded theory research, analytic coding has three steps: open, axial and selective coding. These three analytic coding steps occur in separate phases, as well as simultaneously. Table 8.1 provides a condensed guide to analytic coding and data analysis. For a concept to be coded, interview data should have sufficient meaning in order to create or develop your theory. In the

Table 8.1. Condensed guide to grounded theory data analysis procedures.

Step	Open coding	Axial coding	Selective coding	Memos
What happens	• Events, actions/ interactions or occurrences are identified. • Events, actions/ interactions or occurrences with similarities are grouped into concepts. • Similar concepts are grouped to form categories. • Categories may then be broken down into subcategories based on who, where, why and how.	• Categorical relationships are identified. • Categorical properties and dimensions are elaborated. • Context and conditions (structure) are identified.	• Central category is identified. • Ideas or categories not fitting or contributing to understanding are identified.	• Written records of the researcher's analytic thoughts and reflections.
Result	• Categorical properties and dimensions are easily identifiable. • Theoretical explanation and prediction is possible.	• Answers who, with what results, when, why, how and consequences. • Indicates issues and problems within phenomenon. • Indicates how persons or groups respond.	• Categories are integrated. • All categories are related back to central category. • Theoretical scheme is developed. • Ideas or categories not fitting or contributing to understanding are discarded.	• Theoretical sampling decisions. • Categories are identified. • Hypotheses developed. • Contradictory evidence recorded. • Subsequent interviews developed. • Diagrams of developing theory. • Data are abstracted. • Analytic trail.

example study, coded interview data had sufficient meaning regarding constraints to leisure, learning to swim and coping. Analytic coding is a continual process throughout the study, leading to further refinement and development of the theory.

Open coding

Analytic coding begins with open coding. Open coding is detailed or microanalysis of raw (uncoded) interview data. During this phase of coding, data can be broken down by word, line, sentence or paragraph. Important topics are identified, coded and grouped based on similarities, or separated based on differences. When topics are coded and grouped, this forms concepts. Then concepts sharing meaning or characteristics are grouped forming categories. Table 8.2 provides an example of open coding of raw interview data from the example study. Table 8.3 shows the 49 initial codes and five categories created from data during open coding.

Axial coding

Axial coding identifies subcategories, relationships between categories, categorical dimensions or levels, and how categories affect each other. Table 8.4 provides an example of axial coding, showing subcategories and how data was re-coded and grouped during axial coding.

Selective coding

Selective coding is the final step in analytic coding. During selective coding, categories are integrated and connected and the theoretical framework is pulled together. Selective coding occurs even up to the phase of writing the final theory narrative. Figure 8.1 shows the outcome of selective coding, presenting a flowchart of the final theoretical framework and how categories and relationships were integrated in the example study.

Table 8.2. Open coding of raw interview data examples.

Body image	'I was glad the instructor was a female, just for the fact that I have such a gorgeous body, I guess! Yeah, I mean, I wondered would it be male or female. I did not really care, but female is easier for me, I think. Yeah, because I just, you know, like I said, my body is in such bad shape. My body is horrible, and getting worse!'
	'Well no. It was just that, what bothered me was, he had never seen me in a bathing suit, and even though I was not overweight by even an ounce, I was worried about, what is he going to think of me in a bathing suit? I was worried about the bathing suit part. I wasn't thinking about anything else.'
	'And then, self-image. You know, did I want to be in a class with a bunch of other people with my cellulite, and my granny boobs.'
	'I think as women a lot of that comes from not wanting to get in our bathing suit in front of everybody.'
Parental influence	'My parents said, 'You better not go near that water, you'll get drowned.'
	'I would not go near the water. You would have gotten a beaten. If they say you to, "Stay away," you better stay away. It was just the day. Back in the days, that is just how it was.'
	'As a child it probably never really was reinforced from the parents that we should know how to swim.'

(Continued)

Table 8.2. Continued.

	'My mom said, "I swam as little as I could – I hated it." But she is not a swimmer. I think it might have affected us learning to swim. I think maybe she did not search out opportunities for us to swim so much.'
Lack of facility	'One thing back early in my life is that is wasn't a place to swim. You know we didn't have like now, you know the Y and all that. We didn't have things like that that in my day, in my time you know.'
	'Back then you know it just wasn't, you know swimming pools and things back then. Now they call them streams but back then they called them branches. Some people would take sand and build it up to make them a little place to swim but we weren't allowed to do anything like that.'
	'Because they didn't have access to the pool years ago. So, and then they didn't even have Twin Lakes back then in those days. I didn't know of any lakes. The Twin Lakes, they started building that. People might have a pond for the cows to drink water out of that, something like that and they would go and damn up a branch and make them a pool, a place to swim. I can remember these guys were living on the farm and that is what they did. They damned up this branch and made this place to swim. And they didn't have bathing suits then to swim in. They would just jump in and strip off. That was just the days.'
	'Woods Lake had closed down. The opportunities that we had that were affordable had closed down. The high schools down here did not have pools like the high schools up North used to. And we were poor, so we did not belong to neighbourhood pools. So there wasn't the opportunity.'

Table 8.3. Initial codes and categories created during open coding.

Category	Code
Causal conditions	1. Age or self-image 2. Body image 3. Childhood socialization or experience 4. Cultural 5. Family responsibilities 6. Fear 7. Fear of embarrassment 8. Time period 9. Geographic area 10. Inconvenient activity 11. Lack of facility 12. Lack of time 13. No opportunity or access 14. Not what social group did 15. Parental influence 16. Personality 17. Physical limitation 18. Political 19. Socioeconomic 20. Work responsibilities

(Continued)

Table 8.3. Continued.

Category	Code
Leisure is constrained	21. No participation 22. Limited participation 23. Decreased enjoyment
Catalysing experience	24. Age 25. Determination or priority 26. Family influence or support 27. Health reasons 28. Increase skill level 29. Money 30. New access to pool 31. Peers or work environment 32. Safety 33. Showing off 34. If she can do it, I can do it 35. Wanted to participate fully in activity
Negotiation of constraints	36. Find appropriate lessons 37. Participate in area person feels comfortable 38. Alter daily routine 39. Use other people as positive examples 40. Support from family and friends 41. Prepare self mentally 42. Schedule time for activity 43. Make goals 44. Find affordable lessons 45. Plan ahead 46. Locate facility 47. Get more information about activity
Participation	48. Learn to swim 49. Swim for leisure

Table 8.4. Example of axial coding.

Category	Sub-category	Code
Inhibiting conditions	Psychological issues	1. Age 2. Body image 3. Personality 4. Fear 5. Fear of embarrassment
	Social/cultural/political	6. Cultural 7. Childhood socialization 8. Time period 9. Not what social group did 10. Political 11. Parental influence

(Continued)

Table 8.4. Example of axial coding.

Category	Sub-category	Code
	Physical limitation	12. Physical limitation
	Life responsibilities	13. Family responsibilities 14. Work responsibilities 15. Lack of time
	No access/opportunity	16. No facility 17. No swimming instructor 18. Socioeconomic
Leisure is constrained		19. No participation 20. Limited/modified participation 21. Decreased enjoyment
Catalysing experience	Life review	22. Age
	Social pressure	23. Family influence or support
	Health	24. Health reasons
	Overestimated skill level	25. Increase skill level
	Missing out	26. New access to pool 27. Safety of kids 28. Wanted to participate in activity
	Self-efficacy improvement through vicarious experience	29. If she can do it, I can do it
Increased motivation	Swimming is made a priority	30. Priority
	Determination	31. Determination
Negotiation of constraints	Personally	32. Find appropriate lessons 33. Participate in comfortable area
	Temporally	34. Alter daily routine 35. Schedule time for activity
	Socially	36. Modelling 37. Support from family and friends
	Logistically	38. Locate facility 39. Plan ahead
	Economically	40. Find affordable lessons
	Cognitively	41. Get more information about activity 42. Make goals 43. Prepare self mentally
Participation		44. Learn to swim 45. Swim for leisure

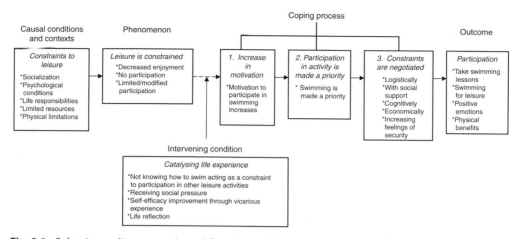

Fig. 8.1. Selective coding example and flowchart of theoretical framework for example study.

Memos

Memos are another part of data analysis of grounded theory studies. Analytic memos are recorded throughout data analysis. Memos serve as written records of reflection, interpretation, and theory development. Memos provide a record of your thought process at different phases of theory development and are ongoing until the theory is completely developed. Memos assist you in making connections, creating codes and categories, contemplating meaning of data, and developing the theoretical framework. In the example study, analytic memos were handwritten and organized in a three-ring binder.

Member Check

Member checks are another component of grounded theory research. The purpose of a member check is to make sure you have correctly understood the meaning of what study participants are saying during interviews. Conducting member checks can be as simple as repeating information back to study participants and asking participants if what you are saying is what they are truly communicating. In instances where there is a discrepancy, you can ask for clarification and elaboration.

Another option for a member check is once the final theoretical framework has been developed, you can write a simple, condensed narrative of your theory. Then you can discuss your theory

with participants face-to-face as a group or individually or over the phone. The narrative can also be sent to study participants via e-mail or postal mail, along with a brief questionnaire regarding the accuracy of the theory. Participants can be asked if he/she agrees the theory is an accurate description of his/her experience. Participants should be given the opportunity to provide any comments regarding the accuracy of the theory or otherwise.

In the example study, participants were mailed by post or e-mailed a brief narrative description of the theory. Participants were asked in a brief survey if he/she agreed the theory was an accurate description of why he/she did not swim earlier in life and how he/she decided to take swimming lessons as an adult. Participants were given the opportunity to write any comments regarding the accuracy of the theory.

Theory Presentation

In grounded theory research, findings can be presented in three ways: (i) as a set of interrelated concepts or categories via a diagram or flowchart (Fig. 8.1); (ii) as a narrative description; or (iii) as proposition statements (Strauss and Corbin, 1998). A diagram or flowchart provides a visual picture of the theory, identifying categories and relationships. This often helps people understand relationships and grasp the theory as a whole. A narrative presentation includes a concise, tightly written story or description of the theory, followed by a thorough discussion of categories, conditions and relationships. Proposition statements are statements of relationship and also include descriptions of categories. Participant quotes are used in narrative and propositional statements to provide evidence of how the theory was developed from or grounded in data (Strauss and Corbin, 1998). Using a diagram or flowchart along with a narrative description or proposition statements is useful in assisting readers to understand the theory.

Evaluation of Research

Strauss and Corbin (1998) developed criteria to evaluate the research process and the empirical grounding of grounded theory studies. Questions evaluating the research process assist you, as the researcher, in determining how closely you followed grounded theory method guidelines. Empirical grounding evaluation criteria measures whether or not your theory was developed from research data. Addressing these criteria can assist you and others in determining the quality of your research and findings. Below are the criteria established by Strauss and Corbin (1998) to address the research process and empirical grounding of grounded theory research.

Research process

Criterion 1: How was the original sample selected? On what grounds?

Criterion 2: What major categories emerged?

Criterion 3: What were some of the events, incidents, or actions (indicators) that pointed to some of these major categories?

Criterion 4: On the basis of what categories did theoretical sampling proceed? How did theoretical sampling guide data collection? Were categories representative of data?

Criterion 5: What were some of the hypotheses pertaining to conceptual relationships among categories and on what grounds were they formulated and validated?

Criterions 6: Were there instances when hypotheses did not explain what was happening in data? How were these discrepancies accounted for? Were hypotheses modified?

Criterion 7: How and why was the central category selected? Was selection sudden, gradual, difficult or easy? On what grounds were final analytic decisions made? (Strauss and Corbin, 1998, p. 269)

Empirical grounding

Criterion #1: Are concepts generated?

Criterion #2: Are the concepts systematically related?

Criterion #3: Are there many conceptual linkages, and are the categories well developed? Do categories have conceptual density?

Criterion #4: Is variation built into the theory?

Criterion #5: Are the conditions under which variation can be found built into the study and explained?

Criterion #6: Has process been taken into account?

Criterion #7: Do theoretical findings seem significant, and to what extent? (Strauss and Corbin, 1998, pp. 270–272)

Final Considerations

Grounded theory methods outlined by Strauss and Corbin (1990, 1994, 1998) allow theoretical frameworks to be developed that describe and predict behaviour and actions specific to tourism and recreation settings. Results from grounded theory research may be used by recreation and tourism practitioners to develop interventions and facilitate changes in recreation and tourism behaviour. This chapter outlined step-by-step how to conduct grounded theory research. An example study using the specific recreation activity of swimming was used to illustrate the basic tenets of grounded theory research including: writing an appropriate grounded theory research question, sampling, data collection, data analysis, conducting a member check, theory presentation, and research evaluation. Grounded theory methods allow researchers to ask and answer different questions than typical quantitative or survey research. Therefore, when deciding what type of research you may like to conduct, first ask yourself what you want to answer. If you want to understand how a specific phenomenon or situation occurs and/or want to develop an intervention, grounded theory may be the most appropriate research method.

Key Terms

Abstract: General or less specific.

Category: Group of related concepts (Strauss and Corbin, 1998).

Coding: Assigning a name or label to a piece of data.

Concept: An abstract phenomenon (Strauss and Corbin, 1998).

Convenience sampling: Picking persons from a population to be included as participants in a research study based on the ease of locating or enlisting potential study participants.

Coping: To face or deal with an issue.

Constraints to leisure: 'Factors that limit people's participation in leisure activities, people's use of leisure services (e.g. parks and programmes), or people's enjoyment of current activities' (Scott, 2005, p. 280).

Diagram: A figure, line drawing or illustration.

Dimension: Properties or levels of something.

Empirical: Guided by research.

Flowchart: Illustration or drawing showing relationships and direction of action.

General: Less specific or broad in understanding.

Interpretation: Meaning or explanation.

Memo: Written records of thoughts, analytic interpretation and reflection (Strauss and Corbin, 1998).

Member check: Researcher assesses his/her understanding of what the study participant is communicating with what the study participant is actually attempting to say, striving for accuracy of information.

Methodology: 'A way of thinking about or studying social reality' (Strauss and Corbin, 1998, p. 3).

Methods: 'A set of procedures and techniques for gathering and analysing data' (Strauss and Corbin, 1998, p. 3).

Microanalysis: Detailed analysis of data (Strauss and Corbin, 1998).

Narrative: A story.

Phenomenon: An event or occurrence.

Practitioner: Person that works in a field of study or profession.

Proposition statements: Formal statements of relationship.

Quantitative: Using numerical data or measurements.

Sampling: Picking persons from a population.

Saturation: No new information emerges in data (Strauss and Corbin, 1998).

Subjective: In a person's mind or personal opinion and interpretation, not fact.

Systematic: Following a set of established procedures.

Theoretical sampling: Sampling based on developing concepts, variation, and gaps in data (Strauss and Corbin, 1998).

Theory: Concepts connected through statements of relationships, comprising and integrated framework useful in explaining or predicting phenomena (Strauss and Corbin, 1998).

Transcribe: Turning audio-recorded conversations into a verbatim script.

Discussion Questions

1. When is grounded theory the appropriate research method to utilize?

2. What are other recreation and tourism examples or settings where grounded theory research methods may be useful?

3. Can you write a research question for a grounded theory study?

4. Why is it important to use theoretical sampling in grounded theory research?

5. Why is it important to use memos during grounded theory research?

6. Why is it important to conduct member checks in grounded theory research?

7. Why is it important to evaluate grounded theory research?

8. How can results from grounded theory research be utilized?

9. How is a grounded theory research different from quantitative or survey research?

References

Charmaz, K. (1990) Discovering chronic illness: Using grounded theory. *Social Science Medicine* 30, 1161–1172.

Charmaz, K. (2000) Grounded theory: objectivist and constructivist methods. In: Denzin, N.K. and Lincoln, Y.S. (eds) *Handbook of Qualitative Research,* 2nd edition. Sage Publications, Thousand Oaks, California, pp. 509–535.

Charmaz, K. (2002) Qualitative interviewing and grounded theory analysis. In: Gubrium, J.F. and Holstein, J.A. (eds) *Inside Interviewing: New Lenses, New Concerns*. Sage Publications, Thousand Oaks, California, pp. 311–330.

Creswell, J.W. (1998) *Qualitative Inquiry and Research Design: Choosing among Five Traditions*. Sage Publications, Thousand Oaks, California.

Creswell, J.W. (2007) *Qualitative Inquiry and Research Design: Choosing among Five Approaches*. Sage Publications, Thousand Oaks, California.

Glaser, B. (1992) *Basics of Grounded Theory Analysis*. Sociology Press, Mill Valley, California.

Schram, T.H. (2006) *Conceptualizing and Proposing Qualitative Research*. Pearson, Upper Saddle River, New Jersey.

Scott, D. (2005) The relevance of constraints research to leisure service delivery. In: Jackson, E.L. (ed.) *Constraints to Leisure*. Venture Publishing, Inc., State College, Pennsylvania, pp. 279–293.

Strauss, A. and Corbin, J. (1990) *Basics of Qualitative Research: Grounded Theory Procedures and Techniques*. Sage Publications, Newbury Park, California.

Strauss, A. and Corbin, J. (1998) *Basics of Qualitative Research: Techniques and Procedures for Developing Grounded Theory*. Sage Publications, Thousand Oaks, California.

Strauss, A. and Corbin, J. (1994) Grounded theory methodology. In: Denzin, N.K. and Lincoln, Y.S. (eds) *Handbook of Qualitative Research*. Sage Publications, Thousand Oaks, California, pp. 273–280.

chapter 9

Evaluation Research Methods in Leisure, Recreation and Tourism Research

Gayle R. Jennings

Learning Objectives

After reading and engaging in the learning experiences provided by this chapter, you should be able to:

1. Understand the background and purpose of evaluation;

2. Compare and contrast a number of evaluation perspectives, processes and strategies;

3. Critically discuss the role of research methods in evaluation;

4. Identify and analyse ethical and responsible practice issues associated with evaluation research;

5. Critique the evaluation research reports of others;

6. Plan and develop an evaluation research project in an applied context.

Chapter Summary

The chapter focuses on evaluation and evaluation research. Evaluation aims to determine through the involvement of various stakeholders the benefit of processes and outcomes associated with leisure, recreation and tourism phenomena. There are different types of evaluation, such as formal and informal. Evaluation within tourism and recreation usually focuses on personnel, performance, products, practices, strategies, experiences, policies, processes, planning, proposals and programmes and technologies. There are a number of evaluation perspectives, processes and strategies. Perspectives include: (i) scientific-experimental tradition including quasi-experimental, objectives, econometrically, theory-driven evaluation; (ii) management-oriented and systems models such as PERT, CPM, UTOS and CIPP; (iii) qualitative/anthropological models; and (iv) participant-oriented models, which use processes such as AEIOU. The chapter also presents strategies of formative evaluation and summative evaluation and ends with discussions on the meaning of ethical and responsible research practice.

What is Evaluation?

Put simply, '[e]valuation is a structured, staged process of identifying, collecting and considering information' (Commonwealth of Australia, 2001). Various synonyms have been used, such as, measurement, grading, accountability, assessment, appraisal (Popham, 1975) and monitoring. Over time and across disciplines, professions and practices, a number of definitions have been developed. Table 9.1 provides an overview of some of the definitions from various sources to demonstrate to you the differing interpretations that relate to evaluation.

As is intimated by Weiss (1972) in Table 9.1, and as stated by Patton (1982, p. 35), 'no single-sentence definition will suffice to fully capture the practice of evaluation'. That being said, and given the diversity in the definitions presented in Table 9.1, a working definition will be posited for application in leisure, recreation and tourism contexts. The following is a generic adaptation of the various definitions of evaluation presented in Table 9.1, to assist our discussions in this chapter. Evaluation is both a formal and informal process that aims to determine the benefit of processes and/or outcomes associated with leisure, recreation and tourism, and

Table 9.1. Examples of evaluation definitions over time.

Definition	Reference
Evaluation is constituted of formative and summative types.	Scriven (1967)
Evaluation . . . an elastic word that stretches to cover judgements of many kinds.	Weiss (1972, p. 1)
A type of disciplined inquiry undertaken to determine the value (merit and/or worth) or some entity – the evaluand – such as a treatment, programme, facility, performance and the like – in order to improve or refine the evaluand (formative evaluation) or to assess its impact (summative evaluation).	Lincoln and Guba (1986, p. 550)
The process of establishing value judgments based on evidence.	Smith and Glass (1987, p. 31)
Evaluation refers to the process of determining the merit, worth or value of something, or the product of that process.	Scriven (1991, p. 139)
Evaluation is a political act in a context where power, ideology and interests are paramount and influence decisions more than evaluative feedback.	Shadish et al. (1991, p. 448)
Evaluation as a learning process takes place throughout the lifespan of every . . . initiative, including one-off projects, ongoing programmes, the management of services or resources, or the development of policy.	Webster and Raphael (2001, p. 5)
Evaluating (i.e. determining the merit, worth, or significance of) . . . programmes, policies, projects and technologies. . .	Schwandt (2001, p. 214)
Evaluation is a structured, staged process of identifying, collecting and considering information.	Commonwealth of Australia (2001, p. 1)
Systematic evaluation is conceptualized as a social and politicized practice that nonetheless aspires to some position of impartiality or fairness, so that evaluation can contribute meaningfully to the well-being of people in that specific context and beyond.	Mark, Greene and Shaw (2006, pp. 5–6)

which involves various stakeholder groups across diverse social, cultural and political contexts.

Types of Evaluation

Evaluation may be either formal or informal. Informal evaluations differ from formal evaluations by nature of the degree of systematic processes utilized (Worthen, Sanders and Fitzpatrick, 1997). Table 9.2 provides an overview of other differences between formal and informal evaluation. An example of an informal evaluation can be evidenced in work environments with the informal evaluation of people, performance, programmes, policies, strategies, processes and outcomes. While we may informally evaluate these as employees in the organisation on a personal and individual level, we can also draw on formal evaluation strategies to evaluate these areas in order to affect some change. To do this we need to shift from the personal, internal processing associated with informal evaluation to the more public, transparent, external processing associated with formal evaluation. However, since all evaluations incorporate human beings, elements of informal evaluation will be in attendance; the degree of their incorporation into the formal

Table 9.2. Informal and formal evaluation counterpoints.

Informal evaluation	Thematic counterpoint	Formal evaluation	
		Qualitative perspective	**Quantitative perspective**
Activities involve an unscheduled agenda	Nature of the process	Activities may be both scheduled and unscheduled	Activities involve a scheduled agenda
Adaptive and responsive actions	Nature of the activities	Considered, adaptive and responsive actions	Measured and considered actions
In-depth empirical materials	Nature of empirical materials and data interpreted and analysed	In-depth empirical materials	Precise data
Enables understanding	Efficacy	Enables understanding	Enables quantification, and/or comparability
Subjective orientation	Bias	Subjective orientation, socially constructed	Objective orientation
Naturalistic	Nature of the evaluation setting(s)	Naturalistic	Controlled
Localized and specific	Conclusions	Localized and specific	Representative
Subjectively determined	Applicability	Subjectively and socially determined	Objectively and at times subjectively determined depending on decision-maker perspectives

(Developed from Williams and Suen, 1998.)

evaluation processes will depend on the evaluation perspective inherent in the overall evaluation design. Refer to Table 9.2 for differences between qualitative and quantitative perspectives. Other perspectives regarding evaluation will be introduced and discussed in the following section.

Having already outlined what is informal evaluation, we conclude this section by considering what is formal evaluation? Formal evaluation is associated with making value judgements based on systematic processes in order to affect change in personnel, performance, products, policies, proposals and programmes. Scriven (1991, 1999) identifies these six items as the 'six Ps'. Examples of these six types of evaluation foci within leisure, recreation and tourism literature are presented in Worked Example 9.1, at the end of the chapter. In the appendix and elsewhere in this chapter, the six Ps have been extended to fit recreation and tourism contexts more specifically, hence you will see inclusion of the terms participants, strategies, experiences and technologies.

To reiterate, the focus of the remainder of this chapter are more formal processes of evaluation unless otherwise stated.

Evaluation Models, Perspectives, Processes and Strategies

In 1978, House, drawing on the work of Stake (1976), Popham (1975), and Worthen and Sanders (1973), identified a number of evaluation models based on the particular focus of the evaluations. Nine different frames were categorized: systems analysis (efficiency based), behavioural objectives (achievement of objectives, productivity, accountability based), decision making (effectiveness based), goal free (social utility based), art criticism (improved standards based), accreditation (professional acceptance based), adversary (resolution based) and transaction (diversity based). See also House (2005). An alternative framework to that proposed by House classifies evaluation strategies into four broad orientations based on their 'philosophical' perspectives or connections: scientific-experimental models, management-oriented systems models, qualitative/anthropological models, and participant-oriented models (Trochim, 2002). These are briefly described in the following sections; you will notice some overlap between Trochim and House's frameworks.

Scientific-experimental models

These models hold a hegemonic (dominant) position within evaluation perspectives, process and strategies. They align with quantitative perspectives of formal evaluation processes noted in Table 9.2. In particular, these models draw on the traditions of:

- Experimental (Campbell, 1969; Suchman, 1967) and quasi-experimental research (Campbell and Stanley, 1966; Rossi and Freeman, 1993).
- Objectives-based research; refer to Cracknell (1996).
- Econometrically oriented research, especially, cost-effectiveness/cost-benefit analyses; refer to Yates (1998).
- Theory-driven evaluation; see discussion by Chen (1994, 2004).

Management-oriented systems models

These models are derived from the placement of evaluation as an integral component within broader organisational strategies. A number of models appear in the literature and are used in practice:

- PERT - Programme Evaluation and Review Techniques
- CPM – Critical Path Method
- UTOS – Units, Treatments, Observations and Settings
- CIPP – Context, Input, Process, Product, see discussion by Stufflebeam (2004)

Qualitative/anthropological models

This model of evaluation is predicated upon phenomenological or naturalistic principles; refer to the qualitative perspectives of formal evaluation in Table 9.2 and see also Shaw (1999). This model acknowledges the social construction and interpretation of phenomena associated with recreation and tourism evaluation. In particular the traditions of interpretive social sciences, constructivism, constructionism, 'Fourth Generation' or naturalistic inquiry (see Guba and Lincoln, 1989), critical theory and grounded theory (see Glaser and Strauss,

1967; Strauss and Corbin, 1998; Charmaz, 2005) are used to amass and interpret empirical materials related to the evaluation.

Participant-oriented models

Participant-oriented models are based on stakeholder involvement and may be connected to action learning approaches. For example, one model, the AEIOU model, which is explained in the next section, utilizes evaluation as a process of 'continuous learning' (Commonwealth of Australia, 2001). In particular, participant-oriented or participatory evaluation supports the principles of a learning organization (Cousins and Earl, 1992), wherein stakeholders socially construct innovative actions/responses informed by shared experiences (memories) of the organization (see discussions by Argyris and Schön, 1978; Levitt and March, 1988; Senge, 1990; Rogers and Williams, 2006).

In addition to the four frames provided by Trochim (2002), Greene (2006) provides a different albeit complementary set of frames. These are outlined here, including the theoretical paradigms (see Jennings, 2009 and 2010 for further details on paradigms) informing their foci: democratic evaluation (constructivism and interpretivism), deliberative democratic evaluation (scientific realism, see Pawson and Tilley, 1997a, 1997b), participatory evaluation (constructivism, critical theory orientation), critical evaluation (critical theory orientation, feminisms) and cultural and contextually responsive evaluation (see Stake, 2004) and indigenous evaluation (constructivism, interpretivism, queer theory, indigenous epistemologies). Demonstrating some synergy with Pawson and Tilley's classification is Herman, Morris and Fitz-Gibbon's (1987) set of four programme evaluation models: goal-oriented, decision-oriented, responsive evaluation, evaluation research, goal-free evaluation, advocacy adversary and utilization-oriented evaluation.

Alkin (2004) provides background information for interested readers regarding various evaluation frameworks and their related theoretical/philosophical underpinnings or roots. He also incorporates several other frames: empowerment, utilization and responsive evaluations in his work. These are explained in turn below.

Empowerment Evaluation: Empowerment evaluation uses personally determined goals of programme participants to frame evaluation processes, in order to empower participants to effect positive change for themselves (Wehmeyer, 2002). This type of evaluation is considered to be a democratic way to foster self-determination (Clarke, 1999). Subsequently, empowerment evaluation entails a continuous modification of programmes based on participants 'self-evaluation and reflection' instead of an externally, objectively derived end-point evaluation (Fetterman, 1996, pp. 5, 6; see also Fetterman, 2000). External evaluators operate as facilitators, coaches and advocates. Some writers link empowerment evaluation with participant-oriented evaluation (Clarke, 1999; Patton, 2002; Greene, 2006), fourth-generation evaluation (see Clarke, 1999; Greene, 2006) or critical evaluation (see Greene, 2006).

Utilization-focused Evaluation: Patton (1986) identified the political nature of evaluation (see also Rossi and Freeman, 1993) and subsequently, for him, utility of evaluation was and is an imperative that requires cooperation between researchers, sponsors and users of evaluation research (Clarke, 1999). The process targets specific stakeholders who will apply or become direct recipients of the evaluation. 'A focus on intended use by intended users undergrids and informs every design decision in evaluation' (Patton, 2002, p. 173; see also Patton, 2004).

Responsive Evaluation: Responsive evaluation (Stake, 1975, 2004) is 'based on what people do naturally to evaluate things: they observe and react' (Stake, 1975, p. 9). This approach emphasises interpersonal engagements throughout evaluation processes, such as identifying issues and concerns, information gathering, strategy formation, and reporting especially matching of appropriate genres to various audiences. House (1978) classifies responsive evaluation as a form of transactional evaluation. It is subjective in nature and is particularly useful in formative evaluation. House (1978) accords responsive evaluation with democratic pluralism.

No doubt you will be aware now that evaluation is not as simplistic as you might have first thought. There are many frames and various authors have developed their own body of related writings. You might refer back to Case Study 9.1 at this point, to see several of the preceding frames used in an applied way. The previous synthesis of an expansive literature has been presented here in order that you are familiar with as many frames as possible so that you are able to choose in an informed way the frame or frames that best suits or suit your evaluation purposes as well as to encourage you to seek out related additional supporting literature. With that said, a note of caution in making your choice, be aware of critiques of various frames. For example, despite the dominance of experimental and quasi-experimental approaches, scientific realism (Pawson and Tilley, 2003) and realistic evaluation are said to challenge the tenets of experimental and quasi-experimental evaluation (Farrington, 2003). The latter is more concerned with 'what works' and the former is more concerned with 'testing theories, especially about linkages between contexts, mechanisms and outcomes' (Farrington, 2003, p. 51). Cronbach (1982) provides a further critique of experimental approaches regarding their focus and emphasis on measurement.

In the end, ensure you are fully informed of the mechanics of each of the frames, their similarity with related frames, and their critiques to enable more informed decision-making as well as their processes for conduct and reporting. For as Owen (1999) comments, equal attention needs to be given to the planning of evaluation processes as well as the dissemination of evaluation findings. Not only does an evaluator require knowledge and skills related to qualitative, quantitative, mixed methods and indigenous methodologies for the conduct of evaluations, but also knowledge that the planning phases of an evaluation require interpersonal skills and the dissemination phase requires communication skills. Of course, interpersonal and communication skills are also important for the conduct of the evaluation itself. Subsequently, as an evaluation researcher you need a fully rounded suite of related skills.

Evaluation Processes

As you are now aware, evaluation strategies and models are manifold. The models may be presented as simple to more sophisticated versions depending on the nature, range and approach utilized. For example, the AEIOU model mentioned earlier is portrayed as a simple model involving five steps. The steps are tied to the mnemonic AEIOU:

Step 1: **A**sk critical questions.

Step 2: **E**xamine ways, perspectives, methodologies and methods to achieve answers to the critical questions.

Step 3: **I**nitiate information gathering and interpretation.

Step 4: **O**ptions for future directions and changes.

Step 5: **U**ndertake change strategies to enable best practice (Commonwealth of Australia, 2001).

The empowerment model, on the other hand, entails only four steps:

1. Establishing a baseline.
2. Setting goals and objectives.
3. Co-constructing processes and strategies to achieve the above.
4. Co-identification of constructs to determine progress (Wehmeyer, 2002).

While these two have been relatively simple models, more technically sophisticated evaluation models may be derived from longitudinal study designs using multiple methods, a mix of methods and/or multiphase approaches.

Types of Evaluation Strategies

Evaluation can be organized into two frames: formative and summative evaluation. This framing is associated with the work of Shriven (1967) and particularly evaluation of educational curricula. Today, these two frames have been accepted across disciplines, and fields of study including recreation and tourism. The dominant views of summative and formative evaluation follow. One view of summative evaluation is the process of determining the failure or success of projects by matching outcomes to goals; while formative evaluation is the process of determining the achievement of project benchmarks in order to refine project strategies in the course of project implementation (Hernández, 2000). Scriven (1967) described summative evaluation as endpoint evaluation and formative as progress evaluation, others have critiqued this duality. In particular, McKenzie and Smeltzer (2001) suggest that there is a blurring of boundary lines between the two, since formative and summative, both involve evaluation before, during and at the end of evaluation processes.

Formative evaluation

Examples of formative evaluation are needs assessments, structured conceptualization, implementation, process evaluation and evaluability assessments (Trochim, 2002).

Needs Assessments: Needs assessments involve the determination of key stakeholders needs, the severity of such needs and the relevant programme to address those needs (Trochim, 2002). The community-oriented needs assessment (CONA) model (see Neuber, 1981), for example, can be used to enable interaction and communication between community stakeholders and, for our purposes, leisure, recreation and tourism providers to distinguish requisite leisure, recreation and tourism services whilst simultaneously engaging the key stakeholders in planning, implementation and evaluation phases. This method has comparability with participatory oriented approaches. CONA methods include secondary analyses and key informant interviews (see also McKillip, 1998).

Structured Conceptualization: Structured conceptualization assists stakeholders in developing appropriate programmes, practices, experiences and/or technologies. It enables the identification of target populations as well as the matching of outcomes to the programme and focus population (Trochim, 2002).

Implementation Evaluation: Implementation evaluation engages evaluators in ongoing assessment, that is, monitoring of the effectiveness and quality of programmes, practices, policies and/or technology during the course of their conduct (Trochim, 2002).

Process Evaluation: Process evaluation hones in on programme or technology delivery processes, including different delivery procedures to ensure maintenance or improvement of quality in the course of implementation (Trochim, 2002).

Evaluability Assessment: Evaluability assessment reflects on stakeholder involvement in the design of evaluation in order to ensure the effectiveness of evaluation. It also identifies whether or not an evaluation is possible and practical (Trochim, 2002).

Summative evaluation

Summative evaluation can also be subdivided into outcome evaluations, impact evaluations, cost-effectiveness and cost-benefit analysis, secondary analysis and metaanalysis (Trochim, 2002).

Outcome Evaluations: These types of evaluations attempt to determine whether stated outcomes of recreation and tourism were achieved as well as the degree of their effectiveness (Trochim, 2002).

Impact Evaluation: Impact evaluation is related to ascertaining whether the specific aims of performances, strategies, practices, products, experiences, policies, programmes and technologies have achieved stated progressive and endpoint outcomes. Empirical materials and data collected are associated with knowledge, skills, attitudes, behaviour and awareness (McKenzie and Smeltzer, 2001). Methods used include experiments and quasi-experiments, regression-discontinuity, comparative change, criterion population and time series designs as well as qualitative methods (Mohr, 1995).

Cost-Effectiveness and Cost-Benefit Analysis: These are financially based evaluations, which determine the feasibility of strategies, programmes, products, experiences, policies, technologies with regard to monetary costs and return for investment (Trochim, 2002). Approaches include cost-effectiveness analysis, cost-benefit analysis and cost-utility analysis (see Levin and McEwan, 2001). Cost-effectiveness analysis compares costs of two or more strategies with their respective outcomes; usually a ratio is utilized to determine the effectiveness. Cost-benefit analysis includes contingency analysis wherein people assign monetary values of worth to a particular phenomenon (Neuman, 2000). For example, what would you have to be paid not to fish a particular area? A second way is actual cost evaluation (Neuman, 2000). Neuman (2000) commented that cost-benefit analysis assumes that all things have a price, and subsequently moral–political elements are masked by economic considerations. Conversely, cost utility does not always consider benefit in financial terms, albeit the benefit will be represented in a quantitative form such as an index.

Secondary Analysis: Secondary analysis reconsiders available empirical materials and data to reflect on more recent issues or implementation strategies which are novel or without previous application (Trochim, 2002). Sources include government information such as census, and government documents, syndicated commercial and non-government sources, computer-assisted information such as CD Rom and online materials (Stewart and Kamins, 1993; see also Cooper and Lindsay, 1998).

Table 9.3. Types of evaluation and some examples from recreation and tourism literature.

Formative evaluation	Summative evaluation
Needs assessments, see Bricker and Kerstetter (2006).	*Outcome evaluations*, see Oliver (1977); Hunter *et al.* (2006); Burke and Lindblom (1989); Stergiou and Airey (2003).
Structured conceptualization, see Proctor and Dreschler (2003).	*Impact evaluations*, see Dwyer *et al.* (2004); Carlsen *et al.* (2001).
Evaluability assessments, see Heller (1992).	*Cost-effectiveness and cost-benefit analysis*, see Smith (1971); Jurowski *et al.* (2006).
Process evaluation, see Bogaards, *et al.* (2000).	*Secondary analysis*, see Whitford *et al.* (1999)
Participatory evaluation, see Proctor and Dreschler (2003); Daniels and Pennington-Gray (2006).	*Meta-analysis*, see Bricker *et al.* (2006); Oliver (1977).

Meta-Analysis: Meta-analysis synthesizes results from many related studies to determine an informed summation upon which to make decisions relating to a specific evaluation question or questions (Trochim, 2002). Auditing and meta-evaluation have linkages, which can be leveraged to facilitate the success of either scientific-experimental or naturalistic models of meta-evaluation (Schwandt and Halpern, 1988).

Examples of some of the various types of summative and formative evaluations previously discussed as used in recreation and tourism fields are presented in Table 9.3. You are encouraged to see the related works for further details.

Evaluation Research Methods

'What distinguishes evaluation research from other research is not method or even subject matter, but intent – the purpose for which it is done' (Bond, 1996). In particular, evaluation research involves the monitoring of 'objectives, strategies, and programs . . . to determine their degree of success and failure as well as the underlying causes of their impact (Weiss, 1972)' (Ritchie 1994, p. 16). Essentially, evaluation research methods reflect the same research methods used in social science research. The methods are informed by either a qualitative or quantitative methodology, which, in turn, is related to two paradigmatic (set of beliefs) perspectives about the way the world may be understood. These paradigms are represented in earlier discussions of scientific experimental and quasi-experimental and qualitative/anthropological models. Further discussion of the paradigms may be found in Jennings (2009, 2010). According to Stake (1995, p. 96), quantitative evaluations focus on 'productivity and effectiveness of criteria' and report findings using measurements and scales, whereas qualitative evaluations are more concerned with 'quality of activities and processes' and report interpretations using narrative style.

In addition to these two paradigmatic representations, there has been a growth of the mixing of methods. Mixed methods have also been referred to as methodological pluralism (Lawrenz and Huffman, 2006). Past practice has been to use quantitative methods as primary evaluation methods especially outcomes with qualitative evaluation methods assisting with evaluation of programme processes (Caracelli and Greene, 1993). Along a similar line, Chatterji (2005) recommends the use of Extended-Term Mixed Method Evaluation (ETMM) designs in order to achieve rigour in evaluation processes by preceding experimental designs with 'appropriate descriptive research methods' in the beginning phases of programme lifecycles to capture the complexity of the broader societal and organization contexts and settings in which the programme operates.

Greene *et al.* (1989) in a review of 57 evaluation studies developed a fivefold typology in regard to the purposes for the use of mixed methods in evaluations:

1. Triangulation, corroboration of findings through the use of different methods (at least one qualitative and one quantitative method).

2. Complementarity, using either a qualitative or a quantitative method to augment the findings of the other.

3. Development, lock-step connectivity between use of one or the other method (qualitative or quantitative) to enhance the efficacy of the next method and its findings.

4. Initiation, challenging and 'testing' questions and findings from one method with that of the alternate method.

5. Expansion, using both qualitative and quantitative methods to widen the scope and nature of evaluations.

According to Berk and Rossi (1999, p. 2), 'commonsense program evaluation has evolved into *evaluation research*, a heterogeneous mix of substantive issues and procedures'. The challenge for evaluation researchers is the comment that evaluation researchers 'need to identify when and where to use methodologies, appropriate ways to merge data collected using diverse methodologies [including indigenous methodologies], and how to fairly report the results to a variety of audiences' (Lawrenz and Huffman, 2006, p. 31).

An overview of dominant evaluation methodologies and accompanying examples of methods as well as applications in tourism and recreation fields is provided in Worked Example 9.2.

Goals of Evaluation Research

Given the definitions already discussed, and presented in Table 9.1, it would seem self-evident what the goals of evaluation research are. However, these will be articulated here. The goals of evaluation research are to effect change for the better, whether this be in regard to personnel, participants, performance, strategies, practice, tourism and recreation products and experiences, leisure, tourism and recreation policies, planning, proposals, programmes and technologies, and, for the purposes of this chapter, in recreation and tourism settings. The degree to which evaluation research may affect or influence the aforementioned, according to Cousins and Leithwood (1986), is dependent on:

1. Information requirements of organizations, as well as primary stakeholders along with their core beliefs, values and attitudes towards the evaluation process;

2. The nature of the decision-making circumstances, that is, whether actions associated with evaluation recommendations are contentious, challenging, unpalatable, innovative, untested, an imperative or critical;

3. Organizational climate and political contexts, which may be influenced by both internal and external factors, such as internal power disputes, external and internal pressures, auditing responsibilities or tensions with external funding agencies;

4. Incorporation or utilization of alternate information sets, that is, the degree to which evaluation processes have acknowledged and addressed other available and related information sources within evaluation processes;

5. The role of management and leaders with regard to their expertise, understandings, experiences, skills and styles;

6. The 'buy-in-ness' of those with the power to make decisions regarding the evaluation, whether they are committed to, neutral or against the evaluation.

An additional element has been added by Alkin *et al.* (1985):

7. The evaluator, her or himself, with regard to experience, style or approach, skills and competence.

A further complementary set of considerations has been proffered by Alkin (1990):

1. Quality and overall integrity of the evaluation;

2. Professional skill set and standing of the evaluator;

3. Quality and integrity of evaluation reporting (and Babbie, 1988, would add readability by multiple stakeholder audiences);

4. Match of evaluation findings with regard to evaluation purpose and brief;

5. Propitiousness of evaluation with regard to decision making timelines.

Neuman (2006) outlines a number of constraints that may impinge on evaluations. These include sponsors limiting the focus of studies and specifying outcome foci as well as ethical and political consequences of evaluations (see the next section). Such constraints need to be considered by evaluation researchers. The nature of evaluations as political acts has also been noted by a number of writers; for example, see Lincoln and Guba (1986), Clarke (1999) and Alkin (1990).

Having considered the goals of evaluation research, these goals may not be achievable for all stakeholder groups. Implicit in evaluation research as with other research are issues of ethics and responsible behaviour. In particular, because of the various stakeholders who may be affected by any evaluation outcomes, researchers need to be cognizant of the role they will be performing and ensure that they are ethically and socially comfortable with their roles.

Ethical and Responsible Practice Issues Associated with Evaluation Research

Evaluation is about improving or determining the value of something. Ethical issues related to evaluation research include:

- Fulfilling responsibilities associated with ethical codes of conduct.
- Ensuring no physical, psychological, legal or other harm comes to participants (see Neuman, 2006).
- Attending to ethical principles associated with any participation of minors, people with disabilities, cross-cultural and indigenous issues, the aged, people unable to make rational decisions (National Health and Medical Council, 2005).
- Undertaking a reasonable search for existing knowledge associated with the evaluation process.
- Acting ethically regarding recruitment of participants and stakeholders.
- Gaining informed consent regarding participation.
- Minimizing the risks and maximizing the benefits of the evaluation research.
- Addressing confidentiality/privacy issues responsibly and ethically.
- Considering and ameliorating power imbalances, which may occur in the course of evaluation research processes.
- Reflecting on conflict of interests and ethically and responsibly addressing the same (Neuman, 2006).
- Ensuring that the results are legitimate and ethically determined.
- Providing feedback to stakeholders for informed decision-making purposes and for reciprocity reasons.

Issues of responsible practice associated with evaluation research include:

- Professional conduct.
- Conflicts of interest.
- Authorship.
- Data storage.
- Legal privacy issues.
- Workplace health and safety.
- Avoiding misconduct.

A number of critiques have been levied regarding ethics and responsible practice of evaluation research. These include critiques of traditional programme evaluation being limited in scope since goal setting is the responsibility of funding sources or management and not programme recipients (Council on Quality and Leadership in Supports for People with Disabilities, 1997). House and Howe (1999) remind us that interplay between facts and values related to both quantitative and qualitative evaluation processes and issues can arise in contract evaluations. Additionally, other critiques of evaluations are associated with evaluating compliance with procedural mechanisms and that this does not necessarily achieve an effective evaluation of the quality of programmes (Wehmeyer, 2002).

Uses of evaluation research

As noted by Stufflebeam and Shinkfield (1985, p. 151), 'The most important purpose of evaluation is not to prove but to improve'. As a consequence, this section now considers the uses of evaluation research. Weiss (1986) classified seven uses of evaluation research:

1. Knowledge-driven model, wherein basic research informs applied research and subsequent real world applications.
2. Problem-solving model, where specific and related empirical research informs specific current and future issues.
3. Interactive model, which engages relevant stakeholders to generate knowledge.
4. Political model, which recognizes that political leanings influence acceptance or rejection of evaluation outcomes.
5. Tactical model, which utilizes research in progress to subsequently avert critique or actions being taken.

Case Study 9.1. Recreation policy evaluation.

The purpose of this case study is to demonstrate some of the different ways that evaluation may be undertaken, as well as an example of research tools that may be used to assist evaluation processes.

In the past, the allocation of land and resources in British Columbia for recreation and tourism industry operators has been of lesser importance than the more economic and resource intensive extractive industries, such as plantation forestry. However, towards the end of the 1990s, as a consequence of a wide-ranging review of planning and management of land and resources, traditional land and resource allocation practices were ameliorated. One of the outcomes of this review was the development of a number of policies, which enabled several recreation/tourism industry sectors previously restricted from participating in tenure agreements with government land to be able to do so. In 1998, the Commercial Recreation on Crown Land Policy (British Columbia MELP, 1998) paved the way for greater participation by commercial recreation operators in regard to crown land and resource usage.

An evaluation of the piloting of the policy in Squamish Forest District was undertaken by Curtis (2003). Curtis, using a case study approach, focused on the Transition Plan (see British Columbia MELP, 1995) implementation from September 2000 to November 2001. His evaluation perspective was situated in policy evaluation, specifically, effectiveness and efficiency evaluation, that is, systems analysis, objectives-based evaluations, impacts evaluation and stakeholder evaluation models. Curtis' research addressed process evaluation (input–output studies) and had linkages with participant-oriented evaluation. His complementary research methods for empirical material collection utilized interviews with stakeholders, and a review of land processes. His analysis was based on identifying key thematic units. As a consequence of his evaluation, Curtis found that, in the main, stakeholders were accepting of the Transition Plan programme and that Commercial Recreation (CR) Policy objectives were not completely achieved due to a number of barriers. Critique of the programme related to 'environmental stewardship', 'public access and use' issues, as well as the 'agency's relationship with First Nations', knowledge of agency's earlier planning strategies to address carrying capacity issues, and lack of incorporation of public recreational values in early planning phases. Curtis made some 30 criteria-related recommendations and 24 process recommendations for the agency. He also identified the following areas as requiring further research:

1. Identification of a system of indicators suitable for use in recreation carrying capacity management programs;
2. Identification of ways to create direct economic benefits for First Nations from Commercial Recreation, CR, management programs;
3. Assessment of the value of CR activities in relation to other types of resource use.

Source: This case study is based on Curtis, N. (2003) *Managing Commercial Recreation on Crown Land in British Columbia: a Policy Evaluation*. M.R.M. research project no. 337, School of Resource and Environmental Management. Simon Fraser University, Burnaby, British Columbia.

---

6. Enlightenment model, wherein evaluation research outcomes are made known to publics, who in turn influence policy.
7. Intellectual enterprise model, in which evaluation research sways intellectuals and policy makers to shape public thought and are in turn shaped by public thought.

Additionally, Alkin (1985) classified four influences on use value of evaluation that you should bear in mind: evaluator characteristics, stakeholder/user participation in process, evaluation context and integrity of the evaluation process itself.

Key Terms

Evaluation: Evaluation is both a formal and informal process that aims to determine the benefit of processes and/or outcomes associated with recreation and tourism, and which involves various stakeholder groups across diverse social, cultural and political contexts.

Formal evaluation: Formal evaluation is associated with making value judgements based on systematic processes in order to effect change in personnel, performance, products, policies, proposals, programmes, strategies, experiences and technologies.

Summative evaluation: Summative evaluation is the process of determining the failure or success of projects by matching outcomes to goals. It is sometimes referred to as end-point evaluation.

Formative evaluation: Formative evaluation is the process of determining the achievement of project benchmarks in order to refine project strategies in the course of project. Formative evaluation has been described as progress evaluation.

Discussion Questions

1. What is the difference between formal and informal evaluation?

2. What is the purpose of formal evaluation in recreation and tourism?

3. Consider the various perspectives, processes and strategies of evaluation. When would you use each and why?

4. In your opinion, what is the role of research in recreation and tourism evaluation?

5. What are the key ethical and responsible practice issues for evaluations in recreation and tourism?

Worked Example 9.1.

Types of evaluation foci and examples from recreation and tourism literature

Evaluation type	Foci	Examples from recreation and tourism literature
Personnel/ participants	Assessing intercultural competence of tour guides.	Yu (2003) used mixed methods (semi-structured interviews and questionnaires).
	Customer satisfaction with service reliability and responsiveness.	Andaleeb and Conway (2006) used mixed method approach secondary sources, qualitative interviews and a questionnaire.
Performance	Performance: Evaluation of the use of evaluation research by a National Tourism Board.	Oliver (1977) used survey method.
	Performance: Comparative performance analysis of Turkey to other destinations.	Yüksel and Yüksel (2001) used modified expert.
Practice	Practice: Assessment of usage practices and importance of event evaluation by tourism destination authorities.	Carlsen, Getz and Soutar (2003) used a Delphic survey to develop standardized criteria for pre- and post- event evaluation.
	Practice: An evaluation of factors influencing customer loyalty in the restaurant industry.	Wilkins and Hwang (2004) used participant observation to evaluate customer loyalty.
Strategies	Strategies: Direct response marketing.	Burke and Lindblom (1989) used conversion studies.
Products/ experiences/ participants	Product/experience: Customer satisfaction of full service restaurants.	Andaleeb and Conway (2006) used the transaction-model, see Teas (1993) and Parasuraman et al. (1994). Design used mixed method approach secondary sources, qualitative interviews and questionnaires.
	Experience: Evaluation of 1987 Southeast Therapeutic Recreation Symposium.	King (1988) used mixed methods to achieve triangulation.
	Experience: Formative evaluation to determine appropriate strategies for school leavers' celebrations.	Bogaards et al. (2000) used mixed methods - interviews with different stakeholders, participant observation; and triangulation.
	Experience: Visitor evaluations of crowding and other recreational impacts.	Manning (2003) critiqued the work of Stewart and Cole (2001) in relation to crowding and solitude.

(Continued)

Worked Example 9.1. Continued.

Evaluation type	Foci	Examples from recreation and tourism literature
	Experiences: Resident attitudes and perceptions of tourism impacts.	Brougham and Butler (1981) and Davis *et al.* (1988) used segmentation analysis.
		Gursoy *et al.* (2000, 2002) used structural equation modelling.
Policies	Determining recreation and tourism options based on various stakeholder inputs.	Proctor and Dreschler (2003) applied multi-criteria evaluation via Citizens' jury.
	Determining economic impacts to assist policy formulation.	Dwyer *et al.* (2004) critiqued multiplier analysis and input–output models. Authors proposed Computable General Equilibrium (CGE) as a viable alternative.
Planning/Proposals	Determining the recreational potential of water resources.	Smith (1971) used cost-benefit analysis.
	Determining residents' interpretations of benefits and costs of tourism.	Jurowski *et al.* (2006) reported on a study using mail questionnaires supplemented by face to face interview technique.
Programmes/ Participants	Determination of effectiveness of state-funded tourism programmes.	Heller (1992) used an evaluability assessment model.
	Effectiveness of free-choice learning programmes in museum sector.	Kelly (2004) used transaction approach and audience research.
	Evaluation of Summer camp for chronically ill children.	Hunter *et al.* (2006) used mission-based programme evaluation.
Technologies	Determination of website advertising effectiveness and conversion studies.	Stergiou and Airey (2003) used conversion studies; and Tierney (2000) used conversion studies and tracking.

Worked Example 9.2.

Research methodologies, some associated methods used in evaluation research and applications in tourism and recreation

Qualitative methodology		Quantitative methodology		Mixed methods		Indigenous methodology	
Method	Tourism/ recreation application	Method	Tourism/ recreation application	Method	Tourism/ recreation application	Method	Tourism/ recreation application
Direct observation – participant observation	Impacts of farm tourism operations on farm and family life (Jennings and Stehlik, 2001)	Experimental design	Formative evaluation of an interpretive brochure in a marine park setting (Moscardo, 1999)	Questionnaires and participant observation	Formative evaluation of an interpretive brochure in a marine park setting (Moscardo, 1999)	Participant observation	Study of an indigenous business' success factors (Radel, 2005)
Ethnography	Study of long term ocean cruisers, provides an evaluation of mainstream society (Jennings, 1999)	Quasi-experimental designs	A study of the effectiveness of Hawaii Visitors' Bureau advertising campaign (Mok, 1990)	Focus groups and questionnaires	Socio-economic impact study of defence training activities in recreational spaces (Stehlik et al., 2004)	Focus groups	Scoping study for the development of Australian Indigenous tourism research strategy (Boyle, 2001)
In-depth interviews	Study (evaluation) of British travel companies of provision of travel experiences for midlife women travelling alone (Jordan, 1998)	Questionnaires	Effectiveness evaluation of a tourism promotional website (Tierney, 2000)	Questionnaires, in-depth interviews focus groups	Formative evaluation of school leavers' celebrations on Rottnest Island. (Bogaards et al., 2000)	In-depth interviews	In-depth interviews related to self determination and Aboriginal tourism planning (Nielsen, 2004)

Focus groups	Investigation of leisure and travel experiences of international students provides an evaluation of leisure and travel opportunities (Junek et al., 2008)	Focus groups/ Delphic technique	Delphi study of event evaluation usage (Carlsen et al., 2001)	Questionnaires, In-depth interviews, citizens' jury and documentary analysis	Evaluation of recreation and tourism options. (Proctor and Dreschler, 2003)	Focus groups/ community consultation	Study of lived experience of conservation in Nepal (Gurung, 2008)
Participatory action research	Study of white-water rafting guiding experiences (Jonas, 1999)	Participatory action research	Responses to public responses to planning changes in natural and marine park settings. Refer to Great Barrier Reef Marine Park Authority (2007)	Participatory action research	Responses to public responses to planning changes in natural and marine park settings. Refer to Great Barrier Reef Marine Park Authority (2007)	Participatory action research	Participatory action research study of the development of an indigenous tourism enterprise (Bennett, 2004)
Case studies	Evaluation of effectiveness and efficiency of interim commercial recreation policy (Curtis, 2003)	Case studies	Study reports on cognitive and affective domain influences on image assessment of Lanzarote, Spain (Beerli and Martin, 2004)	Case studies	Study of use of relationship and ITD factors influencing Small, Medium Enterprises, SMEs' use of destination marketing systems (Hornby, 2007)	Case studies	A reflexive report on the use of cross-cultural research methods in indigenous research using Cook Islands as a case study (Berno, 1996)

Due to overlap between some traditions and methods, examples may appear in more than one location.

References

Alkin, M.C. (2004) *Evaluation Roots: Tracing Theorists' Views and Influences*. Sage, Thousand Oaks, California.

Alkin, M.C. (1985) *A Guide for Evaluation Decision Makers*. Sage, Beverley Hills, California.

Alkin, M.C. (1990) *Debates on Evaluation*. Sage, Newbury Park, California.

Alkin, M.C., Jacobson, P., Burry, J., Ruskus, J., White, P. and Kent, L. (1985) *Guide for Evaluation Decision Makers*. Sage, Beverley Hills, California.

Andaleeb, S.S. and Conway, C. (2006) Customer satisfaction in the restaurant industry: an examination of the transaction-specific model. *Journal of Services Marketing* 20, 3–11.

Argyris, C and Schön, E. (1978) *Organizational Learning: A Theory of Action Perspective*. Addison-Wesley. Reading, MA.

Babbie, E. (1988). Evaluation research: Formulating the problem. *The Practice of Social Research*. Wadsworth Publishing Company, Belmont, California.

Beerli, A. and Martin, J.D. (2004) Tourists' characteristics and the perceived image of tourist destinations: A quantitative analysis – a case study of Lanzarote, Spain. *Tourism Management* 25, 623–636.

Bennet, J. (2004) Indigenous entrepreneurship, social capital and tourism enterprise development: lessons from Cape York. Unpublished PhD thesis, LaTrobe University, Australia.

Berk, R.A. and Rossi, P.H. (1999) *Thinking about Program Evaluation,* 2nd edn. Sage, Thousand Oaks, California.

Berno, T. (1996) Cross-cultural research methods: content or context? A Cook Islands example. In: Butler, R. and Hinch, T. (eds) *Tourism and Indigenous Peoples*. International Thomson Business Press, London, pp. 376–395.

Bricker, K.S., Daniels, M.J. and Carmichael, B.A. (2006) Quality tourism development and planning. In Jennings, G. and Nickerson, N. (eds) *Quality Tourism Experiences*. Elsevier, Burlington, Massachusetts, pp. 171–191.

Bricker, K.S. and Kerstetter. D. (2006) Saravanua ni vanua: exploring sense of place in the rural highliands of Fiji. In: Jennings, G. and Nickerson, N. (eds) *Quality Tourism Experiences*. Elsevier, Burlington, Massachusetts, pp. 99–111.

British Columbia MELP (Ministry of Environment, Lands and Parks) (1998) *Commercial Recreation on Crown Land Policy*. Victoria, British Columbia.

British Columbia MELP (Ministry of Environment, Lands and Parks) (1995) *Commercial Backcountry Recreation (Interim) Policy*. Victoria, British Columbia.

Bogaards, T.R. Midford, R. and Farringdon, F. (2000) *School leavers' celebrations on Rottnest Island: Formative Evaluation Report*. Western Australia, Curtin University of Technology for the School of Drug Education Project, pp. 1–93.

Bond, S. (1996) Evaluation research. In: Cormack, D. (ed.) *The Research Process in Nursing,* 3rd edn. Blackwell Science, Oxford, pp. 190–201.

Boyle, A. (2001) *Australian Indigenous Tourism Research Strategy Scoping Study*. Workshop Report, Darwin.

Brougham, J. and Butler, R.W. (1981) A segmentation analysis of resident attitudes to the social impact of tourism. *Annals of Tourism Research* 8, 569–590.

Burke, J.F. and Lindblom. L.A. (1989) Strategies for evaluating direct response tourism marketing. *Journal of Travel Research* 28, 33–37.

Campbell, D.T. and Stanley, J.C. (1966) *Experimental and Quasi-experimental Designs for Research*. Rand McNally, Skokie, Illinois.

Campbell, D.T. (1969) Reforms as experiments. *American Psychologist* 24, 409–428.

Caracelli, V.J. and Greene, J.C. (1993) Data analysis strategies for mixed method evaluation designs. *Educational Evaluation and Policy Analysis* 15, 195–207.

Carlsen, J., Getz, D. and Soutar, G. (2001) Event evaluation research. *Event Management* 6, 247–257.

Charmaz, K. (2005) Grounded theory in the 21st century: applications for advancing social justice studies. In: Denzin, N.K. and Lincoln, Y.S. (eds) *The Sage Handbook of Qualitative Research*, 3rd edn. Sage, Thousand Oak, California, pp. 507–535.

Chatterji, M. (2005) Evidence on "what works": An argument for extended-term mixed-method (ETMM) evaluation designs. *Educational Researcher* 34, 14–24.

Chen, H.-T. (1994) *Theory-driven Evaluations*. Sage, London.

Chen, H.-T. (2004) The roots of theory-driven evaluation: current views and origins. In: Alkin, M.C. (2004) (ed.) *Evaluation Roots: Tracing Theorists' Views and Influences*. Sage, Thousand Oaks, California, pp. 132–152.

Clarke, A. with Dawson, R. (1999) *Evaluation Research: an Introduction to Principles, Methods and Practice*. Sage, London.

Clemisky, E. and Shadish, W. (eds) (1997) *Evaluation for the 21st Century*. Sage, Thousand Oaks, California.

Commonwealth of Australia (2001) *Evaluation: a Guide for Good Practice*. Department of Health and Aged Care, Canberra.

Cooper, H.M. and Lindsay, J.J. (1998) Research synthesis and meta-analysis. In: Bickman, L. and Rog, D.J. (eds) *Handbook of Applied Social Research Methods*. Sage, Thousand Oaks, California, pp. 315–338.

Corbett, D.C. (1996) Chapter 10: Evaluation. *Australian Public Sector Management*. Allen & Unwin, St Leonards, Australia, pp. 180–195.

Council on Quality and Leadership in Supports for People with Disabilities (1997) *Personal outcomes measures*. Council on Quality and Leadership in Supports for People with Disabilities, Towson, Maryland.

Cousins, J.B. and Earl, L.M. (1992) The case for participatory evaluation. *Educational Evaluation and Policy Analysis* 14, 397–418.

Cousins, J.B. and Leithwood, K.A. (1986) Current empirical research on evaluation utilization. *Review of Educational Research* 56, 331–365.

Cracknell, B. (1996) Evaluating development aid. *Evaluation* 2, 23–34.

Cronbach, L.J. (1982) *Designing evaluations of educational and social programmes*. Jossey-Bass, San Francisco, USA.

Curtis, N. (2003) *Managing commercial recreation on Crown land in British Columbia: a policy evaluation*. M.R.M. research project no. 337, School of Resource and Environmental Management. Simon Fraser University, Burnaby, British Columbia[URL:http://www.rem.sfu.ca/pdf/curtis.pdf#search=%22MANAGING%20COMMERCIAL%20RECREATION%20ON%20CROWN%20LAND%20IN%22]

Daniels, M.J. and Pennington-Gray, L. (2006) Introduction to political economic construction of quality tourism experiences. In: Jennings, G. and Nickerson, N. (eds) *Quality Tourism Experiences*. Elsevier, Burlington, Massachusetts, pp. 159–170.

Davis, D., Allen, J. and Cosenza, R.M. (1988) Segmenting local residents by their attitudes, interest, and opinions toward tourism. *Journal of Travel Research* 27, 2–8.

Dwyer, L., Forsyth, P. and Spurr, R. (2004) Evaluating tourism's economic effects: New and old approaches. *Tourism Management* 25, 307–317.

Farrington, D. P. (2003) Methodological quality standards for evaluation research. *Annals, AAPSS* 587, 49–68.

Fetterman, D.M. (2000) *Foundations of Empowerment Evaluation*. Sage, Thousand Oaks, California.

Fetterman, D.M. (1996) Empowerment evaluation: an introduction. In: Fetterman, D.M., Kaftarian, S. and Wandersman, A. (eds) *Empowerment Evaluation: Knowledge and Tools for Self-assessment and Accountability*. Sage, Thousand Oaks, California, pp. 3–48.

Glaser, B.G. and Strauss, A.L. (1967) *The Discovery of Grounded Theory Strategies for Qualitative Research*. Aldine, New York.

Great Barrier Reef Marine Park Authority (2007) *Public participation*. Downloaded 14 January 2007. URL: http://www.gbrmpa.gov.au/corp_site/management/management_philosophy#Public

Greene, J.C. (2006) Evaluation, democracy, and social change. In Shaw, I.F., Greene, J.C., and Mark, M.M. *The Sage Handbook of Evaluation*. Sage, London, pp. 118–140.

Greene, J.C., Caracelli, V.J. and Graham, W.F. (1989) Toward a conceptual framework for mixed-method evaluation designs. *Educational Evaluation and Policy Analysis* 11, 255–274.

Guba, E.G. and Lincoln, Y.S. (1989) *Fourth Generation Evaluation*. Sage Publications, Newbury Park, California.

Gursoy, D., Chen, J., and Yoon, Y. (2000, June 11–14). Using structural equation modeling to assess the effects of tourism impact factors and local residents support for tourism development. *Thirty-first Annual Travel and Tourism Research Association Conference Proceedings*. San Fernando Valley, California, pp. 243–250.

Gursoy, D., Jurowski, C. and Uysal, M. (2002) Resident attitudes: A structural modeling approach. *Annals of Tourism Research* 29, 79–105.

Gurung, H. (2008) Fusioning: A grounded theory of participatory governance in the Annapurna conservation Area, Nepal. Unpublished PhD, Griffith University, Australia.

Heller, V.L. Jnr, (1992) Determining the effectiveness of state-funded tourism programs. Doctorate of Public Administration Dissertation, Arizona State University, Arizona.

Herández, O. (2000) Evaluation. In: Day, B.A. and Monroe, M.C. (eds) *Environmental Education & Communication for a Sustainable World: Handbook for International Practitioners*. Academy for Educational Development, Washington, DC, pp. 61–65.

Herman, J.L., Morris, L.L. and Fitz-Gibbon, C.T. (1987) *Evaluator's Handbook*. Sage Publications, Newbury Park, California.

Hornby, G. (2007) The influence of inter-organisational relationships on tourism operator participation in destination marketing systems. Unpublished PhD thesis. Griffith University.

House, E.R. (1978) Assumptions underlying evaluation models. *Educational Researcher* 7, 4–12.

House, E.R. (2005) Qualitative evaluation and changing social policy. In: Denzin, N.K. and Lincoln, Y.S. (eds) *The Sage Handbook of Qualitative Research*, 3rd edn. Sage, Thousand Oaks, California, pp. 1069–1081.

House, E.R. and Howe, (1999) *Values in Evaluation and Social Research*. Sage, Thousand Oaks, California.

Hunter, H., Rosnov, D, Koontz, D. and Roberts, M. (2006) Camping programs for children with chronic illness as a modality for recreation, treatment, and evaluation: An example of a mission-based program evaluation of a diabetes camp. *Journal of Clinical Psychology in Medical Settings* 13, 64–77.

Jennings, G.R. (2010) *Tourism research*, 2nd edn. John Wiley, Brisbane.

Jennings, G.R. (2009) Methodologies and methods. In: Jamal, T. and Robinson, M. (eds) *The SAGE Handbook of Tourism Studies*, Chapter 37. Sage, London.

Jennings, G.R. and Stehlik, D. (2001) Mediated authenticity: the perspectives of farm tourism providers. *2001: A Tourism Odyssey: TTRA 32nd Annual Conference Proceedings*, June 10–13.

Jennings, G.R. (1999) Voyages from the Centre to the Margins: an ethnography of long-term ocean cruisers. PhD thesis. Murdoch University Digital Theses Program, Australia. Downloaded 13 January 2007. URL: http://wwwlib.murdoch.edu.au/adt/browse/view/adt-MU20060323.161346

Jonas, L. (1999) Making and facing danger: Constructing strong character on the river. *Symbolic Interaction* 22, 247–267.

Jordan, F. (1998) Shirley Valentine, where are you? Tourism provision for mid life women travelling alone. In: Aitchison, C. and Jordan, F. (eds) *Gender, Space and Identity: Leisure, Culture and Commerce*. Leisure Studies Association Publications, Eastbourne, UK.

Junek, O., Jennings, G. and Killion, L. (2008) Leisure and travel experiences of international students studying at an Australian university. *CAUTHE 2008 Annual conference*, Gold Coast, Australia, 11–14 February.

Jurowski, C., Daniels, M. and Pennington-Gray. L. (2006) The distribution of tourism benefits. In Jennings, G. and N. Nickerson (eds) *Quality Tourism Experiences*. Elsevier, Burlington, Massachusetts, pp. 192–207.

Kelly, L. (2004) Evaluation, research and communities of practice: program evaluation in museums. *Archival Science* 4(1–2), 45–69.

King, K.B. (1988) *The use of triangulated methods as implemented in the evaluation of the 1987 Southeast Therapeutic Recreation Symposium*. Educational doctorate dissertation. University of Georgia, Georgia.

Lawrenz, F. and D. Huffman (2006) Methodological pluralism: The gold standard of STEM evaluation. *New Directions for Evaluation* 109, 19–34.

Lincoln, Y.S. and Guba, E. (1986) Research, evaluation and policy analysis: heuristics and disciplined inquiry. *Policy Studies Review* 5, 546–565.

Levin, H.M. and McEwan, P. J. (2001) *Cost-effectiveness Analysis*, 2nd edn. Sage, Thousand Oaks, California.

Levitt, B. and March, J.G. (1988) Organizational learning. *Annual Review of Sociology* 14, 319–340.

Manning, R.E. (2003) What to do about crowding and solitude in parks and wilderness? A reply to Stewart and Cole, *Journal of Leisure Research* 35(1) 107–118.

Mark, M.M., Greene, J.C. and Shaw, I.F. (2006) The evaluation of policies, programs, and practices. In: Shaw, I.F., Greene, J.C. and Mark, M.M. (eds) *The Sage Handbook of Evaluation*. Sage, London, pp. 1–30.

Mathison, S. (2005) *Encyclopedia of Evaluation*. Sage, Thousand Oaks, California.

McKenzie, J. and Smeltzer, J. (2001) Chapter 13: Evaluation: An overview. *Planning, implementing and evaluating health promotion programs: A primer*. Allyn and Bacon, Boston, pp. 269–280.

McKillip, J. (1998) Needs analysis, process and techniques. In: Bickman, L. and Rog, D.J. (eds) *Handbook of Applied Social Research Methods*. Sage, Thousand Oaks, California, pp. 261–284.

Mohr, L.B. (1995) *Impact analysis for program evaluation*. Sage, Thousand Oaks, California.

Mok, H.M. (1990) A Quasi-experimental measure of effectiveness of destinational advertising: Some evidence from Hawaii. *Journal of Travel Research* 29(1), 30–34.

Moscardo, G. (1999) Communicating with two million tourists: A formative evaluation of an interpretive brochure. *Journal of Interpretation Research* 4(1), 21–37.

Murray, T.R. (2003) *Blending qualitative and quantitative research methods in theses and dissertations*. Corwin Press, Inc., A Sage Publications Company, Thousand Oaks, California.

National Health and Medical Council. (2005) *Human Research Ethics Committees*. Australia. Downloaded 3 January 2006 [URL: http://ww.nhmrc.gov.au/publications/hrecbook/02_ethics/20.htm].

Neuber, K.A. (1981) *Needs Assessment, a Model for Community Planning*. Sage, Thousand Oaks, California.

Neuman, W.L. (2000) *Social Research Methods: Qualitative and Quantitative Approaches*. Pearson Education Company, Needham Heights, Massachusetts.

Neuman, W. L. (2006) *Social Research Methods: Qualitative and Quantitative Approaches*, 6th edn. Allyn and Bacon, Boston.

Nielsen, N. (2004) The need for aboriginal driven planning in in regional NSW. Working Paper. 2004 Council for Australian Tourism and Hospitality Education conference, February, Alice Springs, Australia.

Oliver, R.A. (1977) An evaluation of the use made of evaluation research in a National Tourist Board. *Journal of Market Research Society* 19(4), 151.

Owen, J.M. and Rogers, P.J. (1999) *Program Evaluation: Forms and Approaches*. Sage Publications, London.

Parasuraman, A., Zeithaml, V. and Berry, L. (1994) Reassessment of expectations as a comparison standard in measuring service quality: Implications for further research. *Journal of Marketing* 58(1), 111–124.

Patton, M.Q. (1982) *Practical Evaluation*. Sage, Beverley Hills, California.

Patton, M.Q. (1986) *Utilization-focused Evaluation*, 2nd edn. Sage, Beverley Hills, California.

Patton, M.Q. (2002) *Qualitative Research and Evaluation Methods*, 3rd edn. Sage, Thousand Oaks, California.

Patton, M.Q. (2004) The roots of utilization-focused evaluation. In Alkin, M.C. (ed.) *Evaluation Roots: Tracing Theorists' Views and influences*. Sage, Thousand Oaks, California, pp. 276–292.

Pawson, R. and Tilley, N. (1997a) *Realistic Evaluation*. Sage, London.

Pawson, R. and Tilley, N. (1997b) An introduction to scientific realist evaluation. In: Clemisky, E. and Shadish, W. (eds) (1997) *Evaluation for the 21st century*. Sage, Thousand Oaks, California, pp. 405–418.

Popham, W.J. (1975) *Educational Evaluation*. Prentice Hall, Englewood Cliffs, New Jersey.

Proctor, W. and Drechsler, M. (2003) Deliberative multi-criteria evaluation: A case study of recreation and tourism options in Victoria, Australia. *European Society for Ecological Economics, Frontiers 2 Conference*, Tenerife.

Radel, K. (2005) *Indigenous tourism research: Influences and reflections of epistemological standpoints* presented at the Council for Australian University Tourism and Hospitality Education Conference (CAUTHE), February 1–5 2005, Alice Springs, Australia.

Ritchie, J.R.B. (1994) Roles of research in tourism management. In Ritchie, J.R.B. and Goeldner, C.R. (eds) *Travel, Tourism and Hospitality Research: A Handbook for Managers and Researchers*. John Wiley & Sons, Inc., New York, pp. 13–21.

Rossi, P.H. and Freeman, H.E. (1993) *Evaluation: A Systematic Approach*, 5th edn. Sage, Newbury Park, California.

Schwandt, T.A. (2001) *Dictionary of Qualitative Inquiry*. Sage Publications, Thousand Oaks, California.

Schwandt, T.A. and Halpern, E.S. (1988) *Linking Auditing and Metaevaluation, Enhancing Quality in Applied Research*. Applied Social Research Methods. Sage, Newbury Park, California.

Scriven, M. (1967) The methodology of evaluation. In: Tyler, R.W., Gagne, R.M. and Scriven, M. (eds) *Perspectives of Curriculum Evaluation*. Rand McNally, Chicago, pp. 39–83.

Scriven, M. (1991) *Evaluation Thesaurus*, 4th edn. Sage, Thousand Oaks, California.

Scriven, M. (1999) The nature of evaluation part ii: *Practical Assessment, Research and Evaluation*, 6(12). Downloaded August, 2006. URL: http://PAREonline.net/getvn.asp?v=6&n=12

Senge. P. (1990) *The Fifth Discipline: The Art of Practice of Organisational Learning*. Doubleday, New York.

Shadish, W.R., Cook, T.D. and Leviton, L.C. (1991) *Foundations of Program Evaluation: Theories of Practice*. Sage, Newbury Park, California.

Shaw, I.F. (1999) *Qualitative Evaluation*. Sage, London.

Smith, M.L. and Glass, G.V. (1987) *Research and Evaluation in Education and the Social Sciences*. Prentice-Hall, Englewood Cliffs, New Jersey.

Smith, R.J. (1971) The evaluation of recreation benefits: The Clawson method in practice. *Urban Studies* 8(2), 89–102.

Stake, R.E. (1975) Program evaluation, particularly responsive evaluation. Keynote address at the conference "New trends in evaluation," Institute of Education, University of Goteborg, Sweden (October). In: Stake, R.E. (1975) Program evaluation, particularly responsive evaluation. Center for Instructional Research and Curriculum Evaluation, University of Illinois at Urbana-Champaign, Occasional Paper Series, Paper No. 15 (November).

Stake, R.E. (1995) *The Art of Case Study Research*. Sage, Thousand Oaks, California.

Stake, R. (1976) *Evaluating Educational Programmes: The Need and the Response*. Paris: Organization for Economic co-Operational Development.

Stake, R.E. (2004) Stake and responsive evaluation. In: Alkin, M.C. (ed.) *Evaluation Roots: Tracing Theorists' Views and Influences*. Sage, Thousand Oaks, California, pp. 203–217.

Stehlik, D, Jennings, G.R. and Dwyer, L. (2004) *The socio-economic impacts of defence activities in Central Queensland*. Report to the Australian Department of Defence. Rockhampton, Australia: The Centre for Social Science Research. Downloaded 13 January 2007. URL: http://www.defence.gov.au/publications/CQU_study.pdf

Stergiou, D. and Airey, D. (2003) Inquiry conversion and tourism website effectiveness: assumptions, problems and potential. *Tourism and Hospitality Research* 4(4), 355–366.

Stewart, W. and Cole, D. (2001) Number of encounters and experience quality in Grand Canyon backcountry: consistently negative and weak relationships. *Journal of Leisure Research* 33(1), 106–120.

Stewart, D.W. and Kamins, M.A. (1993) *Secondary Research: Information Sources and Methods*, 2nd edn. Applied Social Research Methods.

Strauss, A. and Corbin, J. (1998) *Basics of Qualitative Research: Techniques and Procedures for Developing Grounded Theory*. Sage, Newbury Park, California.

Stufflebeam, D.L. (2004) The 21st-Century CIPP model: origins, Development and use. In: Alkin, M.C. (ed.) *Evaluation Roots: Tracing Theorists' Views and Influences*. Sage, Thousand Oaks, California, pp. 245–266.

Stufflebeam, D.L. and Shinkfield, A.J. (1985) *Systematic Evaluation: a Self-instructional Guide to Theory and Practice*. Kluwer Nijhoff, Dordrecht.

Suchman, E. (1967) *Evaluative Research*. Sage, New York and London.

Teas, K. (1993) Expectations, performance evaluation, and customers' perceptions of quality. *Journal of Marketing* 57(4), 18–34.

Tierney, P. (2000) Internet-based evaluation of tourism web site effectiveness: Methodological issues and survey results. *Journal of Travel Research* 39, 212–219.

Trochim, W.M.K. (2002) Introduction to evaluation. In: *The Research knowledge base*. Downloaded 25 July 2006. URL: http://www.socialresearchmethods.net/kb/intreval.htm

Webster, I. and Raphael, B. (2001) Foreword. In: Commonwealth of Australia. *Evaluation: a Guide for Good Practice*. Department of Health and Aged Care, Canberra.

Weiss, C.H. (1972) *Evaluation Research*, Prentice Hall, Englewood Cliffs, New Jersey.

Weiss, C.H. (1986) The many meanings of research utilization. In: Blumer, M. *et al.* (eds) *Social Science and Social Policy*. Allen and Unwin, London, pp. 31–40.

Wehmeyer, M.L. (2002) Chapter 6: Program evaluation (Empowerment evaluation and personal outcomes). *Teaching students with mental retardation: Providing access to general curriculum*. Paul H. Brookes, Baltimore, pp. 95–105.

Whitford, M., Bell, B. and Watkins, M. (1999) Aboriginal and Torres Strait Islander tourism policy: contextual and ideological impacts. *Conference on Peak Performance in Tourism and Hospitality Research*. Council for Australian University Tourism and Hospitality Education, Melbourne.

Wilkins, H.C. and Hwang, J. (2004) An evaluation of factors influencing customer loyalty in the restaurant industry, *Journal of Hospitality and Tourism* 2, (1).

Williams, B. and Suen, H. (1998) Formal vs. informal assessment methods. *American Journal of Health Behavior* 22(4), 308–313.

Worthen, B.R. and Sanders, J.R. (eds) (1973) *Educational Evaluation: Theory and Practice*. A. Jones, Worthington, Ohio.

Worthen, B.R., Sanders, J.R. and Fitzpatrick, J.L. (1997) *Program Evaluation: Alternative Approaches and Practical Guidelines*, 2nd edn. Longman, New York.

Yates, B.T. (1998) Formative evaluation of costs, cost-effectiveness and cost-benefit: Toward cost, procedure, process, outcome analysis. In Bickman, L. and Rog, D.J. (eds) *Handbook of applied Social Research Methods*. Sage, Thousand Oaks, California, pp. 285–314.

Yu, X. (2003) Conceptualizing and assessing intercultural competence of tour guides: An analysis of Australian guides of Chinese tour groups. Unpublished PhD thesis, Monash University, Melbourne.

Yüksel, A. and Yüksel, F. (2001) Comparative performance analysis: Tourists' perception of Turkey relative to other tourist destinations. *Journal of Vacation Marketing* 7(4), 333–355.

chapter 10

Experimental Research[1]

Harmen Oppewal

Learning Objectives

After reading this chapter you should be able to:

1. Describe the key features and focus of a true experiment;

2. Explain the validity issues involved in quasi-experimental designs;

3. Explain the advantages and disadvantages of using experiments;

4. Describe the difference between a blocking and experimental factor;

5. Explain the advantages of using a factorial design;

6. Describe the main benefit and limitation of a fractional factorial design;

7. Decide how to analyse data from a simple experimental design.

observed outcome of the experiment are ruled out. The keys to internal validity are standardization, statistical control of external variables and random allocation of test units to experimental conditions. Conducting experiments in field settings can enhance external validity. Including so-called blocking factors can enhance the efficiency of an experiment. Multiple experimental factors can be crossed to allow testing for interactions between factors. Having multiple factors, however, increases the number of conditions that need to be observed. Fractional designs can be used to partly overcome this limitation. The chapter concludes that experiments are not just a type of research but a way of thinking about research. A worked example concerning a museum trying to increase its visitor numbers is presented throughout the chapter.

Chapter Summary

This chapter discusses why you need to conduct experiments and presents the basic principles of the design and analysis of experiments. Experimental research aims to assess cause-and-effect relations and therefore gives priority to maximizing the internal validity of a research design, which means that alternative explanations for the

Experiments in Leisure, Recreation and Tourism: a Museum Shop

To illustrate the usefulness of experiments, this chapter discusses the case of a museum that is looking for means to enhance its attraction to potential visitors and its revenue. Museums increasingly have to look for additional means of revenue to be able to continue fulfilling their principal tasks of curatorship, scholarship, conservation and education. Strategies to increase revenue include organizing special exhibitions, for which extra fees can be charged, and the development of museum shops to commercially exploit the artefacts on display in the museum.

Our example museum plans to convert several of its exhibits into interactive displays and also wants to develop a promotional campaign to attract more people to its shop. The museum management is, however, keen not to 'jump into the deep end' too quickly. There are many questions they would like to have answered before making their final decision. These include: what is the effect of interactive displays; will they attract extra visitors, make visitors stay longer, and make them spend more in the shop? And regarding the promotion: prior research, including some focus groups, suggested that several museum visitors do not visit the shop because they believe the items are too expensive and there is nothing they would really want to purchase. Interviewees who had visited the shop, however, indicated that the shop had much more to offer than they expected. The problem therefore seems to be how to get people to visit the store, more than making changes to the store itself. But how can visitors be attracted to the shop?

Although answers to these questions can be derived from experience gained at other museums and retail stores, there is uncertainty about what is the best approach for this museum. The management therefore wishes to try various solutions within their own museum. This case, and chapter, focuses on only a few aspects of this complex problem and will look at how experiments can be conducted to assess the effects of introducing interactive displays on visitor numbers and the effects of various types of promotions on visitor expenditures in the museum shop. We will explore and demonstrate how an experimental approach can help finding the best solution for the museum in terms of maximizing its visitor numbers and sales. We will, however, also encounter the limitations of experimental research, the most important ones being that experiments can vary only a limited number of variables and that they often require more preparation than is typical for other research methods.

Why we Conduct Experiments

Although many people associate scientific experiments with laboratories, white coats and guinea pigs, experiments have a much wider use. Experiments are sophisticated versions of trial and error, or plan–act–evaluate cycles of behaviour: we try something, observe the outcome, and draw conclusions regarding the effects of our actions.

At the heart of experimental research is the question of whether an observed relationship between an action and an outcome is a true **causal effect** or a mere **spurious relationship.** Causality concerns relationships between variables where a change in one variable necessarily results in a change in another variable. For a detailed discussion see Shadish *et al.* (2002). Philosophers have debated for centuries whether there is such a thing as causality. Can we ever know the true causes of anything? Empiricists like the 18th century Scottish philosopher David Hume argued that all we can see are the observable associations between events. Causes are only in our minds and we can never be sure they really exist. Nevertheless, causal knowledge is one of our most powerful resources because it tells what can or should be done to obtain a desired consequence or avoid an undesirable outcome. Causal knowledge is especially useful if it includes knowledge about the effects of variables that we have active control over – in our example case these are variables such as introducing interactive displays, entrance fees and types of promotion.

There are **three requirements** for a causal relationship, according to John Stuart Mill, an English philosopher from the 19th century. For example, are clouds a cause for rain to occur? Or in general, as shown in Fig. 10.1a, when is X a cause for Y? First, there has to be co-variation: if X varies then

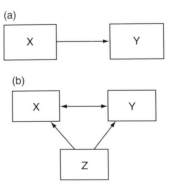

Fig. 10.1. (a) True causal relationship between X and Y. (b) A spurious relationship between X and Y.

Y should vary too. If there are clouds (X), then it may start raining but if there are no clouds, it should not rain, or we would be very surprised, as it violates a basic piece of causal knowledge that is well engrained in our shared understanding of how things work in our world: clouds are a prerequisite for rain.

Second, there should be a sequence in time: first X changes and then Y changes. We would be very suspicious, to say the least, if it first rained and clouds would appear only later. So, if Y changes without X changing or before X has changed, then there is no causal relationship.

These two requirements, although essential, are quite straightforward to assess. The third requirement is less easy to determine: no other, or 'third variable', should co-vary with X and Y. If there were a variable Z that varies with X and Y, Z instead of X could be the true cause for the variation observed for Y. This relationship is shown in Fig. 10.1b. In our museum example, visitor satisfaction (X) and store sales (Y) may be highly correlated but does this mean that by increasing visitor satisfaction levels the museum can increase its store sale revenues? It may well be that overseas visitors compared to domestic visitors are more satisfied, because they did not know much about the museum, but spend more because they are seeking to purchase souvenirs. The relationship between satisfaction (X) and (Y) is spurious because both variables directly depend on the origin of the visitors (Z).

Our museum provides another example of a third variable problem. Suppose the museum has refurbished and converted one room into interactive displays and reopened the exhibit supported with a commercial on local television. If in the following month the museum observes an increase of the number of visitors, has this increase been caused by the new exhibit? It is possible, but there are potential alternative explanations for the increase. For example, there may be a seasonal effect: the holiday season just started in this particular month. Or there may be other external causes such as a few weeks of poor weather, making more people than usual want to visit the museum (especially if this weather coincided with the start of the school holidays). In both these cases, the third variable is clearly distinct from the original variable (opening of the exhibition) and the relationship between the opening and increase in visitor numbers is spurious.

Alternatively, the true cause may indeed be the new exhibit, especially given the advertising support it received. However, this raises the question, what is the true cause: was it the advertising in general, causing increased awareness of the museum, was it the specific nature of the advertisement featuring the new exhibit, or was it the interactive nature of the actual exhibit driving the increase? If the cause was the advertising, will this mean that advertising and publicity is the key to attracting extra visitors? Would any promotional work have this effect or was the visitor increase associated specifically with the promotion around the new exhibit? In contrast, if the mere availability of the interactive exhibit adds appeal to the museum overall, this may be a more permanent effect, and a further and sustained increase may be expected, even without advertising, because the attraction will promote itself through free publicity and word-of-mouth.

As the example illustrates, in applied research the definition of 'cause' and 'effect' is not always easy and straightforward and requires careful attention. There may be multiple causes. In the example, the visitor increase may be partly caused by the start of the holiday season and may partly be due to the advertising around the exhibit opening. Causes themselves may comprise combinations of factors. In the example it seems the visitor increase is due to the launch of the exhibit supported by television advertising, but will other promotional activities result in similar effects? What kinds of promotions will have such positive effects? Are television advertisements a prerequisite for a successful launch? If so, this means that the true cause is the combined or interactive effect of having a new event (exhibit opening) and supporting promotional activities. The success of these factors may even depend on the time of the year.

In sum, causal knowledge is valuable but difficult to attain. Not only are there alternative explanations, often we are not sure what exactly the 'active ingredient' is in our observed causes. This is a crucial but often underestimated issue in applied research. Indeed, too often researchers spend a lot of time developing, implementing and analysing a design without the careful consideration of the essential question: what do we think we are studying and does it match what we are actually studying? This is the question of construct validity.

Validity

Four types of validity are typically distinguished (Cook and Campbell, 1979). **Construct validity** concerns whether the operations and variables in the experiment correctly represent the theoretical constructs as intended. **Statistical conclusion validity** is whether statistical assumptions and procedures are correctly applied in the analysis. The other two types are internal and external validity.

Internal validity

Experiments focus heavily on **internal validity**, which concerns whether an observed relationship is a true causal relationship. The internal validity of a study is the extent to which alternative explanations for an observed relationship between variables can be ruled out. The aim is to rule out any alternative explanation of the relationship observed in the experiment between the independent variables and the dependent variables. To rule out such third variables, experimental designs comprise two core features: **control** and **randomization**. Control means that the researcher actively controls and manipulates the factors of interest while keeping as many other variables as possible constant. This is why experiments are typically conducted in controlled environments. Test conditions are standardized to avoid other factors co-varying and influencing the outcomes. In addition, often a range of variables is measured in addition to the main independent and dependent variables. These extra variables may be used as statistical controls.

Randomization takes over where control cannot be achieved by other means. **Random assignment** involves assigning test units to different conditions based on mere chance, as determined by throwing dice or using a probability generator available in most statistical packages. It is the allocation of test units (e.g. participants) to different conditions through a random draw (like a lottery draw). Test units can be survey respondents, organizations or settings, for example, different rooms in a museum. Whatever the nature of the unit, if random assignment is used there are only two possible sources of variation to drive the differences in outcome between conditions: the actual manipulated differences between the conditions, and the combined effects of all other possible variables on

which the test units differed. This is where statistical theory comes in: because units were randomly assigned, we can calculate the chances of the groups displaying different mean outcomes based on mere random allocation. If an observed outcome is too unlikely to have been caused by random allocation we can safely conclude that the only other possible cause is the difference between the conditions. So, for the combined effect of all these other variables we can determine the chances of them resulting in a systematic difference between the groups, whether age, gender, or any other characteristic of the test units.

The implementation of random assignment requires that the researcher sets the stage and 'manipulates' the conditions according to the pre-determined plan that includes a procedure for random assignment. This means the researcher cannot just wait until the conditions have emerged. If this were the case the natural occurrence of the condition may be a result of underlying unobserved third variables.

Such levels of control and active **manipulation** (experimental manipulation occurs where a researcher actively creates changes in conditions as prescribed by the experimental design plan) are not always feasible in practice. Applied research often uses existing groups or sites and typically these cannot easily be split and allocated to different conditions. Similarly, it may be difficult, or even unethical to create different conditions. This is obviously an issue in medical research; think of testing a potential cure for cancer – is it ethical to place someone in a control condition where participants only receive a 'placebo' treatment (i.e. an identical treatment but without the active ingredient)? But ethical issues also apply in leisure and tourism. For example, providing survey respondents with a chance of winning a holiday trip is deemed unethical by some university ethics committees as a way of incentivizing people to participate in research. Or in research on the effect of promotions it may be seen as unfair to give some people (e.g. children) a gift and others nothing.

External validity

Although the focus in experiments is on internal validity, which is best achieved under homogeneous and specific circumstances, there is always a trade-off with external validity. **External validity** concerns whether the observed relationships can be generalized to other samples of people, situations, or times. Especially in applied research there is often a strong call for studying 'real' situations, and for good reasons. If a study is conducted in more realistic settings, then there is a smaller gap between the test situation and the setting that actually needs to be understood, making generalizability, which always remains a leap of faith, less of an issue. The more similar the test situation to the target situation, the less burden there is for the researcher to show that the results will apply to the target situation. **Field experiments** are experiments that are conducted using such real or realistic settings. Sometimes the situation allows maintaining proper levels of control and randomization without any artificiality to the setting. Such studies are, however, exceptional and often depend not only on the situation but also on the ingenuity of the researchers to find a clever design.

We can test how children interact with museum displays by inviting them to a lab setting where the main features of displays are replicated in different conditions. This allows controlling for many disturbing variables but also excludes variables that may be important determinants of behaviour in practice, for example, the presence of parents and other children, or the promise of a visit to the museum shop. Alternatively, we can observe children in different conditions created in a natural museum environment. In that case it is, however, much more difficult to control other variables and to assign units randomly to conditions.

Indeed, often researchers have to live with the design limitations that the study setting or budget imposes and random assignment of individual test units cannot be achieved. This is, for example, the case where existing groups or conditions are utilized, such as when different student classrooms are exposed to different destination advertisements and asked to rate the destination attractiveness. Another example is when promotional stands are tested at arrival gates at an airport, each gate receiving a different stand. The differences observed between the various stands will not only depend on the stand differences but also on the differences between passenger gates. Although some differences can be measured and accounted for, such as gender, age and origin of travellers, there will be many other variables that may have an influence and that cannot all be

measured. For example, one incoming flight may have been delayed, causing travellers to be more rushed and moody and therefore less receptive to the promotion. Whenever strict randomization cannot be applied the research design becomes a **'quasi-experimental' design**. Quasi-experimental designs are designs where variation in one or more factors is obtained by seeking out participants or conditions from existing situations instead of creating variations through manipulation. Because no proper randomization can be applied, statistical theory cannot be used to automatically rule out 'third variable' effects. As a consequence the burden is on the researcher to argue explicitly, and where possible to demonstrate, that no third variables have influenced the outcomes.

An argument that is often used by experimenters is that if no relationship can be established under controlled circumstances there is no point looking at external validity. External validity is not relevant if there is nothing to generalize. But if the relationship has been established, further testing of the 'boundary conditions' of the relationship is at least as important as the establishment of internal validity. Unfortunately, research focusing on the replication of previous findings and the testing of boundary conditions seems less highly valued in our discipline than the development and testing of new ideas, resulting in literature abundant with isolated findings and ideas that require further testing before they can be applied to a specific problem.

Threats to Internal Validity

For almost any study context there is a host of possible third variables to consider. A comprehensive list of types of third variables is, however, available that can be applied as a checklist for virtually any research project. The list is by Cook and Campbell (1979), who distinguished the following threats to internal validity in quasi-experimental designs.

History effects

There may be external events occurring at the time of the experiment that influence the dependent variable. The change in the dependent variable can therefore not be uniquely ascribed to the experimental procedure. While the new exhibit was opened, another museum in town may have been closed for a refurbishment, resulting in more people visiting our museum. Or a movie may have been released about a museum coming to life at night, resulting in an increased interest in museums. History effects are the summary term for any such external changes.

Maturation

While history concerns external changes, maturation effects are any changes in the experimental subject, whether a respondent, organization or site. This includes mere organic growth, learning effects, and any other 'natural' evolvement influencing the scores on the dependent variable. If such changes coincide with the experimental procedure, this means the experimental results are confounded and cannot uniquely be attributed to the experimental treatment. In our example, the timing of the new exhibit may have coincided with the public expecting museums to be more interactive. So it is not the new exhibit but the fact that it has interactive features and that these features are still a novelty that causes the increase in visitors. Novelty may wear off and the public may 'mature' to no longer being easily excited about interactive museum displays.

Testing

Prior exposure to the experimental measures may result in a change in behaviour. If residents in our town have been surveyed about their interest in visiting a museum, this may have made the people in the town more aware of the museum and the new exhibit, resulting in an increased number of visitors. The increase cannot therefore unequivocally be attributed to the new exhibit.

Instrument variation

Using different measurement instruments for different experimental groups or different times of measurement may result in observing differences between groups. Such differences are confounded with any differences caused by the experimental manipulations.

Our museum may have changed the way it counts its number of visitors; for example, a turnstile may have been replaced with an electronic counting device. Or during the experiment, the museum may have decided to change its definition of visitor from those visiting the museum for any purpose to those purchasing tickets to see the new exhibition.

Statistical regression

If participants are selected for different groups based on their performance on some test, there will be a tendency for the group with high scores to display somewhat lower scores if a similar test is conducted next time, for example, after the experimental manipulation. The opposite is likely to happen to participants with a low initial score; they are more likely to have somewhat higher scores. This 'regression towards the mean' is a statistical phenomenon that will result in changes between experimental groups if the groups have been created on a prior measure that is related to the experimental measure. If the museum selected visitors who showed the greatest interest in the exhibit to first visit the new exhibit, this group will have a somewhat lower level of interest the next time they are asked to indicate their interest. This is not due to being disappointed with the new exhibits but can be totally due to statistical regression.

Experimental mortality

Sometimes experimental conditions differ in the extent to which respondents complete the experimental tasks. One of the conditions may take longer time to complete, resulting in more people dropping out. Some interactive exhibits may take some time to complete and only those who are sufficiently interested may stay long enough to receive the questionnaire that is administered at the end of the exhibit. This survey will therefore not include visitors who did not complete the interactive part of the display.

Selection bias

This is the most severe threat and concerns any systematic difference between the experimental groups not accounted for through standardization or randomization. Quasi-experiments, which use existing groups, are all under threat of selection bias. In true experiments, however, the above-mentioned threats are only an issue if they occur in combination with 'selection'. For example, respondents in different conditions may be different in how they respond to a prior measure of interest or attitude (selection by testing effects) or respondents in particular conditions are more likely to drop out from the experiment, resulting in biased results (selection by mortality effects).

Design Types and Principles

Research design is the whole range of decisions required to assure that a study will be relevant and economical in answering the research question. In experimental design this includes decisions about the units of analysis, the setting in which the experiment is to be conducted, the creation of experimental stimuli and observation instruments, and decisions regarding the number of conditions to create and how many test units to include, and how to assign units to the conditions. The main distinctions between designs are whether they are quasi-experimental or true experiments, how many experimental and blocking factors they include, whether they

include all possible conditions or only a subset of conditions, and whether they include within-subject factors, between-subject factors, or both. Any of these types can be implemented in field or laboratory settings and they all are based on a few key principles that this section will first present.

A notation system for design types

Before discussing various types of design it is useful to introduce the notation system used to display graphically the characteristics of the various designs and discuss the principles of design and analysis.

Each test condition, or group, undergoes a sequence of events consisting of '**treatments**' (X) and **observations** (O) of the dependent variable. Figure 10.2a shows three **pre-experimental** designs. They include a treatment group and one or more observations but there is no comparison or control group to act as a benchmark for assessing the effects of the treatment. They therefore are not true experiments; they are not designs that automatically rule out the 'third variable' alternative explanations discussed earlier.

Experimental designs include at least two groups (conditions), one being the experimental group and one the control group. The **control group** does not receive the experimental treatment.

(a)

One shot case study
$$X \qquad O1$$

One-group pre-test–post-test design
$$O1 \qquad X \qquad O2$$

One-group time-series experiment
$$O1 \qquad O2 \qquad O3 \qquad X \qquad O4 \qquad O5 \qquad O6$$

(b)

G1:   X   O1
G2:   O2

(c)

G1 (R):   X   O1
G2 (R):   O2

Fig. 10.2. (a) Pre-experimental designs; (b) Two-group quasi-experimental design; (c) Two-group post-test only experimental design.

An example is shown in Fig. 10.2b. However, despite the presence of a control group, the design displayed in Fig. 10.2b is only a quasi-experiment because one feature is missing: randomization (R).

An example of a quasi-experiment is the case alluded to above, where different promotional displays are tested at different airport arrival gates. Passengers arriving at different gates will differ on a range of variables, which may result in differences in observed scores for measures such as destination attractiveness or intention to visit certain attractions. As a result, differences observed between O1 and O2 cannot exclusively be attributed to X.

Figure 10.2c presents a two group **post-test-only** experimental design. It is a post-test-only design because the measures are taken only after the treatment has been administered. Each unit ('subject') is in only one condition; it is therefore a **between-subjects** design. In a between-subjects design, each participant receives only one treatment; in contrast, within-subject designs expose each participant to a sequence of treatments. It is a true experimental design because individual test units are randomly assigned to the conditions. In the example of airport arrival gates, arriving passengers cannot be randomly assigned to gates; however, instead the study could be designed to have observation periods (e.g. hourly slots) at gates as the actual units and randomly assign these slots to different treatment conditions.

Museum shop worked example (part 1) – a one-factor design

To increase its revenues our museum operates a shop. Suppose the shop management considers introducing a promotional scheme to increase the number of visits and sales. To test the effects of different promotions they decide to run an experiment for one week. All museum visitors will receive a voucher with their ticket. The vouchers are scratch cards that will give the bearer a chance of either a free gift to be collected from the shop (treatment X1), a 5% discount in the shop (treatment X2), or nothing (the control condition). Shop expenditures are observed over two days for each condition, resulting in observations O1, O2 and O3 for the three conditions. So, the design can be graphically displayed as in Fig. 10.3.

Table 10.1 lists the expenditures in the museum shop for 24 visitors. The visitors are numbered and grouped into the three conditions and their numbering shows the random sequence in which the visitors obtained the various scratch cards (eight in each condition). There is a clear difference in mean spend, with those receiving the discount spending almost $32, those receiving the free gift spending $21 on average, and those without a voucher spending only $16 on average. This suggests a substantial effect of the promotion, with the discount resulting in the greatest increase in sales (especially if we assume the listed amounts are the actual sales after applying the discount). The results are, however, based on only a small sample. What is the chance that these differences are mere sampling variation?

We can test for this alternative explanation by running an Analysis of Variance. The results are shown in Table 10.2 and indicate that the chance of observing these group means, even if there is no 'real' effect of the promotion, is 15%. This is too high to reject the idea that the results are indeed a mere chance fluctuation. But if a similar difference in means had been observed for a sample of 80 in each condition the difference would have been statistically significant.

Statistical rationale

The previous example demonstrated a type of analysis typically conducted on experimental data. To determine the effect of treatment X on the dependent variable O, the means of group 1 and group 2 are compared and tested for statistical reliability using a t-test or Analysis of Variance (ANOVA; assuming the observations have been measured at interval level). If O1 has a statistically significant higher (or lower) mean than O2 this will be attributed to group 1 receiving treatment X. This is because all pre-existing differences between individuals were

G1 (R):	X1	O1
G2 (R):	X2	O2
G3 (R):		O3

Fig. 10.3. Experimental design for promotion study.

Table 10.1. Museum shop expenditures of 24 visitors in three promotion conditions.

Day	No discount/gift		Free gift		Discount	
	Respondent	Amount spent ($)	Respondent	Amount spent ($)	Respondent	Amount spent ($)
1	1	30	4	50	5	55
1	2	50	6	20	7	35
1	3	15	11	15	8	25
1	9	5	12	30	10	55
2	13	20	15	20	14	30
2	17	0	20	5	16	20
2	18	5	22	10	19	10
2	23	5	24	20	21	25
Mean		16.3		21.3		31.9
SD		16.9		13.8		16.0

Table 10.2. ANOVA results for the museum shop example.

Source of variation	ANOVA					
	SS	Df	MS	F	p-value	F crit
Between groups	1018.75	2	509.38	2.09	0.15	3.47
Within groups	5121.88	21	243.90			
Total	6140.63	23				

controlled by randomly allocating them to groups 1 and 2. Adopting the conventional 5% level of significance means that chances of observing this difference due to mere chance (or, actually, due to the combined effect of all unobserved third variables) are less than 5%. That is, there is only 5% probability of drawing the wrong conclusion that there is a difference, while in 'reality' there is no effect (this is called the **Type I error**; a Type I error is committed when it is incorrectly concluded that an effect exists; Type II errors concern incorrectly drawing the conclusion that an effect does *not* exist). This percentage is normally deemed too low to accept the interpretation that the effects are caused by mere chance. Instead, the only other possible interpretation is accepted, which is that X caused the difference between O1 and O2.

If no significant difference is observed between O1 and O2 this may be either because there is really no effect of X, or the effect may exist but could not be detected. The latter means the design lacks sufficient '**power**' (statistical power is the complement of Type II error and is the probability of detecting an effect of certain size, if it exists) and the researcher runs the risk of committing a 'Type II error', falsely concluding there is no effect. This can occur firstly when the sample sizes for the two groups are too small. Means for smaller samples display a larger variance and it is therefore more likely that differences of certain size occur even if there is no effect of X. The researcher can therefore not decide whether the observed difference is due to a real effect of X or due to mere chance. A second reason for possibly not detecting a true effect of X on O is the influence of other (unobserved) factors influencing the individual the variation in units' scores for O1 and O2 (independently from X), thereby increasing the variance in sample means for O1 and O2.

These two reasons for a lack of power of the design each have their own remedy: (i) the sample size can be increased; or (ii) the variation in measures of O1 and O2 can be reduced. The effects of increasing sample size are the same as for any random sampling: any doubling of precision requires a quadrupling of sample size (or stated differently: precision increases with the square root of sample size). Increasing sample size is an obvious candidate for improving a design, but can be costly in terms of money and time. And if the researcher realizes the limited power only after the data have been analysed (and no effects were found) it may be difficult, if not impossible, to replicate the exact experimental conditions to allow the collection of extra responses, especially given the requirement of random assignment. Merely topping up the numbers for one group is not sufficient, extra respondents should be randomly assigned as in the original experiment or one will end up with a quasi-experimental design.

Reduction in variance, which is the second method for enhancing power, can firstly be achieved by design. Standardization of test circumstances will reduce the variance in the dependent variable. However, after the data have been collected the variance can only be reduced by means of statistical control. By including additional variables in the analysis that 'pick up' or 'explain' some of the variance in O the variance to be explained by X reduces, thereby increasing the chances of detecting an effect of X, if it exists. In terms of data analysis this means that extra independent variables are included in the analysis as covariates using ANCOVA or multiple regression methods. Good covariates are variables that themselves are not affected by the treatment and that correlate substantially with the dependent variable. Typical candidate covariates are demographics such as age or gender, attitude measures, or prior observations on the dependent variable, which are called pre-test scores.

Using blocking factors

The general discussion so far has assumed that we always aim to assign experimental units randomly to the various treatment conditions. There is, however, substantial efficiency to be gained from the incorporation of so-called blocking factors. **Blocks** are existing groupings of units that are assumed to show systematic differences in their scores on the dependent variable. By completely or partly repeating the experimental treatments within each of the blocks, these differences can be taken into account in the analysis. This reduces the variance in the dependent variable, thereby providing more scope for the effect of the experimental treatment to be detected.

There are three main types of blocking designs: randomized block designs, incomplete block designs and Latin square designs. In **randomized block designs** all experimental conditions appear equally often within all blocks. In the example below an equal number of experimental vouchers from the three conditions is handed out on two different days. It is not, however, always feasible to administer all treatments in all blocks. A solution may be to use an **incomplete block design**. This means that only a subset of all treatments is administered in each block while it is ensured that each of the treatments appears equally often with each other treatment. Incomplete blocks are only available for specific numbers of treatments and blocks. Yet another type of blocking design is the **Latin square design**, which incorporates two independent blocking factors. This design can be used if two different variables are used to define the blocks. Each experimental condition is administered to only one combination of variables while ensuring that each combination of blocking variable and treatment occurs equally often. In our example this could involve that we not only block on day of the week but also on type of visitor, for example, local visitors versus tourists. Like incomplete block designs, Latin squares exist for only particular types and numbers of factors.

Museum shop worked example (part 2) – a blocking factor

Returning to our museum shop experiment, recall the 24 visitors that had been observed over two different days. Suppose these were a weekday and a weekend day and an equal number voucher types had been distributed on these two days. If we expect weekday visitors to be different from weekend visitors, for example, weekends attracting more local parents with children and weekdays attracting more tourists who typically spend more, then we can include this as a blocking factor in the analysis, realizing that we in fact implemented a randomized block design. By including the blocking factor in the ANOVA, we may be able to 'explain' some of the variance in expenditures, leaving more scope for detecting differences, if they exist.

The average weekday spend is $32 while the average weekend spend is only $14, which suggests that the blocking factor will be useful to include. The results are shown in Table 10.3 and reveal that, indeed, the promotion effect is now much less likely to be based on mere random sampling variation, with a p-value of only 8%. This is still not as low as the conventional level of 5%, but because the 5% is for two-sided tests and we had prior expectations that any promotional effect on sales should be positive, it is defendable that this effect is substantial enough to conclude that, for this particular experiment, the promotion does have an effect on sales.

Suppose we would like to avoid the use of scratch cards and instead have certain times where our promotional vouchers are personally handed out to visitors by a staff member. The personality of the staff member may influence the results as well as, again, the day of the week. Suppose we wish to conduct the experiment on three days, Thursday, Friday and Saturday. Our best option is

now to use a Latin square design. Latin squares have one experimental group for each possible combination of the blocking variables. An example is given in Table 10.4. With only nine combinations it is ensured that each combination of staff and day appears once, similarly each combination of staff and treatment type appears once, as does each combination of day and treatment type.

Including pre-test scores

Pre-tests are observations obtained for each test unit prior to receiving the treatment. By including such 'pre-test' scores in the analysis, the statistical power of the analysis can increase substantially and a same size difference between the post-test means can now become statistically significant. Such a design is called a '**pre-test–post-test** experimental design'. The basic form of this design is shown in Fig. 10.4, for a case with one experimental and one control group. Note that pre-test measures O1 and O3 are not used to directly assess the effects of X, they only act as control variables in the analysis. The actual analysis of a pre-test–post-test design often involves recoding the dependent variables into a new variable representing the difference for each unit between the post-test and pre-test scores.

Table 10.3. ANOVA Results for the museum shop example, with blocking factor.

ANOVA						
Source of variation	SS	Df	MS	F	p-value	F crit
Day (block)	1926.04	1	1926.04	10.98	0.00	4.41
Promotion	1018.75	2	509.38	2.90	0.08	3.55
Interaction	39.58	2	19.79	0.11	0.89	3.55
Within	3156.25	18	175.35			
Total	6140.63	23				

Table 10.4. Latin square design for assigning visitors to treatments (without using scratch cards).

	Thursday	Friday	Saturday
Staff member 1	None	Free gift	Discount
Staff member 2	Free gift	Discount	None
Staff member 3	Discount	None	Free gift

G1 (R):	O1	X	O2
G2 (R):	O3		O4

Fig. 10.4. Pre-test–post-test experimental design.

Although there are clear advantages to having a pre-test measure, there is one main concern: exposure to the pre-test measurement may influence the post-test measures to the extent that they no longer can reflect the effect of X. This is the testing effect discussed earlier. An example from advertising is as follows: in normal circumstances there is no effect of being exposed to advertisement X but exposure to a pre-test of the advertisement sensitizes respondents with the result that they do notice the advertisement and O2 and O4 show significant differences. In this case the real cause (or treatment) is not just 'exposure to X' but 'receiving pre-test followed by exposure to X'.

A design that allows us to detect and separate these possible **carry over** effects from the pure effects of X is the so-called **Solomon four group design**, shown in Fig. 10.5.

A comparison of the means of O2, O4, O5 and O6 will allow inferring the effect of X with and without prior exposure to the measurement instrument as follows:

Effect of X without pre-test exposure = O5–O6
Effect of X with pre-test exposure   = O4–O2
Effect of pre-test only   = O4–O6

It is sometimes possible to make more efficient use of available respondents and increase the sample sizes for different conditions by having respondents complete multiple conditions. If respondents are not completing one but multiple treatment-measurement sequences, then more

observations are obtained from the same respondent. However, this gain in efficiency comes with a cost, similar to introducing a pre-test. The exposure to the first treatment may have carry-over effects and change the response generated by the second and following treatments. The use of such **within-subjects designs** therefore requires special precautions and they should be used only after consideration of these possible biasing effects and how to account for them in the analysis. One compromise solution is to administer the second treatment and measurement but include a sufficient number of respondents to allow conducting the main analysis based on only the observations for the first treatment. This is shown in Fig. 10.6. The first part of the design, with measures O1, O3 and O5, comprises a separate between-subjects three-group design, the total design is a mixed between- and within-subjects design. Analysis of within-subjects designs typically involves so-called **repeated measures** analysis, which is a special type of MANOVA (multivariate analysis of variance); in a repeated measures design multiple observations are obtained for the same experimental unit.

Including multiple factors

So far we have considered only two or three experimental groups, each receiving one or two different experimental treatments or comprising a separate

G1 (R):	O1	X	O2
G2 (R):	O3		O4
G3 (R):		X	O5
G4 (R):			O6

Fig. 10.5. Solomon four-group design.

G1 (R):	X1	O1	X2	O2
G2 (R):	X2	O3	X1	O4
G3 (R):		O5		O6

Fig. 10.6. Within-subjects design with control group.

control group. Each treatment, however, can be made up of a combination of factors. An **experimental factor** is an independent variable describing one facet of the experimental condition or stimulus. Factor levels are the discrete and fixed conditions for the factor to which units are randomly assigned.

Although technically there is little difference between a blocking factor and a true experimental factor, the important conceptual difference is that experimental units are randomly assigned to the conditions of the experimental factor while the conditions of the blocking factor comprise previously existing groups. With blocking, the researcher has no control over the allocation of units to blocking conditions and therefore differences between block means are merely descriptive and cannot be used to infer causal effects of the block factors.

Factorial designs

Factorial designs have two or more factors that are 'crossed' to observe all possible combinations of factor levels. The simplest factorial design is a 2 × 2 ('two by two') factorial design, comprising four experimental groups. The main advantage of factorial designs is that they allow studying the effect of changes in two or more factors at the same time. They therefore allow for the exploration and testing of interaction effects. An **interaction effect** is any effect on the dependent variable that depends on a combination of independent variables; the effect is unique in that

it cannot be described as a mere summation of the 'main effects' of the individual factors.

Interaction effects can be analysed and statistically tested using ANOVA or multiple regression. To interpret an interaction effect it is usually advisable to plot the effects in a line graph. This is illustrated in part 3 of our museum example.

Museum shop worked example (part 3) – factorial experiments

When considering how to implement the promotion, the museum management are concerned that handing out the vouchers at the entrance may lead to visitors not noticing the voucher. The promotion might be more effective if visitors separately received the voucher from a person that can also give extra information and give people directions. An additional factor is therefore included in the design – visitors will receive the voucher either with the ticket or from the separate shop representative. Randomization is implemented by drawing different hourly slots and assigning these slots to one of the two conditions. So any hour, by random assignment, visitors either receive the voucher with their ticket or from the separate shop representative.

Table 10.5a and b present results observed for 24 visitors; 12 in each condition and within these conditions there were four visitors for level of promotion. The cell and marginal means are displayed in Table 10.5b. The marginal means suggest across the promotional conditions the highest level of

Table 10.5a. Museum shop expenditures by 24 weekday visitors randomly assigned to conditions of a 2 × 3 factorial design.

Handout	Control amount spend ($)	Free gift amount spend ($)	Discount amount spend ($)
Separate	15	50	5
Separate	30	40	25
Separate	10	20	15
Separate	5	30	45
With ticket	10	5	30
With ticket	5	5	20
With ticket	15	10	35
With ticket	0	20	35

Table 10.5b. Mean spend in the 2 × 3 factorial design.

Handout	Average shop spend ($)			
	Discount	Free gift	Control	Grand total
Separate	22.50	35.00	15.00	24.17
With ticket	30.00	10.00	7.50	15.83
Grand total	26.25	22.50	11.25	20.00

expenditure occurs in the discount condition ($26 versus $22 for the free gift and only $11 for the control condition) whereas of the two hand-out conditions the separate hand-out condition has the highest expenditure ($24 versus $16 for the ticket condition). These marginal effects, however, do not reveal effects for particular sub-conditions. Indeed, when the actual cell means are inspected it appears the largest spend is by visitors who receive the free gift voucher in the separate hand-out condition.

The pattern becomes more visible when graphically displayed as in Fig. 10.7. The figure shows the interaction of the two experimental factors. Of course, this interaction may be a mere chance result. However, testing the effects of the factors in a two-way ANOVA (Table 10.6) reveals that the effect is statistically significant: the

F-statistic for the interaction components has a p-value of less than 0.05, therefore we accept that the observed effect is not just a random effect.

The figure displays the nature of the interaction: whereas a discount voucher is resulting in an increased level of sales regardless of method of distribution, the free gift is only effective if accompanied by a personal approach. Perhaps visitors who do not receive a separate explanation discard the free gift as not worthwhile, for example, because they don't trust free gifts. A personal approach, perhaps with an explanation about the nature of the promotion, has a different effect. Note that this again raises the issue of 'what is X' – what is the 'active ingredient' of the 'promotion with personal hand-out'. Possibly, it is the friendliness of the handout person, or the fact that visitors could see examples of the gift?

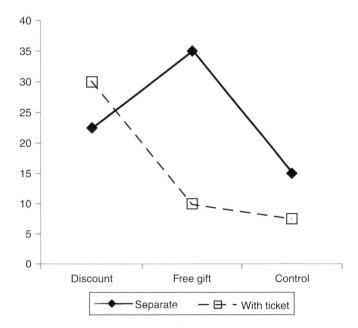

Fig. 10.7. Plot of interaction of two experimental factors.

Table 10.6. ANOVA results for 2 × 3 factorial design.

Source of variation	SS	df	MS	F	p-value	F crit
ANOVA						
Handout	416.67	1	416.67	3.49	0.08	4.41
Promotion	975.00	2	487.50	4.08	0.03	3.55
Interaction	1058.33	2	529.17	4.43	0.03	3.55
Within	2150.00	18	119.44			
Total	4600.00	23				

Answering these questions would require follow-up exploratory, and possibly experimental, research.

Fractional factorial designs

Factorial designs are very useful and are the backbone of a lot of experimental research. They have, however, one main limitation: as the number of factors increases the number of conditions to be observed increases dramatically. Each addition of one two-level factor results in a doubling of the number of conditions. This is easy to see: a 2 × 2 has 4 conditions, a 2 × 2 × 2 has 8, and so on. A factorial design of 7 two-level factors comprises 2^7 or 128 different conditions, a full factorial of 15 two-level attributes consists of 2^{15} or 32,768 different treatments conditions. This number of conditions may be difficult or expensive to produce or to administer.

To overcome this limitation, fractions of factorial designs are often used. **Fractions** are balanced subsets from the full factorial design. They have the property that although not all possible interactions can be tested, at least the 'main effects' of all factors can be observed and tested independently of each other. Whereas a 2^7 factorial design has 128 different treatment combinations, the smallest fractional factorial design with 7 two-level factors comprises only 8 treatment combinations and a fraction design for a study with 15 factors can be as small as only 16 treatment combinations.

This reduction in treatment combinations, however, comes at a major cost. When applying fractional designs one has to assume that most or even all interactions between the independent variables can be ignored. That is, not only can they not be observed and tested, they are actually completely **confounded** with each other and the main effects (confounding of two variables means that they vary together and therefore their separate effects cannot be detected). This means that, while the researcher assumes that main effects are measured, what is actually measured and tested is the combined effect of a factor and a selected set of interactions.

Fractional factorial designs have been used in particular in two related methods for studying consumer preference and choice, called conjoint analysis and choice experiments. In **conjoint analysis** respondents rate the attractiveness or purchase likelihood of hypothetical alternatives that are presented to them one by one. Instead in **choice experiments** respondents are repeatedly asked to makes choices between different alternatives (e.g. Louviere *et al.*, 2000; Hensher *et al.*, 2005). Alternatives can be products, destinations, travel options, sites or any other relevant choice option. Alternatives are described by their main features, called attributes. These can be any feature such as, in the case of travel options, mode of transport, destination names or types, travel cost, local attractions, accommodation types, etc. Different combinations of attributes result in different hypothetical options. From the observed ratings and choices the researcher infers the relative importance of each feature, typically using regression-based methods. The approach uses experimental design methods, especially fractional factorial designs to create the different option descriptions.

Although this author has conducted numerous choice experiments, the focus of this chapter was on the general principles of experimental design and not specifically on choice experiments. The general principles, however, also underlie choice experiments and should be understood before someone seriously attempts conducting experiments, whether traditional experiments or choice experiments.

Conclusion

This chapter explained the main principles behind experimentation. The aim of most experimental research is to test causal relationships. Causal relationships give decision makers control and are a basis for deciding what actions to take to obtain desired outcomes. Experiments are powerful but require careful preparation. Also they can accommodate only a limited number of variables at any time. Experiments are therefore often conducted as a sequence of different tests. They are also typically only conducted after extensive exploratory research through interviews, surveys or observational methods. The research literature obviously is another important source of information to allow the development of ideas in sufficient detail to make experiments worthwhile.

Finding a good design depends on the particular setting, what variables need to be controlled for, the opportunities for applying randomization, and the trade-off between internal validity, which requires homogenous conditions, and external validity, or the extent to which the test situation is representative of the target application situation. In addition to internal validity, which is about assessing causality, another main issue is construct validity: a treatment may have had a reliable effect and all alternative explanations have been ruled out, but often the question remains what is the actual 'active ingredient' of the treatment, and does this active ingredient correspond with the constructs in our theories?

To conclude, experiments are the best method for testing causal relationships but only a limited number of relationships can be tested in any applied setting. The greatest benefit of an understanding of experiments is, however, not that they allow one to conduct experiments but that they make one aware of the limitations of other research approaches. Experimentation is not just a research approach, it is a mind-set.

Discussion Questions

1. Many destination choice studies include gender and age as independent variables. Can you think of an example of how these variables can be studied experimentally?

2. Destination choice studies often include measures of prior destination knowledge. Discuss the different ways in which such measures can affect relevant dependent variables.

3. Many people associate experimental studies with lab studies. Labs are useful because they allow controlling for many external factors. What are some of the factors that tourism and leisure researchers often would like to control for?

4. Experimental studies are often conducted in artificial settings, for example, they use experimental choice scenarios in which respondents have to imagine a situation and then state what they would do if the situation were true. Consider the validity of results observed in such artificial findings.

5. Suppose a researcher wishes to test how travellers will respond to two new destination advertisements, one promoting a winter sports destination and one promoting a beach holiday destination. Outline how you would design a study that measures consumers' responses to these advertisements. Compare the advantages and disadvantages of using a within- or a between-subjects design for this study.

Key Terms

Blocks: Pre-existing groupings of experimental units that are assumed or expected to have different means for the dependent variable.

Carry-over effects: When exposure to one measurement or treatment influences the effects of later treatments or measurements for the same experimental unit.

Causality: Relationships between variables where a change in one variable necessarily results in a change in another variable. For a detailed discussion see Shadish *et al*. (2002).

Choice experiments qualitative research Experiments in which respondents are presented with scenarios in which they are to choose among experimentally designed sets of alternatives.

Confounding: Two variables vary together and therefore their separate effects cannot be detected.

Conjoint analysis: Respondents rate the attractiveness of experimentally designed alternatives that vary in terms of their key features or attributes.

Construct validity: Whether the operations and variables in the experiment represent the theoretical constructs as intended.

Control condition: The condition where no manipulation or only a neutral manipulation is implemented. The control provides a benchmark for assessing the effects of the experimental treatments.

Experimental factors: The independent variables for which the values (levels) are set by the experimenter.

External validity: The extent to which relationships between variables, for example, as observed under controlled experimental conditions, can be generalized to other populations and conditions.

Interaction: A result that is unique for a specific combination of factors; the effect is unique in that it cannot be described as a mere summation of the 'main effects' of the individual factors.

Internal validity: of a study is the extent to which alternative explanations for an observed relationship between variables can be ruled out.

Random assignment: The allocation of test units (e.g. participants) to different conditions through a random draw (like a lottery draw).

Statistical conclusion validity: Whether statistical assumptions and procedures are correctly applied in the analysis.

Statistical power: The probability of detecting an effect of certain size, if it exists. It is the complement of a Type II error.

Treatments: The different conditions to which participants or experimental units are exposed.

Type I error: An error that is committed when it is incorrectly concluded that an effect exists.

Type II error: Incorrectly drawing the conclusion that an effect does *not* exist.

Third variable: A variable, possibly yet unidentified or unobserved, that is the true cause for changes observed in two other variables of interest.

Worked Example 10.1. Example Experiments in Tourism and Leisure With Exercise Questions

Compared to other fields of research, tourism and leisure have made little use of experiments but a handful of studies been published in journals such as the *Journal of Travel Research* and *Tourism Management*, among others. Four example studies are presented in this Appendix. For each some discussion questions are included. The first two are general examples of experimental studies. They concern studies of memory for pictures of tourist destinations and the effectiveness of included tour leader information in holiday brochures. The third example studies effects of presenting information about holiday packages in different formats. It incorporates a so-called conjoint analysis task, which is a method where respondents are asked to rate the attractiveness of different products described in terms of their main features. The last example concerns visitor choices of activities in a theme park and uses (and extends) the method of choice experiments.

Example study 1

Smith, M.C. and Mackay, K.J. (2001) The organization of information in memory for pictures of tourist destinations: are there age-related differences? *Journal of Travel Research* 39, 261–266.

This study investigated age-related differences in memory for pictures of tourist destinations. After receiving encoding instructions, 90 younger and 90 older adults viewed four pictures of tourist destinations and later recalled the content of the pictures. With destination familiarity and education variables statistically controlled, there were no age differences found in pictorial memory performance.

The study gives rise to a 2 (age-group) × 3 (encoding instruction) design. Ninety younger adults (between 18 and 25 years of age) and 90 older adults (between 60 and 75 years of age) were recruited as participants for this study from various community and church groups in a large western Canadian city.

Participants were assigned randomly to one of the three (written) encoding instructions before viewing the destination pictures. One-third of the participants were instructed to pay attention to the features in the pictures, one-third were instructed to pay attention to their impressions of the pictures, and the final third were instructed to pay attention only to the pictures. All participants knew only that they were going to be asked some questions about the pictures that they were about to see. At this point, the destinations were not identified. They were then shown each picture in a slide format for 30 seconds, the order of which was rotated from group to group to avoid primacy and recency effects.

Once the participants had viewed the slides, they completed a 10-minute card-sorting task. This diversion exercise was designed to avoid a short-term memory rehearsal of the slides. Following the sorting task, participants were asked to recall in writing what they had seen in each photograph. At the top of the response sheet, respondents were prompted on the location of the picture (e.g. Halifax, Nova Scotia; Cabot Trail, Nova Scotia; Riding Mountain National Park; and Bermuda). There was no time limit on the recall task. Participants finally rated their perceptions of the attractiveness of each picture, how familiar they were with each tourist destination, and their travel history to these locations.

The study found that after controlling for education and familiarity with the tourist destinations, as well as checking for differences between sexes and direct experience with these destinations, no age-related differences were detected.

Exercise questions

1. What are the experimental factors in this design?
2. Are there any blocking factors?
3. What is the causal relationship being tested?
4. What is the experimental treatment?
5. Are there any carry-over effects?
6. Is this a within-subjects or a between-subjects design?
7. How good is the internal and external validity?
8. How good is the construct validity?

Example study 2

Wang, K.-C., Hsieh, A.-T. and Chen, W.-Y. (2002) Is the tour leader an effective endorser for group package tour brochures? *Tourism Management* 23(5), 489–498.

This study assesses the impact of including information about tour leaders in holiday brochures on advertising effectiveness. It is argued that tour leaders act as endorsers of the package. The study uses one control condition and eight experimental conditions. For each a slightly different brochure was created based on a 2 × 2 × 2 factorial design. The factors were: Endorser's photo (Tour leader or CEO), Personal resume (yes or no), and repetition (once or twice). The control group had no photo or resume and had no repetition.

Participants were 844 students from a business school in Taiwan who received the brochure and next filled out a questionnaire about attitudes and purchase intentions. Five business school departments were selected (with exclusion of the department of tourism) and within each 18 classes were randomly assigned across the nine conditions, resulting in two classes per condition.

Results showed that the addition of the photo and resume had a positive effect on attitude and behaviour, possibly because the endorsement reduces the risk of purchasing an intangible product such as a tour package. Including the CEO had a stronger effect than including the tour leader, which may be a result of the CEO having higher credibility.

Exercise questions

1. Is this a true experiment?
2. What is the experimental unit?
3. What is the causal relationship being tested (if any)?
4. Would any interactions be expected?
5. Are there any alternative explanations for the finding that a photo of the CEO has a greater effect than a photo of the tour leader?

Example study 3

Rewtrakunphaiboon, W. and Oppewal, H. (2008) Effects of package holiday information presentation on destination choice. *Journal of Travel Research* 47, 127–136.

This study investigated the effects of presenting either the destination name or the package price as a header in a holiday package offer. Offers that, for example, appear in a newspaper or online advertisement present only minimal information, consisting of just a few package attributes. Destination marketers and tourism operators need to decide which attribute to highlight as the main header in their advertisements. The study hypothesized that destinations with a less favourable image will benefit from being presented in a format with more attribute information and with a price heading instead of a destination heading.

A total of 400 respondents (200 university students and 200 respondents from the general population in the UK) were asked to evaluate experimentally designed beach package holidays to Mediterranean destinations.

The packages varied on five attributes:

1. Destination name – eight possible destinations were classified into two groups based on market shares and favourability ratings: Greece, Italy, Portugal and Spain were perceived as highly favourable, whereas Cyprus, Malta, Tunisia and Turkey were the group of less favourable destinations.
2. Hotel star rating – this was either 3 stars or 5 stars.
3. Number of nights – 7 nights or 9 nights.
4. Price - £410 or £470.
5. Travel agent - Thomas Cook or Lunn Poly.

Sixteen different combinations of these attributes were selected using a fractional factorial design. Each respondent received a subset (block) of eight of these packages and rated its attractiveness on a seven-point rating scale.

Respondents were randomly placed in one of two conditions: either they received all their packages in a format that displayed the price as the header or their received the destination as the package header. In addition it was varied whether respondents had already seen a destination earlier in the task.

Exercise questions

1. This study was conducted among two samples of respondents, so is it a quasi-experiment or a true experiment?
2. Are there any between-subjects factors?
3. The 16 packages were generated using a fractional factorial design so what assumption was made about interactions between the package attributes? (note: the design actually comprised a design with 32 packages; by using a so-called 'folder over' design it was ensured that all two-way interactions were independent from the main effects).
4. What is the causal relationship that is tested in this study?

5. Can you comment on the external validity of this study?

Example study 4

Kemperman, A., Borgers, A., Oppewal, H. and Timmermans, H. (2003) Predicting the duration of theme park visitors' activities: An ordered Logit Model using conjoint choice data. *Journal of Travel Research* 41, 375–384.

The study introduced a statistical model that allows one to predict the time visitors spend on each of the activities available in a theme park. The model is estimated from experimentally designed choice tasks in a survey that was completed by 357 visitors to an existing theme park in the Netherlands. Visitors indicated their choice of activity and expected time use for various hypothetical scenarios of activity availability.

The respondents' task for each hypothetical choice situation was structured as follows. Respondents were asked to imagine that they could redo their last visit in the park. They were asked to imagine that the park would be somewhat different from their last visit. Some activities would still be available, and some new activities would be added, but some existing activities would not be available. Each choice set represented a new hypothetical park.

For the hypothetical parks respondents were asked to indicate at what time during the day they would visit the various activities, if any, and how much time they would spend on each of the activities. The arrival and departure times could be different from their last visit. They were told that the locations of the activities were the same as in the present park. Respondents were provided a map of the park to help them in finding the location of activities. Respondents were asked to assume that their travel party and the weather were the same as during their last visit.

A fractional factorial design was used to generate 64 different hypothetical parks. Across these parks the presence or absence of 19 possible activities was systematically varied by treating each activity as a factor with levels 'present' or 'absent'. The 19 activities consisted of five theatres, five fantasy characters, five attractions, and four food or other retail outlets. A separate experimental design was used to vary attributes of the different attractions, including location, duration and waiting time. Each respondent completed three choice tasks.

The results provided detailed estimates for each activity of the time that respondents expect to spend and how this time spend depends on the attributes of the activity and the presence or absence of other activities in the park. These results allowed the park management to determine the effects of making changes to the set of attractions in their park.

Exercise questions

1. This study was conducted among a convenience sample of visitors to an existing park, so is it a quasi-experiment or a true experiment?
2. Are there any within-subjects factors?
3. The 64 hypothetical parks were generated using a fractional factorial design. Therefore, what assumption was made about interactions between activities? (note: the design actually comprised a doubled main effects fraction, such that all two-way interactions were independent from the main effects).
4. What is the causal relationship that is tested in this study?
5. How was internal validity guaranteed?
6. Can you comment on the external validity of this study?

References and Further Reading

Cook, Th. D. and Campbell, D. (1979) *Quasi-Experimentation: Design and Analysis Issues for Field Settings*. Houghton Mifflin, Boston, Massachusetts.
Hensher, D., Rose, J. and Greene, W. (2005) *Applied Choice Analysis, A Primer*. Cambridge University Press, Cambridge.
Louviere, J.J., Hensher, D. and Swait, J. (2000) *Stated Choice Methods*. Cambridge University Press, Cambridge.
Montgomery, D.C. (2004) *Design and Analysis of Experiments*, 6th edn. John Wiley & Sons, New York.
Shadish, W.R., Cook, T.D. and Campbell, D.T. (2002) *Experimental and Quasi-Experimental Designs for Generalized Causal Inference*. Houghton Mifflin, Boston, Massachusetts.

[1] Parts of this chapter have appeared in the *Wiley International Encyclopedia of Marketing*, Editors Jagdish Sheth and Naresh K. Malhotra (2010), Wiley-Blackwell. Reproduced with permission.

chapter 11

Cross-cultural Research: Issues and Concerns

Frederic Dimanche

Learning Objectives

After reading and studying this chapter you will be able to:

1. Understand the particularities and requirements of cross-cultural research;
2. Know how to study/research cross-cultural situations;
3. Increase the validity of your cross-cultural research projects;
4. Better understand the concept of culture and how it influences the visitor behaviour you attempt to understand and research;
5. Understand the importance of conducting cross-cultural research to improve leisure, recreation and tourism professional practice;
6. Refer to academic literature for further cross-cultural research guidance.

Chapter Summary

In an increasingly global environment, leisure, recreation and tourism managers are confronted by diverse populations of employees and customers. As managers, you will hire and manage employees who come from multiple cultural backgrounds and nationalities. As marketers, you will attempt to satisfy the needs of customers who are themselves very diverse in terms of culture and/or nationality. You will often need to make marketing or management decisions that should rely on carefully executed research. Yet, as researchers, you will be challenged by numerous methodological issues when conducting studies in cross-cultural contexts, because cultural factors often influence how people respond to research and because this cross-cultural context adds complexity. This chapter examines some of the issues and concerns you should consider and address when planning a cross-cultural study or when reading a document reporting on cross-cultural issues. The chapter proposes methodological guidelines to help you increase the validity and reliability of your cross-cultural studies, and to help you better understand the limitations of some of the studies you will read and use to make managerial decisions.

Introduction

Cultures, nationalities and related factors contribute to determine how people behave and think.

Researchers are always facing many problems when conducting research with people in cross-cultural settings. The purpose of this chapter is to help you to identify several important issues that you are likely to encounter when conducting research in cross-cultural settings. In research, we need to understand how people in different cultures will be affected by a particular research method or strategy. When researchers try to predict behaviour, they need to take into consideration both the individual and the situational factors of the person. At a time of growing globalization and internationalization, the concept of culture becomes increasingly important for managers, marketers and researchers to understand. Although globalization may be perceived as a process of homogenization of cultures through, for example, commerce, media and tourism, it is also an opportunity for many cultures to gain wider recognition. So what is culture? According to Hofstede (2001), one of the most recognized researchers of cultural differences, culture is 'the collective programming of the mind distinguishing the members of one group or category of people from another'. The 'category' can refer to countries, nations, regions, ethnicities, religions, occupations, organizations or gender.

Culture can then be seen as a system of collectively held values. As an example, Hofstede (2001) famously identified five cultural dimensions across nations: uncertainty avoidance; masculinity and femininity; power distance; individualism and collectivism; long-term versus short-term. Overall, people from different cultures do not measure similarly on those factors. As a result, they differ widely in their perceptions of the world, of issues, of concepts. People are different, and assuming that your clients, leisure participants or tourists are all the same would be a major error. There is therefore a need, when conducting programme evaluation research or when identifying visitor profiles, to determine whether culture plays a role in your results. In other words, you need to identify whether the culture of your subjects will affect the way they respond. This is particularly important when you are dealing with a culturally diverse population.

Understanding cultural factors is important because they not only affect people's attitudes and behaviours, they may also influence how people respond to surveys and research. People from different cultural groups are more or less likely to respond to interviewers, or are more or less at ease when responding to some questions. The following three examples highlight this problem: (i) language may be a problem. Can you assume that all your respondents will be fluent enough in English to understand correctly all your questions, and to answer them? (ii) Local customs may make it difficult to interview targeted respondents. For example, in some cultures, women are not allowed to talk to men they don't know; and (iii) your questions should be culturally relevant. Is the concept you attempt to measure equivalent in various cultures? Did you make sure that vocabulary in your questionnaire was carefully chosen to be relevant and meaningful to the cultural group you intend to study? Asking questions can therefore be problematic when conducting research in cross-cultural settings. You must be careful to identify those potential problems when designing your study. A particular group of people who do not respond systematically to specific questions in your questionnaire may threaten your study and lead to invalid or inaccurate results. This represents a serious threat to your research.

Cross-cultural research can be complex; it is also time-consuming. It is important to note that conducting research in cross-cultural settings may require more time for the project to be completed than other research projects. Identifying the

---

Research Box 11.1. Applied research in action.

People from various cultural backgrounds behave differently. Yuksel *et al.* (2006, p. 11) conducted a cross-cultural study to investigate complaint behaviour in tourism settings: 'Complaint handling can have a significant effect on customer retention rates and word-of-mouth recommendations. This study employed the concept of nationality to explore similarities and differences in complaining attitudes and behaviours of hotel customers from Turkey, the Netherlands, Britain and Israel. The research instrument involved a scenario and it was administered to 420 respondents. Results have shown that there are more differences than similarities in complaining behaviours of customers from these countries.'

populations and samples, developing or translating an instrument that is appropriate in more than one culture, gaining access to potential participants or respondents, and collecting data will all contribute to your spending more time on your research.

The next section will give you guidelines and recommendations that will help you identify the main issues to consider when conducting cross-cultural research.

Problem Definition

Cross-cultural research usually takes a comparative approach to a set of questions recreation and tourism managers and marketers have. Whether it is to determine whether a group differs from another or to determine why people behave here differently than there, cross-cultural research responds to numerous questions that will help you improve your organization and the satisfaction of your stakeholders. Your first objective should be to take a step back and to determine the presence of the **self-reference criterion** (SRC) in your approach. Do you use the standards of your own culture to evaluate others or to make assumption about others? In other words, you need to check for ethnocentrism. Imagine that you are product manager for a tour operator and your product, a packaged tour, is very successful with American tourists, which constitute your primary target market. Your marketing manager asks you to sell your product to European travellers. Can you assume that German, Italian or French tourists will be satisfied with the same product you developed for American travellers?

Once you have defined your research problem in your own cultural context and environment, you must try to define the problem again from the perspective of the *other* culture or context. You must familiarize yourself with the other culture and ask yourself what your research questions, the concepts you are trying to measure, your assumptions, mean in this other culture. Are you influenced too much by your own culture? Is the SRC impacting your views? You need to properly address the research problem and limit the influence of your own perspective. Ethnocentrism and ignorance about other cultures may obstruct the development of an objective assessment of cultural differences (Stewart and Bennett, 1991, p. 164). At the very least, we must identify our cultural biases and learn to acknowledge

and interpret them in the studies we conduct. At best, we need to educate ourselves to cultural diversity and learn to discard the lack of interest in or the stereotypes of the 'other'. Cateora and Keaveney (1987) indicated that the most important step in the marketing research process involves correctly defining the problem. They pointed to the difficulty of such a task in international contexts because of the self-reference criterion.

Language Problems

One of the major problems in cross-cultural management and marketing is to determine whether the translation of words, phrases and concepts is equivalent to the original language. A word or a concept in one language is not necessarily equivalent in another language or culture. If you have travelled abroad, you have certainly experienced difficulties in getting yourself understood with the words you attempted to use. For example, one Spanish word may mean one thing in Spain and something else in a Latin American country. Even non-verbal communication differs: you nod in the USA to signify 'yes' and shake your head to say 'no'; in other cultures, the practice may be reversed. Even a translator may not know the nature and meaning of a concept in a target culture or language: there are often significant variations in regional dialects. Idioms (think about all the sports-related expressions in American English: 'To drop the ball', 'a ball park figure', etc.), neologisms (for example, new Internet or social media terms that have not yet been fully adopted everywhere) and slang (across a country or even across generations) are all potential causes of misunderstanding.

The same problem applies to research. Cross-cultural researchers have long pointed out the difficulties of translating and evaluating the appropriateness of translations (e.g. Brislin, 1993). Several types of problem occur when translating questionnaires or other data collection instruments. Without going into the details of those problems, we can recommend four basic translation methods that can be used, either individually or in combination, to increase the validity of a translation: (a) **back translation**; (b) the **bilingual technique**; (c) the **committee approach**; and (d) **pre-test procedures**:

(a) Back translation refers to the use of two bilingual people who will alternatively translate, for example, a set of questions for a questionnaire. A bilingual person is able to use two languages with equal or nearly equal fluency. Individual 1 translates the document from the source language to the target language. Then Individual 2 is asked to translate back from the target language to the original language, without having knowledge of the original material. The researcher can then, without having necessarily knowledge of the target language, make a judgment about the quality of the translation by comparing the two documents in the first language: the original one and the back-translated one. Sentences or questions that would yield different responses can then be identified.

(b) The bilingual technique uses bilingual individuals who are asked to take a test or respond to a questionnaire in two languages. The items or questions that yield different responses can then be identified and corrected.

(c) In the committee approach, a bilingual group translates from the source language into the target language. The members of the group can then work together to identify discrepancies and to agree on a common translation.

(d) Finally, the pre-test procedure consists of testing a questionnaire in the field to make sure that subjects have a good understanding of the questions and terms that are provided. With the feedback from the pre-test, you can go back to refine some items or questions that were poorly understood or that do not match well the culture of the target population.

You will increase the reliability and the validity of your questionnaire by combining at least two of these methods. Also, when reading the results of cross-cultural studies, if target populations were surveyed in different languages, you should check for adequate translation procedures.

Experiential and Conceptual Equivalence

Beyond the technical translation of language problems (e.g. vocabulary equivalence, idiomatic equivalence, and grammatical and syntactical equivalence), which are linguistic considerations, we must deal with issues of experiential and conceptual equivalence. Experiential equivalence refers to the idea that for a translation to be effective from one language or one culture to another, it must use words that refer to things, experiences, or concepts that are familiar or similar in both cultures. This is also called cultural translation. It means that a questionnaire item must have the same cultural meaning in the two languages and cultures. A common example is the 'on time' concept. Being on time does not have the same meaning in the USA, in Mexico, or in France. The expression 'on time' can easily be translated and understood in those three countries. Yet, its true meaning is different in the three countries: there are cultural differences in valuing time.

As another example, consider conducting research on biking and bicycle use in the USA and China. You will find that motivations, attitudes and behaviours are totally different: most Americans bike for recreation and health reasons, while Chinese mostly use bicycles as a means of transportation. In leisure, recreation and tourism contexts, one can think of concepts such as health, wellness, adventure, image, quality of life or satisfaction, just to name a few, that can pose problems of equivalence across cultures.

None the less, in conducting research, we must attempt to use instruments that are equivalent in such a way that they will allow us to describe or measure an experience or a phenomenon in different cultural settings with similar validity. Factor analysis is usually used to assess cross-cultural

---

Research Box 11.2. Research in action.

Researchers from the University of New Orleans conducted a study to help the New Orleans Convention and Visitors Bureau better understand how tourism professionals (event managers, tour operators and travel agents) from Latin America perceived New Orleans as a destination. A questionnaire was developed in English and was then translated in Portuguese (for Brazil) and Spanish (for other Latin American countries) using the back-translation technique. Considering the professional habits of the target population, the questionnaire was sent by fax rather than by e-mail (Dimanche and Moody, 1998).

equivalence by examining the internal structure of a construct. Similarity of factor structure is recommended by Hui and Triandis (1985) or by Davis *et al.* (1981).

Conceptual equivalence refers to the degree to which two concepts are equivalent in the cultures that you want to compare. In order to obtain strong comparability, Bhalla and Lin (1987) recommend that researchers establish equivalence of constructs as well as equivalence of measures across cultures. If you fail to properly establish such equivalence, your research results may be caused not by actual differences in those cultures that you investigate, but by differences in the methods you use.

Measurement equivalence

To the conceptual equivalence discussed above, Hui and Triandis (1985) added three types of measurement equivalence: (a) equivalence in construct operationalization; (b) item equivalence; and (c) scalar equivalence. **Operationalization** is the process of defining variables into measurable factors; it is the transition from theory to measurement. A construct must be operationalized in different cultures so that the instrument may be qualified as equivalent across cultures.

As Hui and Triandis (1985, p. 135) explain, 'A test that lacks item equivalence is in effect two separate tests, one for each culture. If this happens, direct comparison of test scores is misleading and illegitimate.' **Item equivalence** presupposes conceptual and operational equivalence. Then, the construct must be measured in the different cultures by the same instrument. The items have to be identical in the different cultures. In other words, each item should have the same meaning to people in both cultures. Item equivalence is a condition for direct comparison of test scores in two cultures.

Finally, an instrument has **scalar equivalence** for two cultures if the other types of equivalence are present and if 'it can be demonstrated that the construct is measured on the same metric' (Hui and Triandis, 1985, p. 135). A value on a scale should refer to the same degree of the construct regardless of the population. This equivalence is difficult to achieve, but this difficulty can be avoided with the use of standardized instruments employing Likert scales.

Research Methods

The following summary table (Table 11.1) identifies a number of issues that should be carefully addressed and discussed when conducting cross-cultural research. The table follows a five-step research process from problem definition to reporting. You should be familiar with each of those issues. Some of those points are in this chapter, and others are covered in other chapters. You should refer for each of these issues to other chapters in the textbook and think about how a cross-cultural context affects them. For example, beyond the methodological issues, think about how you will report and present your study to another cultural group than yours? Will you be comfortable and ready? Will you avoid the speaker's jokes that won't be understood or appreciated? Again, it is mainly a matter of being aware of potential differences and conflicts, and making sure that your study, your report, your presentation, is as neutral and unbiased as possible. Triandis (1992, p. 232) stated that 'to do research that is ignorant of or insensitive to the major features of the local culture often means to do poor research and thus wastes the time of local subjects, as well as the funds, and that is unethical'.

Conclusion

Cross-cultural research is difficult; it 'presents some unique challenges, numerous environmental and methodological problems, and associated costs' (Kay, 2004). Because of those difficulties, you may either shy away from cross-cultural research questions (despite the fact that our world is increasingly cross-cultural), or run the risk of making design errors and create biases. But the potential benefits for the organizations you will work for, whether they are public or private, leisure, recreation or tourism oriented, should outweigh the costs and difficulties. Globalization is there to stay; we are increasingly experiencing a multicultural world around us. Future leisure and tourism professionals must take this into consideration and learn about their increasingly diverse customers. The purpose of this chapter was merely to introduce you to the challenges of cross-cultural research and to contribute to your understanding of some of the methodological difficulties that need to be

Table 11.1. Issues to consider in the cross-cultural research process.

Problem definition
- Comparability of phenomenon/behaviour/concept
- Isolating the self-reference criterion (SRC) – checking for ethnocentrism

Research design
- Reliability and validity of secondary data
- Appropriate use of qualitative research
- Selection of adequate survey methods
- Establishing language, cultural, and conceptual equivalence
- Questionnaire design – translation techniques; scalar equivalence
- Population and sampling – sampling technique equivalence

Data collection
- Selection, training, supervision and evaluation of interviewers

Data analysis
- Data preparation and standardization
- Sample comparability
- Equivalence
- Level of analysis

Report preparation and presentation
- Interpretation and presentation – checking for SRC and ethnocentrism

Students can refer to Reisinger and Turner (2003), particularly Part 2 of their book, to learn more about hypothesis-testing quantitative methods for cross-cultural analysis in tourism.

addressed. It is hoped that this chapter will encourage you to ask cross-cultural research questions, and that it will give you the methodological tools to get started and the desire to learn more about designing effective cross-cultural research studies. If we are to better manage our organizations and better understand our clients/users, conducting cross-cultural research and using results from valid studies becomes necessary.

In conclusion, the following two cases illustrate the type of situations you might be confronted with as a recreation or tourism professional. Both suggest the need to conduct carefully designed cross-cultural studies.

Case Study 11.1.

Linda is the new recreation programming manager in a large metropolitan area of the USA. After a few days on the job, she realized that municipal recreation programmes do not attract all cultural groups that are none the less part of the city population. She decided to develop leisure and recreation programmes for a diverse population of residents that include African Americans, Asian Americans, Caucasian Americans and Latin Americans. But to make sure that she would properly respond to the needs of the various groups, she first decided to conduct a needs-assessment survey in the city. The survey included questions about recreation needs, recreational habits and behaviours, as well as questions about current satisfaction with the recreation department's existing programmes. Linda started to conduct a telephone survey with a random sample of the resident population, but she quickly realized that many respondents of the minority groups she tried to reach did not want to respond to her questions. Some of them could not even understand her on the phone! She continued to collect information and when she tallied the results, she realized that some of her target respondents were under-represented in her results and that some of the questionnaires had

(Continued)

Case Study 11.1. Continued.

been incomplete: not all questions had been answered. Linda is now questioning the validity of her results; she realizes that she does not have the responses she needs and wonders whether she should have used a different approach to designing her study.

Case Study 11.2.

Jonathan works as a marketing specialist for the French National Tourism Organization. According to the United Nations World Tourism Organization (UNWTO) statistics, France is the leading country in terms of international tourist arrivals worldwide. Yet, despite experiencing annual growth, market share is slowly declining as more countries, particularly in Asia and the Middle East, become more aggressive and demonstrate fast growth rates. Jonathan is in charge of developing a marketing strategy to attract new international markets from the so-called BRIC countries (Brazil, Russia, India and China). These four countries have fast-growing economies and represent key feeder markets for the future. Jonathan wonders whether the marketing communication strategies (brochures, website documents and imagery, etc.) his destination has successfully used to attract Europeans and Americans could be used to woo BRIC travellers. He decides to search and read the tourism research literature and finds strong evidence that people from different cultures react differently to marketing stimuli. In fact, there is evidence that people from different cultures don't give the same meaning to tourism promotional images or pictures (e.g. Dewar *et al.*, 2007). So a picture of a countryside landscape may have much appeal in one culture and very little appeal in another. The same goes for perceptions of quality and tourist satisfaction! As Kozak *et al.* (2004) suggested, 'a comparative analysis of the cultural differences between international tourists and their satisfaction levels becomes a necessity'. Jonathan is puzzled and wonders whether he should test various advertising texts and images to determine their respective effectiveness in the chosen target markets.

Key Terms

Culture: The collective programming of the mind distinguishing the members of one group or category of people from another. (http://www.geerthofstede.nl/culture.aspx)

Cross-cultural research: Research that aims at studying and understanding phenomena and variables in two or more cultures.

Ethnocentrism: A tendency to view other groups or cultures from the perspective of one's own. Ethnocentrism will lead researchers to conduct poorly designed cross-cultural research.

Self-reference criterion (SRC): The unconscious reference to your own cultural values in comparison to another culture.

Discussion Questions

1. Define culture and explain why it is important to understand cultural differences in leisure, recreation, and tourism management and marketing.

2. Why would a researcher's ethnocentrism be a threat to cross-cultural research validity?

3. Discuss how cultural differences can have an impact in how people understand a concept?

4. Identify a research question you have already worked with and re-write it in a cross-cultural context. How does that change your concerns for designing the study?

5. Select a research article reporting on a cross-cultural study, then use the points (if applicable) that are listed in Table 11.1 to evaluate and critique the study.

References

Bhalla, G. and Lin, L.Y. (1987) Cross-cultural marketing research: A discussion of equivalence issues and measurement strategies. *Psychology and Marketing* 4(4), 275–285.

Brislin R. (1993) Some methodological concerns in intercultural and cross-cultural research. In: Brislin, R. (ed.) *Understanding Culture's Influence on Behavior*. Harcourt Brace College, Fort Worth, Texas.

Cateora, P. and Keaveney, S. (1987) *Marketing: An International Perspective*. Irwin, Howewood, Illinois.

Davis, H.L., Douglas, S. and Silk, A. (1981). Measure unreliability: A hidden threat to cross-national marketing research? *Journal of Marketing* 45, 98–109.

Dewar, K., Li, W.M. and Davis, C.H. (2007) Photographic images, culture, and perception in tourism advertising. *Journal of Travel & Tourism Marketing* 22(2), 35–44.

Dimanche, F. and Moody, M. (1998) Perceptions of destination image: A study of Latin American intermediary travel buyers. *Tourism Analysis* 3(3/4), 173–180.

Hofstede, G. (2001) *Cultural Consequences: Comparing Values, Behaviors, Institutions, and Organizations across nations,* 2nd edn. Sage, Thousand Oaks, California.

Hui, H.C. and Triandis, H.C. (1985) Measurement in cross-cultural psychology: A review and comparison of strategies. *Journal of Cross-Cultural Psychology* 16(2), 131–152.

Kay, P. (2004) Cross-cultural research issues in developing international tourists markets for cultural events. *Event Management* 8, 191–202.

Kozak, M., Bigné, E. and Andreu, L. (2004) Limitations of cross-cultural customer satisfaction research and recommending alternative methods. *Journal of Quality Assurance in Hospitality & Tourism* 4(3), 37–59.

Reisinger, Y. and Turner, L. (2003) *Cross-Cultural Behaviour in Tourism: Concepts and Analysis*. Butterworth-Heinemann, Oxford, UK.

Stewart, E. and Bennett, M. (1991) *American Cultural Patterns: A Cross-cultural Perspective*, revised edn. Intercultural Press, Yarmouth, Maine.

Triandis, H. (1992) Cross cultural research in social psychology. In: Granberg, D. and Sarup, G. (eds) *Social Judgement and Intergroup Relations*. Springer, New York, pp. 229–244.

Yuksel, A., Kilinc, U. and Yuksel, F. (2006) Cross-national analysis of hotel customers' attitudes toward complaining and their complaining behaviors. *Tourism Management* 27, 11–24.

Further Reading

Allison, M. (1988) Breaking boundaries and barriers: Future directions in cross-cultural research. *Leisure Sciences* 10(4), 247–259.

Berry, J. (1979) Research in multicultural societies: Implications of cross-cultural methods. *Journal of Cross-Cultural Psychology* 10(4), 415–434.

Crotts, J.C. and Litvin, S.W. (2003) Cross-cultural research: Are researchers better served by knowing respondents' country of birth, residence, or citizenship? *Journal of Travel Research* 42, 186–190.

Dimanche, F. (1994) Cross-cultural tourism marketing research: An assessment and recommendations for future studies. *Journal of International Consumer Marketing* 6, 123–134.

Dunbar, C., Rodriguez, D. and Parker, L. (2002) Race, subjectivity, and the interview process. In: Gubrium J.F. and Holstein, J.A. (eds) *Handbook of Interview Research: Context & Method*. Sage Publications, Thousand Oaks, CA, pp. 279–298.

Malhota, N., Agarwal, J., and Peterson M. (1996) Methodological issue in cross-cultural marketing research. *International Marketing Review*, 13(5), 7–43.

Reisinger, Y. (2009) *International Tourism: Cultures and Behaviors*. Butterworth Heinemann, New York.

Turner, L.W., Reisinger, Y. and McQuilken, L. (2001) How cultural differences cause dimensions of tourism satisfaction. *Journal of Travel & Tourism Marketing* 11, 47–80.

Valentine, K., Allison M.T. and Schneider, I. (1999) The one-way mirror of leisure research: A need for cross-national social scientific perspectives. *Leisure Sciences* 21, 241–246.

chapter 12

Summarizing Data

Seyhmus Baloglu and Ahmet Usakli

Learning Objectives

After completing this chapter, you will be able to:

1. Understand why summarizing data is important;
2. Define descriptive statistics and describe why and when we use it;
3. Distinguish between sample and population, and statistic and parameter;
4. Construct and interpret a variety of statistical graphs used in summarizing data;
5. Distinguish the measures of central tendency and measures of variability;
6. Compute and interpret the measures of central tendency;
7. Compute and interpret the measures of variability.

Chapter Summary

This chapter deals with how to summarize data. Once the data have been collected, it needs to be organized and summarized to reduce a large amount of data to a few meaningful measures that describe the entire data set. There are two basic ways of summarizing a set of data. The first way is to present it in the form of a graph. There are many different graphical methods that can be used to summarize data. The chapter presents the most commonly used graphical representations such as frequency table, pie chart, bar chart, histogram, boxplot, scatterplot, Q-Q plot, and stem-and-leaf display. The second basic way of summarizing a set of data is to compute a numerical measure. The chapter focuses on the three commonly used measures of central tendency (the mode, the median and the mean) and the measures of variability (the range, the interquartile range, the variance and the standard deviation). The chapter also covers two measures of shape: skewness and kurtosis. While skewness refers to the asymmetry of a distribution, the kurtosis indicates the 'peakedness' or flatness of a distribution when compared with normal distribution. Note that in this chapter the data is analysed using SPSS 16.0 for Windows.

Descriptive Statistics

The application of statistics can be grouped into two broad areas: descriptive statistics and inferential statistics (McClave *et al.*, 2008). **Descriptive statistics** are mostly used to describe the characteristics of the population of interest, while **inferential statistics** are used to make inferences about a population of interest based on information obtained from a sample from that population (Ott and Longnecker, 2001). Briefly, the former is used to describe data, whereas the latter is used to draw conclusions or to make inferences from that data.

When one has a large amount of data, it is first necessary to organize and summarize these data to obtain a description of the entire data (Ary and Jacobs, 1978). Descriptive statistics, essential to every quantitative analysis, are employed for this purpose. They are the summaries of the data. They tell us a great deal about the pattern of the scores, i.e. averages, variation, shape, extreme values, missing values, errors, etc. (Leedy and Ormrod, 2005).

Although the descriptive statistics are quite straightforward, their importance should not be underestimated. In most research, they are used for data reduction purposes, i.e. exploring and summarizing the data in an understandable and meaningful way. This analysis is concerned with techniques that will reduce large sets of data (observations) without sacrificing critical information (Kachigan, 1986).

Four Scales of Measurement

Before introducing the methods used in describing data sets, it is necessary to discuss the four scales of measurement since the types of statistics we can use depend on these scales.

Measurement is basically assigning numbers to properties of objects or observed phenomenon. The form of measurements (scales) fall into four types: (i) nominal; (ii) ordinal; (iii) interval; and (iv) ratio (Leedy and Ormrod, 2005).

Nominal scales are used to identify individuals, groups or objects by assigning arbitrary numbers to their characteristics. Nominal measurement divides data into discrete categories. Flight numbers, gender, room numbers, marital status are all nominal measures. For example, you might code gender as 1 = male and 2 = female. Here the numbers are arbitrary and cannot be meaningfully added, subtracted, multiplied or divided. **Ordinal scales** are used to rank-order the data and the order of values are meaningful as we can compare the values in terms of being greater/better or less/worse than one another. However, the distances between the values are not equal. The education level measured as 1 = high school or less, 2 = college, and 3 = graduate is an ordinal scale. **Interval scales** are different from ordinal scales in a way that the distances between the values are equal. The classic example is the temperature scale. Most rating scales used to assess attitudes and satisfaction are often

assumed to be interval scales. One can assign arbitrary '0' to an interval scale (i.e. an overall satisfaction score from 0 to 100). **Ratio scales** are the same as the interval scales, but they have a natural zero point (i.e. total absence of the quantity measured) (Leedy and Ormrod, 2005). Height, weight, money in your bank account, and number of Turkish friends you have can be considered ratio scales.

Methods for Describing Data Sets

Once data has been collected, it must be organized and summarized before the information they contain can be easily understood. Two basic methods for describing data sets are available: one **graphical** and the other **numerical** (McClave *et al.*, 2008). Both play an important role in statistics and should be used together to better understand the description of the data sets. We will first discuss the graphical methods used to summarize data, and then we will continue with the numerical methods.

Summarizing Data Graphically

This section deals with how to visualize a data series, in other words, the graphical methods used in summarizing data. Since there are many different graphical methods used to summarize data, you should determine which type of graph is one that best represents your data. To decide which type of graph to use depends on the type of data you are dealing with. In this section, you will learn the most commonly used graphical methods of summarizing both qualitative and quantitative data.

Frequency distribution and frequency table

The first way of summarizing qualitative data is the frequency distribution. A frequency distribution is a summary of data showing the number of observations falling into each of several non-overlapping classes (Koosis, 1997). It is much more manageable to present data in a frequency distribution than to present the entire set of raw data. A frequency distribution can be portrayed in its simplest form through a frequency table. In Table 12.1, you see the frequency table for whether it is visitors' first visit to Las Vegas.

From the frequency table, one can see the tabulation of different values given by the visitors. The first row is the response No (coded as 0), while the second row is the response Yes (coded as 1). The Frequency column shows us how many people gave each response. In this example, you determine that 213 people visited Las Vegas more than once and for 89 people this is their first visit to Las Vegas. We have a total of 302 valid responses, that is, those who selected one of the two possible valid responses. The Missing row indicates how many people did not respond to this question. In the data file, it was left blank and therefore they were considered 'system missing.' Alternatively, you can code missing values by giving an arbitrary number (e.g. 9, 99 or 999) or use label 'No answer'.

A frequency count may not adequately summarize the data. Instead, percentages, proportion of people selecting each response, would be used (column labelled '%'). The percentages enable you to compare your results across similar surveys. For example, you can tell 69.4% of participants visited Las Vegas more than once and you can compare whether your result is similar to another survey. However, knowing that only 213 people visited Las Vegas more than once not only won't do you much good, but also will prevent you from comparing your results across surveys (Norušis, 2008). The percentages in the 'Valid %' column are calculated by excluding missing responses.

A frequency table is a good summary procedure for categorical variables. A pie or bar chart can also be used as visual display for such data.

Pie chart

The second way of summarizing qualitative data is to display it in the form of a pie chart. A pie chart is a circle graph divided into slices, each displaying a row of the frequency table. In a pie chart, each slice represents a category of the qualitative variable and the size of the slice reflects the number of observations in that category (McClave et al., 2008).

Figure 12.1 shows a pie chart of gender of Canadian visitors to Las Vegas. As you see, it is easy to understand at a glance that more than half of the Canadian visitors to Las Vegas are female.

A pie chart is perhaps the most commonly used graphical method that we see in our daily lives, especially in the mass media because of its quite straightforward interpretation. Although pie charts are useful to show the sizes of categories that make up a whole, it is difficult to interpret them if there are too many categories.

Bar chart

A third way of summarizing qualitative data is to display it in the form of a bar chart. It displays the distribution of a qualitative variable by listing the categories (classes) of the variable along one axis and drawing a bar over each category where the height of the each bar is either the class frequency or class percentage (McClave et al., 2008). The bars should be of equal width.

Figure 12.2 shows a bar chart for the level of education variable. We know that, in a bar chart, the taller the bar represents a category, the more number of observations in that category or vice versa. In this chart, the tallest bar is for visitors with a university degree. You can see that the

Table 12.1. Frequency table of first trip to Las Vegas.

		Frequency	%	Valid %	Cumulative %
Valid	0 No	213	69.4	70.5	70.5
	1 Yes	89	29.0	29.5	100.0
	Total	302	98.4	100.0	
Missing system		5	1.6		
Total		307	100.0		

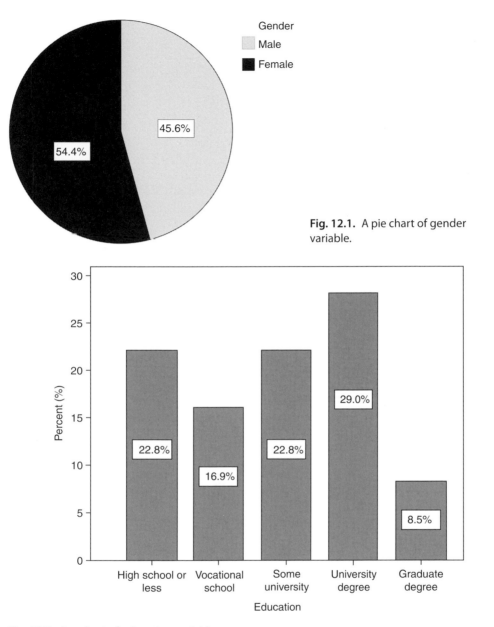

Fig. 12.1. A pie chart of gender variable.

Fig. 12.2. Bar chart of education variable.

education group with the fewest number of visitors is graduate degree; this is determined by looking at the shortest bar. You can also produce bar charts to display the percentage of each category. For example, as shown in Fig. 12.2, 22.8% of visitors have a high school degree or less.

So far, we have discussed the graphical methods used to summarize qualitative data. Now, we

turn to graphical methods used to summarize quantitative data.

Histogram

A histogram is a visual tool that displays the pattern or distribution of a quantitative variable.

It is similar to a bar chart; however, each bar represents a range of values rather than a single value (Buglear, 2000). Thus, one can easily see where the observations are concentrated in the data set.

Figure 12.3 shows a histogram for the overall satisfaction variable. Let's say we asked the visitors to rate their satisfaction on a 7 inch graphic rating scale, a continuous line on which they can place an 'X' anywhere on the line anchored from 'very dissatisfied' to 'very satisfied.' Then, we use a ruler to measure the distance from lower end of the scale to where they have placed the X.

As shown in Fig. 12.3, the vertical axis is the frequencies and horizontal axis is the satisfaction level. Each bar represents a range of satisfaction levels. For example, the bar for which the midpoint is 5.5 includes all ratings between 5.4 and 5.6. The intervals are determined by the observed range of the data. Histograms are very helpful to see how all the values are clustered around a central value and to assess the distribution of the data. In this case, the distribution is not symmetric and has a tail towards lower satisfaction levels.

Although histograms are useful graphical descriptions for quantitative variables, especially in large data sets, they do not let you identify the individual measurements. However, you can see the individual measurements in a stem-and-leaf plot (McClave *et al.*, 2008).

Stem-and-leaf plot

Another way of displaying quantitative data is with a stem-and-leaf plot. A stem-and-leaf plot is very similar to histogram (it resembles a histogram turned sideways) and displays the range of the data, where the observations are concentrated, the shape of the distribution, whether there are any extreme values, and most importantly, the actual values in the data set (Ott and Longnecker, 2001).

A stem-and-leaf plot divides data into intervals. In a stem-and-leaf plot, each piece of data is split into two parts: a 'stem' and a 'leaf.' The stem represents the interval and the leaf represents the

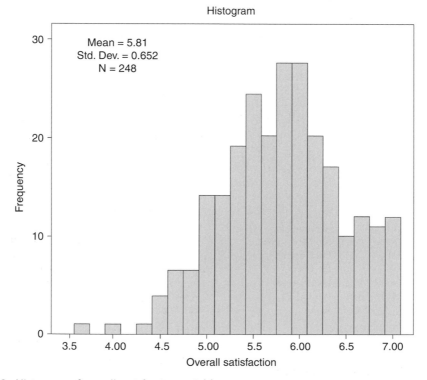

Fig. 12.3. Histogram of overall satisfaction variable.

last digit(s) of the number (McClave *et al.*, 2008). For example, the number 23 would be split as:

Stem	2
Leaf	3

In Fig. 12.4, you see a stem-and-leaf plot for the average room rates of 35 hotels in a tourist destination. To interpret this plot, look at the first row with the stem of 7. The two leaf values in that row are 8 and 9. Before translating the stem-and-leaf values into actual numbers, look at the stem width given below the plot. In this example, the stem width is 10. You multiply the stem value by the stem width and then add it to the leaf value. When you multiply the stem value of 7 with the stem width of 10 and then add it to the leaf value of 8, you find that the first average room rate presented in the first row is $78. With the same formula, you see that the second average room rate in the first row is $79. One advantage to the stem-and-leaf plot over the histogram is that the stem-and-leaf plot displays all of the individual values in a data set; you couldn't do this in a histogram (Norušis, 2008).

From the plot in Fig. 12.4, you can see at a glance that most of the average room rates (23 of 35) are between US$94 and $117. Furthermore, you see that one of the average room rates presented in this plot is US$150 and is considered as 'extreme'.

Boxplot

A boxplot (also known as box-and-whisker plot) is a better way of visualizing the distribution of

Frequency	Stem and leaf
2.00	7. 89
3.00	8. 127
7.00	9. 4456789
9.00	10. 011234578
7.00	11. 0134567
3.00	12. 058
2.00	13. 57
1.00	14. 2
1.00	Extremes (≥150)

Stem width : 10.00
Each leaf   : 1 case(s)

Fig. 12.4. Stem-and-leaf plot for the average room rates.

a variable. It displays several important summary statistics (Norušis, 2008):

- The smallest and the largest observation
- The median
- The lower quartile, the upper quartile and the interquartile range

A boxplot may also indicate which observations, if any, might be considered as outliers or extremes (Marques de Sá, 2003).

In a boxplot, the lower boundary of each box represents the 25th percentile (lower quartile). The upper boundary, on the other hand, represents the 75th percentile (upper quartile). The length of the box represents the interquartile range, the difference between the lower quartile and upper quartile (Freund and Perles, 2004). The larger the box is, the greater the spread of the data.

The vertical line that divides the box is the median. The two lines that are drawn from the lower and upper edges of the box are called whiskers and the lengths of the whiskers are 1.5 box lengths. Any data observation which lies between 1.5 and 3 box lengths from the upper and lower edges of the box are called outliers and are marked with an O. Any data observation which lies more than 3 box lengths from the upper and lower edges of the box are called extreme values and marked with asterisks (*) (Norušis, 2008). Figure 12.5 shows the main parts of a typical boxplot.

Boxplots also provide useful information about the overall shape of the distribution. If the median line is located in the centre of the box, the distribution of the data is symmetric. If not, it is skewed. If the median line is closer to the top of the box, the distribution may be negatively skewed. If the median line is closer to the bottom of the box, the distribution may be positively skewed (Ott and Longnecker, 2001).

Figure 12.6 is a boxplot for the number of previous visits to Las Vegas. What can we tell about our data from the boxplot shown in Fig. 12.6? First, you see that the length of the box is small. That means the difference between the 25th and 75th percentiles is small. From the length of the box, you can also determine the variability. In this case, there is a small amount of variability in the data. You know that the vertical line that divides the box is the median, which is 2 in this example. The line that represents the

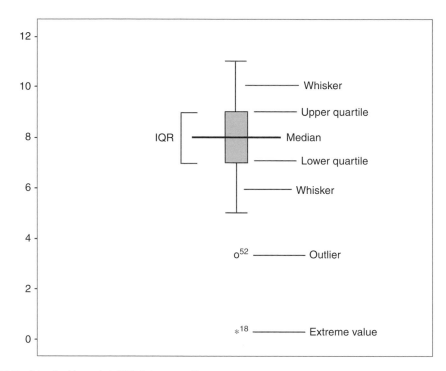

Fig. 12.5. A typical boxplot. IQR, interquartile range.

median is located in the centre of the box. We mentioned that if the median line is located in the centre of the box, the distribution of the data is symmetric. In this example, although the median line is located in the centre of the box, the distribution is not symmetric, instead it is skewed. Additional information about skewness is obtained from the lengths of the whiskers. If one of the whiskers is longer than the other, the distribution is said to be skewed in the direction of the longer whisker (Ott and Longnecker, 2001). You see that there is no lower whisker in this example, meaning that the distribution of the data is positively skewed.

As we have mentioned before, you can see the outliers (identified with O) and extreme values (identified with *) in a boxplot. Boxplots draw attention to extreme values that you need to examine for measurement errors. What should you do if you find outliers or extreme values on your boxplot? In such a case, use the case numbers to find them in your data set and make sure that these values are correct because these values might be the results of measurement or data entry errors.

Scatterplot

So far, we have discussed a variety of graphical displays that show the distribution of the values of a single variable to summarize our data. Now, we will learn a new graphical display, the scatterplot, which shows values for two variables for a set of data. A scatterplot is one of the best graphical tools that display the relationships and patterns between variables (Norušis, 2008).

Scatterplots use horizontal and vertical axes to plot data points. The closer the data points come to making a straight line when plotted, the higher the correlation between the two variables, or the stronger the relationship (Mulberg, 2002). If the data points make a straight line going from the lower left to the upper right of the plot (to high values both on x axis and y axis), then the variables are said to have a positive correlation. If the line goes from upper left of the plot to the lower right, the variables have a negative correlation. If the data points are randomly scattered, then there is no relationship between the two variables (see Fig. 12.7).

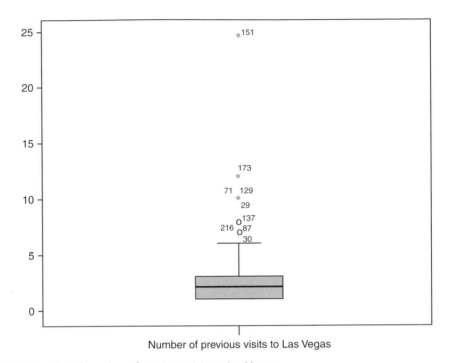

Fig. 12.6. Boxplot of number of previous visits to Las Vegas.

A perfect positive correlation is given the value of 1. A perfect negative correlation is given the value of –1. If there is no correlation between two variables, then the value given is 0. The closer the number is to 1 or –1, the stronger the correlation, or the stronger the relationship between the variables. The closer the number is to 0, the weaker the correlation.

Figure 12.8 is a scatterplot of overall satisfaction and intention to recommend variables. In this example, visitors to Las Vegas are asked to rate their overall satisfaction with Las Vegas using a 7-point Likert-type scale ranging from 'very dissatisfied' to 'very satisfied'. Then, they are asked to indicate their intention to recommend Las Vegas to their friends and/or relatives on another 7-point Likert-type scale. Now we look for whether there is a relationship between these two variables. In this case, intention to recommend is the dependent variable and plotted on the y axis. On the other hand, overall satisfaction is the independent variable plotted on the x axis.

What can you tell from the scatterplot shown in Fig. 12.8? First, you see that the data points are not randomly scattered over the grid, there is a pattern. Next, the data points cluster around a line

that runs from the lower left to the upper right of the plot. This pattern of the data points on the scatter plot reveals that there is a positive relationship between the two variables. Although it is not a perfect positive correlation, it looks like a strong positive correlation. Based on the scatterplot shown in Fig. 12.8, you can say that, as the level of satisfaction increases, intention to recommend increases. Besides displaying the relationship between two variables, a scatterplot also shows if there are any outliers in a data set. In this plot, there aren't any data points that are far removed from the rest of the data.

Q–Q Plot

In most statistical tests, we assume that our sample has a distribution that is approximately normal. Thus, we should check the normality prior to conducting any required statistical tests. Without inspecting the data, it is risky to assume a normal distribution. Although a histogram or stem-and-leaf display can be used to check whether the distribution of a variable follows the normality, the most useful visual tool for assessing normality is the Quantile–Quantile plot or the Q–Q plot for short.

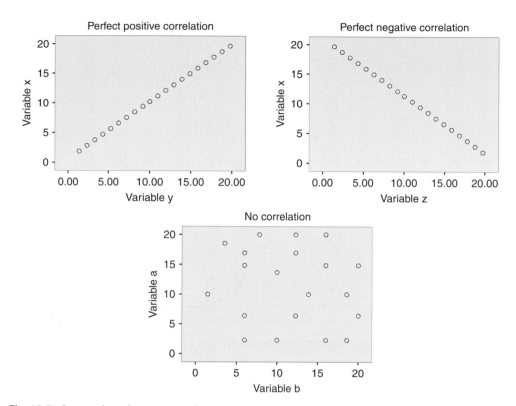

Fig. 12.7. Scatterplots showing correlations.

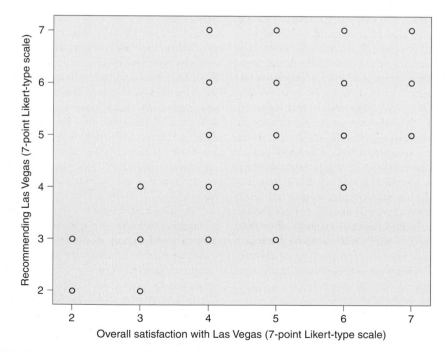

Fig. 12.8. Scatterplot of overall satisfaction and intention to recommend.

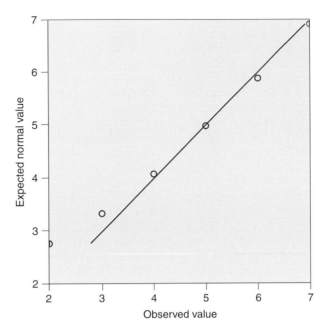

Fig. 12.9. Q–Q Plot for overall satisfaction with Las Vegas.

In a Q–Q plot, the observed values are shown on the horizontal axis and the expected values (the value that are expected if the data are a sample from a normal distribution) are shown on the vertical axis. If the data are a sample from a normal distribution, the data points will cluster along a straight line (Norušis, 2008).

For example, you want to learn whether there is a difference between male and female visitors to Las Vegas regarding their level of satisfaction. Before running the required statistical test, you should check whether your data are a sample from a normal distribution. A Q–Q plot for the level of satisfaction variable is shown in Fig. 12.9. In this plot, the straight line represents what our data would look like if it were perfectly normally distributed. Our actual data is represented by the circles plotted along this line. The closer the circles are to the line, the more normally distributed our data looks. Here, most of our points fall almost perfectly along the line. This is a good indicator that our data are normally distributed.

Summarizing Data Numerically

In the previous section, we have discussed several graphical methods used to summarize and facilitate the understanding of the data, but there are additional methods that may be used for this purpose. In this section, we will discuss the most commonly used numerical methods to summarize a set of data.

Although there are a large number of numerical methods available to summarize quantitative data sets, they can be classified into two categories: the measures of central tendency and the measures of variability. While measures of central tendency are used to convey information about the 'typical values' in a set of data, the measures of variability tell us how the data are spread out around this value (Buglear, 2000). Before discussing the numerical measures used in summarizing data, it is first necessary to introduce the terms statistic and parameter.

A **parameter** describes a population, whereas a **statistic** describes a sample. For example, you have surveyed a group of visitors to Las Vegas in a given period and found that the mean age of these visitors is 45 years. In this case, the people you surveyed are called the sample and the mean age (45) is your **sample statistic**. A statistic is some characteristic of the sample. On the other hand, all visitors to Las Vegas in that period are called the population. You don't know the true mean age of your population. If you had the ages of all visitors to Las Vegas, you would be able to compute the mean age for your population. Let's say the true mean age is 47 years. Here, the true mean age of all visitors to Las Vegas (47) is your **population parameter**. The term parameter refers to some characteristic of the population. The parameter is usually unknown and you must estimate the population parameter based on statistics calculated from sample (Norušis, 2008). As you will see, the distinction between statistic and parameter will clarify your understanding about the numerical measures. Indeed, we use different symbols for statistical measures, depending on whether they are used to describe samples or populations.

Measures of central tendency

The measures of central tendency indicate the 'average' or 'centre' value of a distribution (Freund and Perles, 2004). By measures of central tendency, we mean what the 'average' of a set of data is. The problem is that the term average can have different meanings. There are three commonly used measures of central tendency: the mode, the median and the mean. As you will see, each of them interprets average in a slightly different way.

Mean

The most commonly used measure of central tendency is the arithmetic mean (or simply the mean). It is obtained by adding all the measurements and dividing this sum by the number of measurements in the data set (McClave *et al.*, 2008). For example, the mean or average quiz score is determined by summing all the scores and dividing by the number of students taking the exam.

In statistics, two separate letters are used to express the mean based on whether you are talking about the population mean or the sample mean. The mean of a sample is denoted as $\bar{x}$ (pronounced 'x-bar'). On the other hand, the mean of a population is represented by the Greek letter μ (pronounced 'mu'; Buglear, 2000). We often use the sample mean ($\bar{x}$) to estimate the population mean (μ).

For example, the following set of scores is obtained from a sample of students who take Tourism Research Methods course: 86, 95, 78, 80, 65, 74, 91, 88, 72. The mean of these sample scores is 81 (729 ÷ 9). When you calculate a sample mean, you are only using data from a subset of the population. As a result, $\bar{x}$ (in this case 81) represents your 'estimate' of the true value of the population mean, μ (in this case, the mean score of the entire students who take Tourism Research Methods).

Although the mean is the most frequently used measure for interval and ratio level data, it can be misleading when there are large or small extreme scores (Leedy and Ormrod, 2005). Therefore, the mean may not fully represent the notion of 'average' or 'centre' value for skewed distributions. For skewed distributions, the median may be a more appropriate measure of central tendency (Gerber and Finn, 2005) since it is not affected by extreme scores.

Median

Another measure that describes the central value of a set of data is the median. The median is the midpoint of the distribution and found at the exact middle of the set of [sorted] values (Leedy and Ormrod, 2005). Half of the distribution is located above the median and half is below the median. The symbol for the sample median is m. You can find the median by arranging the values in ascending or descending order (McClave *et al.*, 2008).

With an odd number of observations, the median is the middle value (Marques de Sa, 2003). Consider the following average room rate distribution for seven hotels in Las Vegas: US$149, $175, $132, $129, $152, $89, $99. Before you try to determine the median you must first sort your data in ascending or descending order. In this example, the median room rate is US$132 since it is the middle point; there are three observations above the median US$132 and three observations below it.

With an even number of observations, the median is the average of the two middle numbers (Marques de Sa, 2003). Let's compute the median for the following distribution: 36, 42, 32, 21, 40, 53. In this case, neither 36 nor 40 can be the median. In fact, the median should be somewhere between 36 and 40. When there is an even number of observations in a set of data, the median is computed by taking the 'middle between the two middle observations.' In this case, the median, therefore, would be 38 because it is the middle between 36 and 40, computed as [(36 + 40) ÷ 2]. Note that indeed three numbers are less than 38, and three are bigger, as the definition of the median requires.

The median is most appropriate for ordinal data; however, it is also suitable for interval and ratio level data when there are extreme scores. In such situations, the median may be a better measure of central tendency than the mean because median is less sensitive than the mean to the extremely large or small measurements (McClave *et al.*, 2008). For example, you have the following distribution of income for a group of employees in a restaurant: US$36,000, $38,000, $40,000, $42,000, $45,000, $47,000, $144,000. The mean income of this distribution is $56,000, whereas the median income is $42,000. However, six of the seven employees have an income less than the mean income. Therefore, the mean income of $56,000 is not an appropriate measure to describe the typical value for this distribution. As you see, the income of one highly paid employee ($144,000) has distorted the mean to a disproportionate extent. Thus, the median is a more appropriate measure than the mean when there are extreme values that could greatly influence the mean and distort what might be considered as average.

Mode

The mode is the most frequently occurring value in the data set (McClave *et al.*, 2008). The mode can be determined for both quantitative and qualitative data. For example, the mode for the main purpose of visit is 'to experience new things,' implying the most common purpose of the trip for the visitors to Istanbul in a survey.

Consider the following distribution of ages of ten employees working in a restaurant: 18, 25, 23, 22, 27, 29, 25, 21, 25, 22. By inspection you can see that the mode is 25 because the age 25 occurs more frequently than any of the other values in this distribution. The distribution in this example would be described as unimodal, which means there is only one measurement that occurs most frequently. However, when there are two or more values that occur most frequently, the distribution is bimodal or multimodal. When every score has an equal number of observations (no score occurs with greater frequency than any other), there is no mode (Ary and Jacobs, 1978).

Using SPSS: summarizing the number of previous visits (mean, median and mode)

SPSS is a computer program used for statistical analysis. Table 12.2 contains the measures of central tendency for the number of previous visits to Las Vegas. First, the table indicates the number of valid and missing values for this variable. There are 222 valid cases, meaning that 222 people gave a response to this question. From the Missing row, you determine that 85 people did not respond to this question. Then, the table shows the mean, median and mode for the number of previous visits variable.

You can see that the mean number of previous visits to Las Vegas is 2.81 times. The median is lower than the mean, 2 times. This means, when you arrange the values in ascending or descending order, you will see that the half of the measurements lie above the 2 visits and half lie below the 2 visits. Since the mean (2.81) is greater than the median (2.00), you can conclude that the number of previous visits variable has a tail toward larger values. In other words, the distribution of number of previous visits to Las Vegas is positively skewed. The mode for this variable is 1, which means that the most frequently occurring number of previous visits to Las Vegas is 1. Since there is only one mode, you can conclude that the distribution is unimodal.

Choosing an appropriate measure of central tendency

Each measure of central tendency has certain advantages and disadvantages. So, which of the three measures of central tendency is the most representative? The answer depends on the type of scale represented by your data. Table 12.3 summarizes the appropriate measures of central tendency for a data set based on the measurement scale of the data (Ary and Jacobs, 1978).

Table 12.2. Mean, median, and mode for the number of previous visits to Las Vegas.

Statistics		
N	Valid	222
	Missing	85
Mean		2.81
Median		2.00
Mode		1

Table 12.3. Selecting an appropriate measure of central tendency.

Level of measurement	Appropriate measure of the 'average'
Nominal	Mode
Ordinal	Median
Interval	If the data is symmetric: mean
	If the data is skewed: median
Ratio	If the data is symmetric: mean
	If the data is skewed: median

Measures of variabilty

Although measures of central tendency are quite useful, they do not give a complete picture of the data. For example, they do not tell us anything about how much the observations in a data set differ from one another. To complete the picture, you also need to know how spread out the observations are. Consider the following two sets of average room rates that have the same mean and median.

- Destination A: US$140, $150, $150, $150, $160
- Destination B: US$70, $80, $150, $200, $250

Both samples have a mean and median of $150. However, inspection of the two samples will show that they differ considerably with respect to variability. Indeed, the average room rates in Destination B shows a greater variability than they are in Destination A. So, without the measures of variability the description of a quantitative data set is incomplete (McClave *et al.*, 2008).

Measures of variability indicate how observations are spread out around the central tendency (Buglear, 2000). In this section, you will learn the most common measures of variability: the range, the interquartile range, the variance and the standard deviation.

Range

The simplest measure of variability is the range. It is the difference between the lowest (minimum) and the highest (maximum) value in a data set (Mulberg, 2002).

Range = Maximum value − Minimum value

The following distribution shows the daily high temperatures (in degrees Fahrenheit) for a certain week in Las Vegas: 53, 51, 54, 48, 50, 52, 62. What is the range? The highest temperature is 62° and the lowest temperature is 48°. So, the range is (62 − 48) = 14°.

The range is easy to calculate and easy to understand. It is a rough indication of the variation in a set of data. However, its main disadvantage is that it is based on the two extreme values. Therefore, it can be misleading and may not truly represent the variability of the distribution (Ary and Jacobs, 1978).

A more stable measure of variability is the **interquartile range**. It is the difference between the third quartile (75th percentile) and the first quartile (25th percentile). The interquartile range (IQR) is more stable than the range because it is less influenced by the extreme values (Norušis, 2008).

Variance

A more reliable indicator of the variability or spread in a distribution is the variance. The variance is the average of the squared deviation scores from the distribution's mean. It shows how scores are spread around the mean (Ott and Longnecker, 2001). The larger the dispersion or spread around the mean, the larger the variance. If all the scores are identical, the variance is 0.

While the sample variance is symbolized by s^2, the population variance is denoted by σ^2 (sigma squared). The population variance is usually unknown. We use the sample variance (s^2) to estimate the population variance (σ^2) (McClave *et al.*, 2008).

Table 12.4 contains room rates from three different tourist destinations. Now, we will compute the mean, range and variance for the values presented in this table.

In Table 12.5, you see the SPSS output for the room rate variable. The mean room rate for all three destinations is equal, US$112. However, you can see from the range and variance columns that the three distributions differ in spread. By comparing the variances, you see that the room rates in Destination B are much less diverse than those of the other two destinations and that those for Destination C have

Table 12.4. Room rates from three different destinations.

Destination A (US$)	Destination B (US$)	Destination C (US$)
126	112	140
140	119	84
63	115	133
126	109	91
112	105	84
105	112	140

The standard deviation is simply the square root of the variance (Daniel and Terrell, 1994). Both variance and standard deviation are used to describe interval and ratio level data and are sensitive to large or small extreme scores.

Symbols for Standard Deviation:

s = sample standard deviation

σ = population standard deviation

The sample standard deviation (s) is the estimate of the population standard deviation (σ). Note that σ is almost always unknown. The standard deviation is a more accurate measure of variability. The higher the standard deviation, the more variability you have in the data. The lower the deviation, the less variability you have in the data (Ary and Jacobs, 1978).

Suppose that you have measured the times taken (in minutes) to clean five hotel rooms by two housekeepers. Compare the performance of the two housekeepers using the data in Table 12.6.

One way of comparing the performance of the two housekeepers is calculating the mean time. From Table 12.7, you see that the mean cleaning time for Housekeeper A is 27.52 min, whereas the mean cleaning time for Housekeeper B is 27.64 min. As you see, the mean cleaning times are very similar. So, how can you compare the performance of these two housekeepers? Although the mean scores are very similar, the standard deviations are quite different. You see that the standard deviation score for Housekeeper A is 2.88 min. On the other hand, it is 4.92 min for Housekeeper B. This means that Housekeeper B's cleaning times show more variation than Housekeeper A's. Now, you can say that the performance of Housekeeper A is higher than Housekeeper B based on the standard deviation scores.

the greatest variability. Although the room rates in Destination A have the greatest range, when we consider the deviation from the mean for each destination, the room rates in Destination C vary the most. This is a good example that shows the greater sensitivity of variance as a measure of variability, compared to the range.

The variance is expressed in peculiar units. For example, if the original measurements are in dollars, the variance is expressed in 'dollars squared' (McClave *et al.*, 2008). As you see in Table 12.5, the variance for the room rate variable for Destination B is 23.20 square dollars. To solve this problem, all you need to do is to take the square root of variance; thus you will obtain a measure in the original units rather than squared units (Norušis, 2008).

Standard deviation

The most frequently used measure of variability is the standard deviation because it is measured in the same units as the original data rather than squared units used to calculate the variance.

Table 12.5. The comparison of range, mean and variance for the room rates.

| | N | Descriptive statistics | | |
		Range	Mean	Variance
Destination A	6	77.00	112.0000	725.200
Destination B	6	14.00	112.0000	23.200
Destination C	6	56.00	112.0000	803.600
Valid N (listwise)	6			

Table 12.6. Hotel room cleaning times for two housekeepers.

Housekeeper A Time taken (min)	Housekeeper B Time taken (min)
28.2	32.0
24.3	21.0
32.0	25.2
26.1	32.9
27.0	27.1

Table 12.7. Standard deviation of hotel room cleaning times (in min).

Descriptive statistics			
	N	Mean (min)	Std deviation (min)
Housekeeper A	5	27.5200	2.88045
Housekeeper B	5	27.6400	4.92473
Valid N (listwise)	5		

Using SPSS: summarizing the number of previous visits (range, variance and standard deviation)

In the previous section, we have computed the measures of central tendency for the number of previous visits to Las Vegas. Now, we will compute the measures of variability for this variable.

The SPSS output for the number of previous visits variable is presented in Table 12.8. From this table, you see that the range is 24, meaning that the difference between the highest number of visits and the lowest number of visits is 24. Since the range takes into consideration only the two extreme scores in a data set, it may not be truly descriptive of the distributions. Just a single score can cause greatly fluctuation in the value of the range in a data set. Thus, IQR may be a more stable measure of variability. As you see, the IQR (the difference between the 75th percentile and the 25th) is 1 (3 − 2). In this case, it looks like a better measure of variability than range.

While the variance is 5.95 squared visits, the standard deviation is 2.44 visits. Although we know the standard deviation score, you cannot question

Table 12.8. Measures of variability for the number of previous visits to Las Vegas.

Statistics		
N	Valid	222
	Missing	85
Mean		2.81
Std deviation		2.44
Variance		5.95
Range		24
Percentiles	25	1.00
	50	2.00
	75	3.00

whether it is small or large. You can interpret and use the labels small and large to describe the standard deviation in a relative sense, meaning that a distribution has a small or large standard deviation when compared with the standard deviation of another distribution. But, how can we interpret the standard deviation for a single sample and use it to make inferences? You will learn this in the next section.

Interpreting the standard deviation

We have previously learned how to interpret the standard deviation on a comparative basis. However, we can interpret the standard deviation for a single sample without comparing it with another sample. More specifically, we can draw conclusions about the population variability based on a single sample because the main use of the standard deviation is making inferences about the population which the sample is drawn.

The standard deviation allows us to reach some conclusions about specific scores in our distribution. Assuming that the distribution of scores is normal or bell-shaped (or close to it!), the following conclusions can be reached (Ott and Longnecker, 2001):

- Approximately 68% of the scores in the sample fall within **one standard deviation** of the **mean**, that is, between $\bar{x} - s$ and $\bar{x} + s$ for samples and $\mu - \sigma$ and $\mu + \sigma$ for populations.

- Approximately 95% of the scores in the sample fall within **two standard deviations** of the **mean**, that is, between $\bar{x} - 2s$ and $\bar{x} + 2s$ for samples and $\mu - 2\sigma$ and $\mu + 2\sigma$ for populations.
- Approximately 99% of the scores in the sample fall within **three standard deviations** of the **mean**, that is, between $\bar{x} - 3s$ and $\bar{x} + 3s$ for samples and $\mu - 3\sigma$ and $\mu + 3\sigma$ for populations.

The above conclusions, also known as the Empirical Rule, are shown in Fig. 12.10.

Refer to the standard deviation and mean score in Table 12.8. We have previously calculated the standard deviation score of 2.44 and mean of 2.81 for the number of previous visits variable. Assuming that our sample has an approximately normal distribution, we can say that 68.26% of visitors to Las Vegas have visited Las Vegas between 0 and 5.25 times (2.44 ± 2.81) in the past three years.

In the above example, we did not examine whether our distribution is approximately normal or not, we just assumed it. However, before applying the Empirical Rule, you should determine whether your data are approximately normal.

The following approaches can be conducted to determine the normality (McClave *et al.*, 2008):

1. Construct either histogram or stem-and-leaf display for the data and assess the shape of the graph.
2. Compute the interquartile range (IQR) and standard deviation (σ) for the sample, and then calculate the ratio IQR/σ. If the data are approximately normal, then IQR/σ will be around 1.30.
3. Construct a normal probability plot (Q–Q plot) for the data. If the data are approximately normal, the points will fall approximately on a straight line. A normal probability plot is a scatterplot with the ranked data values and their corresponding expected z-scores from a normal distribution.

There are also some statistical tests of normality such as the one available in SPSS, Kolmogorov and Smirnov test, but they are very sensitive to sample size and slight departures from normality. Therefore, their use is not suggested unless the distribution is perfectly symmetrical and normal.

The normal distribution or bell-shaped (or bell curve) is very important in statistical inference tests. Thus, the distribution of any continuous variable should be approximately normal before one can use any inferential tests.

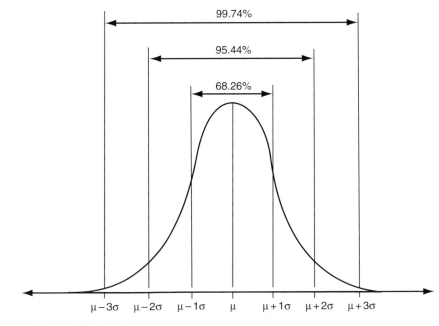

Fig. 12.10. Normal distribution.

Example: In a Food and Beverage Management (FBM) class, the mean score for final exam is 70 and the standard deviation is 10. In a Tourism Marketing (TM) class, the mean is 62 with a standard deviation of 6. Jennifer received 80 on the FBM exam and 74 on the TM exam. What can you say about her performance for the two exams?

On the FBM exam, her score is 80 and it is 1 standard deviation above the mean score (70 + 10). However, on the TM exam, her score is 74 and it is 2 standard deviations above the mean score [62 + (2 × 6)]. Although her score on the FBM is higher than her TM score, her performance relative to the two classes is better in TM than it is in FBM. To better explain what this means, look at Fig. 12.11.

As you see in Fig. 12.11, being 2 standard deviations above the mean score in the TM exam puts Jennifer in a relatively better position than being 1 standard deviation above the mean score in the FBM exam.

In the above example, we have transformed the raw scores into standard scores (z-scores), in other words, we have standardized the two distributions. Once a distribution is standardized, it has a mean of 0 and standard deviation of 1 regardless of the measurement scales used. This new distribution is called the **standard normal distribution** (Daniel and Terrell, 1994). The standard normal distribution allows us to compare different distributions that are differing from each other in mean and standard deviation.

The standard normal distribution and the z-scores are displayed in Fig. 12.12. Note that the interpretation of z-scores is identical to the interpretation of the Empirical Rule (McClave *et al.*, 2008).

Some further descriptions: measures of shape

So far we have discussed the measures of central tendency and variability in a data set. However, a further statistical analysis of the data includes the description of the overall shape of a distribution. Now, we will discuss the two measures of shape: skewness and kurtosis. Skewness and kurtosis give you a more precise idea about the overall shape of your distribution.

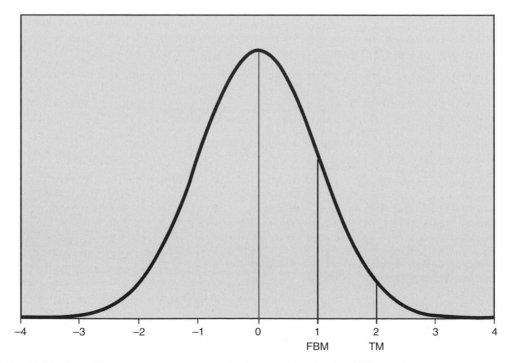

Fig. 12.11. Two different test scores on standard normal distribution. FBM, Food and Beverage Management class; TM, Tourism Marketing class.

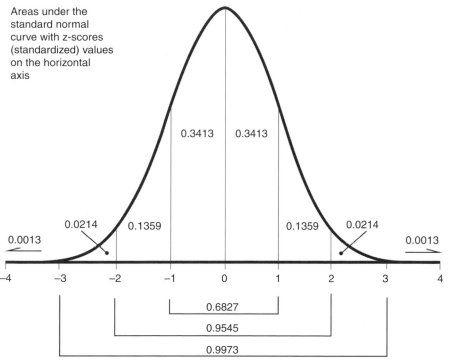

Fig. 12.12. Standard normal distribution.

Skewness

Skewness refers to the asymmetry of a distribution (Wuensch, 2007). In a symmetrical distribution (the normal distribution), the mean, median and mode are in the same location and its skewness is zero (Ott and Longnecker, 2001). A symmetrical distribution is illustrated in Fig. 12.13.

If a distribution is stretching toward one tail, it is skewed. If the tail stretches to smaller values, the distribution is said to be negatively skewed or skewed to the left. On the other hand, if the tail stretches to higher values, it is said to be positively skewed or skewed to the right (Freund and Perles, 2004; see Fig. 12.14).

The skewness value ranges from minus infinity to positive infinity. If a distribution is not skewed, the value for skewness is zero (Wuensch, 2007). With a positive skew, the skewness value will be a positive number or vice versa. By rule of thumb, a skewness value outside the range between –1 and 1 is considered a skewed distribution (Hair *et al.*, 1998). The higher the absolute value the more skewed it is.

Another way of determining whether or not a distribution is significantly skewed is to compare the numerical value for 'skewness' with twice the 'standard error of skewness' and include the range from minus twice the 'standard error of skewness' to plus twice the 'standard error of skewness.' If the value for skewness falls within this range, the skewness is considered not significantly violated. If it doesn't, the distribution is said to be significantly skewed (University of New England, 2000).

For example, the SPSS output in Table 12.9 shows many numerical measures for the number of previous visits variable. The standard error of skewness is 0.163. Twice the standard error of skewness is $2 \times 0.163 = 0.326$. We now look at the range from –0.326 to +0.326 and check if the skewness falls within this range. In this example, the skewness value is 4.259 and it does not fall within this range. We can conclude that the number of previous visit variable is significantly non-normal in terms of skewness. Since the value for skewness is positive, we can say that the distribution is significantly positively skewed.

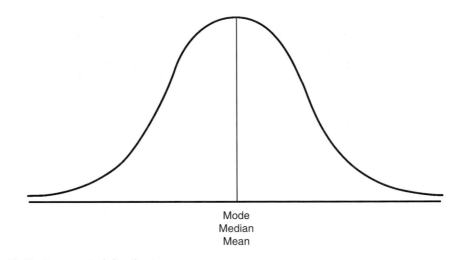

Fig. 12.13. Symmetrical distribution.

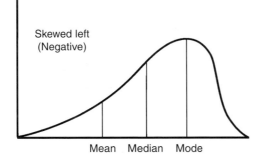
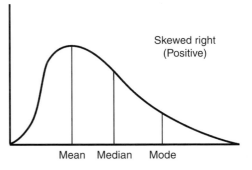

Fig. 12.14. Skewed distributions.

Table 12.9. Determining skewness for the number of previous visits to Las Vegas.

Statistics		
N	Valid	222
	Missing	85
Mean		2.81
Median		2.00
Mode		1
Std deviation		2.44
Variance		5.95
Skewness		4.259
Std error of skewness		0.163
Range		24

You can also determine the skewness by comparing the mean and the median values in a distribution. If a distribution is positively skewed, the median is less than the mean. If a distribution is negatively skewed, the mean is less than the median (McClave *et al.*, 2008). Since the median (2.00) is less than the mean (2.81) in Table 12.9, you can say that the number of previous visits variable is positively skewed.

Kurtosis

Kurtosis is a measure of a distribution's 'peakedness' or flatness when compared with normal distribution (Hair *et al.*, 1998). In peak distributions, the scores pile up in the centre, whereas in flat distributions the scores are evenly distributed and the tails are fatter than those of a normal distribution. Peak distributions will have a positive value and flat distributions will be negative. For symmetric or normal distributions kurtosis is 0 (Tabachnik and Fidell, 2006).

If a distribution is flatter when compared with the normal distribution, it is **platykurtic**. If a distribution is more peaked than the normal distribution, it is **leptokurtic**. If the kurtosis is the same as in the normal distribution, it is **mesokurtic** (see Fig. 12.15).

To determine whether or not the kurtosis is significantly non-normal, the same numerical process is used as in skewness. So, we again compare the numerical value for 'kurtosis' with twice the 'standard error of kurtosis' and include the range from minus twice the 'standard error of kurtosis' to plus twice the 'standard error of kurtosis.' If the value for kurtosis falls within this range, the kurtosis is considered not significantly violated. If it doesn't, the distribution is considered as significantly non-normal in terms of kurtosis (University of New England, 2000).

The kurtosis value (31.491) and the standard error of kurtosis (0.325) for the number of previous visits variable are shown in Table 12.10. Twice the standard error of kurtosis is 2 × 0.325 = 0.650. Now, look at the range from −0.650 to +0.650 and check if the value for kurtosis falls within this range. The skewness value (31.491) does not fall within this range. So, you can conclude that the number of previous visits variable is significantly non-normal in terms of kurtosis, it is leptokurtic. This variable has a peak distribution since it has a positive kurtosis value.

You should bear in mind that these numerical ways of determining if a distribution is significantly non-normal are very sensitive to the numbers of scores you have. Thus, the results can be misleading with small sets of scores (University of New England, 2000).

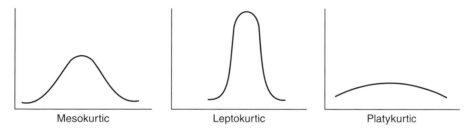

Mesokurtic   Leptokurtic   Platykurtic

Fig. 12.15. Mesokurtic, leptokurtic and platykurtic distributions.

Table 12.10. Determining kurtosis for the number of previous visits to Las Vegas.

Statistics		
N	Valid	222
	Missing	85
Mean		2.81
Median		2.00
Mode		1
Std deviation		2.44
Variance		5.95
Skewness		4.259
Std error of skewness		0.163
Kurtosis		31.491
Std error of kurtosis		0.325
Range		24

Case Study 12.1. 2007 Las Vegas visitor profile.

In this section, we present to you one of a series of visitor profile studies conducted by the Las Vegas Convention and Visitors Authority (LVCVA). The LVCVA is the official destination marketing organization of Las Vegas and is charged with marketing Southern Nevada as a tourism and convention destination worldwide. The Las Vegas Visitor Profile Study is conducted monthly and reported annually to provide a detailed profile of visitors to Las Vegas and to monitor trends in visitor behaviour over time. Here we will be referring to the 2007 study because the study is a good real-life example that shows how descriptive statistics are being applied in tourism industry.

For the 2007 study, a total of 3600 in-person interviews (approximately 300 interviews per month) were conducted between 1 January 2007 and 31 December 2007. The respondents of the study were visitors to Las Vegas (excluding residents of Clark County, Nevada) who were at least 21 years of age. The visitors were intercepted in the vicinity of Las Vegas casinos, hotels, motels and RV parks. To assure a random selection of visitors, different locations were utilized on each interviewing day, and interviewing was conducted at different times of the day. Upon completion of the interview, visitors were given souvenirs as incentives. The interviews were edited for completeness and accuracy, and the information was then analysed using statistical software packages. Finally, bar charts were used to illustrate the results.

The sections of the study include reasons for visiting, travel planning, trip characteristics and expenditures, gaming behaviour and budgets, entertainment, attitudinal information and visitor demographics. The findings of the study are summarized below.

While 19% of the visitors indicated they were first-time visitors to Las Vegas, the remaining 81% was repeat visitors. The primary reason for visiting Las Vegas was vacation or pleasure (42%) followed by visiting friends and relatives (13%). Eleven per cent said they came to gamble. The average number of previous visits over the past five years was 6.3.

Fifty-four per cent of visitors arrived via ground transportation, and 46% arrived by air. The proportion of visitors who reported using a travel agent to plan their current trip to Las Vegas declined to 15% in 2007 from 17% in 2005 and 16% in 2006. Visitors were asked if they used the Internet to plan their current trip to Las Vegas, and 40% said they had done so. Of these visitors, 60% said they booked their accommodation online. The proportion who said they found information online that influenced their choice of accommodation was 34%, down from 37% in 2006.

The average party size in 2007 was 2.5 persons. Eight per cent of visitors had children under the age of 21 in their immediate party. Almost all (99.3%) visitors stayed overnight. Visitors in the 2007 study stayed an average of 3.5 nights and 4.5 days in Las Vegas. Visitors spent an average of US$108.87 per night on lodging in 2007, up from $107.12 in 2006. Fourteen per cent purchased a package trip and the average cost of such a package in 2007 was US$709.90. Over the course of their entire stay in Las Vegas, visitors spent an average of $254.49 for food and drink, and $62.66 for local transportation. Visitors spent an average of $114.50 for shopping, $47.87 on shows, and $8.31 on sightseeing.

Eighty-four per cent of 2007 visitors said they gambled while in Las Vegas. Gamblers spent an average of 3.4 h per day gambling. The average gaming budget in 2007 was $555.64, down significantly from $651.94 in 2006. Nearly half of visitors (48%) said they would be more likely to visit Las Vegas even with the wider gambling choices available to them.

Sixty-three per cent of visitors attended shows during their current stay. Among those who saw a show in Las Vegas, 64% went to a lounge act and 21% attended to comedy shows.

Visitors in 2007 were likely to be married (79%), earning $40,000 or more (80%), and employed (67%). One-quarter were retired (26%). The proportion of visitors who were 40 years old or older was 71%, and the average age was 49. More than one-half of visitors were from the Western United States (52%), with 31% of them coming from California. Twelve per cent of visitors were foreign.

Finally, 89% of visitors reported being 'very satisfied' with their trip to Las Vegas, down from 96% in 2006.

Key Terms

Boxplot: Also called box-and-whisker plot. A very commonly used graphical representation for exploring or describing data. It provides a visual image of the distribution's shape, spread, median and interquartile range.

Descriptive statistics: A group of numerical and graphical methods that are used to look for patterns in a data set, to summarize the information revealed in a data set, and to present the information in a convenient form.

Frequency table: A table listing the frequency (number) or relative frequency (percentage) of observations.

Histogram: Graphical display of the distribution of a single variable. Used to make a visual comparison to the normal distribution.

Inferential statistics: A group of methods that enable the researcher to generalize some findings to a larger group from which the sample was selected.

Interquartile range: The distance between the lower and upper quartiles.

Kurtosis: Measure of the peakedness or flatness of a distribution when compared with normal distribution.

Leptokurtic: A distribution which is more peaked when compared with the normal distribution.

Lower quartile: 25th percentile of a data set.

Mean: Also known as the arithmetic mean. The sum of the measurements divided by the number of measurements contained in the data set.

Median: Also known as middle quartile or 50th percentile. The middle value in a distribution when the observations are arranged in ascending or descending order.

Mesokurtic: A distribution with zero degree of kurtosis. A distribution with the same degree of kurtosis as in the normal distribution.

Mode: The most frequently occurring value in the data set.

Normal distribution (curve): Mathematically defined, symmetrical, unimodal distribution.

Outlier: Observations that are far removed from the rest of the data.

Parameter: Some characteristic of a population. Usually unknown.

Platykurtic: A distribution which is flatter when compared with the normal distribution.

Population: A population is a set of units (people, objects, events, etc.) that are of interest to study.

Q–Q plot: Quantile–Quantile plot. A graphical method for assessing normality. The Q–Q plot graphically compares the distribution of a given variable to the normal distribution which is represented by a straight line.

Range: The difference between the highest and the lowest value in the data set.

Sample: A subset of the units of a population.

Scatterplot: Representation of the relationship between two numerical variables portraying the joint values of each observation in a two-dimensional graph.

Skewed distribution: A distribution that is not symmetrical.

Standard normal distribution: A normal distribution with a mean of 0 and a standard deviation of 1.

Standard deviation: The square root of the variance.

Statistic: A characteristic of a sample. Used to estimate a parameter.

Stem-and-leaf plot: A stem-and-leaf plot is a display that shows the distribution of a variable. In a stem-and-leaf plot, each data value is split into a 'stem' and a 'leaf.' The 'leaf' is usually the last digit of the number and the other digits to the left of the 'leaf' form the 'stem.'

Upper quartile: 75th percentile of a data set.

Variable: A characteristic that can take on more than one value and that differs from individual to individual. For example, age, height, weight.

Variance: The average of the squared deviation scores from the distribution's mean.

Discussion Questions

1. Why do we summarize data?

2. Is it adequate to just compute the measures of central tendency and measures of variability without examining the data graphically?

3. Can graphical displays distort the truth or mislead us? Is it possible to draw graphs for the same group of data which give entirely different impressions?

4. What should you do if you have extreme values in your data set?

5. Which measure of central tendency may be appropriate to report the 'average' in a skewed distribution? Why?

6. Why do we generally prefer the standard deviation to the range or variance as a measure of variability?

7. How do we determine if a distribution is significantly skewed?

8. How do we determine if a distribution has a significant kurtosis problem?

References

Ary, D. and Jacobs, L.C. (1978) *Introduction to Statistics: Purposes and Procedures.* Holt, Rinehart and Winston, New York.

Baloglu, S., Pekcan, A., Chen, S. and Santos, J. (2003) The relationship between destination performance, overall satisfaction, and behavioral intention for distinct segments. *Journal of Quality Assurance in Hospitality & Tourism* 4, 149–166.

Buglear, J. (2000) *Stats to Go: A Guide to Statistics for Hospitality, Leisure and Tourism.* Butterworth-Heinemann, Oxford, UK.

Daniel, W.W. and Terrell, J.C. (1994) *Business Statistics for Management and Economics,* 7th edn. Houghton Mifflin Company, Boston, Massachusetts.

Freund, J.E. and Perles, B.M. (2004) *Statistics: A First Course,* 8th edn. Prentice Hall, Englewoods Cliff, New Jersey.

Gerber, S.B. and Finn, K.V. (2005) *Using SPSS for Windows: Data Analysis and Graphics,* 2nd edn. Springer, New York.

Hair, J.F., Anderson, R.E., Tatham, R.L. and Black, W.C. (1998) *Multivariate Data Analysis,* 5th edn. Prentice Hall, Upper Saddle River, New Jersey.

Hurst, F. (1994) En route surveys. In: Ritchie J.R.B. and Goeldner, C.R. (eds) *Travel, Tourism, and Hospitality Research: A Handbook for Managers and Researchers,* 2nd edn. John Wiley & Sons, New York, pp. 453–471.

Kachigan, S.K. (1986) *Statistical Analysis: An Interdisciplinary Introduction to Univariate and Multivariate Methods.* Radius Press, New York.

Koosis, D.J. (1997) *Business Statistics: A Self-Teaching Guide,* 3rd edn. John Wiley & Sons, New York.

LVCVA (2007) Las Vegas visitor profile: Calendar year 2007. Available at: http://www.lvcva.com/getfile/VPS-2007%20Las%20Vegas.pdf?fileID=107 (accessed 16 February 2009).

Leedy, P.D. and Ormrod, J.E. (2005). *Practical Research: Planning and Design,* 8th edn. Prentice Hall, Upper Saddle River, New Jersey.

Marques de Sá, J.P. (2003) *Applied Statistics Using SPSS, STATISTICA and MATLAB.* Springer-Verlag, Berlin, Germany.

McClave, J.T., Benson, P.G. and Sincich, T. (2008) *Statistics for Business and Economics,* 10th edn. Prentice Hall, Upper Saddle River, NJ.

Mulberg, J. (2002) *Figuring Figures: An Introduction to Data Analysis.* Pearson Education, Harlow, UK.

Norušis, M. J. (2008) *SPSS 16.0 Guide to Data Analysis.* Prentice Hall, Upper Saddle River, New Jersey.

Ott, L. and Longnecker, M. (2001) *An Introduction to Statistics and Data Analysis,* 5th edn. Duxbury/Thomson Learning, Pacific Grove, California.

Tabachnik, B.G. and Fidell, L.S. (2006) *Using Multivariate Statistics,* 5th edn. Allyn & Bacon, Boston, Massachusetts.

Wuensch, K.L. (2007) Skewness, kurtosis and the normal curve. Available at: http://core.ecu.edu/psyc/wuenschk/docs30/Skew-Kurt.doc (accessed 15 February 2009)

University of New England (2000) Determining if skewness and kurtosis are significantly non-normal. Available at: http://www.une.edu.au/WebStat/unit_materials/c4_descriptive_statistics/determine_skew_kurt.html (accessed 15 February 2009).

chapter 13

Inferential Analysis of Data

Kathleen L. Andereck

Learning Objectives

After reading and studying this chapter you will be able to:

1. Define inferential analysis and describe why and when we use it;
2. Calculate the standard error of the mean or proportion for a variable if provided sample size and standard deviation/percentages for the variable;
3. Explain what a confidence interval is;
4. Describe what is meant by statistical significance;
5. Explain how sample size influences standard error and statistical significance.

Chapter Summary

This chapter introduces the concept of inferential data analysis. This form of analysis is used to make general conclusions about a large population based on a sample of that population. The use of inferential analysis relies upon random sampling of members of the larger group of people we are interested in knowing about. The sampling error and confidence interval are directly related to the size of the sample and the amount of variability in the study data. These two aspects of the generated data also influence the statistical significance

of the inferential statistics that we use to test relationships among the variables in the data set. The chapter also provides some further discussion on the importance and meaning of tested relationships from a managerial standpoint.

What is Inferential Analysis?

Most of the time when we conduct research for all of the reasons we have been discussing in this book, we use **samples** of a larger **population**. When the group of people we are studying is too big to ask every single person to provide us with information, we need to select a relatively small number of those people from whom to gather data. For example, in Case Study 13.1, the list of people who ask for tourism information included 18,921 people. Obviously, we could not ask all of those people to evaluate the state travel guide, so we took a stratified random sample of 1200 people to survey. So how do we make conclusions about the entire study population when we only sampled 1200 and even then only had 436 questionnaires returned? The answer is that we use **inferential statistics.** Inferential statistics allow us to generalize the data from the sample to the larger population. In other words, we are able to make assertions about the entire population based on the data from the sample; we can make **inferences** about the population (Babbie, 1986). Because we took an appropriately sized random sample of the population, we assume that the information from the sample represents the entire population. In research articles and reports you will often see this presented as data that is **representative** of the population (Brightman, 1999). You will also see the results of data analysis described as **generalizable** because we assume we can generalize our results to the entire population. We only need to use inferential statistics when we have a sample; if we have a census, or information from the entire population, there is nothing to infer so we do not need this type of data analysis.

Sometimes, inferential statistics consider only one **parameter** (characteristic or measure of a subject) at a time, and are called **univariate** inferences (Babbie, 1986). For example, if we discover that the average, or mean, age of the sample of people who requested tourism information is 51 years old, we assume that this is also true for all of the people who requested information. We can also use more complex types of statistical tests that consider more than one variable to provide more in-depth and potentially useful information, such as discovering relationships among variables, finding differences between groups of people, and predicting or explaining people's opinions or attitudes. This is called **multivariate** analysis. For example, we could determine if there is a relationship between the household incomes of the people in our sample and whether or not they visited Arizona; we could see if satisfaction with the tourism information differed between people who did visit and people who did not; and we could discover whether the satisfaction with the information predicted the average amount of time people stayed in the state during their visit.

Although inferential analysis can tell us a lot about the people we are researching, there are many difficulties that can occur during the research process that create potential problems. There are also a lot of assumptions we make about our sampling when we conduct various inferential statistical tests.

Populations Versus Samples

Probability sampling

One of the biggest assumptions made when we conduct inferential statistical tests on sample data

is that the sample is truly representative of the population. How often is this actually the case when we are doing recreation and tourism research? Probably not very often. To have a sample that is entirely representative of the population we must select a sample that has absolutely no bias in it, or is in fact, random in nature. Every person in the population must have a chance of being selected as part of our sample. The sample also must be large enough to be representative. Then, every person in the sample must respond to our survey and complete the instrument we are using completely and carefully. This is called a **probability sample** (Jaeger, 1983; Henderson and Bialeschki, 1995). Inferential analysis really should be used only when we have a probability sample. This is because with samples such as convenience samples we have no way to figure out the risk of error we may have; this can only be done with a random sample (Hunter and Brown, 1991). We will find out how we can determine how much error is likely to exist in our data in the following paragraphs.

The ability to select a truly random sample is easier in some instances than in others. If we have a list of people that make up our population, such as the list of people who asked for travel information, it is fairly easy to select a random sample, and even better a stratified random sample based on some criteria that are important to the study. There are many times in our field, however, when we do not have such a list. How do we draw a random sample of festival attendees, white-water rafters, visitors to a museum, or fans at a football game? We do not have lists of these people and usually must survey them on-site. Strategies for random selection are beyond the scope of this chapter, but it is important to note that problems with sampling will create problems with data analysis. In addition to the difficulty we sometimes experience with sampling, not everyone is willing to participate in a study resulting in **non-respondents** and **non-sampling error** (Babbie, 1986). It is entirely possible non-respondents have some characteristic in common that make them less likely to participate in the study. This creates a bias in our sample. In the example we have been using, only 41% of the people in our sample actually sent back their questionnaires. This response rate is not unusual. When a follow-up was done to see if the non-respondents were different than the respondents, it was discovered that non-respondents were less likely to have visited than respondents. This introduces a **non-response bias** into our data that we must take into account when doing analysis. This is a particular concern in our case study example because if we did not know visitors were more likely to send back their questionnaires than non-visitors, we would overestimate the number of people from the population who visited and were influenced by the Guide.

We must also have a sample that is large enough to use for analysis. Sample sizes have already been discussed to some extent and we will further consider them from a statistical standpoint later in this chapter. Normally, we select a sample anticipating that we will have non-respondents so our initial sample size will need to be large enough to account for this. In the study we are discussing, an initial sample of 1200 was selected because experience suggested about a 40% response rate would be achieved and a final sample of at least 400 was desired.

As you can see, gaining a truly random sample is difficult and almost never happens in social sciences. Never the less, as long as we keep this in mind and have some idea of the biases in our data, inferential statistics can be a very useful tool. Even if our sampling is perfect and every person responds, the fact that it is a sample means there are probably some errors. We will discuss concepts related to this issue next.

Sampling error

Because we may have a sample that is not 100% representative of our population even if our sampling is perfect, our analysis results are referred to as **estimates** (Jaeger, 1983). We assume that there is probably some level of **sampling error** within our

data and therefore within the results of our analysis. Even when we are very careful, random sampling introduces some chance errors (Pyrczak, 1995). During political elections, you may have heard the results of polls reported with some comment about 95% confident and plus or minus 3% or something similar. What this is referring to is the **confidence interval** and the **sampling error**, or **margin of error**, of the poll. What this means is when we use a sample to estimate parameters for an entire population, we can only say with confidence that our result falls within a range that is likely to include the true proportion (or percentage), the true mean, or other measures of interest for the population (Weisberg and Bowen, 1977). If we find that 82% of our sample of 436 people who requested tourism information about the state are married or have a partner, and the mean age is 51, are these the true statistics for all of the 18,921 people in our population? How sure can we be that the real percentage of people with spouses or partners is not 71% and the real mean age is not 63? We use **probabilities** to answer this question. If we do a good job of sampling and our sample is big enough, the probability that our statistics are close to the true population values are high (Veal, 2006).

From a theoretical standpoint, the **central limit theorem** tells us if we took several samples of our population, in this case the information requesters, and looked at the means for a particular variable for each one of the samples, in this case age of respondents, the means would fall on what is called a **normal curve** or a bell curve (because it is shaped like a bell; Henderson and Bialeschki, 1995). Figure 13.1 shows what a normal curve looks like. In other words, if we took a sample

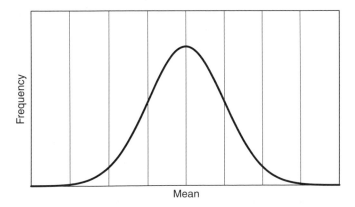

Fig. 13.1. Normal curve.

of 400 people and computed the mean age, then another sample of 400 people and computed the mean age, and so on 100 times, when we produced a graph of the final means we would have a normal curve (Pyrczak, 1995). When we chart the means on the graph it will show us the **sampling distribution** of the means, and most of the **sample means** will be near the **true mean** of the population but a few will not (Weisberg and Bowen, 1977; Pyrczak, 1995). Figure 13.1 shows what this would look like if we actually make a graph of the mean age of our respondents for all 100 of the samples.

The variability in our graph is due to the chance errors created by random sampling. We have taken 100 random samples of our population in the same way over and over, so the only explanation for different means every time is these chance errors. This is called the **standard error** of the mean. Standard error can be computed for statistics other than means too. The standard error can be defined as the standard deviation of the sampling distribution (Pyrczak, 1995). You have already learned about standard deviation and variance, but, to review, remember that the standard deviation measures the spread of our data around the mean. In this case it is the spread of data around our true mean (Jaeger, 1983).

Of course we have a bit of a problem here; we cannot realistically do 100 studies to figure out our standard error. To help us out, there is a formula to determine standard error of the mean using a sample (Pyrczak, 1995). We now must get into actual mathematical formulas, as painful as that might be. First, you need to know the standard deviation and mean of your sample variable. Using SPSS we find that the mean age of our sample of 436 information requesters is 51 years old and has a standard deviation of 13.02 years. The formula to calculate the standard error of the mean and using our sample is as follows (Phillips, 2000):

$$s_{\bar{x}} = \frac{s}{\sqrt{n}} = \frac{13.02}{\sqrt{436}} = \frac{13.02}{20.88} = 0.62$$

Where:

$s_{\bar{x}}$ = estimated standard error of the mean
s = estimated standard deviation of the population (standard deviation of the sample)
n = sample size

Luckily for us, however, SPSS will also calculate standard error at the same time as it calculates the mean, standard deviation and other descriptive statistics, but it is important to see the formula and know how it works to know how we get the number. So what exactly does a standard error of 0.62 mean for the age variable in our study? Keep in mind that the standard error of the mean is an estimate of the standard deviation of the sampling distribution of the mean (Pyrczak, 1995). Again, going back to the concept of standard deviation, when we look at graphs of standard deviations, about 68% of the cases are within one standard deviation of the mean, 95% are within two standard deviations of the mean, and 99% are within three standard deviations of the mean. This is also true of the standard error: about 68% of the cases will fall within one standard error of the mean, 95% will fall within two standard errors, and 99% within three standard errors. See Fig. 13.2 which shows this on a graph.

What this means using our example, is that at least 95% of the sample means will lie within two estimated standard errors of the mean, or 1.24 years using our example (0.62 × 2). In other words, we are at least 95% confident that our sample mean of 51 years is within 1.26 years of the population mean; or we are at least 95% certain that the range 51 ± 1.24 year contains the real population mean (Brightman, 1999). We could also say that we are 68% certain the range 51 ± 0.62 years contains our mean but this is not a very high level of certainty. We could also say that we are 99% certain that the range 51 ± 1.86 years contains our mean but we now have a wider range (Fig. 13.3).

Example 1

Now let's try calculating a standard error for a different example. This study was done at a Native-American-focused special event (Andereck and Ng, 2005b). It is an annual event where Native American artists exhibit and sell their art work, and Native American performers conduct dance and music performances. The study consisted of a short on-site questionnaire and respondents were given a second and more detailed questionnaire to take home and mail back. The sample size for the on-site survey was 468 and for the mail survey 211. Let's use age of respondents again as our example, a question we asked on the mail-back questionnaire. The mean age was 56, with a standard deviation of 13.2. Based on this information, what is the standard error of the mean? Now, let's see how the

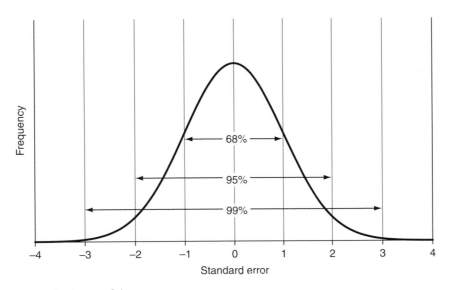

Fig. 13.2. Standard error of the mean.

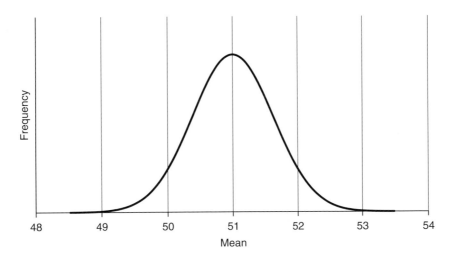

Fig. 13.3. Normal distribution of age.

sample size affects standard error. If we had asked this question on the on-site questionnaire rather than the mail-back what would be the standard error?

The range within which we are certain our mean falls is called the confidence interval. In our example 51 ± 1.26, or 49.74 years old to 51.26 years old, is a 95% confidence interval. We are 95% certain the population mean is within this interval and there is only a 5% chance we are wrong (Brightman, 1999). We use the confidence interval to determine the extent to which the results from our sample precisely describe the population (Veal, 2006). If our confidence interval is 95%, then there is a 95% chance that this confidence interval includes the true mean of the population (Weisberg and Bowen, 1977). The confidence interval is determined partly by the size of our sample, and partly by the standard deviation. When the sample size is larger and the standard deviation smaller we will have more exact estimates of our results (Weisberg and Bowen, 1977).

Usually when we are doing research we would like to have at least a 95% confidence interval, also called a **level of confidence** (Jaeger, 1983).

Although there is nothing magical about 95%, it is a useful margin; clearly a confidence interval of 68% or less is much too imprecise, but the sample sizes required for smaller confidence intervals with high levels of confidence get increasingly large and may be an inefficient use of resources.

A standard error can also be calculated for a percentage, or proportion, as well as for many other statistics (Phillips, 2000). In our sample of information inquirers we find that 73% of the people we surveyed had visited the state before the time of our promotion campaign so obviously 27% had not previously visited. Using this information, we can calculate standard error for a proportion (or percentage) (Babbie, 1986):

$$s = \sqrt{\frac{P \times Q}{n}} = \sqrt{\frac{0.73 \times 0.27}{436}}$$
$$= \sqrt{\frac{0.20}{436}} = 0.02$$

Where:

s = standard error
P,Q = the estimated population percentages for the variable
n = the sample size

Thus, our standard error is 0.02 or 2%. This now tells us the extent to which the sample estimates will be distributed around the population parameter (Babbie, 1986) just like it did for the mean. Remembering that 68% of our values will be within one standard error of our estimate, 95% will be within two standard errors, and 99% with three standard errors we can say that:

- We are 68% certain that 73 ± 2%, or 71–75%, of the people we surveyed had visited the state before the time of the promotion;
- We are 95% certain that 73 ± 4%, or 69–77%, of the people we surveyed had visited the state before the time of the promotion; or
- We are 99% certain that 73 ± 6%, 67–79%, of the people we surveyed had visited the state before the time of the promotion.

Note that for proportions the standard error depends in part on the sample size just like it does for means and that the larger the sample the smaller the standard error. It also depends on the way the respondents split with respect to their answers on the question, similar to the standard deviation for means (Babbie, 1986). Let's see how this works using a different example.

Example 2

The project from which this example is drawn is a survey of visitors to Lake Meredith National Recreation Area and Alibates Flint Quarries National Monument, National Park Service sites north of Amarillo, Texas (White *et al.*, 2004). Visitors do a number of outdoor recreation activities in the area including picnicking, swimming, boating, fishing, off-road-vehicle activities, hiking, camping, and visiting archaeological sites. The purpose was to provide visitor information for the site's management plan. The survey was partly done on-site and partly done by mail. We had a sample of 481 people who completed the on-site portion of the survey. Most of those people were there for the day (74%) while 26% were on an overnight trip. What is the standard error for this estimate? To see how the proportion affects the standard error, let's pretend 95% were on a day trip and 5% were on an overnight visit. What is the standard error?

Testing for Relationships

Hypothesis testing

The next few chapters will teach you how to use inferential statistics to actually test for relationships among variables, but we will cover some of the conceptual considerations in this chapter. Other than simply describing our sample with frequencies, percentages and means, we would often like to try to understand more about the people we are researching. This is referred to as **hypothesis testing**. We want to know differences between people and explanations for why there are differences (Pyrczak, 1995). To do this, we often use a variety of statistical techniques to test relationships among variables and learn more about our population. There are tests for most kinds of relationships you might want to investigate. For example, with our chapter case study in mind, we may want to know not only what percentage of the people in our sample were influenced to visit the state because of the Official State Visitor's Guide, but whether there were differences among the target cities. This could help us decide if we should keep focusing on the same cities for the next campaign. We can do a statistical test to find out.

When we do statistical tests using software such as SPSS, it looks for various patterns in the data to see if the results are likely to be random or whether the pattern indicates there is a relationship between the variables. What the statistical procedure is doing is testing the **null hypothesis** that no relationships exist among the variables in the population and whether any apparent relationship in the sample is due to chance (Weisberg and Bowen, 1977; Jaeger, 1983). The opposite of the null hypothesis is our **alternative hypothesis** that there is a relationship between the variables (Jaeger, 1983; Dunn, 1993). In other words, if we see differences among the target cities in the percentage of people who were influenced to visit by the Visitor's Guide, are the differences 'real' or due to sampling error? If the pattern appears to be more than just a random occurrence, the relationship is **statistically significant.** If there seems to be no particular pattern in the data then the results are non-significant (Katzer *et al.*, 1982). Thus our null hypothesis is:

H$_0$: Respondents in the target cities do not differ with respect to influence of the Official State Visitor's Guide on their decisions to visit the state.

Our alternative hypothesis is:

H$_1$: Respondents in the target cities differ with respect to influence of the Official State Visitor's Guide on their decisions to visit the state.

If we find the relationship between these two variables (target city and influence of the Guide) is statistically significant, it means there's a good chance that there really is a relationship and people in some cities were more heavily influenced than those in other cities. In our example, analysis tells us the relationship between influence of the Visitor Guide and target city is statistically significant at the 0.05 level. We interpret this by saying people in some cities, in this case Chicago, Minneapolis/ St Paul and Dallas, were more heavily influenced by the Visitor's Guide than people in other cities, in this case Denver, Portland and St Louis. From a practical perspective, it probably means that Chicago and Minneapolis are good places to promote the state but we may want to rethink our focus on Portland and Denver. St Louis is a little different because, even though relatively fewer people were influenced to visit by the Guide, it had the total highest number of visitors while just the opposite was true of Dallas. We may also decide we need more information about why the Guide had differing impact levels in the cities and do further research, possibly qualitative research such as focus groups, with residents in those cities.

The ultimate outcome of interferential tests for significance is the probability that there is a 'real' relationship. This probability is designated as α (alpha) and is called the **significance level** or the alpha level of the test (Jaeger, 1983; Mansfield, 1986). Recall our discussion in Chapter 2 about the concept of significance. We usually determine the level of significance we are looking for before we conduct the analysis. In research articles and reports the probability or significance level is usually is designated with a *p*. Using our previous example, our *p* for the test we did (called a chi-square) is 0.05. This means that there is only a 5 in 100 chance that the null hypothesis is true, or in other words that the relationship is due to chance. Again, in statistical terms, significance means 'probably true' (not due to chance), in other words, we might have found something in our sample that is worth telling to others. We usually use 0.05 as the cut-off point for significant relationships, so in our case of the respondents in the target cities we have a statistically significant result. Often, the tests can have even higher levels of significance such as 0.01 or even 0.001. You will frequently see *p* values reported as $p < 0.05$, $p < 0.01$, or $p < 0.001$ rather than a specific value such as 0.03 (Pyrczak, 1995).

There are a few things to keep in mind when using tests of statistical significance. There is an assumption that the tests are conducted on a random sample. The reason we do these tests is because, again, we are testing a sample of the population so just looking at the data alone cannot answer these kinds of questions; we need to do these tests to infer that the relationships hold true for the entire population. Even so, we still cannot be 100% sure that the results for our sample apply to the entire population, so we again use the concept of confidence intervals to gauge the likelihood that our estimates apply to the population. As before, the larger the sample size the narrower our confidence interval, the less likely we are to have an error, and the more likely we are to have a statistically significant result (Weisberg and Bowen, 1977).

Example 3

Midewin National Tallgrass Prairie is located near Joliet, Illinois, USA. It is a new site and managers needed a market study to determine the number of prospective visitors for facility and programme planning. We conducted a mail survey that included a general sample of people living in the region (final n = 356) and a sample of outdoor enthusiasts (final n = 218) (Vogt *et al.*, 2002). We compared the two segments of visitors with respect to their intensions to visit Midewin. We found that the p value for a comparison of the groups was <0.001. Given this limited amount of information, what does this tell you?

Errors

There are two types of errors that can happen when we do hypothesis testing to look for significant results. One is called a **Type I error** and the other a **Type II error**. A Type I error is when we reject the null hypothesis even though it is true; or in other words we find a significant result when one does not really exist. A Type I error is the same as the level of significance or the alpha level of our test (Dunn, 1993). If we see a research article that says the test was significant at the 0.05 level, what it is telling you is that the null hypothesis was tested in a way that the risk of making a Type I error was 5% (Pyrczak, 1995). When deciding on a significance level, you should decide how serious the consequences are of making a Type I error. If you use the 0.05 level you must be sure you are comfortable with the probability of being wrong 5% of the time you find a statistically significant result (Dunn, 1993; Jaeger, 1983). A Type II error is the opposite of a Type I error: we do not reject the null hypothesis even though it is false; or in other words we do not find a significant relationship when one really exists (Jaeger, 1983; Pyrczak, 1995). A Type II error is denoted by β (beta; Jaeger, 1983).

Some Final Considerations

Sample size

One question that researchers must answer when developing their sampling strategy is how big the sample should be. Part of the answer depends on the size of your population and part of the answer depends on what kind of inferential analysis you may want to do later. A larger sample is better, but only up to a point. As we discovered in the exercise above, as the sample gets bigger sampling error is reduced, but it is also more costly to do the survey. Eventually you will reach a point of diminishing returns where increasing the sample size only reduces the sampling error by a very small amount (Pyrczak, 1995). You can continue to reduce your error by increasing your sample size but the cost may not be worth the extra precision.

From the perspective of inferential analysis, you also need to think about the questions you want to answer using analysis of your data. If you want a representative sample with a 95% confidence interval of specific segments, or groups of people, in your sample you may need a bigger sample size. For example, in a study of subscribers to an Arizona travel magazine we found that 40% of the subscribers live in Arizona and 60% live in other states (Andereck and Ng, 2004). Because we wanted a representative sample of both segments, we did a stratified random sample with a target of at least 400 respondents from each segment. As a result, we sent out 2000 questionnaires: 800 to people from Arizona (40%) and 1200 to people from other states (60%). We ended up with 436 returns from Arizona residents and 612 from residents of other states. This provided us with a very good sample, but most importantly it provided an acceptable sampling error for each of the two segment of the sample while largely maintaining the 40–60% proportion.

Substantive significance

While statistical tests may discover statistically significant results, we must also be concerned with whether the findings are substantive from a managerial perspective. Statistical significance should not be confused with managerial significance (Veal, 2006). In other words, are the findings meaningful from a managerial perspective? Because large samples often result in many statistically significant findings when we do analysis, results should be examined for differences from a practical as well as a statistical point of view. For example, let's say we are interested in gender differences with respect to fitness activities and we find that 23% of women and 27% of men in a sample are runners. If this is from a very large sample this difference might be considered statistically significant, but is it practically significant? That may depend on the manager viewing the data and what the data are to be used for, but a 4% difference for many purposes may not be all that meaningful.

Case Study 13.1.

A primary objective of research in recreation and tourism is an evaluation of programmes and activities to determine their effectiveness. As a result, it is important to understand the nature of evaluative research and how it is conducted. It is the primary type of research practitioners may need to do themselves. In this chapter we refer to a study conducted to evaluate the effectiveness of state tourism information on people's decisions to actually visit the state (Andereck and Ng, 2005a). This kind of research is often called a 'conversion' study because it measures how many information inquirers were 'converted' into visitors. At the same time we are discovering how many people who read our information ended up visiting, we can gather quite a bit of other information about visitors and non-visitors. It is important for tourism managers and marketers to know that their promotional efforts are effective. This is even more important when the promotion is done by a government agency since government entities are accountable to the citizens who support these organizations via their tax money.

The primary purpose of this study was to evaluate the effectiveness of one US state's promotional campaign, and the information that was sent to interested people in attracting visitors to the state. The survey was of individuals who entered a sweepstake and requested the travel information after seeing an advertisement or other promotion for the state. There were six cities targeted for the promotion that was done during the winter season. The list of those who responded to the campaign included 18,921 people. In order to generate a representative group of respondents from this population, a **stratified random sample** of 1200 names was drawn from the list, stratified by target city. In other words, a sample proportional to the number of people in the list from each target city was sampled.

The survey instrument was designed by the study manager and agency staff to address the research questions generated for the study. The questionnaires were mailed to the addresses given by those sampled at the time they entered the sweepstake or made their information request. The mailing process followed a method widely accepted in social sciences and marketing research that was originally develop by Dillman and recently updated (Dillman, 2000). The procedure included an initial mailing of the survey packet including a personalized cover letter, the questionnaire, and a return postage-paid envelope; a reminder postcard about 10 days later; and a second mailing of an entire survey packet to remaining non-respondents after another two weeks. To encourage response, an incentive of US$5.00 was offered if the questionnaire was returned. Ultimately, 436 usable questionnaires were returned resulting in a 41% response rate.

The following research questions guided construction of the questionnaire:

- What are the interest levels that information requestors hold for the state as a vacation destination?
- What percentage of information requestors actually visited the state after they received the information?
- What percentage of people who actually visited were in some way influenced by the Official State Visitor's Guide?
- For those individuals who had not yet taken a trip since making the request, do they hold intentions to visit in the future and what factors contributed to their decisions not to visit?
- What were the primary activities and motives with respect to the visit?
- What modes of transportation did travellers use to enter, and travel within, the state and what types of overnight accommodations were used?
- How much money was spent in the state by those who travelled to the state after receiving the requested information?
- What are the demographics of the information requesters (gender, age, household composition, income, education and ethnicity)?

(Continued)

Case Study 13.1. Continued.

From this research, agency staff were able to determine if the target cities promotional campaign was effective (which it was); how satisfied people were with the Visitor's Guide and if it influenced their travel decisions (which it did); and a variety of information about the people who actually did visit and what they did on their trip. This information provided agency staff with additional information about the market they had targeted for the promotion campaign. It also demonstrated that the money spent on the promotional campaign was returned to the state several-fold through tourist spending, a fact that is very important to maintain support and funding from the state government.

Key Terms

Population: Any collect of objects or entities that have at least one characteristic in common (Jaeger, 1983).

Sample: A part of a population . . . consisting of those objects or people we have observed or measured (Jaeger, 1983).

Inferential statistics: A group of methods which enable the researcher to generalize some findings to the larger group from which the sample was selected (Hunter & Brown, 1991).

Representative sample: The aggregate characteristics of the sample closely approximate the same aggregate characteristics of the population (Babbie, 1986).

Generalizability: The extent to which research findings can be applied to the population in general.

Census: A survey of an entire population (Katzer *et al.*, 1982)

Parameter: Some characteristic of a population (Jaeger, 1983). It is the summary description of a given variable in a population (Babbie, 1986).

Univariate: An analysis of one variable at a time.

Multivariate: Statistical analysis that uses more than one variable at once (Katzer *et al.*, 1982).

Probability sample: All members of the population have an equal chance of being selected in the sample (Babbie, 1986).

Non-respondents: Individuals who choose not to participate in a survey.

Non-sampling error: Error in the data arising from a study which used some form of survey research. The error may be due to inadequacies in design, questionnaire construction, interviewing, data analysis, non-response, etc. Non-sampling error may contain bias (Katzer *et al.*, 1982).

Non-response bias: A potential bias in survey data resulting from those who choose not to participate in the survey.

Estimate: A number that is computed by using data collected from a sample that is used as a best guess about the value of a population parameter (Jaeger, 1983).

Sampling error: The degree to which a sample statistic fails to equal the average of an infinite number of determinations of this statistic from the same population (Katzer *et al.*, 1982).

Confidence interval: A range of values within which there is a specified probability that the population parameter will exist, over all possible samples. The specified probability is called the confidence level. A confidence interval is a type of interval estimate (Katzer *et al.*, 1982).

Statistic: A characteristic of a sample…a number that describes some feature of a sample. Each is computed using the data collected on a sample (Jaeger, 1983).

Probability: The theoretical relative frequency of occurrence of a certain kind of event in the long run (Loether and McTavish, 1988).

Central Limit Theorem: As the sample size n becomes large, the sampling distribution of the sample mean can be approximated by a normal distribution with a mean of μ and a standard deviation of $\sigma/\sqrt{n}$, where μ is the mean of the population and σ is its standard deviation (Mansfield, 1986).

Normal distribution (curve): A mathematically defined, symmetrical, unimodal distribution (Katzer *et al.*, 1982).

Sampling distribution: The theoretical distribution of a statistic that results from selecting an infinite number of random samples of the same size from a given population (Rosenthal, 2001).

Sample mean: The mean of the sample (Katzer *et al.*, 1982).

True mean: The mean of the population which may or may not be known.

Standard error of the mean: An estimate of the standard deviation of the sampling distribution of the means which is normal in shape when the sample size is relatively large (Pyrczak, 1995).

Confidence level: If the process of estimating a parameter from a sample statistic were repeated many times, the confidence level would be the percent of the obtained confidence intervals which contain the parameter (which are correct) (Katzer *et al.*, 1982).

Hypothesis testing: A method of statistical inference that leads to the rejection or non-rejection of statistical hypotheses (Katzer *et al.*, 1982).

Null hypothesis: An hypothesis about parameters which is tested statistically. Usually the null hypothesis reflects no relationship, no difference, or the status quo of a phenomenon or relationship (Katzer *et al.*, 1982).

Alternate hypothesis: The hypothesis that the researcher would like to be able to accept if the null hypothesis is rejected with a significance test (Katzer *et al.*, 1982).

Statistical significance: The outcome of significance test in which the results are show to have a low probability of being due to chance alone, thereby eliminating chance as a viable cause of the results (Katzer *et al.*, 1982).

Alpha level: The probability of incorrectly rejecting the null hypothesis with a significance test (Katzer *et al.*, 1982).

Significance level: The alpha level chosen by the researcher for a significance test. It is also sometime used synonymously with *p-value* (Katzer *et al.*, 1982).

Type I error: Finding a statistically significant relationship when one does not really exist.

Type II error: Not finding a statistically significant relationship when one really does exist.

Discussion Questions

1. In what research circumstances is it appropriate and helpful to use interferential analysis?

2. Can you think of any fields of research where a 95% confidence interval like we usually use in social science research may not be precise enough?

3. Why is sample size such an important consideration when we conduct research? Also, why is taking a great deal of care to develop a very good sampling strategy a necessity?

4. Is the significance level of a statistical test always the best way to determine if a relationship is meaningful from a managerial standpoint? Why or why not?

Worked Example 13.1. Research in Action, Gunnison Gorge National Conservation Area

The project from which this example is drawn is a survey of visitors to the Gunnison Gorge National Conservation Area (GGNCA), a Bureau of Land Management (BLM) area in Colorado (Knopf *et al.*, 2002). Visitors do a number of outdoor recreation activities in the area including white water river running, off road vehicle activities, hiking, fishing and camping. The purpose of the research was to provide visitor information for the site's management plan after it was designated a National Conservation Area. The survey was partly done onsite and partly done by mail. We had a sample of 428 people who completed the onsite portion of the survey which provided us with a margin of sampling error of ±4.8% at the 95% confidence interval. We had a response rate of 46% among those visitors for a mail survey sample size of 196. This provided a sampling error of ±7.1% at the 95% level. Though this is not as precise as we normally would like, the resources required to gain a larger sample were not available. Often, sampling in the field, especially in an area that is largely wilderness or backcountry such as the GGNCA, even finding people to contact presents challenges. For the purposes of the planning document, it was determined that the survey results were accurate enough to provide the framework for the plan.

The visitor study data was in addition to the public scoping process that is required of federal agencies doing management plans, and included several focus groups that were held in surrounding communities, and interviews with stakeholder groups such as river outfitters.

The study was primarily intended to feed into the management plan for the area and was founded on the concept of benefits-based management (Knopf *et al.*, 2004). The area was divided into three zones, and statistical tests for differences among recreationists in the zones were conducted. Statistically significant results were found between the zones. As a result, the BLM developed the management plan with these differences in mind. The area where off-highway vehicle activities take place, for example, will be managed to facilitate social and stress release experiences, including high social contact, facilities to encourage social interaction, and high levels of access. Activities will primarily include off-road use, camping and picnicking. Support facilities will be abundant and highly maintained with limited visitor controls. Managers will address problems identified in the area such as litter and depreciative behavior using interpretive information, and increased visitor contact and patrols. This is in contrast to the inner-gorge wilderness area that will be managed for the traditional wilderness values of solitude and natural experiences, with limited contact with other visitors and use level controls.

References

Andereck, K.L. and Ng, E. (2005a) *Arizona Office of Tourism Marketing Conversion Study: Target Cities Promotion 2004.* Department of Recreation and Tourism Management, Arizona State University, Phoenix, Arizona.

Andereck, K.L. and Ng, E. (2005b) *Pueblo Grande Museum Indian Market Evaluation.* Department Recreation and Tourism Management, Arizona State University, Phoenix, Arizona.

Andereck, K. L. and Ng, E. (2004) *Arizona Highways Magazine's Impact on Tourism.* Arizona Department of Transportation, Phoenix, Arizona.

Babbie, E. (1986) *The Practice of Social Research,* 4th edn. Wadsworth Publishing Belmont, California.

Brightman, H.J. (1999) *Data Analysis in Plain English with Microsoft Excel.* Duxbury Press, New York.

Dillman, D.A. (2000) *Mail and Internet Surveys: The Tailored Design Method*, 2nd edn. John Wiley and Sons, New York.

Dunn, J.K. (1993) *Research in Therapeutic Recreation: Concepts and Methods.* In: Malkin, M. and Howe, C.Z. (eds), Venture Publishing, Inc., State College, Pennsylvania, pp. 161–179.

Henderson, K.A. and Bialeschki, M.D. (1995) *Evaluating Leisure Services: Making Enlightened Decisions.* Venture Publishing, Inc., State College, Pennsylvania.

Hunter, I.R., and Brown, R. (1991) The application of inferential statistics with non-probability type samples. *Journal of Applied Recreation Research* 16, 234–243.

Jaeger, R. (1983) *Statistics: A Spectator Sport*. Sage Publications, Bevery Hills, California.

Katzer, J., Cook, K.H. and Crouch, W.W. (1982) *Evaluating Information: A Guide for Users of Social Science Information*, 2nd edn. Random House, New York.

Knopf, R.C., Andereck, K.L., Tucker, K., Bottomly, B. and Virden, R.J. (2004) Building connections among lands, people and communities: A case study of benefits-based management plan development for the gunnison gorge national conservation area. *Proceedings of the Fourth Social Aspects and Recreation Research Symposium,* 146–157.

Knopf, R.C., Andereck, K.L., Virden, R.J. and Fletcher, J. (2002) *Gunnison Gorge National Conservation Area Visitor Study*. Department of Recreation and Tourism Management, Arizona State University, Phoenix, Arizona.

Loether, H.J. and McTavish, D.G. (1988) *Descriptive and Inferential Statistics: An Introduction*, 3rd edn. Allyn and Bacon, Inc., Boston, Massachusetts.

Mansfield, E. (1986) *Basic Statistics with Applications*. W.W. Norton and Company, New York.

Phillips, J.L. (2000) *How to Think About Statistics*, 6th edn. W.H. Freeman and Company, New York.

Pyrczak, F. (1995) *Making Sense of Statistics*. Pyrczak Publishing, Los Angeles.

Rosenthal, J.A. (2001) *Statistics and Data Interpretation for the Helping Professions*. Wadsworth/ Thomson Learning, Belmont, California.

Veal, A.J. (2006) *Research Methods for Leisure and Tourism: A Practical Guide*, 3rd edn. Prentice Hall, London.

Vogt, C.A., Andereck, K.L. and Klenosky, D.B. (2002) *Project Report: Market Analysis, Midewin National Tallgrass Prairie*. Department of Park, Recreation, and Tourism Resources, East Lansing, Michigan.

Weisberg, H.F. and Bowen, B.D. (1977) *An Introduction to Survey Research and Data Analysis*. W.H. Freeman and Company, San Francisco.

White, D.D., Andereck, K., Lankford, C. and Yedlapati, N. (2004) *Visitor Study Technical Report: Lake Meredith National Recreation Area/Alibates Flint Quarries National Monument*. School of Community Resources and Development, Arizona State University, Phoenix, Arizona.

chapter 14

Relationship Analysis: *t*-Tests, Analysis of Variance and Cross Tabulations

Jacinta M. Gau and Dogan Gursoy

Learning Objectives

After reading this chapter, you will be able to:

1. Define the four levels of measurement;
2. Be able to select the appropriate statistical technique based on the level of measurements of study variables;
3. Know the five steps of hypothesis testing;
4. Explain the four types of *t*-tests and the situations in which each one is used;
5. Run *t*-tests using SPSS and interpret the output;
6. Be able to differentiate between ANOVA and *t*-test;
7. Describe the logic of the chi-square/cross tabulation test;
8. Run the chi-square test in SPSS and interpret the results.

Chapter Summary

This chapter introduces the basic uses of two parametric tests (*t*-tests and ANOVA) and one

non-parametric test (χ^2). For each test, it discusses the purposes of the test, the assumptions (if any) underlying it, and the types of data that are appropriate and inappropriate for this test. Moreover, the chapter stresses the difference between statistical significance and substantive meaning. The researcher has an obligation to report fully informative results. The chapter provides discussion on reporting effect sizes and always questioning research results that are not accompanied by effect size estimates.

Introduction

The level(s) of measurement of your independent and dependent variables determines what statistical tests you can use to analyse those variables. The *t*-test and analysis of variance (ANOVA) are appropriate when the independent variable is categorical (nominal or ordinal) and the dependent variable is continuous (interval or ratio). The chi-square test is for use when both the independent variable (IV) and the dependent variable (DV) are categorical.

All of the techniques discussed in this chapter revolve around the central idea of **hypothesis testing**, otherwise known as **inferential statistics**. Chapter 13 introduced you to inferential statistics, so be sure you have a good grasp of that concept before delving into the present chapter. Hypothesis testing begins with the specification of a **null hypothesis**. The null hypothesis is the prediction that the two groups we are comparing are not significantly different from one another and that they differ from one another solely because of fluke variations attributable to sampling error. Think of the word 'null' to mean 'no' or 'none'. The null hypothesis is denoted by the symbol H_0. The null hypothesis is what is tested during a statistical procedure. The **alternative hypothesis** (denoted H_1) proposes that there is a difference between the two variables being tested. Note that we never test the alternative hypothesis directly; we only test the null. If the null is rejected (more on this concept in a minute), then we take that as support for the alternative. If the null is not rejected, then we conclude that there is no support for the alternative.

Means Difference Test: the *t*-test

The first type of statistical test we will discuss is the *t*-test, which is used when the independent variable is categorical and has two levels (or classes) and the dependent variable is continuous. The *t*-test is an analysis of means. The ultimate goal is to determine whether the discrepancy between two means is sufficiently large to be considered a real, true difference, or whether it is more likely to be the product of sampling error.

There are two types of *t*-tests: one-sample tests and two-sample tests. The two-sample *t*-test can be further subdivided into two types: independent samples and matched/dependent samples. Independent-samples *t*-test can be divided further still into pooled variance and separate variance types. Each of these types and subtypes of *t*-tests will be discussed separately below.

One-sample *t*-test

Suppose we are in a situation where we have information about the population mean. The one-sample *t*-test allows us to answer the question, 'Given a population mean (μ) and a sample mean ($\bar{x}$), what is the probability that this sample came from the population with mean μ?' Let's work through the steps of a one-sample *t*-test using an example from the hypothetical data based on the Tropical Hotel survey. One question that a hotel manager may want to know is whether the guests of her hotel are similar in age to the general population or, conversely, whether her hotel attracts people with a significantly different (either older or younger) mean age. The USA census reports that the average age in the population is 36.7 years. You compute the mean of the sample of 90 people who filled out the survey and find a mean age of 46.6 years. There is clearly a difference between these two means: a difference of 9.9 years, to be exact (46.6 – 36.7 = 9.9). Subtraction alone, though, is not enough to establish the existence of a true, bona fide difference between these two values because sampling error could have produced a higher sample mean simply by chance. We do not yet know if this apparent difference truly indicates that Tropical Hotel guests are, on average, older than the general population or whether the age differences are the product of chance variations in the data. A one-sample *t*-test can be used to answer this question.

Here, the null hypothesis is stated as our prediction that there is no difference between Tropical Hotel guests and the general population; that is, that any discrepancies between the average age of the hotel guests and the general population are simply due to sampling variation and are not true statistical differences. We state the null hypothesis as:

$$H_0: \mu = 36.7$$

What this represents, substantively, is that we predict that the Tropical Hotel guest sample is part of a larger population with a mean age of 36.7 years (i.e. we predict that the Tropical Hotel sample comes from the general US population). If we fail to reject H_0, then we will conclude that the Tropical Hotel guests are part of the general US population age distribution.

The alternative hypothesis, then, is a statement predicting that the Tropical Hotel sample *is* not similar to the general US population; in other words, H_1 predicts that there is a **statistically significant difference** between the Tropical Hotel guests' age and that of the general US population. There are two types of alternative hypotheses: one-tailed (aka directional) and two-tailed (aka non-directional). **One-tailed** or **directional hypothesis** tests are appropriate when you have reason to believe that one of the means is greater than the other. One-tailed tests are not typically used in statistics because most software programs default to the more conservative two-tailed tests. **Two-tailed** or **non-directional hypothesis tests** are for use when you do not wish to predict a direction of the difference beforehand. It is harder to reject the null in two-tailed tests than it is in one-tailed tests, so two-tailed are generally preferred because they are more conservative.

In this chapter, only two-tailed tests will be used. A two-tailed alternative hypothesis predicting that the sample mean is significantly different from the population mean is represented as:

$$H_1: \mu \neq 36.7$$

If, at the conclusion of the one-sample t-test, we end up rejecting the null hypothesis, we will conclude that the alternative hypothesis is true, that is, that the sample of 90 survey-takers did not come from the general population but instead from a population with a mean that is different that of the general public.

The appropriate distribution for a t-test is, not surprisingly, the **t-distribution**. Like the z-distribution that you learned about in earlier chapters, the t-distribution is a type of **normal curve**, meaning that it is symmetrical and unimodal. Unlike the z-distribution, however, the t-distribution is actually not just one curve but a family of curves: the exact shape of the t-distribution changes depending on the size of the sample under examination. When the sample size (denoted 'N') is 50 or greater, the t- and z-distributions are nearly identical; when N is less than 50, the t-distribution flattens out. As N gets smaller and smaller, the t-distribution looks less like a bell curve and more like a flat line.

Having identified the distribution we are going to use for the hypothesis test (the t-distribution), the next task is to specify the significance level or, in statistical terms, the **α-level** (alpha-level). The α-level represents the critical region of the t-distribution. The most common α-levels in social science are $\alpha = 0.05$ and $\alpha = 0.01$. An α of 0.05 means that 5% of the area under the t-curve is located beyond that point, while an α of 0.01 means that 1% of the area under the curve is located beyond it. Area and

probability are synonymous in the parlance of statistics. To say that 0.05 (i.e. 5%) of the curve is in the tail of the distribution beyond the critical value is to say that the probability of obtaining a value either greater than (if the critical value is positive) or less than (if the critical value is negative) is less than 0.05. For a two-tailed test, the 0.05 α-level is split in half and each half (that is, 0.025) is located in the two tails of the distribution. If the specified α-level were 0.01, then the area in each of the critical tail regions would be 0.005 for a two-tailed test.

The importance of the α-level is that it allows us to determine the circumstances under which we will decide whether or not to reject the null hypothesis. If the obtained value of the test statistic falls in the area of the curve beyond the α-level cut-off point, then the null hypothesis will be rejected because the probability of obtaining such a result is less than the pre-set α-level (0.05 or 0.01). Since this is such a tiny probability, we conclude that, in all likelihood, it just would not have happened by chance; in other words, it must symbolize a real difference between the two means. In this case, the null would be rejected and the alternative hypothesis would be taken as the true state of affairs. Note, though, that in statistics, one can never be absolutely positive about a conclusion concerning rejection of the null hypothesis; there is always a probability, sometimes an incredibly small probability, but a probability nonetheless, that the null is actually true and has been wrongfully rejected. This is an intractable problem in statistics and one that you should always keep in mind when you do inferential tests and when you evaluate the results of inferential tests done by others.

When you run a statistical test in a software program like SPSS, you will get something called a **p-value**. This can be interpreted as a sort of 'obtained significance level' and should be compared to either 0.05 or 0.01. If the p-value is less than the pre-determined α-level (either 0.05 or 0.01), then the null hypothesis can be rejected and you would conclude that there is a real difference between the two means. If the p-value is greater than the α-level, the null must be retained and the conclusion would be that there is no true difference.

The computation of the test statistic requires that you have access to and be able to use a statistical software program. There are several such programs available, such as SPSS, SAS and STATA. For basic computations such as t-tests, you can even find websites online that will compute them for you. Here, SPSS will be used.

First, click on the 'Analyse' tab at the top of the screen. This opens a drop-down menu from which you can then select 'Compare Means' and, on the menu that opens to the right of that option, 'One-Sample T Test'. Clicking on 'One-Sample T Test' will cause a new dialogue box to open. Move the variable 'age' from the list on the left side to the space on the right side of the box. The 'Test Value' box is where you enter the population mean (μ) that you are testing the sample mean against. In the Tropical Hotel guest example, the test value (i.e. population mean) is 36.7. After the test value has been specified, click 'OK' to produce the output window shown in Fig. 14.1.

To determine if the results are statistically significant or not (i.e. if the null will be rejected or not), take a look at the 'Sig. (2-tailed)' column. The number in this cell is the p-value and the question is, 'Is the p-value less than alpha?' In this case, you can see that $p = 0.000$, which is less than both 0.05 and 0.01, so this is definitely a statistically significant result. We can reject the null and conclude that the hotel guests' mean age is significantly different from that of the population as a whole. This difference is important to you as a manager of the Tropical Hotel because you now realize that your guests somehow stand apart from the general population. You may be catering to a specific group of people; specifically, you are serving a crowd that tends to be older in age. You therefore probably want to focus on providing amenities, activities and forms of entertainment that are popular among older adults.

Two-sample t-test: independent samples

There are many instances when you will want to compare the means of two samples. Two-sample t-tests invoke the concepts of independent and dependent variables and are used when a researcher wishes to know whether a two-class, categorical independent variable affects the mean of a continuous dependent variable.

There are two types of two-sample t-tests: (i) independent samples; and (ii) matched pairs or dependent samples. Pay attention to the differences between these two types because using the wrong test will yield erroneous results and conclusions. **Independent samples t-tests** are for use when the two samples under investigation were drawn independently of one another. Independent selection means that the selection of cases into the first sample did not in any way affect the selection of cases into the second sample; they were drawn independently. **Matched pairs t-tests** and **repeated measures t-tests** are used whenever the two samples under investigation are not independent. Matched pairs tests are used when an initial sample is drawn and then a second sample is constructed by finding people (or objects, depending on the unit of analysis) who resemble the people in the sample on relevant characteristics. If, for example, there was a white, 35-year-old male in the first sample, then you would find a white man in his mid-30s to put in the second sample. Repeated measures tests are used when working with before-and-after research designs in which a sample is measured at one point in time and then a treatment of some kind is applied. After the treatment, the sample is measured again. The purpose is to determine if the treatment caused a statistically significant change in the sample's mean.

Suppose you want to know whether men and women differ in terms of the amount of money they spend on hotel amenities. This would help inform you as to whether you should concentrate on providing those amenities that men prefer, those that women prefer, or whether you should offer an array of gender-neutral services. The independent

One-Sample Test

	Test value = 36.7				95% Confidence interval of the difference	
	t	df	Sig.(2-tailed)	Mean difference	Lower	Upper
How old are you?	5.417	89	0	9.922	6.28	13.56

Fig. 14.1. Output window with *t*-test results.

variable in this test would be guest gender. It is measured as 'male or female' and is therefore a two-class, nominal variable. The dependent variable is 'money spent' and is continuous. No matching or repeated testing was involved in the gathering of the survey data, so the samples can be said to have been selected independently. This is a case for an independent samples t-test.

The null hypothesis for the independent-samples t-test is that there is no difference between the two group means. Formally, the null is stated as:

$$H_0: \mu_{males} = \mu_{females}$$

The two-tailed alternative hypothesis is:

$$H_1: \mu_{males} \neq \mu_{females}$$

The distribution is still t. Since 0.05 is the most common significance level used in social sciences, we will use it again. Two-sample tests present an issue that was not present in the one-sample test. There are two types of independent samples t-tests: **pooled variance** and **separate variance**. Pooled variance tests are appropriate when the two samples have similar variances; that is, when the 'spread' of the data in one sample is similar to that in the other sample. Separate variances tests are needed when the two samples have significantly different variances. Luckily, there is an easy test for determining whether the pooled or separate variances test is more appropriate for a given situation. This test is called Levene's Test for Equality of Variances and it is something that statistical software packages will compute for you. Levene's has its own built-in hypothesis test: the null hypothesis is that there is no significant difference between the variances of the two samples. When the obtained value of the Levene's statistic is significant, the null hypothesis is rejected and the conclusion is that there is a significant difference between the two samples' variances. A separate variances test would be used. If the obtained value of Levene's F statistic is non-significant, then the null is not rejected and we conclude that the variances are not different and that a pooled variance t-test must be employed.

Let's go back to SPSS. We have to actually run the independent samples t-test in order to get the obtained value of the Levene's F statistic so that we know whether we need to use pooled or independent variances. To run an independent samples t-test, use the same menu and dialogue boxes that you used for the one-sample test, except this time, select 'Independent Samples t-test' from the menu. Move the test variable from the left space to the right space and then click on 'Define Groups'. This will open a dialogue box wherein you will need to enter the coding of the grouping variable to tell the program how it should compare the two groups.

Since 'gender' is the independent variable, select it and move it to the 'Grouping Variable' box. You must click on 'Define Groups' and enter the independent variable's coding. Here, males are coded as '0' and females as '1'. The variable labelled 'spent' is the item containing respondents' reports about how much money they spent during their stay; this is the dependent variable and needs to be moved to the 'Test Variable(s)' box. Then click 'OK' and an output window will appear. Figure 14.2 contains the output for this test.

		Levene's test for equality of variances		t-test for Equality of Means						Interval of the difference	
		F	Sig	t	df	Sig (2-tailed)	Mean difference	Std. error difference		Lower	Upper
About how much money did you spend in the Tropical Hotel during this stay?	Equal variances assumed	0.367	0.546	−1.295	88	0.199	−10.595	8.181		−26.854	5.663
	Equal variance not assumed			−1.299	87.269	0.197	−10.595	8.157		−26.807	5.617

Fig. 14.2. Output for independent samples t-test.

The first thing you need to look at when you are examining the output for an independent samples t-test is the Levene's F test. In Fig. 14.2, the obtained value of Levene's F statistic is not statistically significant because the '0.546' in the column labelled 'Sig' to the right of the Levene's F column is greater than 0.05; therefore, the null hypothesis of no difference must be retained.

Since the Levene's test yielded a non-significant result, the pooled variances t-test is the appropriate strategy (had Lavene's been significant, the separate variances test would be used instead). We will therefore refer to the p-value in the 'Equal variances assumed' row of the bottom table in Fig. 14.2. Following this row over to the 'Sig (2-tailed)' column, you can see that $p = 0.199$. This is greater than 0.05, so the null cannot be rejected. This means that there is no significant difference between men and women in terms of the amount of money they spend during their stay at the hotel. It would appear from this study that there is no need to focus on male- or female-specific amenities and services; it would instead be a better idea to offer an array of products and activities that appeal to both sexes.

The matched pairs or repeated measures t-test

The independent samples t-test assumes that the two samples were drawn randomly and independently. Some research designs, however, do not use independent random samples. These designs, as described above, are called matched pairs or repeated measures. Let's go back to the Tropical Hotel. You, the manager, decide that you want to increase the amount of money that your guests spend at the hotel on dining, room service, laundry service, and other amenities during their stay. After the first month-long survey is complete, you implement several changes to the hotel. You redo the restaurant menu and add several new items, you put up more signs around the hotel advertising laundry and room services, you get a new internet service provider and then put up signs advertising faster connection speed, and other things that you think of to boost in-house guest spending.

After six months, you want to know if the changes you made were effective; that is, you want to know if you accomplished your goal of increasing guest spending. To answer this question, you conduct another survey. You are concerned about sampling error, though. Because you cannot retest the same people who took the survey the first time, you want to make sure that you do not inadvertently capture a completely different sample on the second survey. In other words, you want the people who take your second survey to be as similar to those who took the first survey as possible so that you can place more confidence in the validity of your results. To do this, you begin gathering demographic information from your guests as they check in. Every time a new guest's information matches that of a guest from the original pre-survey, you select that new guest and ask her or him to complete the post-survey. Your new guests, of course, are not exactly equal to your original guests, but they are similar in many key respects. This sort of deliberate selection procedure makes the second sample a matched sample because selection into the second group was not random but was, instead, determined by these participants' similarities to the original survey respondents.

The null hypothesis for the matched-pairs or dependent-samples t-test is that the difference between the pairs' mean scores is zero. We can state the null and alternative, respectively, as:

$$H_0: \mu_{before} = \mu_{after}$$
$$H_1: \mu_{before} \neq \mu_{after}$$

Here, the null is predicting that the two means will be equal. If the p-value for the matched-pairs or dependent-samples test is non-significant, we would conclude that the treatment or intervention had no effect. The next step is to pull up SPSS and select 'Paired Samples T Test'. A dialogue box will open that will prompt you to select the groups you wish to compare. Move each group over into the appropriate location in the right-hand box. Then hit 'OK' and the output window featured in Fig.14.3 will appear.

The results are statistically significant, as indicated by the '0.001' in the 'Sig.' column. This is less than 0.01, so the null hypothesis is rejected. It appears as if the new services and amenities significantly increased the amount of money they spend at the hotel. What you did seems to have worked.

Paired Samples Test

		Paired differences							
					95% confidence interval of the difference				
		Mean	Std. deviation	Std. error mean	Lower	Upper	t	df	Sig. (2-tailed)
Pair 1	First Survey: Approximately how much money did you spend in the Tropical Hotel During this stay? Second Survey: Approximately how much money did you spend in the Tropical Hotel During this stay?	−9.51111	25.69713	2.70872	−14.89327	−4.12895	−3.511	89	0.001

Fig. 14.3. Output for guest in-house spending before and after renovation.

Categorical Independent Variables with Continuous Dependent Variables: Analysis of Variance

The t-test allows you to make comparisons between two sample means, but there are many situations where you may want to test three, four, five or more means at once. A t-test is inappropriate in this instance. It may be tempting to do a series of two-mean t-tests on all the means of interest, but such an approach is dangerous because it greatly inflates the **Type I error rate**. The Type I error rate is the likelihood that a true null will be wrongfully rejected. The Type I error rates translate into what is called the **familywise error rate**. As the number of t-tests you conduct increases, so too does the probability that you will make a Type I error. So, what do you do when you are working with more than two means? The answer is that you conduct an **analysis of variance (ANOVA)**. The ANOVA is for use when the DV is continuous and the IV is categorical and has three or more classes. It functions much like a t-test in that it is used to compare sample means.

There are some characteristics about the ANOVA that make it necessary to use caution when employing this technique. The most important assumption that ANOVA makes is that the samples are independent and randomly selected. The assumption of independent, random samples is similar to the assumption we made for the independent-samples t-test: the samples must be mutually exclusive and the selection of cases into one group must not affect the selection of cases into any other group. The precise reason for this is beyond the scope of this text, but it is a very important point, so remember it. The ANOVA cannot be used if the groups are not independent.

The word 'variance' in 'analysis of variance' refers to the variability both of individuals and of groups. In ANOVA, these two types of variability are called **within-group variability** and **between-group variability**, respectively. Within-group variability refers to the variation of scores around their respective group means. The between-group variation is the variability of group means around the grand mean, or the mean for the entire sample, irrespective of group status.

The Tropical Hotel guest survey contained the items 'How satisfied are you with your stay at the hotel?' and 'How much money did you spend on in-house amenities during your stay?' The relationship between these two variables is interesting from a managerial standpoint because satisfaction with the hotel may affect spending: guests who are more satisfied with the hotel overall may spend more money in-house (e.g. eating at the hotel restaurant rather than going out). This question also lends itself to testing via ANOVA because the independent variable (satisfaction with the hotel) is categorical and has three classes ('satisfied', 'unsure' and 'dissatisfied') and the dependent variable (money spent) is continuous.

The procedure will still follow the five steps of hypothesis testing, starting with the statement of the null and alternate hypotheses. The null hypothesis in ANOVA is that all of the groups have the same mean. Applied to the Tropical Hotel example, the null hypothesis states that there is no difference between the different groups on the amount of money spent at the hotel; that is, that satisfaction does not affect spending. For an ANOVA with four groups, the null would be:

$$H_0: \mu_1 = \mu_2 = \mu_3$$

The alternative hypothesis is that at least one of the groups is significantly different from the others. It is written as:

$$H_1: \text{some } \mu_i \neq \text{some } \mu_j$$

The subscripts 'i' and 'j' are used instead of specific group identifications because the alternative hypothesis does not state which group(s) should be different from the others; it merely says that there is a difference somewhere. The location, number, and direction of difference(s) are not indicated by the ANOVA test. (This is the reason why **post-hoc tests** are used; post-hoc tests will be discussed shortly.)

The second step in hypothesis testing is to determine what distribution to use. Analysis of variance is based on the *F*-distribution and utilizes the *F*-statistic. The *F*-distribution looks much different from the normal curve and has its own table of critical values. Conceptually, the *F*-statistic is a ratio of variances between the groups. The equation below represents this ratio:

$$F = \frac{\text{Between-group variance}}{\text{Within-group variance}}$$

Between-group variance can be conceptualized as a real, genuine difference between the groups. The within-group variance is a measure of error, of random variability amongst the people or objects in the study. When the between-group variation is large relative to the within-group variation, the *F*-ratio will also be large and the null will be rejected. If the between-group variation is similar to or less than the within-group variation, then the *F*-statistic will be small and the null will not be rejected.

Going back to SPSS, we can compute the *F*-statistic. The one-way ANOVA is located in the same menu in which the *t*-tests are found. Select the independent and dependent variables you want to use and move them from the left to the right side of the dialogue box. Also click on 'Descriptives' so that SPSS will provide each group's mean. Click 'Continue' to close this dialogue box.

Next, click on 'Post Hoc' to pull up the post-hoc test selection. You will need to choose one or more post-hoc tests. There are several and the relative merits and drawbacks of each have been the subject of much debate that is beyond the scope of this book. Tukey's test is one of the most common

(Bachman and Paternoster, 1997) and most useful (Fox *et al.*, 2002, 2009) of all post-hoc tests. It is powerful (Field, 2000) and it controls for the family-wise error rate. For the present purposes, Tukey's will be chosen. Once you have selected the post-hoc tests you want, click 'OK' on that window and then 'OK' on the main dialogue box. The output shown in Fig. 14.4 will be produced.

It can be seen here that *F* = 3.792 and the obtained significance value (*p*) is 0.026. Since *p* < 0.05, the null hypothesis can be rejected (note, though, that it would have to be retained if the α-level were to be set at 0.01). We can conclude from this that there is a statistically significant difference somewhere.

But where? And how many differences are there? To answer these questions, we turn to the results of the post-hoc tests, which are shown in Fig. 14.5.

Tukey's HSD (honestly significant differences) compares each group to all other groups to determine where the significant differences are. The column you want to pay attention to is the 'Sig.' column. As with all other output we have analysed thus far, you are looking for values of less than 0.05 because that indicates the presence of a statistically significant between-group difference. Figure 14.5 shows that there is only one significant difference between the groups and that it is located between the 'satisfied' and 'dissatisfied' groups. The 'unsure' group is not significantly different from either of the other two.

There is a final concept that must be visited before the discussion of ANOVA is complete. As discussed above, a statistically significant *F*-statistic tells you whether or not the association between the IV and DV is statistically significant, but it does not tell you the strength of the relationship. What is needed is a **measure of association** or, in other words, an effect size. A relationship between two variables can be statistically significant but yet so small in an absolute sense that it is not substantively meaningful. Traditionally, researchers have relied on **eta squared**

ANOVA

Approximately how much money did you spend in the Tropical Hotel during this stay?

	Sum of squares	df	Mean square	F	Sig.
Between groups	10780.259	2	5390.130	3.792	0.026
Within groups	123672.630	87	1421.524		
Total	134452.889	89			

Fig. 14.4. Output for one-way ANOVA.

Multiple Comparisons

Approximately how much money did you spend in the Tropical Hotel during this stay?
Tukey HSD

(I) Overall, how satisfied are you with your stay at the Tropical Hotel?	(J) Overall, how satisfied are you with your stay at the Tropical Hotel?	Mean difference (I–J)	Std. error	Sig.	95% confidence interval	
					Lower bound	Upper bound
Satisfied	Unsure	11.84470	9.35410	0.418	−10.4600	34.1494
	Dissatisfied	27.52970*	9.99687	0.019	3.6924	51.3670
Unsure	Satisfied	−11.84470	9.35410	0.418	−34.1494	10.4600
	Dissatisfied	15.68500	10.06398	0.269	−8.3123	39.6823
Dissatisfied	Satisfied	−27.52970*	9.99687	0.019	−51.3670	−3.6924
	Unsure	−15.68500	10.06398	0.269	−39.6823	8.3121

* The mean difference is significant at the 0.05 level.

Fig. 14.5. ANOVA Post-hoc test results.

(η^2) as a measure of effect size in ANOVA (Bachman and Paternoster, 2009; Thorndike and Dinnel, 2001). This is computed using the formula:

$$\eta^2 = \frac{SSB}{SST},$$

where

SSB = the between-groups sum of squares
SST = the total sum of squares

We can calculate η^2 for the Tropical Hotel guest satisfaction example. Going back to the SPSS output in Fig. 14.4, we can get SSB and SST and plug them into the above equation:

$$\eta^2 = \frac{10780.259}{134452.889} = 0.080$$

Eta squared is a proportion; specifically, it is the proportion of the total variation in the sample that is attributable to between-group differences. The closer it is to 1.0, the greater the association between the independent and dependent variables. Conversely, the closer it is to 0, the weaker the association is. Here, $\eta^2 = 0.080$, so this means that 0.080 or about 8% of the variation is between the groups. This is not very much and means that satisfaction fails to explain 92% of the variation in money spent. This is a good example of a case where the statistical result indicate that there is a relationship between the independent and dependent variables, but that relationship is not meaningful on a substantive level. Improving overall satisfaction with the hotel would

be an ineffective way to boost the amount of money guests spend at the hotel during their stay. It is important to consider not just statistical significance but, also, the strength of a relationship.

Cross Tabulations and the Chi-Square Test of Independence

Until now, we have been working with data wherein the independent variable is categorical and the dependent variable is continuous. Sometimes, researchers want to test for associations between two categorical variables. This is done using the **chi-square (χ^2) test of independence**. (Chi-square is also sometimes referred to as a cross tabulation. The term 'chi-square' will be used here, but understand both terms refer to the same statistical technique.) If the two variables under examination are independent of one another, then there is no relationship and the IV has no predictive power. If, however, the variables are dependent upon one another, then knowing what category a person falls into on the first variable helps predict which category that person will be in on the second variable.

For the χ^2 example, let's revisit the Tropical Hotel data and select two survey items that may offer you, the hotel manager, important information about your guests. The survey asked respondents about the nature of their visit to the hotel (business, pleasure or both) and it asked them what they look for in a hotel (rate, pool/sauna or room service). Note that the IV here (reason for visit) is categorical, as is the DV (most important hotel characteristic), so a chi-square test is the appropriate statistical analysis to use.

The null hypothesis in a chi-square analysis is that there is no relationship between the independent and dependent variables; that is, that they are independent of one another. The alternative hypothesis posits that the variables are related to one another. Chi-square analyses utilize the χ^2-distribution. This sampling distribution, similar to the F-distribution, is positively skewed and bounded at zero. The null and alternative hypotheses for the chi-square test are always:

$$H_0: \chi^2 = 0$$
$$H_1: \chi^2 > 0$$

The null hypothesis represents the prediction that there is no relationship between the two variables. If there is no relationship, then the obtained value of χ^2 will not be statistically significant from zero. The alternative hypothesis is the supposition that there is a relationship between the two variables. If χ^2_{obt} is larger than χ^2_{crit} then the null is rejected and we conclude that the two variables are related.

The χ^2 statistic is based on a comparison between **expected cell frequencies** and **observed cell frequencies**. The expected cell frequencies are those that we would expect to see if there is no relationship between the independent and dependent variables; that is, what is expected under the null hypothesis of independence. Think of this as a sort of random distribution, with no clear pattern or tendency. The observed cell frequencies are what we actually see in the data; they are the empirical pattern of results. If the observed cell frequencies are not significantly different from the expected cell frequencies, the value of χ^2 will be small and the null hypothesis cannot be rejected. If the observed frequencies differ significantly from the expected frequencies, the χ^2 value will be large and the null will be rejected.

To run a chi-square analysis in SPSS, use the 'Analyse' menu. Go to 'Descriptive Statistics' and then click on 'Crosstabs'. Click on the 'Statistics' option to pull up a new dialogue box. This is where you will direct SPSS to run the chi-square test (if you do not request a chi-square test, SPSS will just give you a crosstabs table without the accompanying inferential test). Put a check in the box, then click on 'Continue' and 'OK'. Figure 14.6 shows the output screen that will be produced.

You can see that $\chi^2_{obt} = 11.636$, which you can tell by the significance value of 0.020 is statistically different (i.e. it is less than 0.05). This shows that there is a statistically significant difference between the reason for guests' visit to the area and the things they prioritize when they select a hotel.

The chi-square test carries two important assumptions. The first is that the samples were selected independently. Like the ANOVA and independent-samples t-tests, the chi-square cannot be used with non-independent sampling methods. The second important caveat to the chi-square test pertains to expected cell counts. The formula for the χ^2 test statistic uses the expected cell counts in the denominator of the equation. Small denominators make it more likely that χ^2 will be large and, therefore, statistically significant, but such a result is spurious and due only to the small expected frequency count. Even one cell with an expected frequency of less than five can cause you to find an erroneous χ^2 value. If you see that you have an expected frequency of less than five, you should collapse some of your independent or dependent variable categories (if it makes conceptual sense to do so) or gather a larger sample.

As with F, χ^2 speaks only to the issue of statistical significance and is silent about the actual magnitude of the relationship. When χ^2 is

Chi-Square Tests

	Value	df	Asymp. sig. (2-sided)
Pearson Chi-Square	11.636[a]	4	0.020
Likelihood Ratio	12.017	4	0.017
Linear-by-Linear Association	2.719	1	0.099
N of Valid Cases	90		

[a]0 cells (0%) have expected count less than 5. The minimum expected count is 8.09.

Fig. 14.6. Chi-square test output.

statistically significant, it is imperative to analyse the strength of association between the
independent and dependent variables before you
put any stock in the outcome of the chi-square
test. There are many different measures of association for the chi-square analysis and they are
each appropriate with specific types of variables
and certain table sizes. When both variables are
measured at the nominal level and the table is
2 × 2 (that is, each variable has two classes), the
phi coefficient (ϕ) can be used. The formula for
this is:

$$\phi = \sqrt{\frac{\chi^2}{N}}$$

Here, though, we cannot use phi because the table
is 3 × 3. For tables larger than 2 × 2, **Cramer's V(V)**
is available. The equation for V (see Bachman and
Paternoster, 2009) is:

$$V = \sqrt{\frac{\chi^2}{N(k-1)}},$$

where

k = the number of rows or the number of columns,
whichever is smaller.

Plugging the SPSS-generated numbers into the
equation for V yields:

$$V = \sqrt{\frac{11.636}{90(3-1)}} = \sqrt{0.065} = 0.255$$

Cramer's V ranges from 0 to 1.0, with values closer
to 0 indicating weaker relationships and values closer
to 1.0 indicating stronger relationships. Here, V =
0.254, so it appears that the relationship between
visit type and hotel priorities is moderate; not very
strong, but not meaningless either. As a manager,
visit type is probably something you want to keep in
mind as you develop marketing strategies, but you
do not want to place undue emphasis on visit type.

Case Study 14.1.

Suppose you are the manager of the Tropical Hotel, which is part of a large chain. Knowing that you
have a lot of competition from other hotel chains, you set out to discover what amenities your guests
like and do not like so that you can tailor your hotel's services to meet the demands of the area's tourists
and other travellers. You design a survey and for one month, you ask all your guests to fill out the survey
as they check out of the hotel. Your survey contains seven questions and they are as follows:

1. *What is the most important thing you look for when you decide on a hotel?*
   Rate   Pool/sauna   Room service
2. *How likely are you to refer the Tropical Hotel to a friend?*
   Definitely will   Might   Definitely will not
3. *Prior to this stay, how many times had you stayed at this or any other Tropical Hotel?* _____
4. *What is the nature of your visit to the area?*
   Business   Pleasure   Both
5. *Overall, how satisfied are you with your stay at the Tropical Hotel?*
   Satisfied   Unsure   Dissatisfied
6. *What is your approximate annual household income, in US dollars? (please circle one)*
   $19,000 or less $20,000 - $39,999 $40,000 - $59,999 $60,000 or more
7. *How old are you?* _____
8. *What is your gender? Female   Male*
9. *About how much money did you spend in the Tropical Hotel during this stay, including room service,*
   in-hotel restaurant dining, laundry service, internet, etc.? _____

After one month, you have collected 90 completed surveys. Now what? How will you make sense of
the data? What you need are some techniques for statistical analysis. This chapter will present three
such techniques: Tests for comparing one or two means (*t*-tests), tests for comparing more than two
means (analysis of variance), and tests for comparing two or more categorical variables (chi-square).
These are all types of **bivariate** tests, or tests that seek to explore relationships between two variables.

Key Terms

Bivariate: An analysis involving two variables.

Level of measurement: The type of data that a variable captures. Can be qualitative/categorical or quantitative/continuous.

Hypothesis testing/inferential statistics: The process of analysing a statistic or association in a sample and using probability theory to make an inference about the population value or relationship.

Null hypothesis: Hypothesis predicting that there is no difference between two means (as in the case of *t*-tests and analysis of variance) or that two variables are statistically independent of one another (as in the case of chi-square). This is the hypothesis that is being tested in a given statistical analysis. If the obtained value of the test statistic is greater than the critical value, the null is rejected in favour of the alternative.

Alternative hypothesis: The opposite of the null. This hypothesis is taken to be correct if the null is rejected.

Statistically significant difference: A difference between two or more means that is large enough to allow the conclusion that the means are truly different from one another and that the difference between them is not simply the result of chance or sampling error.

One-tailed or directional hypotheses: Alternative hypotheses that make a prediction about whether one mean will be higher or lower than another mean. Contrast to two-tailed or non-directional hypotheses.

Two-tailed or non-directional hypotheses: Alternative hypotheses that posit only that there is a difference between two or more means and that do not specify whether one mean will be higher or lower than the other. Contrast to one-tailed or directional hypotheses.

t-Distribution: A family of curves that are flattened when the sample size is small and are almost identical to the standard normal curve when the sample size is high.

Normal curve: A curve that is unimodal and symmetrical; a bell-shaped curve. The *t*-distribution is normal when the sample size is large, while the F- and χ^2- distributions are not normal.

α-Level: The level of significance for a statistical test that is set prior to the conducting of the test. Specifies the probability level being used in the analysis and is used to locate the critical value of the test statistic.

p-Value: The obtained significance value that is produced by statistical software. When the p-value is less than the pre-set α-level, the null hypothesis is rejected; when it is greater than α, the null hypothesis is retained.

Degrees of freedom: needed in order to locate the critical value of the test statistic. Refers to the number of elements in a set of data that are free to vary in a given analysis.

Independent selection: Sample selection method whereby the selection of a case into one sample does not affect the selection of a different case into the other sample. Contrast to matched-pairs or dependent samples.

Pooled variances: Independent-samples *t*-test for use when the variances of the two samples are not statistically different from one another.

Separate variances: Independent-samples *t*-test for use when the variances of the two samples are statistically different from one another, as indicated by a significant value of Levene's F-statistic.

Matched cases: Samples wherein cases were chosen based on their similarity to one another on key characteristics. This is a way to try to reduce sampling error in situations where a pre–post treatment design is not possible.

Repeated measures: The repeated measuring of a single sample of cases. The first measurement is done prior to a planned intervention and the second measurement is taken after the intervention to determine if there is a difference in post-intervention measurements.

Type I error rate: The likelihood of finding a statistically significant result by chance or error and incorrectly rejecting the null hypothesis. Based on the α-level, e.g. an α-level of 0.05 carries a 5% Type I error rate. In 100 tests, 5 will be statistically significant just by chance or sampling error.

Family-wise error rate: The result of using repeated *t*-tests and, in so doing, inflating the Type I error rate with each *t*-test that is conducted. The family-wise error phenomenon is the reason why ANOVA must be used when the independent variable has three or more categories.

Within-group variability: The variability (or deviations) of individual scores around their respective group means. Each category of the IV has its own group mean. A measure of how similar the individual cases in a group are to the other cases in that same group.

Between-group variability: The variability of the different group means around the grand mean, or total mean for the entire sample regardless of IV class. A measure of how similar different groups are to each other.

Post-hoc tests: Tests conducted after a finding of a significant *F*-statistic in ANOVA to determine the location and number of between-group differences.

F-Distribution: The sampling distribution used in ANOVA. This set of curves is bounded at zero and positively skewed.

F-Statistic: The test statistic used in ANOVA.

Measure of association: A method of determining the strength of a statistically significant relationship. Relationships can be statistically significant but substantively meaningless, so measures of association provide a way to assess the magnitude of an association.

Eta squared: A measure of association for ANOVA.

Chi-square test of independence: The inferential hypothesis test for use when both the independent and dependent variables are categorical.

χ^2 *distribution*: The sampling distribution used for chi-square tests. This set of curves is bounded at zero and positively skewed.

Expected cell frequencies: The cell count that would be expected if the null hypothesis of independence were true; an equal distribution of cases across the cells.

Observed cell frequencies: The actual, empirical cell counts in a cross-tabulation table. The chi-square test compares the observed to the expected cell frequencies to determine if the differences are large enough to reject the null of independence and conclude that the two variables are dependent.

Cramer's V: A measure of association for the chi-square test when the cross-tabulation table is larger than 2 × 2.

Discussion Questions

1. For *t*-tests, ANOVA and chi-square tests, identify the level of measurement of the independent variable and that of the dependent variable.

2. Explain α-levels and *p*-values. How are they used to determine whether or not the results of a test are statistically significant?

3. Why does the ANOVA require the use of post-hoc tests?

4. Why do ANOVA and chi-square require the use of measure of association?

5. Explain the assumptions underlying ANOVA.

6. Discuss the two types of *t*-tests (independent samples and matched pairs/repeated measures) and the circumstances under which each is used.

References

Bachman, R. and Paternoster, R. (2009) *Statistical Methods for Criminology and Criminal Justice,* 3rd edn. McGraw-Hill, New York.

Field, A. (2000) *Discovering Statistics: Using SPSS for Windows.* Sage Publications, London, UK.

Fox, J.A., Levin, J. and Forde, D.R. (2009) *Elementary Statistics in Criminal Justice Research.* Allyn and Bacon, Boston, Massachusetts.

Fox, J.A., Levin, J. and Shively, M. (2005) *Elementary Statistics in Criminal Justice Research: The Essentials.* Allyn and Bacon, Boston, Massachusetts.

Thorndike, R.M. and Dinnel, D.L. (2001) *Behavioral Statistics for the Social Sciences.* Prentice Hall, Upper Saddle River, New Jersey.

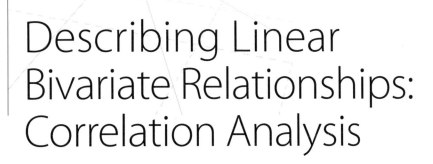

chapter 15

Describing Linear Bivariate Relationships: Correlation Analysis

Chenchen Huang and Lori Pennington-Gray

Learning Objectives

After studying this chapter, you should be able to:

1. Explain and give examples of different types of relationships between two interval and ratio variables;
2. Interpret a correlation table and correlation coefficients as well as scatterplots;
3. Conduct a simple bivariate regression;
4. Use simple bivariate regression as a tool to forecast tourist behaviours;
5. Briefly define and give examples of the basic concepts and techniques of multivariate regression.

Chapter Summary

This chapter addresses two frequently used statistical analyses: correlation analysis and simple linear regression. The chapter explains several types of relationships between two variables and two methods to explore these relationships. In addition, simple linear regression is introduced as a method to predict the value of a dependent variable by the value of an independent variable. Finally, since

tourism researchers and practitioners typically face more complex relationships than merely a bivariate relationship (two variables), multiple regression will also be explored.

What are Linear Bivariate Relationships?

Most studies in tourism involve relationships between variables. In fact, studying these relationships is usually the main purpose of funded research projects. As a start to examining relationships, we will look at the **bivariate** relationship or the relationship between two interval/ratio level variables. The concept of a correlation is to measure the linear relationship between two interval or ratio level variables. Among any two variables, there are three types of relationships: not correlated, positively correlated and negatively correlated. When examining the correlation between two variables, two pieces of the relationship are the strength of the relationship and the direction of the relationship.

There are different ways to describe bivariate relationships. The most common are: (i) the use of a pictorial representation; and (ii) the use of a mathematical representation. With regards

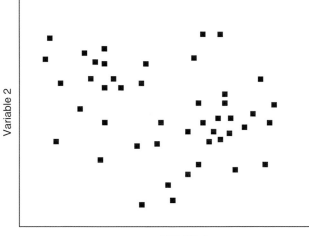

Fig. 15.1. A scatterplot of two variables that have no linear correlation.

to the pictorial representation, a **scatterplot** is a visual demonstration of the relationship between two variables (see Fig. 15.1). For a mathematical representation, **covariance** and **correlation** coefficients can be used to demonstrate the relationship between the variables.

The correlation analysis is based on studying numerical variables. Numerical variables, rather than categorical variables, are indicated by the mean or the expected value and the variance, usually in the form of standard deviation. The variance of a variable represents the average number of intervals each **data point** is away from the mean. If we want to investigate whether two variables are related, we are actually interested in whether changes in one variable are associated with changes in the other variable (Field, 2005). If we observe that when one variable deviates from its mean, the other variable moves away from its mean in the same direction or the opposite direction, we say these two variables covary. **Covariance** describes the combined difference of two variables. A positive covariance shows that two variables vary in the same direction; a negative covariance suggests that two variables vary in the opposite direction.

Although the calculation of covariance is usually performed by computer software such as SPSS, it is helpful to understand the mathematical process of the calculation, as indicated by the following formula. For two random variables X and Y, if the mean of X is indicated by X (hat) and the mean of Y is indicated by Y (hat), the covariance is defined as the average or expected value (E) of the product of each pair of the variance of X and the variance of Y:

$$\mathrm{CoVar}\,(X,\,Y) = E\,\{[X{-}X(\text{hat})]\,[(Y{-}Y(\text{hat})]\}$$

One major constraint with using the covariance is that both variables must be measured on the same scale. As a result, it is inconvenient or even impossible to compare variables if they are measured on different scales. To address this drawback, it is possible to standardize the unit of measurement and covert the covariance into correlation coefficients. There are different correlation coefficients that have been applied in testing bivariate correlation. For example, Pearson's correlation coefficient, Spearman's correlation coefficient and Kendall's correlation coefficient are all options that could be calculated. Here, we will look at Pearson's correlation coefficient, indicated by 'r'. Pearson's r is the standardized value of the covariance. Pearson's r varies between -1 and $+1$.

Because the calculation of covariance and correlation coefficients requires time and mathematical skills, it is common practice to use statistical software to carry out the necessary calculations.

Interpreting a scatterplot by using a regression line

A scatterplot is a graph used to describe the relationship between two variables. A typical scatterplot includes a horizontal axis, a vertical axis, and

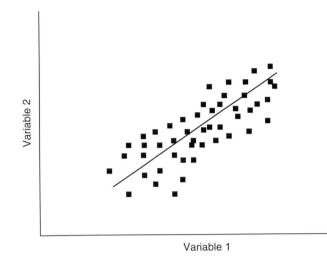

Fig. 15.2. A scatterplot of two variables that have a positive linear correlation.

a collection of dots indicating different observations. In the analysis of two variables, a regression line could also be included in the scatterplot to indicate the trend of the relationship between these two variables. Figures 15.1, 15.2 and 15.3 are a series of scatterplots describing the three types of relationships between two numerical variables.

How to interpret a correlation table

Next, we will look at how to interpret the results of a correlation analysis. Table 15.1 is a correlation table of two variables: number of nights and total expenditure. We can find all the important information, such as the Pearson correlation coefficient, the significance level, the covariance and the sample size in the table. The Pearson correlation (r) along the diagonal of the table is 1 since a variable is perfectly correlated with itself. The covariance between the two variables is 12916.71. Unfortunately, it is difficult to interpret this covariance. However, the Pearson correlation coefficient between these two variables $r = 0.455$, and its significance level is p-value <0.01.

How to interpret correlation coefficients

The Pearson correlation coefficient in the correlation table is 0.455 at the significance level of 0.01.

The significance level tells us that the probability that the correlation is false is very low. Since most of the time social scientists accept the significance level at 0.05, we are confident to say that total nights in the destination and total expenditures are significantly positively related. Because the Pearson correlation coefficient r is a standardized form of covariance, it should be interpreted as the increase of one unit of standard deviation in nights will cause 0.455 unit of standard deviation increase in total expenditure. In other words, the more nights a tourist stayed in a destination, the more money he or she will spend in the destination.

Use of linear bivariate regression as a means of forecasting

Forecasting refers to the methods and practice of predicting what will happen in the future by analysing the data that has currently occurred. Forecasting plays an important role in tourism planning and management because many decisions about tourism supply are based on scientific predictions of the future demand. For example, the decision to build a new hotel in a destination is essentially based on projecting the number of additional incoming travellers in the following years. While there are various and sometimes complicated methods of forecasting, the following part of the chapter will demonstrate one method of forecasting using simple bivariate linear regression.

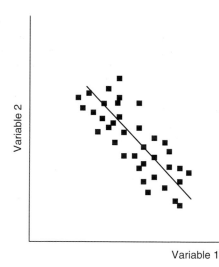

Fig. 15.3. A scatterplot of two variables that have a negative linear correlation.

Table 15.1. The correlation table.

		Nights	**Total expenditure**
Nights	Pearson correlation	1	0.455(*)
	Sig. (2-tailed)		0.00
	Sum of squares and cross-products	286978.69	3125843.97
	Covariance	1087.04	12916.71
	N	265	243
Total expenditure	Pearson correlation	0.455(*)	1
	Sig. (2-tailed)	0.000	.
	Sum of squares and cross-products	3125843.969	234791102.14
	Covariance	12916.71	624444.42
	N	243	377

*Correlation is significant at the 0.01 level (2-tailed).

There are four basic components of a simple bivariate linear regression analysis:

1. The time sequence.
2. The independent variable.
3. The dependent variable.
4. The linear relationship between the independent variable and the dependent variable (Agresti and Finlay, 1997).

Forecasting has an obvious time component because it employs what has happened in the past to predict what will happen in the future. For example, a tourism marketing manager of a city may want to predict how many tourists will visit the city this year. In this case, the number of tourists is the dependent variable, which is often designated as 'y' in regression analysis. The independent variable could be any factor that is independent from the dependent variable but also closely related to it. For example, if the city is located close to a major snow ski attraction, an independent variable the manager could use is inches of snowfall. The independent variable is usually designated as 'x'. In a simple **bivariate** regression, it is assumed that y is caused by x and the relationship between x and y is a linear relationship.

What is the Relationship Between Correlations and Bivariate Regression Analysis?

Simple linear regression is based on the correlation between the independent variable and the dependent variable. However, strong correlation is only a necessary condition for a successful prediction because a strong correlation is just part of a causal relationship. As we have learned in the preceding part of the chapter on correlations, there are some basic rules or assumptions about causal relationships. First, x happens before y. Second, there is a correlation between x and y. Third, x and y are not caused by a third common variable (Agresti and Finlay, 1997). In our ski resort city example, it is reasonable to believe that skiers come to the city after snow falls and snow attracts skiers to come to the city, which account for the time sequence and the correlation between these two variables. However, because we only look at two variables, numbers of tourists and inches of snow, we cannot exclusively say that visitation is not influenced by a third factor. In practical sense, we are 'ignoring' other variables. We will revisit this issue in the section on multiple regression.

In order to understand how efficiently an independent variable predicts a dependent variable, we need to look at the statistical basis for a simple bivariate regression. The relationship between the dependent variable Y and the independent variable X could be expressed by the formula:

$$Y = \alpha + \beta X$$

Prediction equation $Y(\text{hat}) = a + bX + e$

There are two parameters in this formula, α and β. The parameter β is called the slope of the regression line and is also the main interest of regression analysis. The parameter α is called the intercept and is not significant for our purpose.

The slope b describes the relationship between X and Y. The slope is interpreted as one unit change in X which will cause b unit change of Y.

Recall that the correlation between two variables is measured by the Pearson correlation coefficient r. Mathematically the Pearson correlation coefficient is the standardized slope. Since variables have different units of measure, for example, inches of snow and numbers of tourists, a change in the unit of measure of either x or y will change the value of the slope. For the purpose of investigating the relationship between two variables, it is convenient to have a standardized form of variables so that the results are comparable. A common practice is to use the standard deviation of a variable as a unit of measure to rescale a variable and get a standardized form of the variable.

Before we start to learn how to test the regression model and calculate the regression coefficients, it is helpful to understand the mathematical assumptions of simple linear regression. A thorough discussion of the assumptions of simple linear regression and ways to fix violations is beyond the scope of this chapter; please refer to other sources for further explanations.

If we know that our data meet the assumptions of simple linear regression, we need to decide a method to identify the model that fits the data best. Using the regression line method from the previous example (Fig. 15.2), the best fitting line is one which minimizes the difference (the residual) between the predicted Y variable (Y hat) and the actual variable (Y). This is called the method of least squares. This method provides the best model based on a calculation and identification of a regression line that generates the minimum sum of squared residuals.

After we decide the method of least squares as our estimation method, we will study how to decide the goodness-of-fit of the model and to assess the estimated slope b by a hypothesis test. Although we can find the fittest straight line by the method of least squares, we still need to know how well the line fits the data. We introduce the concept of r square, which represents how much variation in Y could be explained by the model. Obviously the value of r square varies between 0 and 1. The bigger the r square is, the better the model fits the data.

Simple linear regression

Based on the Indian River County survey data, a simple linear bivariate regression analysis generates the results shown in Tables 15.2, 15.3 and 15.4.

Table 15.2. Goodness-of-fit summary.

Model summary				
Model	*r*	*r* square	Adjusted *r* square	Std error of the estimate
1	0.455[a]	0.207	0.203	811.372

[a]Predictors: (Constant), people, nights.

Table 15.3. Test of the overall model.

ANOVA[a,b]						
Model		Sum of squares	df	Mean square	F	Sig.
1	Regression	41317677.104	1	41317677.104	62.762	0.000
	Residual	158656515.915	241	658325.792		
	Total	199974193.019	242			

[a]Predictors: (Constant), nights.
[b]Dependent variable: total expenditure.

Table 15.4. Test of the coefficients.

Coefficients[a]						
		Unstandardized coefficients		Standardized coefficients		
Model		*b*	Std error	β	*t*	Sig.
1	(Constant)	534.081	58.755		9.090	0.000
	nights	13.218	1.668	0.455	7.922	0.000

[a]Dependent variable: total expenditure.

In Table 15.2, we can see that the Pearson *r* value 0.455 in the model summary is the same as the value in the correlation analysis in Table 15.1. The square of the Pearson *r*, *r* square, is 0.207, which suggests that 20.7% of the variance in total expenditure is explained by nights. The adjusted *r* square is preferred by many researchers because it adjusts the influence of sample size on *r* square and is more accurate. In this case the adjusted *r* square is slightly smaller than the *r* square. Table 15.3 summarizes the result of the ANOVA test; *p*-value <0.01 indicates that the bivariate regression model fits the data well.

Table 15.4 summarizes the estimates of coefficients and the result of the hypothesis test.

Again we are not interested in the intercept (called 'Constant' in SPSS). The second row indicates that *b* = 13.218. Please notice that the standardized *b* (β) equates to the correlation coefficient (0.455). The *p*-value is less than 0.01. In other words, we are 99% confident that the increase of one standardized unit of total number of nights will increase the total expenditure by 0.455 standardized unit.

Multiple Regression

In the preceding part of the chapter you learned how to do and interpret a simple linear bivariate regression. The reality, however, is that most relationships are more complicated than merely the relationship between two variables. As we have mentioned, the practice of only investigating two variables suggests we have ignored other variables. The benefits of doing so include a simpler statistical approach as well as a simpler mathematical calculation. However, the cost of doing so may be that there is a weak explanatory power associated with only one independent variable, which is evidenced by a small r square.

When we investigated the relationship between total nights in the destination and total expenditure of a tourist group, we ignored other variables which might also play a role in explaining total expenditures. For example, other variables which might affect total expenditures may be number of people in the travel party. Thus, both total nights and number of people in the group could be included in a multivariate regression analysis as two independent variables.

We extend our example to the model with the group expenditure as the dependent variable and nights and the number of people in the group as two independent variables. Tables 15.5, 15.6 and 15.7 are the results of the analysis.

The r square in Table 15.5 is 0.214, which is slightly bigger than the r square in Table 15.2. By adding one more independent variable, the model has improved. About 21.4% of the variance in total expenditure is explained by nights and the number of people. The analysis of variance (ANOVA) Table (Table 15.6) summarizes the result of an F-test of all the independent variables simultaneously. The p-value of the F-test is less than 0.01 and suggests that the model is a significantly good fit of the data.

The coefficients table tells us the estimates of the number of nights and number of people and the results of the two t-tests. The estimates are called partial regression coefficients because they are the result of controlling the other independent variable or keeping the other independent variable constant. For example, the standardized coefficient of nights is 0.451, which means that the increase of nights by one standardized unit will result in 0.451 standardized unit of increase in total expenditure, when keeping the number of people constant. The p-value of nights is less than 0.01 and the variable 'nights' is a significant predictor of total expenditure, while the p-value of people is $0.126 > 0.05$. And the variable 'people' is not significant.

This example is just a simple practical case of a multiple regression. There are some issues you need to keep in mind when you conduct your own multiple regression analysis. First, the independent variables could be either numerical or categorical

Table 15.5. Goodness-of-fit summary.

Model summary				
Model	r	r square	Adjusted r square	Std error of the estimate
1	0.463[a]	0.214	0.208	809.12

[a]Predictors: (Constant), people, nights.

Table 15.6. Test of the overall model.

ANOVA[b]						
Model		Sum of squares	df	Mean square	F	Sig.
1	Regression	42857939.66	2	21428969.83	32.733	0.000[a]
	Residual	157116253.35	240	654651.06		
	Total	199974193.02	242			

[a]Predictors: (Constant), people, nights
[b]Dependent variable: total expenditure

Table 15.7. Test of the coefficients.

Model		Unstandardized coefficients		Standardized coefficients		
		b	Std error	β	*t*	Sig.
1	(Constant)	662.985	102.446		6.472	0.000
	Nights	13.114	1.665	0.451	7.875	0.000
	People	−52.836	34.446	−0.088	−1.534	0.126

[a]Dependent variable: total expenditure.

variables. Dummy variables are used in case of categorical independent variables. Second, there are assumptions about linear multiple regression and those assumptions need to be met to make sure your model is meaningful. Third, the interaction between independent variables could be a major concern. **Multicollinearity** happens when the independent variables overlap and correlate with each other. The methods of testing the interaction between independent variables could be complicated and are not covered in this chapter. You are encouraged to refer to more advanced books for this issue.

Case Study 15.1.

The tourism industry can result in tremendous economic benefits to host communities. Spending patterns within the community by tourists is a good measure of the breadth and depth of economic benefits. In this chapter we examine tourist characteristics and behaviours and how they correlate as well as predict certain behaviours.

Tourism spending is one example of a variable which may correlate with several tourist behaviours. Research suggests these behaviours may include: length of stay, party size, purpose of trip, some demographics (age, income) and activities participated in while on the trip. These correlations are particularly important for Destination Management Organizations (DMOs) to understand to aid in management and marketing functions.

In 2001, officials from Indian River County, a mid-central county of Florida, hired the Center for Tourism Research and Development at the University of Florida to help them better understand visitors to their county. This county is best known for a variety of tourism attractions, such as beaches, rivers, golf courses, museums, theatres, etc. The officials were most interested in having numbers available to justify marketing dollars spent on different market segments. A survey was therefore conducted to collect this data to answer the following research questions (Pennington-Gray and Holland, 2001):

- Who are the tourists visiting Indian River County?
- What is their demographic profile (age, gender, household income, education attainment, employment status)?
- What is the percentage of the tourists who stay overnight in the county? What is the percentage of day-visitors among the tourists?
- What are the most popular types of accommodation chosen by the tourists? What is the percentage of the visitors who are repeat tourists?

(Continued)

Case Study 15.1. Continued.

- What is the primary motive of the tourists?
- What types of information sources do tourists use when they are planning for their trip? When do tourists make decisions about participating in activities in the county?
- What are the most favourite and least favourite aspects of the county among the tourists?
- How much money do tourists spend on food and beverage, transportation, accommodation, shopping, and tickets and admission to events and activities?

As part of the study, statistical analyses were conducted to investigate the relationship between several variables. In particular, total number of nights tourists spent in the county and their total expenditures were examined. The result of the analysis suggested that these two variables were significantly positively correlated. In other words, the more nights a tourist stayed, the more money he or she spent in the county. As a result, officials recognized the need to find ways to increase length of stay in order to generate greater benefits from tourism. The purpose of this relationship was to demonstrate a correlation analysis as statistical technique employed to show the relationship between two interval level variables.

Key Terms

Bivariate regression: A regression that aims at investigating the relationship between two variables only (Vogt, 2005).

β coefficient (also called beta weight): A regression coefficient expressed in standard deviation units. The β coefficient describes the change (measured by standard deviation) in a dependent variable when an independent variable increases or decreases by one standard deviation (Vogt, 2005).

Multicollinearity: A phenomenon that occurs in multiple regression analysis if two or more of the independent variables are related to each other. Multicollinearity has adverse impacts on the development of a multiple regress model and the inferences drawn from the model (Salkind, 2007).

Partial regression coefficient: In multiple regression, partial regression coefficient describes the portion of variance explained by a specific independent variable (Salkind, 2007).

Discussion Questions

1. Under what circumstances would you use a linear bivariate correlation?

2. Can you show how a scatterplot can graphically depict a bivariate relationship?

3. What is the relationship between a correlation analysis and a linear bivariate regression? What parts are similar and what are different?

4. As a manager of a destination management organization, when and how would you want to conduct a regression analysis?

5. Can you think of when use of multiple regression analysis could help with planning in our field?

References

Agresti, A. and Finlay, B. (1997) *Statistical Methods for the Social Sciences,* 3rd edn. Prentice-Hall, Upper Saddle River, New Jersey.

Field, A. (2005) *Discovering Statistics using SPSS*. Sage, Thousand Oaks, California.

Pennington-Gray, L. and Holland, S. (2001) *Visitors to Indian River County-Final Report*. Prepared for Indian River County Chamber of Commerce, 68 pp.

Salkind, N.J. (2007) *Encyclopedia of Measurement and Statistics*. Sage, Thousand Oaks, California.

Vogt, W.P. (2005) *Dictionary of Statistics & Methodology: A Nontechnical Guide for the Social Sciences*. Sage, Thousand Oaks, California.

chapter 16

Communicating Research Results

Patrick Tierney

Learning Objectives

After reading and studying this chapter you will be able to:

1. Define the fundamental types of research reports;
2. Understand common elements of a research report;
3. Identify what is contained in the front matter, body and back matter of a research report;
4. Design and create a professional presentation;
5. Understand the need for and where to find report style and form guidelines and legal considerations.

Chapter Summary

This chapter focuses on communicating and reporting research results and discusses four types of research reports: class assignments, a thesis or dissertation, a research journal article and a technical report. Most comprehensive research reports, such as a thesis, contain all of the following sections: title page, abstract, introduction, literature review, methods, results, discussion, references and appendices. The research report is divided into three sections, 'front matter' containing legal notices, title, an executive summary and listings of contents; the

'body', which is the heart of your report containing your introduction, literature review, methods, results and discussion sections; and 'back matter' consisting of references and appendices. There are two broad types of research presentations covered in this chapter: a thesis or dissertation defence; and a research conference presentation. We present typical steps in the thesis or dissertation defence process and stages in getting accepted and presenting at a research conference. The chapter ends with a discussion of ethical and legal considerations for publishing, presenting and protecting your work.

Communicating Your Research Results

After all the hard work you have put into designing your leisure, recreation or tourism research, collecting and analysing the data and testing your hypotheses, it is time to start communicating your results. This is a critically important final step in the research process. Without proper communications you findings will not be known by others who could benefit from it, you'll not advance knowledge in the leisure, recreation and tourism field and you may not satisfy your research sponsors, course instructors or your academic review committee. In other words, you may not be paid, get a passing grade in class or graduate with a degree.

At this stage in the research process you must pull together all the various parts of the investigation. Many new researchers find at this time that the various elements of the research are scattered in several locations, lack organization, research procedures may have been modified somewhat from the original proposal and results are different from initially hypothesized. Much of the 'fun' parts of the process, such as design and the discovery of new findings, are over and you are left with what some view as the less glamorous need to write and present your findings. You may also lack experience in technical writing, which slows progress. Adding pressure to your situation is that you may be behind on the schedule and running up against contract or graduation deadlines because of unrealistic completion time estimates at first and/or the more typical situation where there were delays getting the research started and completed. Some students completing a thesis find it takes almost as much time to write and obtain approval of the document as it does to design and conduct the research. Taking all these elements together can result in this part of the process being very emotional and stressful, or it can be a smooth completion of the process, resulting in justifiable recognition for your efforts.

There are several documents that will be vital at this communications stage because they describe, in at least in a general way, what you need to communicate. The initial instructor or sponsor guidelines will be the basis for what you will need to communicate. If these guidelines or rubrics are not in writing, then you'll need to verify again their expectations. If you are writing for scholarly purposes, such as a thesis or professional paper, then you probably made an oral or written proposal that was approved by your instructor or research review committee. In this proposal you 'promised', through your research goals, objectives and hypotheses, what you will discuss in the final report or presentation. Use these initial documents to guide your communications of research results.

The Fundamentals of Research Reports

Types of research reports

What is communicated will often vary with the type of research report you are preparing. The following section describes several types of reports, including:

- Class assignment: a brief report on a short term and limited research effort done as part of a class assignment. In this type of report your teacher's instructions are the critical elements to follow. These instructions vary widely but the tendency is for teachers to require students to follow the style and format report requirements of the latest edition of *Publication Manual of the American Psychological Association* (American Psychological Association (APA), 2001) that are described later in this chapter.

- Thesis, professional paper or dissertation: a highly detailed formal research report on original research that is used to satisfy the culminating experience requirements of graduate programmes. A professional paper, required with a master's level professional project, is written in a similar manner to a thesis. The author of a thesis, professional paper or dissertation is required to strictly follow APA guidelines and the submission requirements of their school.

- Research journal article: a concise description of the entire research process that is presented in print or electronic form in a scholarly journal. These are often peer-reviewed and very competitive for acceptance. Your writing, along with the procedures and significance of your research, greatly influences whether your manuscript will be accepted for publication. All journals provide instructions for submittal and frequently now require the use of APA style and format guidelines.

- Technical report: this is a detailed written presentation of the methods and findings for contracted research. The emphasis is more frequently on methods and results. There are a wide range of report styles and formats used. Government agency sponsors now often require adherence to APA guidelines, while there is no one style of reports for private companies.

Common elements of a research report

The previously described types of research reports may include all of the following common report elements, or only a few of them. You will need to clarify what is required with your course instructor, research review committee, research sponsor or publication before commencing the report writing. Most comprehensive research reports for recreation and tourism studies, such as a thesis, contain the following sections:

- Title page
- Abstract
- Introduction
- Literature review
- Methods
- Results
- Discussion
- References
- Appendices

Again, not all research reports contain each of the above sections, but the most comprehensive do. The next part of this chapter divides the research report into three sections, front matter, the body and back matter, and describes typical contents and considerations for each of these sections.

Front Matter

The front matter of a comprehensive research report, such as a thesis, normally contains the following sections:

- The title page
- Notice of copyright (optional)
- Committee recommendation and signatures (if required)
- Abstract
- Dedication (optional)
- Acknowledgements (optional)
- Table of contents
- Lists of tables and figures

Every research report must have a **title page**. Specific style and format requirements must be rigorously followed for a thesis and some technical reports. The title, typed in all uppercase letters, normally must fall between 2 and 2.5 inches from the top edge of the page. It must be centred. The title page of a thesis normally contains: (i) The centred title of your report or thesis; (ii) your name (optional: previous degrees earned); (iii) the degree to be earned (thesis, dissertation, etc.); (iv) fulfils partial requirements statement; (v) school or affiliation; and (vi) and

the report date. In the following pages, we present the thesis formatting requirements for San Francisco State University Graduate Studies (2008), which are typical of many university thesis requirements. Figure 16.1 illustrates the formatting of the title page, while Appendix 16.1 in Worked Example 16 shows an example title page from an actual thesis.

The **notice of copyright** is an optional legal statement that protects 'original works of the author'. The topic of copyrights and why they are used is discussed later in this chapter. An example copyright for a thesis is provided in Appendix 16.2.

The **committee recommendation page**, for a thesis or dissertation, contains a statement that the research committee recommends it be accepted to fulfil partial requirements, the date and it has the signatures of all committee members. Other report types do not have this page. A sample recommendation page is provided in Appendix 16.3.

An **abstract** is a very concise synopsis of the research background, purpose, methods, results and conclusions. It is normally limited to less than 350 words (1 page). This is a very important part of the report because it is the most frequently read section. The formatting of an abstract page is shown in Fig. 16.2. Appendix 16.4 illustrates an actual abstract.

A **table of contents** is a required element of all reports, with the possible exception of a brief class assignment report. It shows the report section names and associated starting page number. See Fig. 16.3 for the formatting of a table of contents. It is normally followed by a **list of tables** and **list of figures**. See Appendix 16 for samples of these pages.

The Body

The body of the research report typically contains the main text of your report. The normal contents of a comprehensive research report, such as a thesis, are the following:

- Introduction
- Literature review
- Methods
- Results
- Discussion

These sections happen to correspond with the typical chapters for a theses or dissertation. So Chapter 1 is the Introduction, Chapter 2 is the Literature

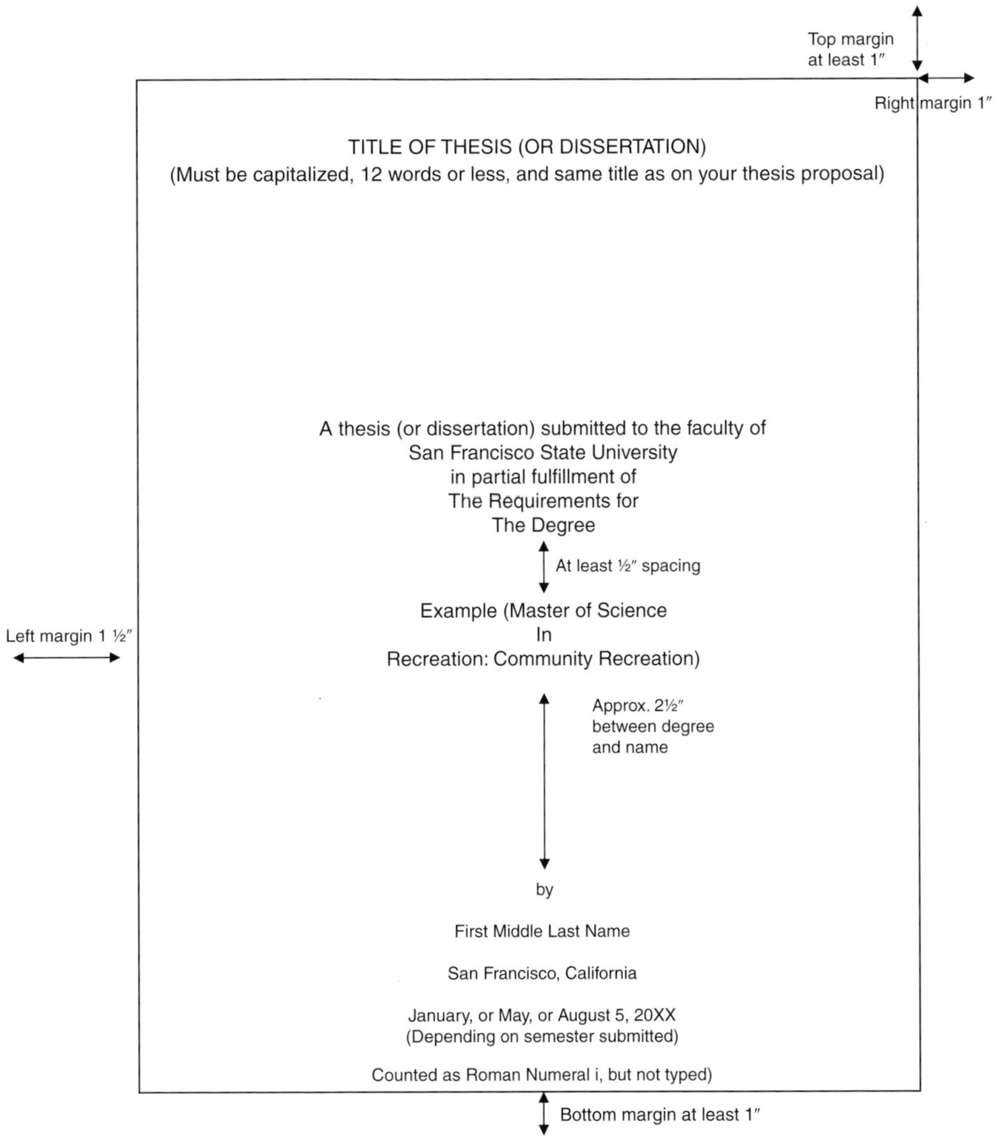

Top margin
at least 1″

Right margin 1″

TITLE OF THESIS (OR DISSERTATION)
(Must be capitalized, 12 words or less, and same title as on your thesis proposal)

A thesis (or dissertation) submitted to the faculty of
San Francisco State University
in partial fulfillment of
The Requirements for
The Degree

At least ½″ spacing

Example (Master of Science
In
Recreation: Community Recreation)

Approx. 2½″
between degree
and name

Left margin 1 ½″

by

First Middle Last Name

San Francisco, California

January, or May, or August 5, 20XX
(Depending on semester submitted)

Counted as Roman Numeral i, but not typed)

Bottom margin at least 1″

Fig. 16.1. Example title page (approximate scale).

review, Chapter 3 the Methods, Chapter 4 the Results and Chapter 5 is the Discussion.

Introduction

The introduction orients the reader to the background of the research topic, the importance and need for the research; a research problem statement (for quantitative research) or guiding questions (for qualitative research), research purpose and objectives and limitations of the study. Hypotheses may also be described after the study purpose and objectives. Each of these elements of the research process has been described in previous chapters. Now you must clearly elaborate what these are to your reader or listeners. This section is extremely critical to introduce the reader to your research, its importance and describe what you hope to accomplish through your efforts.

Top margin
at least 1″

Right margin 1″

TITLE OF THESIS (or Dissertation)
(Must be capitalized, 12 words or less, and same title as on thesis proposal)

At least ½″ spacing

First Middle Last Name
San Francisco, California
20XX

At least ½″ spacing

First line of abstract starts here. Abstract must be double-spaced or 1.5 spaced. Justify text.

Left margin 1 ½″

Last line of abstract finishes here. Abstract must be double-spaced or 1.5 spaced. Justify text.

At least ½″ spacing

I certify that the Abstract is a correct representation of the content of this thesis (or dissertation).

At least ½″ spacing

Chair, Thesis (or dissertation) Committee   Date

(Counted as Roman Numeral iii [or iv], but not typed)

Bottom margin at least 1″

Fig. 16.2. Example abstract page (approximate scale).

Literature review

An excellent literature review will identify prior studies relevant to the research topic and describe why they are important to consider in the current research. There should be a discussion identifying the chronological progression of thought and findings on the topic and providing the theoretical background for it. Theoretical background refers to past and current theories and models. It can also contain information on methods used to address the research topics. How the proposed research will integrate

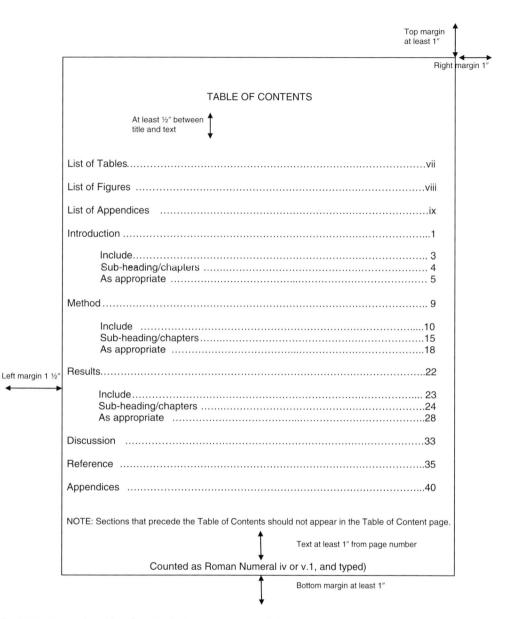

TABLE OF CONTENTS

At least ½" between
title and text

Top margin
at least 1"

Right margin 1"

Left margin 1 ½"

NOTE: Sections that precede the Table of Contents should not appear in the Table of Content page.

Text at least 1" from page number

Counted as Roman Numeral iv or v.1, and typed)

Bottom margin at least 1"

Fig. 16.3. Example table of contents (approximate scale).

into current thinking and theoretical models should be a result of reading this section. This element must support the research need and purpose. It can culminate in a proposed theoretical model or new research approach to be tested in the study. Some authors like to display their hypotheses at the end of this section instead of in the Introduction.

Methods

The methods section describes the data collection actions, any proposed models and the data analysis techniques that were employed. If you do not provide a clear discussion of methods then the reader may question whether your data and results are valid.

It should describe and build upon past research. Specific elements of the methods section normally include: the overall research plan, sampling utilized, design and justification for the data collection instruments, often a proposed theoretical model, the specific methods used for data analysis and how a model was tested. The methods should clearly emanate from the literature cited and be able to provide data to satisfy research purpose and objectives. The methods described should closely follow those in the initial proposal or there must be an explanation of how and why they were changed.

Results

The heart of your research report is the presentation of study findings. This section must relate directly to the study purpose and objectives and emanate from the methods employed. It should contain explanatory tables and charts to help the reader better comprehend your findings. Tables and charts must be designed and titled so that they can 'stand alone' and be understood without the reader needing to refer to the text. Any horizontally oriented graphics must be bound so that the top title part of the page is closest to the binding. You generally just report the results in this section but do not discuss the implications of them, as this is done in the next discussion section. Participant responses to the guiding questions of a qualitative study are addressed here. The results of testing hypotheses are presented. A results summary, which includes a discussion of the most significant and relevant findings related to your research purpose and objectives is provided at the end. Therefore, a typical results section includes the following components: presentation of quantitative and qualitative findings; testing of any proposed models; results of hypothesis testing; and a summary of key findings.

Discussion

In the discussion part of your report you interpret the results presented earlier and describe the implications of your research. The author does not repeat previously presented results; rather you should discuss what these mean and how they change the state of knowledge about the research problem. You may also compare your study results with those of other researchers and describe how and why they differ, or if they align with previous work. You will also interpret any hypothesis testing and the implications for proposed theories and/or models. The discussion section normally includes: conclusions drawn from data collected and a comparison with previous works by other researchers; the implications of testing of a proposed model and if adjustments to the model are needed; recommendations on how you could have improved the current methods to achieve more accurate or useful information; and recommendations for future research on this topic.

Back Matter

The back matter of a research report includes the list of references, or bibliography and any appendices. These help the reader know details about your sources and satisfy legal citation requirements.

References

All research reports must include a list of references in the appropriate form. The reference list for a research report is normally found in the back matter, near the end of the report, but some academic books place them at the end of each chapter. If only the studies referred to in the body of the report are included in the list, then the title of this section should be 'Works Cited', 'Literature Cited' or 'References'. If the list is comprehensive and also includes sources consulted for research and preparation, then it should be titled 'Bibliography'. Normally the reference list is single-spaced within the listing and double-space between the listings. See Appendix 16.8 for an actual reference list page from a thesis by Howe (2007). It illustrates the formatting of the reference list.

Appendix

An appendix contains very detailed and supportive information that would be too lengthy in the report body. Examples of what might be found in an appendix include a lengthy survey instrument;

maps or very detailed data analysis results that are useful but not critical to the research objectives. It is optional for the author of a research report to have appendices. If there is more than one appendix, then they are given a letter name, such as Appendix A.

Writing Style and Form

Research reports are technical writing that almost always must follow strict writing style and form requirements. Consistent style and form, such as font type and size, margins and reference format, makes it easier for readers to follow and quickly find what they desire. Publications require specific style and format to ensure quality and to present a consistent image that distinguishes them from other journals. However, different styles and formats can make it more difficult for authors to know exactly what is required. The author will need to be sure about the exact style and form specifications of your sponsor and oversight entity since there is no one universal style and form for all research reports. But more research reports are now being required to follow consistent style and form guidelines. There are several frequently used style and form manuals, including:

- Campbell, Ballou, and Slade (1982) *Form and Style: Theses, Reports, Term Papers*. Houghton Mifflin Co., Boston.
- Turabian (2007) *A Manual for Writers of Term Papers, Theses and Dissertations*, 7th edition. University of Chicago Press, Chicago, latest edition.
- American Psychological Association [APA] (2001) *Publication Manual of the American Psychological Association*, 5th edition. The American Psychological Association, Washington, D.C.

Many journals now require authors to follow the guidelines detailed in the 5th edition of the *Publication Manual of the American Psychological Association*. This guide is used extensively and is referred in the document as APA. Whatever style and form guidelines are required, the author must strictly follow them throughout the research report.

Guidelines for page and figure layout

The following are some frequently employed style and form requirements used in recreation and tourism reports, theses and journals:

- Margins
- Print font
- Line spacing
- Page numbering
- Paper weight
- Headings
- Figures and tables

Consistent **margins** are needed for binding and copying. The minimum margin standards, including figures, tables and appendices are: Top: 1 inch; bottom: 1 inch; right: 1 inch; left (binding edge): 1.5 inch.

The most standard **print font** is 12-point Times New Roman, but another font may be required. Regardless of type used, a consistent font size and style must be employed throughout the report text. The same font should be, but is not required, in figures, tables and appendices. Most universities allow italics to be used for quotations, words in a foreign language, or for emphasis in a thesis.

All theses must be **double spaced** or one-and-a-half spaced. The same spacing is required in the abstract, acknowledgments and introduction. Reference list entries, footnotes, listed items, and appendices may or may not be single-spaced, depending on your specific type of report and sponsor. Check with your adviser to confirm what the requirements are.

A research report must normally have all **pages numbered**, with the exception of the notice of copyright page and title page. The bottom centre of the page is the recommended placement of page numbers. In the front matter of a report the page numbers are lowercase Roman numerals. The first page of the report body begins with the number '1'.

A special heavier **paper weight** is required by many universities for a thesis or dissertation. All other types of research reports can use 20-pound, standard grade, white, 8 ½" × 11" paper. **Print colour** is normally black, but colour copies are accepted for illustrations in a thesis but are not accepted by most print journals.

Research report **headings** help the reader find their way around the document. There is no one universal style for headings, but they must be used and presented consistently throughout in terms of capitalization, placement on the page, font style and font size used. All first level report sections must begin on a new page and whenever the heading of a subsection appears near the bottom of a page, it must be followed by at least one line of text, or moved to the top of the next page.

Figure and table location are normally presented within the body after their reference in the text for a term paper, thesis or technical report. The arrangement of figures and tables for a journal article manuscript is usually at the end of the back matter in continuous numeric order. There is a line stating at the location in the body where the figure should be located. This is done because considerations by the publisher in the final print layout will dictate where it is ultimately placed. A figure too large in size to fit on one page may be divided or folded. Figures can be numbered using either a straight sequence (1, 2, 3, 4, etc.) or a decimal system (1.1, 1.2, 2.1, 2.2, etc., where the first digit relates to the chapter number and the digit following the decimal point is the figure number). A single-spaced caption must be provided for each figure/table and they may appear above or below it.

Guidelines for references

Every research report must reference materials and sources of information you used. A later section of this chapter discusses the legal and ethical issues related to why and when reference materials and sources of information must be referenced. In this section guidelines for the location, style and form of references are provided. The topic of reference format is complex and a full documentation of all styles and forms is beyond the scope of this book. For a detailed listing of reference styles and forms see APA (2001). However, examples of common reference situations and forms are provided below. There are two basic kinds of references, citations in the body, including footnotes/endnotes; and the reference list found in the end matter.

In-text and footnote citations

When the author uses verbatim the words or ideas found in another published or unpublished document in their research report the authors must be referenced. The most common form is the in-text citation. APA (2001) requires that the first letter of the author's last name be capitalized followed by the date of publication in parentheses. Two examples of a **two author in-text citation** are shown below:

> Research by Crompton and Williams (1994) showed that visitors were more likely to be male. Visitors were much more likely to be male (Crompton & Williams, 1994).

When the author is an **organization** or **agency**, present the organization in the citation the first time you cite the source.

> According to the International Special Events Society (2007)....

If the organization reference will be used more than once it can be cited as:

> According to the International Special Events Society [ISES] (2007), . . .
> Then subsequently as: (ISES 2007)

When there are two or more studies in the same line then place the author last name and date in parentheses, as shown in below, and in the same order in the reference list:

> (Berndt, 2002; Harlow, 1983)

In the situation where you are citing interviews, letters, e-mails, and other person-to-person communication, cite the communicator's name, that it was personal communication, and the date of the communication. You must not include a personal communication in the reference list. See the example below.

> (E. Robbins, personal communication, January 4, 2001)

An **indirect source** is one which you used is referenced in another source. List the secondary source in your reference list and the original source in the text when citing indirect sources. An example is provided below.

> Jamison believed that . . . (as cited in Johnson, 2006, p. 3)

When you use information from a website article that has an author, cite it the same way you would in the text body as any other document, but also show the website address and retrieval date. If there is no author on the website information then list the website address and retrieval date, as shown below:

> An excellent source on APA formatting is the Purdue Online Writing Lab (2010).

APA (2001) guidelines suggest that when there is a long explanation that is not directly related to the line of thought expressed in the text that a **footnote** or **endnote** can be used. In the text body, place a superscript number right after the text where more information is needed. Illustrated below is an example footnote:

> Researcher at Stanford investigated the relationship of sense of place.[1]

Reference list

The most commonly followed style and form rules for the reference list in the back matter are provided by APA (2001). Refer to this manual for detailed instructions and case studies. Below are listed a few of the basic rules, as cited in the Purdue Online Writing Lab (2010), for creating a reference list.

- Indent the first line of each new reference one-half inch from the left margin.
- List the authors last name first, followed by initials of first name, unless there are more than six authors.
- List entries in alphabetical order based on last name of first author.
- If there is more than one work by the same person or multiple-author reference same authors, they are listed in order of year of publication, earliest first.
- If you are referring to a web page, book or other work not in a journal, then capitalize only the first letter of the first word of the title, the first word after the colon or a dash in the title, and proper nouns.
- All major words in a journal title should be capitalized.
- The titles of longer works, such as books or journals, should be italicized.
- The titles of shorter works, such as journal articles or essays, should not be italicized.

Appendix 16.8 presents an example of an actual reference list.

Paper Presentation

There are two broad types of research presentations: a thesis or dissertation defence; and a research conference presentation. Each of these two types is discussed below, with background on how they are set up and guidelines to help you submit a presentation proposal and make your presentation.

Thesis or dissertation defence

Many universities require that the graduate school candidate make an oral presentation to their faculty committee in defence of their research before the committee can approve the final written thesis or dissertation. Each school has its own specific requirements and procedures so the researcher should be exceptionally clear about the defence presentation requirements. In general, the thesis candidate works with their advisor and submits draft chapters of their thesis to the advisor for suggestion and needed revisions. When the advisor believes that the draft document is of high enough quality for presentation, the student candidate submits the thesis to the full committee and arranges for a defence. When planning a defence presentation a student will benefit greatly from talking with their advisor about the defence process, time limits and what should be the focus of the presentation. Like any presentation, you must know your audience and what their particular interests are. The presentation must be a concise summary of all thesis chapters, normally with a focus on methods and findings. You will need to time the presentation carefully to fit within the period available to you. You should not just read from a paper, rather you should have an outline that will guide your discussion. The use of PowerPoint® slides to serve as both your discussion outline and to illustrate key points is strongly encouraged. See Research Box 16.1 below about conference presentations for additional presentation tips and suggestions. At the end of the candidate's presentation the committee members will ask detailed questions. It is normal to have to make some revisions to your draft thesis based on committee concerns expressed during the defence presentation.

Conference presentation

An alternative to publishing your leisure, recreation or tourism research report in print or electronic form is to make a verbal presentation of your research findings at a research conference. Presentations can often reach a wider audience than a strict scholarly journal so your findings may impact practitioners as well as academics. A presentation also gives you the opportunity to get helpful feedback about your work that could assist you in writing a report or journal manuscript. There are many leisure, recreation and tourism conferences held each year so you have a great number of presentation venues and theme options. The conference presentation process usually starts when you submit a 1–2 page abstract to conference organizers so that a panel of peers can conduct a 'blind review' and make a decision to accept or reject your proposed presentation. If accepted, then you may be given the option to submit a 1–8 page paper for publication in the conference proceedings. See Research Box 16.1 for more details on how to get accepted and what to expect once you are. Below are a few guidelines and suggestions for making a presentation at a leisure, recreation or tourism research conference.

In almost all cases, a written paper and its presentation at a research conference are quite distinct. A technical report or written paper that is 10–50 pages long, for example, is many times longer than would be possible to read in the 15–20 minutes normally available for a conference presentation. Therefore, it is best for the presenter to deliver a conversational-style summary of the paper. You do not read a paper, but rather deliver it in a more spontaneous way. This is the preferred style because it engages and keeps the audience's attention more than just reading from a paper. A most crucial factor for a successful presentation is to decide what are your most important findings and conclusions and to organize your presentation around these. But you will also need to at least touch on all parts of the research report, from problem statement, literature, methods to discussion. Therefore, it is highly recommend to create an outline of the key points and to cover them in your presentation in natural, conversational speech. Today the expectation is to also present the outline and key results visually to the audience through a PowerPoint® type presentation on an LCD projector. Always save your presentation to several storage devices (i.e. flash drive, CD and accessible website) in case of corrupted files. You should make copies of the presentation available and these could be a 'handout' from PowerPoint® with six slides per printed page.

Every presenter is strictly required to complete their presentation in the time allotted. The presentation session chair will end your presentation when your time has expired, regardless of whether you have finished or not. Therefore, it is crucial that you do not include too much information and you pace the presentation such that you are able to complete it and give a coherent ending within the time allowed. A general rule to use for determining presentation timing is; no more than one slide for every two minutes. It is strongly recommended that you practice your presentation repeatedly until you can comfortably complete it in the available time. Arrive very early to the presentation room to make sure you can open the files and the equipment is working properly.

Research Box 16.1. The conference presentation process: from acceptance to proceedings.

If you have not been involved in a presentation at a state or national conference, the process for getting your research accepted for presentation, the required steps after acceptance, presentation limitations and publication in a conference proceedings can be a mystery. The first step in the acceptance process is for the researcher to determine whether the conference will consider research of the type and content of their work. Conferences have clear guidelines on research topics they will consider. Find these on the conference's website. If congruent with the conference's areas of interest then the author writes and submits an 1–2 page abstract of the research, without author identification (other than on the title page) to the conference coordinator by a deadline that is 4–6 months in advance of the conference. The coordinator then removes the title page and author identification and sends the abstract out for a 'blind review' to an expert(s) in the research topic. A written review with comments and separate evaluation of whether the abstract should be

(Continued)

Research Box 16.1. Continued.

accepted for presentation is sent to the coordinator by the reviewer(s). The coordinator then compares the number of acceptable abstracts with the time available for all the presentations and selects the most highly rated abstracts and contacts the authors.

The accepted author usually has a limited amount of time to make suggested or required revisions and resubmit it. If these are completed then the author is given an acceptance letter with the date and time of presentation, maximum length of time for presentation and other presentation details. In most conferences there is a written or electronic conference 'proceedings' published with abstracts or in some cases, more lengthy papers, that were accepted for presentation. The author must submit the final abstract or full-length paper for the proceedings well before the actual conference begins. Finally, the day arrives for the presentation at the conference and the researcher meets the assigned room facilitator, loads their slides on the provided laptop computer and then must give their presentation within the strict time limits. At some conferences the researcher will be asked to make a limited number of abstract copies available for distribution in the room before or after their presentation. Other conferences provide this opportunity for researchers whose abstract has been accepted but there was not enough time for it to be verbally presented, or to anyone accepted to be part of a 'poster session'. These sessions are where the author places printouts of key slides from the presentation on walls at the conference site during a specified time and is present to answer questions from attendees. The future holds prospects for online conferences where 'attendees' do not physically travel to a location, but hear and see the presentations and can ask questions all while online.

Ethical and Legal Considerations

The research communications process has several important ethical and legal considerations. Paying attention to these considerations will help you avoid severe fines, loss of your 'intellectual property' and even graduation problems. This section of the chapter discusses the ethical issue of plagiarism and the more serious matter of copyright infringement. These guidelines and laws have been developed to encourage fair treatment and to protect both your 'intellectual property', such as a written article, photograph, graphic or web page, and that of past authors and publishers.

Copying statements or using ideas from a past student paper, published recreation or tourism journal, music, a website, or a government report without citing it is considered plagiarism. To avoid plagiarism you must properly cite the work of others. All universities now have severe penalties, ranging from an F grade on a paper to expulsion from the school, for students found engaging in plagiarism, especially graduate students. Therefore, it is critical that the writer of a research report be very aware of where they get information presented in their report, how it is presented (used verbatim, paraphrased or rewritten in your own words), give credit and cite other authors and sources where appropriate.

Plagiarism

A rapidly growing serious concern at schools worldwide is the ethical issue of plagiarism. A commonly used concept of plagiarism is:

> A specific form of cheating which consists of the misuse of the published and/or unpublished works, written or on a website, of others by misrepresenting the material as one's own work (Center for Teaching and Faculty Development, 2010).

Copyrights

The topic of copyrights has two main dimensions: (i) how to avoid copyright infringement; and (ii) protecting your own work with a copyright.

Avoiding copyright infringement

A more serious form of plagiarism is the actual outright copying of copyrighted intellectual property, such as text, figures, software or music, because this is illegal under US law. Significant fines can be imposed on those found violating a copyright. Copyright law protects 'original works of authorship' which are 'fixed in any tangible medium of expression'. Legal use of copyrighted work, without acquiring written permission, is limited to 'fair use' of the work. If a research report is published this is not necessarily 'fair use'. Fair use is a complex evolving legal issue so the reader is referred to two excellent resource on this subject, Crews (2000) and Nolo (2010), for details on the subject and the latest legal interpretations. The author of a research report is responsible for getting proper permissions for using copyrighted materials. In 'Guide 5; Copyright and Your Dissertation or Thesis', Crews (2000) suggests the following should have written permission:

- Long quotations from pre-existing materials that extend more than one and one-half single-spaced pages.
- Reproduced publications. Examples include copies of standard survey instruments or journal articles. This applies even if you are one of the authors of the original work, as the publisher may have the copyright.
- Graphic or pictorial works. The material should be closely related to your research

objectives, tied to critical analysis and not supersede the market for the original.

Finally, if you have images in your research report where individual people can be easily identified, then you may need to have a signed 'model release' giving you permission to use their picture.

Using a copyright to protect your materials and reports

Currently a copyright notice or symbol is not necessary to maintain copyright because a copyright is considered to be in place upon creation of the work. However, it is suggested that you copyright your work by providing a copyright statement like one of the two forms shown below:

Copyright 2006, Patrick T. Tierney or © 2007 Patrick T. Tierney.

The formal registration of your copyright in the USA can be accomplished by contacting the U.S. Copyright Office, 101 Independence Avenue SE, Washington, D.C. 20559. Your research report is then a public record. One cannot generally file an infringement lawsuit without registration.

Case Study 16.1.

Clearly and effectively communicating the results of your recreation or tourism research is a critically important final step in the research process. In this chapter we will be referring to research undertaken for the US Forest Service, Pacific Southwest Research Station on the use of undeveloped natural areas (parks and protected areas located outside of cities) by residents of Barcelona, Glasgow Los Angeles (LA) and Morelia, Mexico. The results were published in the *Journal of Tourism Management* (Tierney, Dahl, and Chavez, 2001) and later presented at the 2004 Social Aspects of Recreation Research Symposium (Tierney et al., 2004). The LA studies compared motives for visitation, barriers and actual visitation, while statistically controlling for differences in demographic variables, between three ethnic groups, African Americans, Asian Americans and Anglo Americans. Later the overall LA data on constraints and visitation were compared with data collected from a similar survey instrument translated and administered in the other three cities by researchers there. The publication of the article in an international journal and presentation of results at an international conference are good examples of how the findings of research are communicated to various audiences. Even though the results were not communicated as part of a thesis, professional paper or dissertation, most of the elements of a research report described in this chapter (introduction, literature review, methods, results and discussion) were required parts of both the article and the presentation. In the case of the scholarly journal, the authors were required to submit a detailed manuscript, a concise (15 page) description of the entire research and discussion of results, for peer review. If the manuscript writing is not clear and exact, then it is rejected outright or must be resubmitted after suggested

(Continued)

Case Study 16.1. Continued.

revisions are made. The peer-review process of submittal, review and re-submittal for this journal article lasted almost four months. An even shorter (1–2 pages) abstract and re-focused version of the article manuscript was later submitted to the Social Aspects conference organizers for review. The manuscript and abstract later became the foundation from which the presentation outline and slides were developed and used by the researcher. The author spent almost six hours re-evaluating results and developing the final presentation which lasted 20 minutes but was seen by a room full of researchers keenly interested in the research topic.

Key Terms

Abstract: A very concise synopsis of the research background, purpose, methods, results and conclusions.

Back matter: Those sections of a research report which include the literature cited, or bibliography, and any appendices.

Bibliography: A comprehensive list of not only sources referred to in the body of the report but also studies consulted for the preparation of the research.

Blind review: Process of review where a professional peer(s) with expertise in the research subject area evaluates an abstract or manuscript without knowing who the author is and writes their decision to accept or reject it for a future presentation or publication based only on the merits of the submittal.

Copyright: A legal right that protects the original works of an author which are fixed in any tangible medium of expression, from use and copying by another. It must be formally filed with the federal government in order to be able to file an infringement lawsuit.

Discussion: The section of your report where you interpret the results presented earlier and describe the implications of your research findings on professional practice, as well as past and future research.

Dissertation: A formal, theory-based research report on original research that is used to satisfy the culminating experience requirements of a doctoral degree programme.

Front matter: The first sections of a comprehensive research report that normally include: notice of copyright, title page, committee recommendation and signatures, abstract, dedication, acknowledgements, table of contents and lists of tables and figures.

Hypothesis: A suggested explanation for a phenomenon that can be tested by research and written in such a way that it can be either accepted or rejected by research findings.

Intellectual property: Your own original photographs, graphics, web pages, designs, logos, ideas, written material, journal articles, books, music or inventions.

Literature cited: Studies referred to in the body of the report included in a list of sources used in the research.

Notice of copyright: An optional legal statement included in a thesis or research report that protects original works of the author.

Professional paper: A scholarly comprehensive written paper that describes research, a creative activity or applied project which demonstrates knowledge gained through coursework, research, and professional experience.

Plagiarism: A specific form of cheating which consists of the misuse of the published and/or unpublished works, written or on a website, of others by misrepresenting the material as one's own work.

Technical report: A detailed written presentation of the methods and findings for contracted research.

Thesis: A highly detailed formal report on original research that is used to satisfy the culminating experience requirements of a master's degree programme.

Thesis defence: Many universities requires the graduate candidate make an oral presentation to their faculty committee and the public about how they conducted and the findings of their research before the committee can approve the written thesis.

Theoretical model: A conceptual framework that seeks to explain the relationships between several variables.

Discussion Questions

1. What are common situations in which it would be most appropriate to use one of the four cited research report types over the others? Is it always better to prepare a formal written research report or are their cases where if might be better to just make a verbal presentation of results?

2. What are the main purposes of the front matter of a formal research report? What is typically contained in the front matter of a thesis?

3. In what section(s) of the thesis should a theoretical model be discussed? How is the model linked to the content of other report sections?

4. How does the material presented in the 'discussion' section of the formal report differ from the results section? Are data repeated in these two sections to clarify technically difficult or very important findings? Why or why not?

5. What are the two primary sources of guidelines to develop the format and style of a formal research report. Why is attention to detail and precise formatting required for the reference list?

6. What is plagiarism and copyright infringement? How can the authors of: (i) a university class assignment paper; and (ii) a master's thesis, ensure they avoid these two legal concerns when writing assignment paper or a thesis?

References

American Psychological Association (2001) *Publication Manual of the American Psychological Association.* American Psychological Association, Washington, DC.

Campbell, W., Ballou, S. and Slade, C. (1982) *Form and Style: Theses, Reports, Term Papers.* Houghton Mifflin Co., Boston, Massachusetts.

Center for Teaching and Faculty Development, San Francisco State University *Academic integrity and plagiarism at SFSU.* Accessed 22 September 2010 from http://ctfd.sfsu.edu/feature/academic-integrity-and-plagiarism-at-sf-state.htm

Crews, K.D. (2000) *Copyright Essentials for Librarians and Educators.* American Library Association, Chicago, Illinois.

Graduate Division, San Francisco State University. Sample thesis and dissertation pages. Accessed 9 September 2010 from http://www.sfsu.edu/~gradstdy/forms/thesis-dissertation-sample-pages.pdf

Howe, A. (2007) The effects of entertainment technology on youth participation in active recreation. Unpublished master's thesis, San Francisco State University, San Francisco, California.

Nolo *The Fair Use Rule: When Use of Copyrighted Material is Acceptable.* Accessed 9 September 2010 from http://www.nolo.com/legal-encyclopedia/article-30100.html

Purdue Online Writing Lab *The Purdue Online Writing Lab.* Accessed 15 September 2010 from http://owl.english.purdue.edu

Tierney, P., Dahl, R. and Chavez, D. (2001) Cultural diversity in use of undeveloped natural areas by Los Angeles County residents. *Journal of Tourism Management* 22, 271–277.

Tierney, P., Barkin D., Burnett K., Chavez D. and Miranda J. (2004) Leisure travel, vacations, constraints and visitation to natural area attractions: A comparison of residents of Barcelona, Glasgow, Los Angeles and Morelia, Mexico. *Proceedings of the 4th Social Aspects and Recreation Research Symposium,* 6 February, San Francisco, California.

Turabian, K. (2007) *A Manual for Writers of Term Papers, Theses and Dissertations.* Latest edition. University of Chicago Press, Chicago, Illinois.

Worked Example 16.1. Research in Action, Examples of Pages from a Thesis

The following pages contain key pages from an actual master's thesis. These are intended to illustrate one commonly used thesis format and style type, but the researcher must check with their graduate programme before assuming these are acceptable at their university. This author wishes to acknowledge the support and give credit to Ashley D. Howe (2007) for allowing the use of pages from her master's thesis at San Francisco State University titled *The Effects of Entertainment Technology on Youth Participation in Active Recreation*. The following pages are provided.

- Title Page
- Notice of Copyright Page
- Committee Recommendation and Signatures Page
- Abstract
- Sample page from a Table of Contents
- Example page from a List of Tables
- Sample Introduction Page
- Example page from a Reference List

Use these examples to see the format, level of detail and style that is typically found in a thesis.

APPENDIX 16.1 EXAMPLE OF TITLE PAGE

The Effects of Entertainment Technology
on Youth Participation in Active Recreation

A thesis submitted to the faculty of
San Francisco State University
In partial fulfillment of
The requirements for
The degree

Master of Science
in
Recreation and Leisure Studies

by
Ashley D. Howe
San Francisco, California
January, 2007

APPENDIX 16.2 NOTICE OF COPYRIGHT PAGE

Copyright © 2007
by
Ashley D. Howe

APPENDIX 16.3 EXAMPLE OF COMMITTEE RECOMMENDATION AND SIGNATURE PAGE

CERTIFICATION OF APPROVAL

I certify that I have read *The Effects of Entertainment Technology on Youth Participation in Active Recreation* by Ashley D. Howe, and that in my opinion this work meets the criteria for approving a thesis submitted in partial fulfillment of the requirements for the degree: Master of Science in Recreation & Leisure Studies at San Francisco State University.

_____

Patrick Tierney
Professor of Recreation and Leisure Studies

_____

Erik Rosegard
Professor of Recreation and Leisure Studies

APPENDIX 16.4 SAMPLE OF ABSTRACT PAGE

The Effects of Entertainment Technology
on Youth Participation in Active Recreation

Ashley D. Howe
San Francisco State University
2007

This study was designed to identify relationships between playing video games, computers, the Internet, and television and youth participation in active recreation. A review of literature was conducted focusing on the relationship of youth obesity with entertainment technology, urban development, perceived safety, and methods of marketing food and beverage products to youth. Data were obtained from surveys of 69 students from two middle schools in Marin County, California. The results showed there was no significant difference between the lengths of time respondents played video games and the total monthly minutes spent participating in active recreation. However, a statistically significant difference was found between the length of time respondents watched television and total monthly minutes engaged in active recreation. A statistically significant difference was also found between the number of times respondents used the Internet per week and total monthly minutes reported participating in active recreation.

I certify that the Abstract is a correct representation of the content of this thesis.

_____   _____

(Chair, Thesis Committee)   (Date)

APPENDIX 16.5 SAMPLE PAGE FROM TABLE OF CONTENTS

TABLE OF CONTENTS

APPENDIX 16.6 SAMPLE OF LIST OF TABLES

LIST OF TABLES

APPENDIX 16.7 SAMPLE INTRODUCTION PAGE

Chapter 1

INTRODUCTION

Background of the Study

The types of recreational activities that youths pursue are undergoing a change, as are their levels of participation in the activities chosen. Fewer children today select to engage in informal activities like climbing trees or playing outdoors than in past generations. Research implicates that as entertainment technology (video games, the Internet, and television) continues to advance and attract a larger audience of sedentary users, urban development becomes more centered around cars than ease of walking, and congestion of cities and urbanization of neighborhoods threaten safety (actual or perceived), has resulted in the youth obesity epidemic will continue to prevail in the United States.

Many Americans believe changes in youth recreation and leisure activities are greatly due to advances in entertainment technology. Americans have also expressed concern with the amount of time youth spend in front of computers and video games rather than being outdoors and engaging in an activity that requires some level of physical movement and aerobic conditioning.

Dennis Cauchon, author of the article *Kids are Living Under House Arrest Says USA Today* (Cauchon, 2006), said, 'in generations past, children's play tended to be open-ended, following whatever game or adventure a child's imagination could generate. Children and parents now prefer structured entertainment, whether it's a video game or a day at the pool.'

APPENDIX 16.8 EXAMPLE OF REFERENCE LIST

REFERENCES

Annenberg Public Policy Center of the University of Pennsylvania (APPCUP) *Television in the home: The 1997 survey of parents and children*. Philadelphia: University of Pennsylvania; 1997.

Bundred, P., Kitchiner, D., Buchan, I. (2001) Prevalence of overweight and obese children between 1989 and 1998: population based series of cross sectional studies. *British Medical Journal*. 2001;322:326–8.

Cauchon, D. (2006) *Kids are living under house arrest says USA Today*. White Dot, the international campaign against television. Retrieved on October 24, 2006 from: http://www.whitedot.org/issue/iss_story.asp?slug=sedentary+kids

Cole, T., Bellizzi, M., Flegal, K., Dietz, W. (2000) Establishing a standard definition for child overweight and obesity worldwide: international survey. *British Medical Journal*. 2000;320:1240–3.

Collins, A. (2003) Teenage obesity How to prevent teenage obesity . *Fitness and Kids*. Retrieved March 4, 2004, from http://www.fitnessandkids.com/teenage-obesity.html

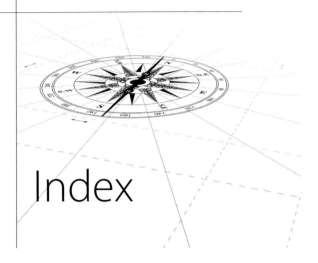

Index

Page numbers in **bold** refer to illustrations and tables